MY WORLD OF
THEATRE

GEN. SIR AUGUSTINE DAUBENY

GEN. SIR HUBERT DAUBENY

FIELD-MARSHAL SIR ADHEMAR DAUBENY

GENERAL SIR RUPERT DAUBENY

GEN. CONFORMITY DAUBENY

GEN. SIR LAMBERT DAUBENY

SIR ALARICK A DAUBENY

SIR PIRBRYTE DAUBENY

DAUBENFREED BONETOOTH

SIR GUILLAUME A D'EAU BENIT

DAUBINIUS PRAETOR

PILTDAUBENY

Are you really worthy of the Tradition?

The family tree of Peter Daubeny as seen by Peter Ustinov

MY WORLD OF THEATRE

PETER DAUBENY

WITH A FOREWORD AND AFTERWORD BY
RONALD BRYDEN

JONATHAN CAPE
THIRTY BEDFORD SQUARE LONDON

FIRST PUBLISHED 1971
© 1971 BY PETER DAUBENY
FOREWORD AND AFTERWORD © 1971 BY JONATHAN CAPE LTD

JONATHAN CAPE LTD, 30 BEDFORD SQUARE, LONDON WCI

ISBN 0 224 00537 5

PRINTED AND BOUND IN GREAT BRITAIN
BY BUTLER & TANNER LTD, LONDON AND FROME

ACKNOWLEDGMENTS

I should like to thank all my friends in the world theatre for their help and encouragement throughout my work on *My World of Theatre*. Without their enthusiasm and friendship this book would not have been possible.

To my staff, Timothy Mason, Janet Carroll, and to my personal assistant, Neil Mundy, I should like to say a grateful 'thank you' for all their great patience and help.

Material previously published in various newspapers and journals reprinted by kind permission of the Beaverbrook Foundations, the New York Times Company, the *Spectator*, the *Sunday Telegraph*, *The Times* and *Vogue* Magazine.

CONTENTS

ILLUSTRATIONS

Frontispiece The family tree of Peter Daubeny as seen by Peter Ustinov (*Author's collection*)

9

LIST OF MAJOR PRODUCTIONS, COMPANIES AND SEASONS PRESENTED IN LONDON BY PETER DAUBENY

The Gay Pavilion by William Lipscombe	April 1945	(Piccadilly)
Jacobowsky and the Colonel by Franz Werfel adapted by S. N. Behrman	June 1945	(Piccadilly)
Day after Tomorrow by Kieran Tunney and Simon Wardell	1945	(Fortune)
The Wind is 90	May 1946	(Apollo)
But for the Grace of God by Frederick Lonsdale	Sept. 1946	(St James's
Our Betters by W. Somerset Maugham	Oct. 1946	(Playhouse)
Power without Glory by Michael Clayton Hutton	April 1947	(Fortune)
We Proudly Present by Ivor Novello	May 1947	(Duke of York's)
The Way Back (retitled from *Home of the Brave*) by Arthur Laurents	Jan. 1949	(Westminster)
The Late Edwina Black by William Dinner and William Morum	July 1949	(Ambassadors)
Fallen Angels (with *Fumed Oak*) by Noël Coward	Dec. 1949	(Ambassadors)
The Gay Invalid adapted from Molière's *Le Malade imaginaire* by Sir Barry Jackson and Robert Brenon	Jan. 1951	(Garrick)
Rosario and Antonio	June–July 1951	(Cambridge)
Les Ballets des Champs-Élysées	Aug. 1951	(Cambridge)
Ballet Espagnol de Pilar Lopez	Sept. 1951	(Cambridge)
Grand Ballet du Marquis de Cuevas	Oct. 1951	(Cambridge)
Mrinalini Sarabhai and her Hindu Ballet	Nov. 1951	(Cambridge)
Rosario and Antonio	Nov.–Dec. 1951	(Cambridge)
Katherine Dunham and her Company	Jan.–March 1952	(Cambridge)
Coros y Danzas de España — National Spanish Company of Dancers, Singers and Instrumentalists	Feb.–March 1952	(Stoll)
Carmen Amaya and her Company of Spanish Gypsy Dancers	April–May 1952	(Cambridge)
Yugoslav State Company in *Slavonic Rhapsody*	May–June 1952	(Cambridge)

Italian Opera Company	Sept.–Oct. 1952	(Stoll)
Teresa and Luisillo—*Spanish Fiesta*	Oct.–Dec. 1952	(on tour)
Caravana Española with Paquita León	Nov.–Dec. 1952	(London Casino)
Ram Gopal with his Indian Dancers and Musicians	Nov.–Dec. 1952	(King's, Hammersmith)
Italian Opera Company	May–June 1953	(Stoll)
Sacha Guitry—*Écoutez bien messieurs*	June 1953	(Winter Garden)
Bulbul and his Oriental Ballet	June 1953	(Scala)
The American National Ballet Theater	Aug. 1953	(on tour)
Ballets de Paris de Roland Petit	Aug.–Sept. 1953	(Stoll)
Walter Gore Ballet	Sept.–Oct. 1953	(Princes)
Ballet Espagnol de Pilar Lopez	Oct. 1953	(Stoll)
Ballets de Paris de Roland Petit	Dec. 1953	(Stoll)
Grand Ballet du Marquis de Cuevas	Jan.–Feb. 1954	(Stoll)
Antonio and his Spanish Ballet	Feb.–April 1954	(Stoll)
Martha Graham and her Dance Company	March 1954	(Saville)
Ballets de France de Janine Charrat	April 1954	(Stoll)
Moscow State Dance Company—Beryozka	April–May 1954	(Stoll)
Sergei Obraztsov's Moscow State Puppet Theatre	July 1954	(London Casino)
The Yugoslav National Opera and Ballet	Jan. 1955	(Stoll)
Antonio and his Spanish Ballet	Feb.–April 1955	(Palace)
Italian Opera Company	March 1955	(Stoll)
Maurice Chevalier	April 1955	(Palace)
Jan Kiepura and Martha Eggerth Company in Franz Lehar's *Merry Widow*	May–June 1955	(Palace)
Les Compagnons de la Chanson	July 1955	(Palace)
Compagnie Edwige Feuillère in *La Dame aux camélias* by Alexandre Dumas *fils*	Sept. 1955	(Duke of York's)
Italian Opera Company	Sept.–Oct. 1955	(Palace)
The Classical Theatre of China (Peking Opera)	Oct.–Nov. 1955	(Palace)
The Moisseyev Russian Dance Company	Oct.–Nov. 1955	(Empress Hall)
The Soviet Baltic Fleet	Oct. 1955	(Empress Hall)
Ballet Espagnol de Pilar Lopez	Nov.–Dec. 1955	(Palace)
The Salzburg Mozart Opera Company in Mozart's *La Finta Semplice* (bi-centenary celebration production)	March 1956	(Palace)
Trevallion—comic opera by Roy Phillips	March 1956	(Palace)

Les Ballets Africains de Kieta Fodeba	April 1956	(Palace)
Jean Vilar's Théâtre National Populaire in *Dom Juan* by Molière, *Marie Tudor* by Victor Hugo and *Le Triomphe de l'amour* by Marivaux	April–May 1956	(Palace)
Les Ballets de Paris de Roland Petit	May–June 1956	(Palace)
The House by the Lake by Hugh Mills	May 1956–Feb. 1958	(Duke of York's)
The Hungarian State Company of Dance, Song and Music	June–July 1956	(Palace)
Greta Garbo Film Season	July–Aug. 1956	(Palace)
The Red Army Choir	July–Aug. 1956	(Empress Hall)
Les Ballets Africains de Kieta Fodeba	Aug. 1956	(Palace)
The Berliner Ensemble in *Mother Courage, The Caucasian Chalk Circle* and *Trumpets and Drums* (adapted from the play by George Farquhar) by Bertolt Brecht	Aug.–Sept. 1956	(Palace)
Antonio and his Spanish Ballet	Sept.–Nov. 1956	(Palace)
Compagnie Madeleine Renaud — Jean-Louis Barrault in *Le Chien du jardinier* by Lope de Vega, adapted by Georges Neveux, *Le Misanthrope* by Molière, *Occupe-toi d'Amélie* by Feydeau, *Christophe Colomb* by Claudel and *Intermezzo* by Giraudoux	Nov.–Dec. 1956	(Palace)
The Polish State Dance Company of 100 — Mazowsze	Jan.–March 1957	(Stoll)
Compagnie Edwige Feuillère in *La Dame aux camélias* by Alexandre Dumas *fils*, *La Parisienne* by Henry Becque with *Le Carrosse du Saint-Sacrement* by Prosper Mérimée, and *Phèdre* by Racine	March 1957	(Palace)
Ballet Espagnol de Pilar Lopez	Aug.–Sept. 1957	(Palace)
Chinese Classical Theatre from Formosa	Sept.–Oct. 1957	(Drury Lane)
New York Negro Ballet	Sept.–Oct. 1957	(on tour)
Moscow Art Theatre in *The Cherry Orchard, The Three Sisters* and *Uncle Vanya* by Chekhov and *The Troubled Past* by Leonid Rakhmanov	May–June 1958	(Sadler's Wells)
Comédie–Française in *Le Dindon* by Feydeau, *Les Femmes savantes* by Molière, and *Les Fourberies de Scapin* by Molière with *Un Caprice* by Alfred de Musset	March–April 1959	(Princes)

The Old Vic Company in *Ghosts* by Ibsen	April 1959	(Princes)
The Swedish Malmo City Theatre Company in Ingmar Bergman's production of *Urfaust* by Goethe	May 1959	(Princes)
Ballet Espagnol de Pilar Lopez	May 1959	(Princes)
The Aspern Papers adapted for the stage by Michael Redgrave from the novel by Henry James	Aug. 1959–July 1960	(Queen's)
Jerome Robbins's *Ballets: U.S.A.*	Sept. 1959	(Piccadilly)
Compagnie Marie Bell Racine Season — *Phèdre, Bérénice* and *Britannicus*	March 1960	(Savoy)
Zizi Jeanmaire and her Company	Nov. 1960	(Royalty)
Chin-Chin by François Billetdoux, adapted by Willis Hall	Nov. 1960–March 1961	(Wyndham's)
The Connection by Jack Gelber	Feb.–April 1961	(Duke of York's)
Jerome Robbins's *Ballets: U.S.A.*	Aug. 1961	(Saville)
Photo Finish by Peter Ustinov	April–Nov. 1962	(Saville)
Micheál Mac Liammóir Season — *The Importance of Being Oscar* and *I Must Be Talking To My Friends*	April–May 1963	(Aldwych)
Vittorio Gassman and his Teatro Popolare Italiano in *The Heroes*	May 1963	(Aldwych)

World Theatre Season 1964   (Aldwych)
(in celebration of the four hundredth anniversary of Shakespeare's birth)

March 17th to June 13th (13 weeks)

Comédie — Française	*Tartuffe* by Molière
	Un Fil à la Patte by Feydeau
Schiller-Theater — West Berlin	*Andorra* by Frisch
	Clavigo by Goethe
Peppino de Filippo's Italian Theatre	*Metamorphoses of a Wandering Minstrel* by Peppino de Filippo
Abbey Theatre — Dublin	*Juno and the Paycock* by O'Casey
	The Plough and the Stars by O'Casey
Polish Contemporary Theatre	*The Life Annuity* by Fredro
	What a Lovely Dream with *Let's Have Fun* by Mrożek
Greek Art Theatre	*The Birds* by Aristophanes
Moscow Art Theatre	*Dead Souls* by Gogol
	The Cherry Orchard by Chekhov
	Kremlin Chimes by Pogodin

World Theatre Season 1965   (Aldwych)
March 22nd to May 22nd (9 weeks)

Théâtre de France	*Andromaque* by Racine
	Le Piéton de L'air by Ionesco
	Ne te promène donc pas toute nue by Feydeau
	Le Soulier de satin by Claudel
	Oh! les beaux jours by Beckett
Compagnia dei Giovani — Italy	*La Bugiarda* by Fabbri
	Six Characters in Search of an Author by Pirandello
Greek Art Theater	*The Birds* by Aristophanes
	The Persians by Aeschylus
Habimah National Theatre — Israel	*The Dybbuk* by Anski
Actors' Studio Theater — U.S.A.	*Blues for Mister Charlie* by Baldwin
	The Three Sisters by Chekhov

World Theatre Season 1966   (Aldwych)
March 21st to May 21st (9 weeks)

Czech National Theatre	*The Insect Play* by Karel and Josef Čapek
Compagnia dei Giovani — Italy	*The Rules of the Game* by Pirandello
	Six Characters in Search of an Author by Pirandello
National Theatre of Greece	*Hecuba* by Euripides
	Oedipus Rex by Sophocles
	Oedipus at Colonus by Sophocles
Polish Popular Theatre	*The Wedding* by Wyspianski, adapted by Hanuszkiewicz
	Crime and Punishment adapted from Dostoyevsky's novel by Hubner
	The Columbus Boys: Warsaw 44–46 adapted from Bratny's novel by Hanuszkiewicz
Leningrad Gorky Theatre	*The Idiot* adapted from Dostoyevsky's novel by Tovstonogov
	Grandma, Uncle Iliko, Hilarion and I by Dumbadze and Lordkipanidze

World Theatre Season 1967   (Aldwych)
March 27th to June 3rd (10 weeks)

National Theatre of Poland	*The Glorious Resurrection of Our Lord* by Nicolas of Wilkowiecko
Comédie-Française	*Le Cid* by Corneille
	Le Jeu de a' Amour et du hasard by Marivaux with *Feu la mère de Madame* by Feydeau

B

Nō Theatre of Japan	**Programme One:** *Hagoromo* by Zeami with *Bo Shibari* (Anon.) and *Tsuchi-Gumo* (Anon.) **Programme Two:** *Kiku-Jido* (Anon.) with *Kazumo* (Anon.) and *Aoi-No-Ue* by Zeami
Bremen Theatre—West Germany	*Spring Awakening* by Wedekind *Die Unberatenen* by Valentin and Muller
Cameri Theatre—Israel	*King Solomon and the Cobbler* by Gronemann
Greek Art Theatre	*The Frogs* by Aristophanes *The Birds* by Aristophanes *The Persians* by Aeschylus
Piccolo Theatre of Milan	*The Servant of Two Masters* by Goldoni
Theatre on the Balustrade—Czechoslovakia	*The Trial* adapted from Kafka's novel by Grossman *The Fools* (or *A Strange Dream of a Clown*) by Fialka

World Theatre Season 1968 (5th Anniversary Season) *April 15th to June 22nd* (10 *weeks*)	(Aldwych)
Theatre on the Balustrade—Czechoslovakia	*The Clowns* by Fialka *The Fools* (or *A Strange Dream of a Clown*) by Fialka *King Ubu* adapted from Jarry by Macourek and Grossman
Théâtre de France	*Partage de midi* by Claudel *Il faut passer par les nuages* by Billetdoux *Le Barbier de Seville* by Beaumarchais
Rome Stabile Theatre	*Naples by Night, Naples by Day* by Viviani
Abbey Theatre—Dublin	*The Shaughraun* by Boucicault
Royal Dramatic Theatre—Sweden	*Hedda Gabler* by Ibsen
Bunraku National Theatre of Japan	**Programme One:** *Kanadehon Chushingura* by Takeda with *Tsuri Onna* (Anon.) and *Tsubosaka Kannon Reigenki* by Kako **Programme Two:** *Kanjincho* by Namiki with *Sonezaki Shinju* by Chikamatsu

World Theatre Season 1969 (Aldwych)
April 14th *to June* 7th (8 *weeks*)

Théâtre de la Cité—France — *Bérénice* by Racine
Georges Dandin by Molière
Theatre behind the Gate— — *The Three Sisters* by Chekhov
 Czechoslovakia — *The Single-Ended Rope* by Nestroy
An Hour of Love by Topol with
 The Green Cockatoo by Schnitzler
Negro Ensemble Company—U.S.A. — *Song of the Lusitanian Bogey* by
 Weiss
God is a (Guess What?) by McIver
Greek Art Theatre — *Lysistrata* by Aristophanes
Oedipus Rex by Sophocles
Anna Magnani Company—Rome — *La Lupa* by Verga

World Theatre Season 1970 (Aldwych)
April 13th *to June* 6th (8 *weeks*)

The Činoherní Klub of Prague — *Mandragola* by Machiavelli
Whose Turn Next? by Vostrá
The Government Inspector by Gogol
Schiller-Theater—West Berlin — *The Captain of Köpenick* by Zuck-
 mayer
Krapp's Last Tape by Beckett
Intrigue and Love by Schiller
Comédie-Française — *La Navette* by Becque with
 Amphitryon by Molière
Dom Juan by Molière
Catania Stabile Theatre—Sicily — *Liolà* by Pirandello
Moscow Art Theatre — *The Seagull* by Chekhov
Lenin—The Third Pathétique by
 Pogodin

World Theatre Season 1971 (Aldwych)
March 24th *to May* 22nd (9 weeks)

Théâtre Michel—Paris — *La Ville dont le Prince est
un Enfant* by Montherlant
Theatre behind the Gate— — *The Three Sisters*
 Czechoslovakia — by Chekhov
Ivanov by Chekhov
Royal Dramatic Theatre—Sweden — *The Dream Play*
 by Strindberg
Schiller-Theater—West Berlin — *Krapp's Last Tape* by Beckett
 with *Endgame* by Beckett
Yvonne, Princess of Burgundy
 by Gombrowicz

Genoa Stabile Theatre — Italy	*The Venetian Twins* by Goldoni
Dormen Theatre — Turkey	*A Tale of Istanbul* by Günaydin
Nuria Espert Company — Spain	*The Maids* by Genet

TO MOLLY

FOREWORD

Early in 1963, someone on the *Sunday Telegraph* noticed that the
following year was the four hundredth anniversary of Shakespeare's birth, and suggested that the newspaper help to promote
a celebration of some kind. Presumably on the premise that the
theatre itself was too vulgar a place for so hallowed an event, the
initial idea was to get up a music festival. An emissary was sent
to ask Yehudi Menuhin whether he would organize something
on the lines of the annual fortnight of opera and chamber music
he then ran at Bath. Sensibly, Menuhin replied that in his opinion
the appropriate way to celebrate the birth of the world's greatest
playwright was with a festival of plays from all over the world.
He recommended that the newspaper get in touch with his friend
Peter Daubeny.

In the years since 1964, the World Theatre Season has become a
fixture of the London calendar and one of the strongest justifica-
tions of the city's claim to be the world's theatrical capital. Nothing quite like it exists anywhere else. Paris's Théâtre des Nations,
which operated for some years on a similar basis, never reached
the same scale and has now dwindled from sight. Venice's
attempts at an *avant-garde* equivalent have been dogged by the
same *avant-garde* crises and power struggles as its film festival and
Biennale. Only in London does each spring usher in a cavalcade
of the world's great theatrical companies—the Comédie-Française, the Moscow Art Theatre, Dublin's Abbey, Israel's Habimah,
the Nō Theatre of Japan—bringing their wares to market at the
Aldwych Theatre while the resident Royal Shakespeare Company,
host to the visiting companies, girds itself for the new season. Like
the World Cup and Wimbledon, these glittering theatrical fairs
have become global occasions, drawing tourists from both hemi-
spheres, famous wherever there are actors and audiences. Distinguished companies vie for invitations like small boys wrangling
over marbles. Politico-cultural crises have been provoked in
countries which go in for such things by approaches to theatres
livelier than the august official ensembles. Yet the impresario

responsible for this phenomenon remains virtually anonymous. The man himself is as unknown, except as a name, as the companies he presents are renowned.

It is hard to see why. Certainly, the impresarios who catch the public eye seem usually to be those who, like Barnum, Daly or Ziegfeld, purvey freaks or beautiful girls; and Daubeny's brand of showmanship is not theirs. Still, for twenty years he has been London's foremost provider of the best international dance and drama, doing more than any other man to keep open the British theatre's channels of communication with the rest of the world. When the history of our post-war stage is written, it will be difficult to name anyone who influenced it more profoundly than the man who first imported Brecht's Berliner Ensemble, the Moscow Art Theatre, the Living Theatre of New York, and the talents of Ingmar Bergman, Jacques Charon, Karolos Koun, Josef Svoboda, Vittorio Gassman, Edwige Feuillère, Innokenti Smoktunovsky and Jerome Robbins. Apart from this, he is himself, as his autobiography's modest emphasis on other people cannot wholly conceal, a uniquely remarkable figure in the world theatre.

He is remarkable in that, coming to the theatre from a background utterly remote from its tight web of kinship and jealously guarded skills, he has pursued it with a passion matched by few born professionals. As he tells, he comes from a military family with no theatrical traditions and most of their caste's mistrust of artists. To break out of that world into the one he has made his own must have taken a courage and determination barely hinted at between the amusing lines describing his schoolboy efforts to get on terms with his first culture-heroes, Hugh Walpole, C. B. Cochran and Godfrey Winn. It must have taken even greater courage, when the loss of an arm at Salerno in 1943 put an end to his acting ambitions, to embark on a new career in the hostile, Machiavellian corridors of West End management. Most remarkable of all is the way in which he (though too loyal to notice it himself) has grown with his career past those early struggles and enthusiasms, into one of the most discerning and knowledgeable connoisseurs of the theatre arts living today.

One of the most? No, he is unique in his knowledge. No one else in the world could have written a book like this one, for no one else has had his peculiarly intimate and embracing experience of the theatre in Europe, Asia and America. He has not only seen it all, in his capacity as buyer and ringmaster for his astonishing spring Dionysia, he has known its makers, the men and women who have created it and its historic occasions, with the intimacy of friendship and, once or twice, the even greater intimacy of hatred. His theatrical travels have covered ground trodden by no one else in more senses than one, as he flies each year in search of new, undiscovered dramatic excitements to such cities as Warsaw, Prague, Moscow, Delhi, Rome, Tokyo or Tel Aviv. He has known the great actors, directors and dramatists of his time not only in their private vanities and vulnerabilities, but in that most private place of all in an artist's life—at work.

Look at the list of names. Starting his career in a theatre still dominated by the mid-Atlantic giants of the inter-war comedy of manners, he snared plays from four of the largest: Lonsdale, Coward, Maugham and S. N. Behrman. His reminiscences of them alone would make this an invaluable source book. But his search for talents not yet corralled by the monopolists of Shaftesbury Avenue led him to America at a time when few Europeans were aware of the new forces stirring there. Long before their names became household words, he encountered Lee Strasberg's Actors' Studio and its brilliant graduate, Montgomery Clift; Elia Kazan; the tempestuous Becks; the new American musical theatre ushered in by Jerome Robbins's and Leonard Bernstein's *On the Town*.

That last seems to have been the germ of his interest in modern dancing, and those memorable seasons which brought to London Roland Petit's Ballets de Paris, Martha Graham, Antonio and Rosario, Katherine Dunham, the Peking Opera, Jerome Robbins's own company. But it also led him, evidently, to his fascinating, unsuccessful attempt to stage Molière's *Imaginary Invalid* with A. E. Matthews and Elisabeth Bergner (the only effort anyone has made since the war to furnish the greatest European actress of her time with a London vehicle worthy of her) as the comedy-cum-ballet-cum-masque it was intended to be. It was clearly a turning point. After it Daubeny could no longer be content with the haphazard, catch-as-catch-can production methods of the com-mercial West End theatre. He had glimpsed the possibility of a total, integrated work of theatrical art, combining acting, mime, dancing, music and painting in one ensemble effect, feasible only with the sort of permanent company Britain did not yet possess. And so he became an importer of the world's great ensembles; the man who showed Britain the necessity of what we have finally achieved in the National Theatre and Royal Shakespeare companies.

That is not to say that he disbelieves in individual genius, the star actor or director. His accounts of the great companies he has brought to London are accounts of the brilliant individuals who have provided their focus: Jean-Louis Barrault and Madeline Renaud; Edwige Feuillère, Marie Bell, Sacha Guitry; Helene Weigel; Anna Magnani; Rosella Falk and Giorgio de Lullo; Otomar Krejča; Katina Paxinou and Alexis Minotis; Micheál Mac Liammóir and Cyril Cusack; the superb Neapolitan clown Peppino di Filippo and Japan's 'Intangible Cultural Asset' Cumas Hashioka, who headed the Nō group which came to the Aldwych in 1967. With each account comes a glimpse of the friends who have helped and guided him in his quest for undiscovered theatrical gold: the Lunts, Orson Welles, Erwin Piscator, Pierre Fresnay and Yvonne Printemps, Jean Vilar, Maurice Chevalier, Sean O'Casey, Ivor Novello, Peter Ustinov, Michel Saint-Denis.

It is hard to think of an important name in the modern theatre he hasn't encountered, presented, befriended or been befriended by. His story of his career is a unique personal guide-book to the stages and backstages of almost every country in the world where the theatre is a live art. So much so that it seems incredible that only eight years ago there was no such thing as the World Theatre Season; that it was possible for anyone to contemplate celebrating Shakespeare's quater-centenary with anything but an international festival of plays and, when he asked who might organize such an event, need prompting with the name 'Peter Daubeny'. Who else?

London, 1971   RONALD BRYDEN

PART ONE

PART ONE

I

Tripoli and Youth

Noël Coward seemed the natural person to tell first about my decision to go into theatrical management. His ENSA concert in Tripoli was the first thing for many weeks that I felt had given me a reason to look forward to anything at all.

Sweating under my mosquito-net in the Libyan military hospital, I had decided, with what I hoped was a philosophical detachment, that life had nothing more to offer. It was no longer the pain that dominated. Nor was it the remorseless monotony — the days' distorted rhythm of early meals, the chromium tray of dressings wheeled down the ward. It was the future that filled my mind: a future blank as the ceiling around which the flies wheeled above me. The matron's announcement came as the most important I had ever heard. It set a limit to negation, re-establishing a sense of time, even of purpose.

From my ward to the concert hut was a perilous journey across a strip of desert waste. The ground plunged drunkenly under my feet like the deck of a ship. The sun struck up from it in a dizzying glare. Suddenly I felt very sick. The crammed, sweltering hall swam in front of my eyes in a pattern of white bandages and khaki. Someone led me to a chair near the front. I thought, what an ordeal! What guts he must have! In the previous life where I had known Noël, I too had been an actor of a kind. Through my drugged drowsiness, I could feel the stirrings of vicarious stage-fright, anxiety lest he exasperate or rub up the wrong way an audience still numbed and battered from the Salerno beach-head.

The curtains parted, to grudging applause. Noël was revealed, sleek, over-trim and debonair as usual, grinning from ear to ear. He was dressed as a Desert Rat, but somehow had managed to give his disguise a Cartier finish. I trembled again for him: how would they take it? I need not have worried. What I was about to witness was an extraordinary triumph of personality over environment.

This audience was hardly to be enraptured by the delicate sorcery of Noël's talent, but it was swiftly bludgeoned into submission by his sheer vitality and determination. Following with doped vision the quickening angularities of his technique, I had almost the impression of a Keystone comedy played by a one-man army.

He finished with 'I'll See You Again'. The audience roared, stamped and shouted for encores, using every flattering artifice to keep him with them, like children being kissed good night. His triumph was complete.

A brigadier on the platform, swelling with pride in his warden-ship of Tripoli's sole cultural attraction, told me tartly that Mr Coward would visit all wards later. I walked straight past him into the improvised dressing-room where Noël was changing into a dry shirt. 'What on earth are you doing here?' he asked, surprised and apparently delighted to see me. Before I could answer, his eyes strayed to my empty sleeve. I explained that I had been hit by a mortar bomb. For a few seconds he was acutely moved. Tired out by his performance, he had no resistance against the surge of emotion which brought tears to his eyes. Putting his arm round me, he led me to the brigadier's car. They drove me back to my ward, Noël promising to return after his round of the others to spend the remainder of the day with me.

The news of Noël's imminent visit was coldly received by my room-mate, Bill Gore-Langton, an ex-adjutant of my Coldstream battalion who had undergone the amputation of his right arm on the battlefield without anaesthetic. Bill was an admirable soldier, handsome and fearless, with a rare gift for bawdy anecdote and a natural sense of showmanship which made him the regiment's proudest ornament on parade. But he shared the guardsman's traditional distrust of anything to do with the stage, and made it clear that his friendship for me was by way of a personal concession. Tradition reared its head again at the prospect of meeting Noël. Normally eloquent only when discussing the etiquette of the hunting field, his beloved shires and the gentle art of hooking a salmon or a blonde, Bill now waxed rhetorical against the short-comings of 'the profession'. 'The trouble with actors', he snarled, 'is that they never talk about anyone but themselves.'

Noël appeared, and within minutes Bill had surrendered without firing a shot. It was the same phenomenon I had observed the first time I met Noël, during my apprenticeship as an actor with the Liverpool Rep. He had the actor's trick of dominating an occasion while flattering you with the sense that his performance was offered solely for your approval. I too had succumbed delighted to his astounding armoury of technical imperatives: the commanding forefinger, the swift glance to ensure that everything was in place, the staccato precision with which the sparse yet showy wit rapped out like Morse code. Although he dominates any room he enters, he creates a climate towards which everyone there is able to respond and contribute.

When Noël and Bill had talked themselves to exhaustion, I found myself bringing out importantly the plan which was on my mind. I told Noël how, with a small group of brother officers, I had formed a backing syndicate to launch myself into theatrical management. At the word 'syndicate' I detected a flicker of sardonic amusement. Not that he was patronizing, but it was incongruous to hear that Wall Street term dropped in a fly-blown North African hospital ward. The aspirations of four young men, whiling away boredom by planning such a future while still under imminent threat of extinction, must have seemed as far-fetched as a village dramatic society bidding for Drury Lane. But Noël was friendly, encouraging. Simply by listening without laughing, he made my idea seem more real.

The evening wound up with iced beer, laughter and a promise from Noël that our small holiday from war would continue next day. 'What a grand chap,' Bill murmured complacently as we settled for the night. 'And the odd thing is, he didn't say a word about himself.'

Lying there in darkness, I reflected that Noël, with the chameleon instinct of a born actor, had painted in all sincerity a portrait of himself which corresponded in every particular to Bill's ideal of a cruising companion. Every good actor is subtly changed by each different individual he encounters; I had often noticed it. Was I a good actor? I also had played instinctively the part for which Noël cast me, as I realized when I read his account of our meeting in his *Middle East Diary*, published at the end of the war.

It was heartening talking to these two boys, both of them a million per cent English, both of them Guards Officers and both so utterly different from each other and so unmistakable

in type ... Between them they created an atmosphere of well-
bred, privileged England at its best, I had a mental picture of
Sycamores, tennis courts, green lawns and rather yellowing
white flannels. 'Stands the church clock at ten to three and
is there honey still for tea?'

Noël's Rupert Brooke image of me as the spirit of Young
England fresh from the playing fields was undeserved, not to say
glamorized. Even at my prep. school, Selwyn House at Broad-
stairs, I had been hopelessly unsporting, a small stage-struck
bookworm. Where the imagination of other boys was fired by
cricket heroes or myth-inspiring figures like Lawrence of Arabia,
the visions which fixed my attention and held me momentously
enthralled were entirely to do with the theatre. The memories
from my early development which fed my visions derived from
scattered visits with my parents in the mid-'thirties to Shaftesbury
Avenue and the Theatre Royal in Brighton. They were of Elisabeth Bergner and Griffith Jones in *Escape me Never*, of the young
Laurence Olivier playing Bothwell in Gordon Daviot's *Queen of
Scots*, of Gertrude Lawrence and Douglas Fairbanks, Jr, in
Moonlight is Silver, of Diana Wynyard in *Sweet Aloes*, of John
Gielgud in *Richard of Bordeaux*, and of Ralph Richardson in *The
Amazing Dr Clitterhouse*. The fact that some of these were to
become my friends fifteen to twenty years later would at that time
have been inconceivable. My mind was a brilliant album of snap-
shots of them, walking like deities, defined with a clear luminosity.
They haunted, like a passion, my choice of reading later at Marlborough: David Fairweather's magazine *Theatre World*, Godfrey
Winn's 'Personality Parade' column in the *Daily Mirror* and the
entire literary output of Hugh Walpole.

At least I suppose it was something theatrical, larger and more
limelit, at once sharper and vaguer than life, which drew me at
fourteen to the characters of *The Herries Chronicle*, *The Cathedral*,
The Dark Forest and the rest of Walpole's novels. I galloped
through them all and, overcome with admiration, wrote a fan-
letter to their author. 'I hate school', I declared proudly, 'and
most of all games. I like acting, and I love your books.' I was
astounded to receive a reply which ended, 'Write to me again
whenever you like.'

This released from me a torrent of hero-worship. Walpole

accepted it graciously, never failing to answer my letters. The correspondence exhilarated me so much that finally I wrote inviting him to lunch with me during my next holidays, at the Ritz. Walpole replied by postcard: 'No, what you shall do is lunch with me, one sharp, Piccadilly, any day you choose.'

On the agreed day I was put on to the train at Haywards Heath by my parents, who were uncertain whether to be curious or amused. Had my father known where the day's adventure was to lead, his prevailing emotion would probably have been alarm. Living in the gentle quietude of military retirement, he shared fully the army's mistrust of the stage. He had already been alarmed about a year earlier, when he had accidentally let fall that he actually knew an actor—Allan Aynesworth, the original Algy in *The Importance of Being Earnest*, who belonged to his shooting syndicate at Horsham. When I heard this I made a huge commotion over the breakfast table. My own father, on hobnobbing terms with one of the legendary names from *Theatre World*! Through him I might actually penetrate back-stage, meet one of my imaginary demigods in the flesh! Urgently pleading, wild with joy, I dragged him up to a matinée of Mr Aynesworth's current play, and afterwards towards the stage door, gateway of the forbidden kingdom I longed to enter.

Mr Aynesworth, wearing a long black dressing-gown, seemed to gleam with a terrible antiquity, like some ancient thoroughbred groomed and shining for his last royal funeral. He still had a powerful kick, however. 'For God's sake keep him off the stage,' he pronounced with imperious dismissiveness. 'It's no place for a gentleman.' We boarded the train home to Sussex as silent and self-conscious as two mortuary attendants escorting a coffin. Even my father felt, I think, that his friend had been unnecessarily sharp, while I, watching the lights of the dormitory towns and lone farms pass and fall behind us in the dusk, saw the brilliant marquees of Shaftesbury Avenue receding with them.

But now, with the confidence of almost fifteen years, my hopes rose again as I boarded the train for my meeting with Hugh Walpole.

I arrived far too early at the block of chambers on the corner of Half Moon Street. With studied unconcern I dallied before the sumptuous window displays of Messrs Dare and Dolphin, idling away the minutes which weighed so fearfully. At one o'clock I rang the bell lettered 'Day'. A small monkey-faced man with white hair appeared suddenly and, without asking my name, shuffled me into the entrance hall. 'Mr Walpole is expecting you,' he said, leading the way up a staircase which circled the lift-shaft. Reaching the first floor, he fumbled with a door-key and ushered me into the Presence.

I was confronted by one of the friendliest figures I had ever encountered: a great jolly, red-faced farmer, bulkily proportioned, with spectacles which lent him an owl-like wisdom and benevolence. He stared at me through them, exuding cosiness and simplicity. 'You know, Peter,' he said, 'you're exactly what I thought you'd be.' My fears vanished. The imaginary world was as I had always dreamed and I felt at home.

Walpole too was just as I had imagined him. The atmosphere of his room, with its details of fussy well-being—and its glowing fire, which sparkled now in a defiant burst of winter sunshine—was somehow that of his novels, lacking only the sense of dark things lurking outside. I had never seen a room like it, and he listened indulgently while I devoured it with admiration. It was a miniature art gallery. Paintings of innumerable styles and colours struggled to catch the eye in every nook and cranny. Abstract designs hung beside landscapes of photographic realism. It was disconcerting and fascinating. 'Is that what you call modern art?' I asked, pointing to one particularly inscrutable canvas. Walpole turned towards it gravely. 'There is no such thing as modern art,' he said conclusively. 'There is good art and bad art.'

That lunch was one of the most important events of my life. Nobody under forty can properly grasp the position Hugh Walpole held in the London of the early 1930s. Then in his middle fifties, he was a viceroy of the literary world, a figure of Victorian power and munificence. His novels, in their discreetly splendid uniform green-and-gold binding, seemed as safely destined for immortality as, in those days, did Bennett's and Galsworthy's. He was Chairman of the Book Society. His weekly book column in the *Daily Express* made and broke reputations.

Walpole was naive enough to enjoy his power, and he guarded against its waning. Although a patron of the young, always championing the new and *avant-garde*, he did so out of a lonely fear of falling behind the times rather than from any real sense of community with their modernity, and they were aware of it. 'The son of a bishop,' as one of them, V. S. Pritchett, has written of him, 'he bounded about literature as if it were his diocese.' He probably did, but in those days it was.

Walpole's only rival on the London scene at that time was Somerset Maugham, and it did not take long to discover the sharp insecurity this rivalry inspired in him. At our second meeting he spoke with a kind of pained bewilderment of Maugham's acid caricature of him as Alroy Kear in *Cakes and Ale*.

One of the things Walpole most envied in Maugham was his success in the theatre. He himself, he confided to me, had once had an ambition to act, and later had tried to write plays, but 'could never think of plots'. (In the later 1930s his novels *The Cathedral* and *The Old Ladies* were successfully adapted for the stage, but by other writers — an experience which curiously echoes that of Henry James, with whom, as a young man, Walpole had struck up a lifelong friendship after writing *him* a fan-letter.) I could imagine Walpole as an actor. He was one of those people driven to enlarge and colour life, as an actor does. Since his death his popularity has gone into an eclipse, and I suppose posterity is unlikely to rate him a highly important writer. But lovers of London may still be drawn to his romantic image of the city, and readers who enjoy a compelling story to his brooding sense of the sinister. He once wrote to me, 'I am a kind of macabre romantic, and have a narrative gift which most of my contemporaries lack. I shall live in the Lakes as a kind of guide-book, but *Above the Dark Circus* and *The Old Ladies* are real works.'

To me he was always loyal in a way consistent with that first impression of simple, rubicund kindliness. I like best to remember him as I once glimpsed him, with a pang of envy, in the West End during one of my Christmas holidays from school. A lighted taxi sped by, filled with excited children, evidently on the way to or from a pantomime. In their midst Hugh Walpole beamed with a rosy Pickwickian benevolence. He was the first person to encourage me by taking me seriously, treating me as an adult, and I poured into his sympathetic ear ambitions confided to no one else. I told him how I planned to produce *Richard of Bordeaux* at school, and asked how I should go about becoming an actor. He told me to let him think about it — during the next year or so we should come to some conclusion together. At half past three on the day of that first luncheon I said goodbye to him, feeling reassured and enormously flattered.

Looking back, I realize that he tactfully deferred his promise of help towards an acting career, probably expecting that by the time I left Marlborough my enthusiasm would have faded. He could not know how I was nourishing it daily with draughts of glamour from a heady source. Every day at school I devoured the world through the eyes of Godfrey Winn in his column in the *Daily Mirror*. To me Godfrey Winn was the Saint-Simon of the day. He preached the gospel of a supernal reality which I believed in passionately. His column was, to use an apt description of D. H. Lawrence's, 'like a lamp-post that everything in the world comes and pisses on'. I devoured the photographs of Gertrude Lawrence with her *retroussé* wonder-stirring profile; of Noël Coward with his elongated cigarette-holder, which evoked for me an unexplored world of sophistication, an attitude of mind. Then, to root these magic personalities in accessible experience, there was the cosy background of the Winn cottage-*ménage* at Esher: Mr Sponge, his dog; Penny, his secretary; Mum, for ever pruning roses in the garden. Such worldly insight, such ability to walk with kings yet keep the common touch, seemed to me urgently necessary for my school production of *Richard of Bordeaux*. Seizing my pen, I wrote to inform Mr Winn, with what seemed the mildest leavening of truth with civility, that I considered him to be a greater writer than Sir James Barrie and anxiously desired his acquaintance. By return of post I received an invitation to call at his *Daily Mirror* office in my next holidays.

I journeyed to London, keyed up for a major performance: a man-to-man—no, artist-to-artist—discussion of the problems of theatrical production. I arrived at the *Daily Mirror*—and fell through a door into reality: a small clerical parlour where I found myself facing a clear-eyed Mr Winn. My powers of self-projection withered and flagged, overpowered by a sense of spatial embarrassment. When Mr Winn asked how *Richard of Bordeaux* had gone, I felt like a pianist who has forgotten even how his piece begins. I stumbled over the first bars, and halted miserably. Gallantly Mr Winn took over. With unerring panache he pinned down, summed up, encapsulated and disposed. It was a bravura performance. He ended his recital, and our meeting, with the words 'And I expect you used flags, and all that.'

I have thought so much about that sentence that it has stayed with me ever since. Meant kindly, it showed with awful, shaming clarity my total failure in the interview. My humiliation was extreme. As I walked down Fleet Street I felt my universe had been reduced to a rubble of illusions and one ineradicable phrase.

Yet in the same year that I began my friendship with Hugh Walpole I also first met C. B. Cochran. I presented at his office in New Bond Street a letter of introduction from a friend of my father, who had by then become resigned to my theatrical aspirations.

To me, Cochran's name on the brass plate downstairs represented all the glamour and adventure of the theatre. A perfume, heady as incense, billowed even more overpoweringly about me in the magic arcade above to which he welcomed me courteously. Paying me the enormous compliment of treating me as an equal, he showed me solemnly through his staggering collection of Impressionist paintings and photographs of the great names he had presented—Bernhardt, Duse, Pierre Fresnay and Yvonne Printemps, Bergner, Guitry, Chevalier, Noël Coward and Gertrude Lawrence—while from the bowels of his domain echoed declaiming Spanish voices and the stampings of Cuadro Flamenco.

I was lucky in my friendship with this 'Sun King' of the theatre. He was one of those who did most to help me enter the shining world of heightened reality which haunted my schoolboy imagination. And he also brought me into personal contact with its apostolic succession, the founding immortals of the modern theatre. It amused him wryly to recognize that he would be remembered as the presenter of 'Mr Cochran's Young Ladies'; and by the glittering string of revues and musical comedies for which he was responsible, from Noël Coward's *On With the Dance* to A. P. Herbert's *Bless the Bride*. He resigned himself to the fact that people would forget, as they already have, his part in creating *The Miracle*; his importations of Duse and Bernhardt; the fact that he gave London its first production of a play by Eugene O'Neill —*Anna Christie*, with Pauline Lord; and the memorable *première* of Sean O'Casey's *The Silver Tassie*, in which Charles Laughton played the crippled footballer Harry Heegan.

Another friend who put me into direct touch with theatrical roots which went even further back was Graham Robertson, a surviving veteran of the Victorian and Edwardian theatre, largely forgotten in the post-war world and living in seclusion. As with Hugh Walpole, I was first led to seek him out through a passionate enthusiasm for his writing. I cannot remember now how I stumbled on his autobiography *Time Was*, but turning its first pages was like straying into a golden wonderland from whose magic there was no escape. Its author had known all the *monstres sacrés* of the turn of the century: in his pages Oscar Wilde jested again, Irving held the Lyceum gallery with an eye glittering like the Ancient Mariner's, Sarah Bernhardt laced herself once more into the tunic of l'Aiglon. A whole cavalcade of legends came to life in his memories.

Most tantalizing of all was the revelation on the last page that the author, whose life had mingled with these great ones half a century before, had written his book at Witley, only a few miles from my home at Haslemere. Could he still be living there, perpetuating their fragile mortality in his own?

One blazing afternoon I set out on my bicycle to discover if the world he personified was wholly extinct, or if it might still survive so near at hand. I arrived hot and tired at the foot of Witley Hill, and was bracing myself for the steep ascent when a postman freewheeled by in the opposite direction. I shouted to him and he pulled up. 'Could you tell me, please, the way to Mr Graham Robertson's house?' I waited anxiously while he considered gravely. Would he tell me that the gentleman was deceased? Then he pointed matter-of-factly up the hill. 'Through Witley—turn right at the top. Keep on till you come to Sandhills.'

I pedalled with a leaping heart through that almost intolerably picturesque village. Time, through a shimmering bee-drowsy silence, proclaimed that here it could indeed stand still. Under the signpost which pointed at Sandhills I propped my bicycle against a hedge which was the original bank of the winding lane, and walked through a white gate down a sloping path to a Victorian villa whose outlines were furred by creeper. At the door I stood suddenly paralysed by the absurdity of my journey. What would I do with the Grail if I found it; what on earth could I say to Graham Robertson, even if he were at home? I was about to turn and flee, my last vestige of nerve deserting me, when the gravel crunched behind me.

I turned and recognized the ghost of Sargent's most memorable portrait. The man facing me looked like an early golfer in his plus-fours, white tie, shaggy hat and unseasonably woolly cloak. Yet, behind the outlandish costume, there survived a faint recollection of that poignantly boyish Victorian dandy, as slim as his jade-handled cane, exquisitely fine-drawn in his long black overcoat.

He was as disconcerted as I was. Stumblingly I apologized for my intrusion, explaining how much I had enjoyed his book; so much so that I could not rest until I had met its author. 'In that case', he said tolerantly, 'you had better come in and have a cup of tea.'

His small drawing-room was hung with part of the magnificent collection of Blake drawings which he was to bequeath to the Tate. It breathed the chilly serenity of houses once inhabited by famous men and since turned into museums. The only signs of modernity were one or two new books, fresh flowers and a signed photograph of the Lunts on a table.

Despite my desperate conversational sorties, the tea-party was not a success. My host, it seemed, was even shyer than I was. It was a relief when he suggested showing me his garden and, re-equipping himself with hat and cloak, led the way through a densely green apple-hung orchard to the barn which he used as a studio and storehouse for his pictures.

My taste in art then, largely formed by Hugh Walpole, had no room for the faint afterglow of Pre-Raphaelitism which was the essence of Robertson's style. That afternoon I was silently merciless to his graceful but somewhat anaemic portraits of Ellen Terry and Ada Rehan. Later on I came to see them as reflections of the faded splendour of that high noon at which Graham Robertson had stopped his clocks for ever. For him, the immortal yesterday in which he had been a sun had been replaced mysteriously by something so odious that he found it sacriligious even to concede its existence. So long as they stayed with him, his visitors returned to an age of tranquil gaslight and simmering copper baths. No telephone, wireless or newspapers were there to remind them that today was not yesterday. The book at their bedside would be some volume of fashionable ephemera; but its fashion would be of sixty years before, its fly-leaf, as likely as not, inscribed 'To dear Graham, from Oscar'.

Graham Robertson had lived in Arcadia with Irving, Tree and Ellen Terry, and refused to forsake it. He represented a living bridge to the age of the last great actor-managers, a vanished, prehistoric past he continued to inhabit until his death, refusing to admit that its enchanted world of illusions had grown empty and outmoded.

Meanwhile I continued to prepare for my acting career. During the Christmas holidays—I was then sixteen—I took voice and acting lessons from Molly Hartley-Milburn, the wife of Charles Hickman, at my aunt's small flat in Hill Street. It was through her that I met my next actor, Alec Guinness, then twenty-two and playing small parts at the Old Vic.

I was very nervous, and could sense Guinness's own shyness. There was something curiously unemotional, inaccessible, beyond his gentleness. Even then he had the kind of intellectual humility which was described by Matthew Arnold: 'You must get yourself out of the way to see things clearly.' But he listened kindly and with understanding, as if in a confessional—and, indeed, the sort of help our meeting gave me was similar to that which I might have obtained by pouring myself out to a priest in some shadowy cathedral stall. I came away feeling relieved of a psychological wound which, like any physical one, had needed airing to prevent it from festering. I suppose I simply felt I needed witnesses so as to convince myself of the truth of my theatrical destiny. And I was not doing too badly in gathering them—two actors, a famous author and the twentieth-century 'Saint-Simon'.

Alec Guinness in particular gave me one piece of positive, direct advice. The only acting school worth training at, he told me, was the London Theatre Studio, which had been set up in London the year before by Michel Saint-Denis and George Devine. Rather to my surprise, Hugh Walpole seconded the suggestion. When I returned after my seventeenth birthday in 1938 for the promised decision about my future, he accepted that I was determined upon the stage and agreed that Saint-Denis's school was the best place to prepare myself for my career. Long before most people in England, Walpole had become aware of the importance of Stanislavsky, and he recognized Saint-Denis as Stanislavsky's apostle in the West.

'You can't get away from Stanislavsky,' he declared buoyantly. 'You'll like him.' I was reminded of the cheerful confidence of this understatement years later in Leningrad, emerging from a documentary film about the life of Lenin with a charming enthusiast who had borne me off to see it. When I tried to stem her flow of eager questions about my response to the Father of the Revolution with the remark that he seemed to have a delightful personality, she clapped her hands, crying, 'I knew you would like each other!'

I am afraid I have to confess that I hated every moment of the year I spent under Saint-Denis in the disused chapel in Islington which had been converted into an acting school. It looked like a gymnasium, and its curriculum, it seemed to me, was one more suitable for a seminary of psychiatric therapists than students of drama. Day after day we would improvise solemnly on what seemed to me extravagantly bizarre themes. 'Now you're a dinosaur in labour'; 'Now you're a bush in a snowstorm'; 'Now you come home to find there's no tea and your mother has been raped.' I suppose it stretched and tested our imagination, but at the time I found it only incomprehensible, boring and grotesque, lacking the mystery and excitement of either Stanislavsky's books or, for that matter, of Saint-Denis's own productions, then dazzling London, of *The Three Sisters*, *The White Guard* by Michael Bulgakov, and *Twelfth Night*.

I failed at the time to see what significance these studio exercises could have in the English theatre. However, one of my fellow-toilers in the thickets of the subconscious was to find an application for them which our instructors can scarcely have foreseen. Peter Ustinov used to travel on the same bus with me each morning, enlivening the ride with graphic anticipations of whatever new fantasies the day might hold in store for us. Saint-Denis once described Peter as possessing 'a dangerous facility' which would need counteracting with discipline. This discipline he, in common with most of Peter's previous teachers, signally failed to impose.

Peter always maintained that he had been driven to acting by a process of elimination. At Westminster he had been abandoned as a hopeless case by his English master, who declared that he would never be able to write grammatically. His only success at school was as a goal-keeper. 'My natural corpulence', he has explained, 'blocked more of the goal than any other boy could.' He had left school at sixteen without taking his School Certificate. As he admitted candidly, it was obvious that he would fail it, and in any case he had no intention of entering any profession for which exams or diplomas were necessary.

In fact, Peter was cut out for the theatre by a varied artistic heredity. His great-great-grandfather had been a director of the Imperial Theatre in St Petersburg. His great-uncle was Alexandre Benois, the brilliant designer of Diaghilev's early ballets, and his mother, Nadia Benois, was also a designer and painter. On the occasion of Peter's first appearance in the West End, Alexandre Benois wrote to him, 'For centuries our family has been prowling around theatres. We have built them; we have designed sets and conducted orchestras; at last, one of us has had the nerve to scramble on the stage itself.'

I do not think Peter made much more than I did of our exercises with Saint-Denis. Already there was nothing that did not provide grist for his satiric reflex; but I suspect that, like me, he was at root slightly intimidated by our master. In spite of the affable, cosily bourgeois exterior—beret, puffing pipe, the smile which appeared to invite intimacy—there was something withdrawn and more awesome than approachable about Saint-Denis, who was a father to everyone but no one's friend. He seldom let himself go. Once, when we were devising our own improvisations, I mimed a soldier escaping under fire. Darting across the stage, I flung myself to the floor and, miscalculating my momentum, cut my chin wide open—I still have the scar. He ticked me off severely for not having proper control of my body. Control was a master-notion with him.

Behind the mask, however, lay a marvellous kindness and good humour, on which I have relied many times during our subsequent friendship. But then I was too inexperienced to absorb the ideas which were to make him a pioneer influence on the British post-war theatre. I longed to reach out to him, to talk to him and make him understand my problems. While he tried to develop our inner resources, what I desperately needed was reassurance that I had any such resources, that I could ever hope to be an actor at all. When he and George Devine held classes for actors already established in the profession, I lurked in the small passageway, marvelling at the comings and goings of the giants—Michael Redgrave, John Gielgud, Glen Byam Shaw and many others. But the only one with whom I made contact was John Fernald. He smiled at me and asked how I was getting on. The mere presumption that I was getting on at all, that I was sufficiently a member of the profession to be noticed by him, was new and cheering.

In those days—by now it was the summer of 1939—I turned again, as ever in time of trouble, to Hugh Walpole, telling him of my despair of ever making an actor. He replied hearteningly that even bushes in snowstorms may hide the light of budding talent, and that one day he would see 'the Hamlet and Richard II of my dreams'. Meanwhile he promised to write to William Armstrong, the well-known Director of the Liverpool Repertory Theatre, asking him to take me on as a student. Leaving the dinosaurs to labour in the primeval ooze of Islington, I packed my bags for the banks of the Mersey.

2

Liverpool and the War

Willie Armstrong was a legend among young actors of that period. His capriciously brilliant judgment had singled out and launched Michael Redgrave, Robert Donat and Diana Wynyard, but had missed Rex Harrison, whom he had advised to give up the stage because he showed such a singular lack of talent. This story he told with the pride and self-admonitory amusement of a schoolmistress who has failed a future prime minister. I asked Rex Harrison, a great actor whose friendship I have enjoyed for twenty-six years, whether this was true. 'Certainly,' he said. 'He told me I was not good enough, and I quite agreed; so I took to the road for ten years.'

Willie was a remote, majestic figure with a slight stoop and a bronchial wheeze which echoed eerily down the *coulisses*. He ran his company with amiable offhandedness. During my first weeks at Liverpool he seemed totally unaware of my existence. The only work I was given was playing a monkey in the Christmas production of *The Swiss Family Robinson*, adapted from Wyss's children's classic by James Laver, whose brilliant *Nymph Errant* had given Gertrude Lawrence and Cole Porter one of their greatest hits two years before. Now the portrayal of a monkey was to launch me on my acting career, and the play's adapter, James Laver, was many years later to become one of my most valued friends.

After several weeks at Liverpool I was thinking of writing again to Hugh Walpole, asking him to sponsor me elsewhere, when I heard behind me as I left the theatre one evening a thin, bronchial baying. I turned, and faced an upholstery of greatcoat and mufflers from whose depths peered the pink whimsical countenance of Willie Armstrong. I waited respectfully for him to pass, but he stopped, holding out a script. He explained that Alan Webb, who had no understudy, had a bad sore throat and might be sickening for flu. 'You may have to go on for him. See what you can do.'

44

The part, originally created by tall, sardonic Raymond Massey, was that of Raymond Dabney in *The Man in Possession* by H. M. Harwood and Tennyson Jesse, and it demanded the confident insolent charm of a Ritz-bar *maquereau*. A neatly contrived if somewhat improbable plot tells how Raymond, having served a prison sentence for some car-dealing offence, is disowned by his family and gets work as a bailiff's man; in this capacity he visits the divorcee to whom his brother is engaged. To save her face he poses as the butler at a dinner party to which his own family is invited, and then, in a daring seduction scene, replaces his brother in the lady's affections—the part of a lifetime for a mature and polished comedian.

I was aghast at Willie Armstrong's suggestion, knowing that on the stage I only looked about thirteen, and that even theatrical convention could not invest with plausibility the climax of the play—my seduction of the massive Miss Ena Burrill. Eloquently I pointed out the hazards, erotic and technical, of an engagement so unequal. I naturally expected to be relieved of this responsibility, but William, patting me on the head, reassured me that, if my love-making did not burn the topless towers of Ilium, it would at least arouse the maternal instincts of the Liverpool housewives. 'Don't worry,' he hoarsely whispered, 'it's the sort of chance every actor waits for all his life.' And leaving me holding the script the kindly muffled figure wheezed his way into the foggy night.

If it had happened in a novel, I should have been word-perfect next morning and a star twenty-four hours later. As it was I just about managed to fulfil the first half of the traditional legend by sitting up all night with the script. But a special rehearsal the following morning drained away any confidence I might have built up. Miss Burrill threw my cues at me in a manner which suggested that the whole business was a great waste of everyone's time. Whenever I got into my stride, her dog, which she always insisted on bringing with her to rehearsals, would cause a disturbance that threw me out completely.

By lunch-time I felt small and panic-stricken and adjourned to a near-by café, in no way consoled by the assurances of my imperious leading lady that Mr Webb would undoubtedly be able to play his role. It proved wishful thinking on her part. By two o'clock Mr Webb had failed either to put in an appearance or to

notify the theatre of his movements. Gingerly and with trepidation, I rigged myself out as a Mayfair roué in a suit of Alan
Webb's which did not fit, subdued my pink cheeks to a Worm-
wood Scrubbs pallor and presented myself to the director. Willie
Armstrong was in a dressing-gown, scratching around his office
for something. It turned out to be a packet of glucose tablets,
which he pressed on me. 'It's a wonderful chance,' he repeated,
'but suck these, just in case.'

I waited in the wings, sucking hard, while the other actors
built up to my entry with extravagant descriptions of my charm,
virility and sex-appeal. Then I was on. The audience took the shock
good-humouredly, and I managed to play the short scene without
drying. At the fall of the first-act curtain, Willie hurtled through the
pass-door. Everything was fine, he said, apart from the fact that,
sitting in the fourth row of the stalls, he had not heard a word.

Not to be put out, raising my voice and adopting a carelessly
truculent attitude, I cruised through the second act to the ex-
cruciating quick-change which revealed me as the butler. But
every time I moved towards Miss Burrill my dickey, as ill-fitting
as the rest of my suit, popped out with rude self-assertiveness.
Persevering against these setbacks I worked up to the climax
where Crystal, lying back on the sofa and inviting Raymond to
pounce, croons: 'Who are you? Tell me.' My great moment had
come, the cue to move forward and overpower her in my embrace. I moved. Once more, for the last time that afternoon, my
dickey popped out with a starchy 'plop'. Raising my voice, I
answered: 'Just ... the man in possession!'

The curtain fell to laughter which still rings in my ears. Twenty
years later, asked by the B.B.C. to take part in a series of programmes in which people described the most embarrassing
moments of their lives, I needed no pause for reflection before
naming this as mine. Yet in his office afterwards William Armstrong had been very cheerful, if slightly disconcerted by Miss
Burrill's forcible expression of her feelings. He was grateful to
me for keeping the curtain up, and, instead of the instant dismissal I had expected, offered as a reward to put me on the company pay-roll at a salary of eight pounds a week. I also received
several letters of encouragement and a very special tribute from
an old lady of eighty, who informed me that I was better than
Robert Donat.

At eighteen, then, I could at least claim to be a professional actor working in the best repertory theatre in England, playing the usual astonishing range of leading or supporting roles associated with repertory work. Willie and I became great friends. In his gay if somewhat impersonal rooms in Huskisson Street in Liverpool he would talk the nights away after our evening performances, reminiscing with endearing high-pitched giggles about his days as leading man to Mrs Patrick Campbell, the great actress and notorious wit for whom Shaw wrote the part of Eliza Doolittle in *Pygmalion*. He abounded in anecdotes of her ferocious wit. Pinero's 'fragile creature of Italian origin' had become, by the time Willie knew her, a substantial wasp, the sting of whose humour grew increasingly venomous.

A tolerant amusement, easy and undogmatic, was Willie's great strength as a director. He approached a script as he approached life, with a casual, intuitive adaptability which made him as much at home in the bohemian anarchy of the theatre as in the social order of the great houses which he loved. Early in the 1920s he had gone for a time to Madresfield, the seat of the Beauchamps, as a kind of dramatic coach-tutor to the Lygon family. In many ways it must have been a humiliating and painful experience. He found that he was expected to eat at a separate table, like an upper servant, and to act as a sort of moral warder to the unfortunate Hugh Lygon, whom he adored and who was later to be Evelyn Waugh's model for the character of Anthony Blanche in *Brideshead Revisited*. But the beauty of the house, evoked so magnificently by Waugh in his novel, had bred in Willie a permanent affection and respect for the grand style of English country living—the deer cropping the park, the visitors' book in the hall, tea under the cedars on a well-kept lawn. Madresfield, which later I visited with him in 1956, was one of the high points of his life, an experience which stood him in good stead when he came to direct the artificial comedies of society—by Lonsdale, Maugham and Coward—at which he excelled.

He talked brilliantly, always over the tinny whine of his gramophone, playing popular songs of the day. Even now, when I try to recall his voice, I seem to hear it inextricably mixed with that of Noël Coward faintly crooning 'Poor Little Rich Girl' on a scratchy record.

Yet my richest occasion with Willie was one afternoon during the war when I took him to tea with Graham Robertson. They took to each other instantly, and sat delightedly capping each other's stories about Mrs Patrick Campbell. Graham recalled a meeting with her, in the years after her figure began to spread, when he complimented her on a smart black-and-yellow ensemble she was wearing. 'Nonsense,' she snapped. 'It makes me look like a wasp in an interesting condition.' Willie, who played opposite Mrs Pat in *Hedda Gabler*, was able to bring Graham *au courant* with her wanderings in America—telling of the occasion when, giving a reading in the Southern States with Beerbohm Tree, she watched him thread his way to the platform through a predominantly Negro audience and, leaning forward to greet him, hissed in her most penetrating stage-whisper, 'Herbert, how *white* you look!'

Graham collapsed when he heard Willie's 'insecticide story'. Mrs Pat was being shown round an insecticide laboratory by a famous entomologist at Oxford, and he was giving her his appreciation of the ant world. 'There are the regiments, the brigades, the companies, the platoons, and even the scouts—it is a marvellous army all of their own!' There was a long pause as she looked at him with expectation. Finally Mrs Pat said, 'But do tell me about their navy.'

These memories were the sunset of a tradition that had stretched back to Alleyn and Burbage. Mrs Pat herself is a legend embellished by time and retelling, who totally captivated four of my friends: Graham Robertson, Willie Armstrong, Anew MacMaster (the Irish actor-manager) and Bobbie Andrews, whose wit ran a close second to her own.

My short period of acting for Willie Armstrong greatly boosted my self-confidence. He taught me much—far more than I should have learned but for his implicit suggestion that he found me worth teaching. Shortly after going to Liverpool I got a letter from Hugh Walpole:

Just a line to say how glad I am you stuck with Willie. You have plenty of time ahead of you, and I think that loyalty and generosity of heart are the two most important things; plus a few brains, of course, and the power to see yourself as a cock-a-doodle-doo. All these qualities you seem to have, and a small list like this is just the thing. God bless you.

Eighteen months after writing it, Walpole was dead. I received the letter in September 1939, a week or two after the outbreak of war.

My first war-time service was not carried out in uniform, but in heavy disguise. I was playing the leading role in a play called *The Astonished Ostrich* when the entire Liverpool Repertory Company was called up, conscripted by ENSA to brighten the lives of our brave boys in khaki during the nervous months of the phoney war. For some reason this particular little comedy was considered suitable for the job, and under Willie's spirited captaincy we set out to tour the army camps. Alas, even in those days of trial we were not to be spared the company of Miss Burrill's dog.

On tour we reverted to the discipline of the school dormitory. My memory is of a cheerless succession of grey military hostels where, under the steely surveillance of formidable matrons (where on earth, so far from any site of classical archaeology, did they manage to dig up all those stony ladies?), we felt that at any moment the figure of the headmaster would round a corner, poised to rap our knuckles for some innocent but briskly reported misdemeanour.

The headmaster in question was Basil Dean. He had been given the impossible job of mobilizing the enormous, amorphous British entertainment industry for the maintenance of troop morale during the dreary, bewildering climate of those early months of war. Inevitably he was to attract the fire of everyone's criticism. But he did a fine job in a confused period. The theatre and everything else were as dislocated as the train services by which we, and dozens of other quickly recruited troupes of ill-assorted talents, travelled around in a blacked-out country.

It was natural for Basil Dean to enrol Willie Armstrong as one of his first proconsuls in ENSA's war-time entertainment empire. He had been Willie's predecessor at Liverpool; in fact, he was the first director of the Repertory Theatre, establishing there before the First World War the tradition of ensemble acting which he had learned as a junior member of Miss Horniman's Gaiety Company in Manchester, and which Willie later carried on.

Now, as the theatre more or less collapsed under the initial stresses of war, it was natural for Willie to enlist under his old master's banner. I suspected that he was not unhappy at being called to these particular colours, for the job relieved him of the strains of thirty years of administration. For the course of the war he was to huddle in the stalls of Drury Lane, more heavily muffled than ever, reviewing for Basil Dean an endless pageant of plays and variety shows and indulging to the full a wonderful capacity for poetic idleness which had always seemed to me to be the secret of his artistic success.

It was in fact at Drury Lane, a few weeks after my final performance in *The Astonished Ostrich* at Pirbright, that I said farewell to him—and to my career as an actor. Years earlier, because of a family connection with the regiment, my name had been put down for the Coldstream Guards. That early enrolment, regarded by me with horror at the time, now came in handy. After an icy journey from Amesbury on Salisbury Plain, one of the camps where our caravan was resting, for an interview with the colonel at Wellington Barracks, I found myself summoned to present myself at Caterham as a candidate for the Brigade Squad.

Nobody can know everything that lies concealed in his subconscious, that immense uncharted ocean of the heart and mind where our innumerable alternative selves float. Nothing in one's history is unalterable fact. In recalling a particular memory, perhaps in effect we choose only one image from among a gigantic repository of undeveloped negatives. Later, chance experiences may superimpose others: what we had thought was an objective memory becomes overlaid and altered by time and subsequent events. We ourselves change with our experiences.

In a book written eight years afterwards I tried to recapture in all their fiery detail the furies of battle. I shall not attempt to do so now; the lightning flash, the growl of thunder, which at that time could burst over my mind at any moment, no longer exist. I see the war now in different focus, through the prism of Evelyn Waugh, whose trilogy of novels, *Sword of Honour*, has assimilated my experience of war, and I imagine that of thousands of others, into its distinctive mode of galloping tragi-comedy.

Guided by Waugh, escorted by the familiar shades of Guy Crouchback, and Apthorpe clutching his thunder-box, I am now capable of returning light-heartedly to scenes which were formerly agonizingly charged with frustration and ignominy: to that first encounter with my colonel at Birdcage Walk, now recognizable in the same terms as the minor farce played out by Basil Seal in

Put Out More Flags; to Caterham, a Prussian lunatic asylum where we learned the art of spit-and-polish and of marching and wheeling with a crispness the Tiller Girls have yet to attain.

I can even consider without qualm that ultimate initiation into communism: the twelve-seater field latrine—the Big Bertha of all thunderboxes—where a dozen of us squatted side by side in the Syrian desert, six in front, six behind, separated by a single sheet of corrugated iron, all titles, ranks and dignities ruthlessly levelled by nature. The sharp, astringent memories of that torture-instrument of war have been rendered by Waugh's Apthorpe in *Men at Arms* into a nostalgic, softly yellowing snapshot on which I look back now with amused detachment. Only vignettes, equally faded, remain of the journey leading up to it: the long weeks of monotonous seascape as our troopship crawled round Africa to the sullen, liverish shallows of the misnamed Red Sea; war-time Cairo, paradise of pimps; the dusty jolting waste of Sinai; the skyscrapers of Tel Aviv; Jerusalem, where, leaving my brother officers to tinkle John Collinses at the King David Hotel, I called on my ancestor Philip D'Aubigni, whose tomb, though handsomely restored by Sir Ronald Storrs during his governorship, inspired me only with a contrary resolve that nothing, save total necessity or utter mischance, should make me leave my bones outside Europe.

The hills of Syria where I finished my training were superbly green, except for the grey bowl of dust which our staff, with that infinite capacity for taking pains said to constitute genius, had managed to find for our encampment. Nothing grew there but exasperation. Fortunately our time-table allowed opportunities to escape with a truck to more romantic haunts, such as the Krak des Chevaliers, possibly the world's most dramatic piece of military architecture. Its towers and long curtain-walls, like those of a castle in some blossom-misted Burgundian landscape from the illuminated manuscript pages of *Les Très Riches Heures du Duc de Berry*, rose rather out of hot, arid rock into a sky of merciless clarity.

From there, a few months after Alamein, we lurched in our trucks to another graceless extreme of warfare: the Western Desert, mile after mile of anonymous dunes, littered with shabby debris. It was strewn with burnt-out tanks, empty jerrycans, a radio gone silent just when everything hinged on its liveliness.

Indeed, an uncanny silence emanated from that derelict moon-scape of sand and twisted metal as our convoy passed through it.

One morning, when we had almost forgotten that there was anything in the world but sand, we noticed a change in the colour of the horizon. Across a pale yellow sea we seemed to be approaching a dark coastline. It was the vegetation of southern Tunisia, whose Arabic name means 'The Green'; there, in the southern spurs of the Mareth Hills, the major part of Rommel's armoured strength lay concealed. On a plain bare as an aerodrome we crouched for a day and a night in slit trenches, listening for any suspicious sound from the sombre range of mountains rising ominously ahead of us. Darkness had turned to grey and greyness to a full daylight as I peered for the hundredth time across the plain's shimmering emptiness, when what looked like a mass of grey slugs began oozing towards us from the shadowed foothills. They disappeared into a depression, then, after an interminable moment, reappeared much closer: giant metallic grey cottage loaves, crawling with a demoniac life of their own, like creatures out of the imagination of Hieronymus Bosch. Now we could hear the roar and clatter of their engines—a hundred and forty or so of Rommel's tanks, seemingly implacable, irresistible. Surely nothing could stop them from overrunning our lines. Behind them the German infantry was fanning out to form a continuous line of attack.

Then the hills behind our own lines seemed to heave, with a sound like the roll of a gigantic drum. It was our artillery, tremendous and unexpected in its strength, perfectly sighted, bursting into action. In a moment the plain was ablaze with burning tanks, but still the survivors came on, the infantry behind them. Yet we held our fire until they were entering our chosen range. Then I gave the order, and my machine-guns began their intolerable rattle. With exultation I thought, 'I'm in action at last.'

It was deceptively, exhilaratingly simple, that first battle, and virtually won from the moment our anti-tank guns opened up. The machine-guns had only to clean up behind them, and in this phase my platoon was like the lucky gun in a grouse-drive. The whole line of German infantry came within arcs of our fire, presenting ridiculously easy targets as we raked them down like ninepins at a fair. In what seemed little more than half an hour, the survivors turned tail for the hills, leaving the plain bare save for dead and wounded and the red-hot skeletons of tanks. In that brief encounter Rommel had wasted a large part of his available infantry and some 40 per cent of his armour. It was actually his last action in Africa, one from which his forces never recovered. Our total casualties on that day did not reach a hundred and fifty.

The realities of war, however, were to burst on me savagely a few nights later in a disastrous attack through many acres of minefield on the strongest advance section of the Mareth Line. For an hour and a half before the crucial advance we crouched helplessly in the Wadi Boru-Remli under incessant German shelling. Later in the night I found myself with a party of five men pinned down in the minefield by fire from a German machine-gun post. Leaving three men to cover us, I ordered an N.C.O. to crawl forward with me to try and knock it out by lobbing grenades. I had gone about eight yards when I realized that I was alone. I looked back through the dark. The N.C.O. had not moved. I bawled at him; still he did not budge. With horror, I realized that, immobilized by fear, he had disregarded my order. I was appalled, more by my predicament than by any moral indignation. The conventional gesture of shooting him seemed absurdly inappropriate: he was an excellent N.C.O., for whom I had a great liking. In a flash I remembered a letter from him to his wife which had come to me for censorship that morning. She was expecting a baby; the young husband had written with touching solicitude, assuring her of his safe, imminent return. I crawled on alone into the darkness, hurled my grenade ineffectually, then led my party forward on to the wire. Three minutes later the young N.C.O. was blown to pieces on a mine.

But although several battles still lay ahead of us, the North African campaign was by now virtually at an end. Suddenly we found ourselves motoring freely through positions from which we had been bloodily repulsed a few nights earlier. From the west the First Army was racing to link up with us for the final killing of the Afrika Korps on Cap Bon, perhaps the most complete and spectacular victory achieved in any modern war. Apart, however, from an epic image of our aircraft diving towards the great columns of smoke rising from olive groves and vineyards into the Mediterranean sunlight, my remaining memories of Tunisia have a peripheral, Waugh-like frivolity. I recall racing down long

Tunisian roads in a Mercedes Benz, consigned to us coyly, along
with his liberty, by a German general, its supercharger screaming
past the sprawling pens which our ever-mounting, embarrassing
haul of captives was erecting for their own incarceration. I remember a long summer night in Von Arnem's villa at Tunis with
Beatrice Lillie, who had been stricken with dysentery but remained immaculately serene and poised; and a swim in the warm
blue sea, which promised a future as tranquil and undarkened as
its clear depths, in the elegant company of Vivien Leigh and
Dorothy Dickson. Rumours grew daily in pleasurable intensity of
our battalion's imminent return to England. Italy was tottering;
on the Russian Front the Wehrmacht was bleeding to death before Stalingrad. It seemed that a time had come at last when to
be light-hearted it was no longer also necessary to be brave.

Not even the memory of half our brigade sacrificed on the
Mareth Line to the ruthless genius of Montgomery, nor the
arrival of Bill Gore-Langton as our new adjutant, gleaming with
Pirbright spit-and-polish and keenness for battle, could quite
make us weep in those days. The tragi-comic invasion of Pan-
telleria, the Italian island in the Sicilian Channel, scarcely interrupted our day-dreaming about the life of peace so soon to dawn.

On that rocky, flea-invested island, where Mussolini had im-
prisoned his political opponents, I bathed in hot sulphur springs
with Christopher Soames. We lolled in the bubbling grottoes like
decadent Roman senators and discussed the post-war theatre,
where he thought half-seriously of joining me. How could such
a future be far away? Had we not stood together in the sunny
streets of Tunis, watching the triumphal entry of the great architect of victory himself, shamelessly forking his fingers in the sign
of victory, bulkily unaware that one of the slim, pink-faced
officers lining his garlanded route would one day be his son-in-
law?

Our bubble was too bright not to burst. Reinforcements
arrived from England; then we were ordered back to Tripoli.
Early in September we learned that another battle lay ahead and
that landing-craft were waiting to take us to Salerno. After our
orgy of hope the prospect of new danger was almost unbearable.
It was as if a sufferer from cancer, assured after several operations
that his malignant growth had been destroyed, had learnt that
yet another operation was necessary. I sweated with fear under my

mosquito-net. The idea of the future I had built up in my imagination seemed completely shattered.

One night I had a dream. It had none of the panic of a nightmare, but the detached clarity of an experience happening to someone else. I was under fire, and suddenly I knew I was wounded: not from the pain, but from an immensely lucid awareness that the worst that was going to happen had happened, and I was still there to know it. I knew I had been hit in the arm; I knew, with a sense of both fatality and deliverance, that it was my left arm, not my right. Then, somehow, I was back in England, in my aunt's flat, waiting for her to enter the room and discover I was wounded, and knowing that her discovery was the worst thing I had to face.

Our embarkation came. For four days we clung to that strip of Italian coastline, facing waves of infantry and tank attacks. In the bay behind us the navy stood by, ready to take us off the minute the order came. It was the critical day of the invasion. Between periods of extreme violence there were uncanny lulls, when the Italian landscape lay tranquil and classical, glistening with dewy lyricism. But we knew that it masked ugly, imminent danger; that hidden eyes watched us and something dark manœuvred unseen, threatening to devour us. From glittering foliage only a few yards away would come sudden, staccato barks of orders in German. We lay tense, waiting, half-believing that the next moment might bring some eerie manifestation of evil.

It was during one of those lulls that the mortar-bomb whined down and exploded.

3

First Productions

After being demobilized at the beginning of 1945, I immediately set about realizing my ambition of entering theatrical management. A year before, Ivor Novello had warned me of the perils facing me. 'From now on,' he said, 'you can trust very few. The theatre is the most exciting profession in the world. It is also a very dangerous and treacherous one. Never mind what people think of you. Follow your own judgment, and no one else's. And if ever in trouble over anything, come to me. I will never let you down.' Ivor was to demonstrate his practical support in due course by presenting one play with me and writing another for me.

Did I realize, at that stage, what the term 'theatrical management' implied? I hardly think so. I am barely beginning to realize it now. I only knew then that no other choice was open if my passion for the theatre was to be satisfied. I had studied the situation with what I thought was the necessary objective detachment, and decided that I had arrived at the only possible solution. Acting, now that I had lost my arm, seemed out of the question, and anyway I feel in retrospect that in the long run I should never have followed it through as a career. To be dependent for bread and butter on catching and retaining the whimsical fancy of a fickle public, a public that supports its idols not necessarily for their acting ability but for some indefinable appeal in their personalities, had in any case come to seem too precarious and frustrating.

I wanted, moreover, to embrace the whole range of theatrical experience, with all its prismatic facets. I wanted to choose and cast my own plays, select my own designers, pick my own directors, and even to undertake the direction myself if I felt like it. How else could I achieve this ambition, except by becoming what in England is described as a theatrical manager, in Europe as an impresario and in America as a producer?

What were my qualifications? Apart from having flirted with

the professional fringe of acting and production, none whatsoever. On the other hand, I possessed a brazen confidence, an unquenchable enthusiasm, an ardent desire to learn everything and, within the new territory which faced me, an army of carefully cultivated contacts and some genuine friends.

I was, of course, entirely ignorant of the prevalent working conditions in the theatre, and for that matter had very little detailed knowledge of how it had functioned over the previous twenty years. I seemed to be embarking on a career without any of the necessary experience in dealing with all its highly intricate departments; but I felt that the combination of my youthful enthusiasm and the sober guidance of staunch, experienced friends would in the end lead to a more imaginative and creative outlook than if I spent years studying each individual department of the theatre.

What, then, was the state of the West End theatre that confronted me at that period, and how did it function? The situation was grave. During the war the bombing of London had taken its toll: in Shaftesbury Avenue alone, two theatres had been demolished, others needed drastic repair and no new ones would be built for many years. Elsewhere, some had fallen into the hands of speculators, who bartered them with neither policy nor taste. Leases had changed hands a great many times, and through this fast sub-letting the rent charged to the producing manager had increased three or four times over. A theatre costing £80 a week before the First World War now cost, basically, £300 as a guarantee against a high percentage of the takings. Today, twenty-five years later, a commercial theatre will cost between £600 and £800 a week.

The most formidable factor in my favour, I now thought hopefully, was not the condition of the theatres or the prices; it was the presence of Hugh ('Binkie') Beaumont, managing director of H. M. Tennent, whom I had met through Willie Armstrong. It was through me that the 3rd Battalion Coldstream Guards had joyfully welcomed his concert party in Tunis. I therefore fully expected some gesture of response on my return from war.

He had fought his war with glorious success, and, helped by the generosity of Lord Keynes, the great economist, who was given war-time responsibility for apportioning Government subsidies to keep the arts alive, he had taken over many of the best theatres in London with the unobtrusive ease of an occupying general. At the age of thirty-six, Hugh Beaumont was omnipotent and invulnerable. He was a major force totally dominating the lives of actors, directors and playwrights. It was not unusual to find fourteen Tennent productions running at the same time. He moved about his empire with patience, wariness and smooth refinement. But, in spite of Ivor Novello's intervention, he seemed to be entirely indifferent to my difficulties and my attempt to get into the theatre, so my hopes were dashed to the ground.

Like Ivor Novello, Hugh Beaumont had come from Cardiff. He started in his career as an assistant to Mr Woodcock, manager of the Prince of Wales Theatre there. Mr Woodcock lodged at Mrs Beaumont's boarding-house in Cathedral Road. Opposite, at number eleven, Ivor Novello lived with his father and his mother, the great Madame Clara Novello Davies.

Bobbie Andrews, a fine actor with a mordant wit, whom both Ivor and I knew, tells a story which reads like a Dickensian anecdote of how he first met Hugh Beaumont in Cardiff. Bobbie was touring in a play called *Eternal Spring* with Lillian Braithwaite and Dennis Eadie. He was making up for a matinée, when a soft knock at his door was followed by the appearance of 'a plump boy of fifteen' who asked him for his autograph. Bobbie told him that he should also get the autographs of the other actors, but the boy replied that he was too shy to ask them. So Bobbie volunteered to get them for him, and through this act of kindness they became friends. The boy's name was 'Binkie' Beaumont.

From the Prince of Wales Theatre in Cardiff Binkie went to work as business manager for Philip Ridgeway, an adept director of Chekhov, at the Barnes Theatre, where John Gielgud made frequent appearances. Binkie later joined Moss Empires at Cranbourne Mansions, where he first became an assistant to the booking manager, Harry M. Tennent, and finally his co-director. It was as a result of this friendly liaison that H. M. Tennent Ltd was founded in 1936. On the death of Harry Tennent, Binkie ascended the throne.

'If his long reign as the monarch of his particular realm can be seriously criticized,' Tyrone Guthrie has written in his book

A Life in the Theatre, 'it is because, for all his courage and buoyant ingenuity, he has broken so little ground. He had been content to farm with splendid efficiency soil which had proved its fertility and to leave the pioneering to others.' For theatregoers and actors, H. M. Tennent was in what he gave to the public as comfortable and glamorous as a Boots lending-library. You finished a Dodie Smith and took out a Du Maurier, which you then replaced with a Terence Rattigan. But, although a man with a bland philosophy of art, he was far more dangerous, I felt, than the people I had been fighting.

In April 1945, however, with the help of Ivor Novello, who recommended it, I got my first break and managed to put on my first production in my least favourite theatre—the Piccadilly. I presented William Lipscombe's *The Gay Pavilion*, the first play to be produced in London after V.E. Day. It dealt not ungenerously with the early amours of the Prince Regent and Mrs Fitzherbert; it was, to use the words of Stephen Williams, writing in the *Evening News*, 'a charming love story, tenderly and sympathetically told'. W. A. Darlington, the critic of the *Daily Telegraph*, summed up the general tenor of criticism by describing it as 'enchanting to the eye and pleasant to the ear'. Indeed, everyone went on their knees before the glittering 1705 decor which John Fowler and Sibyl Colefax designed, and the play contained some superb performances. I still feel gratitude at the thought of Mary Ellis's tender, moving portrait of the royal mistress, at the vision of Frank Allenby, elegant and witty as the Mephistophelean Sheridan, and at the joyful domestic potterings of Muriel Aked as the Queen who simply *had* to re-arrange the furniture wherever she went. Unfortunately it did not have the mysterious extra ingredient which makes a box-office success, and ran for barely a month. It was not an encouraging beginning.

Through my friend Hamish Hamilton I had met Sam Behrman, the eminent American playwright and master of sophisticated light comedy, whose plays, such as *The Second Man* and *No Time For Comedy*, show a curious amalgam of cynicism and moral purpose. He had been in London reporting the V1 attacks when an account of my difficulties which reached him aroused all the eccentric generosity of his character. Impulsively he offered me his latest success, *Jacobowsky and the Colonel*, an adaptation of a play by Franz Werfel which was just completing a two-year run on Broadway. I was enchanted at this gesture, and even more enchanted by the play when I read it. Rachel Kempson and Karel Stepanek took leading roles, and Michael Redgrave, as eminent and brilliant a star then as he is now, doubled as director and as the stiff-necked Polish officer who escapes across collapsing France in 1940 with an unheroic but practical Polish Jew. Beginning by despising his strange companion, the Colonel ends by revering him.

This was, of course, almost the formula of *The Admirable Crichton*; and, like Barrie's earlier comedy, it told the story of how a kind heart turned out to be much more efficient than a coronet; like it again, *Jacobowsky and the Colonel* transcended mere satire to become almost a tract for the times. It drove home the lesson that blue blood, by its indifference to the common humanities, tends to bring calamity upon itself. The story, however trite in essence, was told with such cunning alternations of tears and laughter that the audience felt itself infallibly seduced. Nothing, I thought, could prevent the repetition in London of the triumph the play had already enjoyed in New York.

The prospect of success seemed immeasurably to increase the enthusiasm of Michael Redgrave, who showed great courage by offering to work for an independent producer. I knew that he could give to the character of the Colonel just the quality of mixed grandeur and silliness which the part needed.

Experience has taught me to doubt the practical wisdom of the actor-director, however gifted an individual he may be. While it is always an asset for a director to have acted, I believe it to be almost a disadvantage for him if he happens also to be a great actor. Inevitably the actor who plays in his own production will tend to see the whole play from the viewpoint of his own part, equilibrium thereby being bound to suffer. Moreover, I hold that it does a great actor's art no good to be bereft of all discipline excepting that which he chooses to impose upon himself. All art, save perhaps for the conceptions of a few geniuses, is the better for the restraint imposed on it by others, or by the limitations of the medium, however exasperating it may seem at the time. So far as the actor goes, in general he positively needs an authority above his own to check and guide the way a role develops. Of course there are exceptions to this generalization:

Laurence Olivier, John Gielgud and Jean-Louis Barrault come immediately to mind. Yet they serve only, I believe, as exceptions which prove a rule.

However, in the case of *Jacobowsky and the Colonel* Michael Redgrave admirably combined his talents as both actor and director and the play was excellently received. It did business good enough to justify a long run in the case of a normal production. Playing, as we were, to takings in the region of £1,900 a week, we should have been more than satisfied in ordinary circumstances. However, the play had been expensive to put on, and its running costs were comparable with those of a musical comedy. Consequently, after a run of a couple of months, I sadly decided to withdraw it. With this second failure I seemed to be back where I had started, my prospects of breaking into London theatre dimmer than ever. With his customary grace Sam Behrman was quick to advise me in no way to be disconcerted; he would offer me his new comedy, *Dunnigan's Daughter*, which the Theatre Guild were about to produce in New York.

So now I was to attempt a new start, withdrawing as far as possible *pour mieux sauter*—as far as the New World itself. I needed a pause to reflect upon the crowded and worrying hazards of the previous few months. Besides the beginnings of my career as an impresario, these had included the closing stages of my military career, with my getting accustomed to my empty sleeve; and, in particular, one moment on a Sunday morning in June 1944, when at twenty past eleven, out of the bright sky over Queen Anne's Mansions, a flying-bomb had dived straight upon Wellington Chapel, where many of my friends were at service. At that moment I was dismissing the King's Guard a bare fifty yards away. If the chapel's massive walls had not withstood most of the bomb's blast, we too should inevitably have been blown to pieces. It had seemed ironical to have survived the horrors of Mareth and emerged from Salerno still alive if not entirely whole, only to witness on Birdcage Walk the most horrifying scene of my military career.

At least I had gained one thing from the last few months, from my abortive forays into Shaftesbury Avenue: the knowledge that this was the career in which I most desperately wanted success, the only one in which my passion for the theatre could be satisfied.

4

America in the Forties

During the war we in Europe had forgotten the meaning of the word 'metropolis'. Above all, I found I had forgotten those infinite resources of light that a city could command. Light to defy darkness or gloom, light to transform the most humdrum building into a legendary palace. The black-out had by no means vanished from London when I left in August 1945. The impact of New York's lights was consequently overwhelming. New York in the hot nights of that first month of peace was a beacon, a phosphorescent sea, a dragon flaming on the clouds. Evening after evening I would stroll down Broadway towards Columbus Circle, past theatres that were shut during the hot weather, through a milling haze of multi-coloured neon which blazed into a breathless sky.

It was curious too to find oneself in a city which revelled with no sense of guilt in the luxuries it could afford. In war-time England we had grown into the habit of apologizing for every extravagance, feeling a twinge of conscience if we ate a good meal. In America anyone with money took frank pleasure in the prodigious quantities of food it would buy, pride in giving lavish parties.

My primary reaction to Broadway was that I was witnessing a unique revolution. Its theatres were a dizzy harvest of plenty. Coming from London, I was astounded by the number and range of independent productions. In New York, even though a majority of theatres were owned by the powerful Shubert group, there was at least a score of managements competing to rent them and no question of owners cautiously tying themselves to one production company. New dramatists had a far greater chance of a hearing, and the New York theatre seethed with rising talents. This accounted for the extraordinary experimental vitality of the American theatre, a theatre which had hardly existed as an independent organism forty-five years before. It was Jane Cowl, that vibrant catalyst and great actress, who, over innumerable cups of coffee at the Algonquin, pointed out to me that Eugene O'Neill was the first American playwright to be taken seriously in Europe and to influence European theatre. Yet *Anna Christie* had been written as recently as 1921.

She told me that Eugene O'Neill was a disciple of Strindberg and Nietzsche. In the 1930s Elmer Rice, Thornton Wilder, Clifford Odets and Lillian Hellman had carried on the tradition he began, while on the lighter level Sam Behrman, Robert Sherwood and Philip Barry moved with sophisticated ease over the European scene. The aim and intention of the first group was to give the essence, almost the smell, of American life — particularly the harsh strident life of the back-streets, the waterfront, the broken-down saloon; and from this material, from situations which could occur nowhere but in America, they distilled, sometimes with great success, a rough poetry.

The trouble, to European tastes at least, was an affectation of 'toughness' which, in nine cases out of ten, covered a core of sentimentality — a nut with a marshmallow centre.

As I ran the gamut of the New York theatre from the hit of the season, *The Glass Menagerie*, the first play by Tennessee Williams to catch the public imagination, to Jerome Robbins's and Leonard Bernstein's *On the Town*, I came to realize that almost the only element held in common by the American and the British stage was language, and that largely by coincidence.

In America two subjects which in 1945 were entirely taboo for British theatrical managers had become part of the playgoer's staple fare: mythology and political satire. And I was fascinated also by the emergence, under my eyes as it seemed, of a completely new formula for musical comedy which was destined to revolutionize the musical show. For fifty years the musical chorus had been dressed for the garden-party in the first act, for the beach and the tennis-court in the second, and for the ballroom in the third; and this tradition persisted almost until the Second World War on both sides of the Atlantic, and could even be detected in the brilliant screen collaborations of Fred Astaire and Ginger Rogers.

Then, all at once, America gave birth to *Carousel*, *Annie Get Your Gun*, *South Pacific* and *Oklahoma!*, and to a formula which appeared to us to be entirely new. Perhaps on analysis we shall find that at root it represented a return to origins in the Viennese operetta; but if this was the original model, it remained unrecognizable under a score where languor gave way to rhythmic sparkle in settings—Pacific war-base or cowboy fair—that strove for democratic realism with, at the back of it all, a meticulous choreography created by Agnes de Mille or Jerome Robbins.

The revival of the American musical was due in no small part to the work of the adventurous and exciting Theatre Guild, which for thirty years stood out as the most solid managerial group in America. They had fallen briefly into a decline, but had been saved by a production of Philip Barry's *Philadelphia Story* in 1939, and then went from strength to strength with productions of *Oklahoma!* and *Carousel*. Directed by Laurence Langer and Theresa Helburn, these were the most beneficent influences on the American theatre of the first post-war years.

A generation of young Stanislavsky-orientated actors was rising from the ashes of the Group Theater at that time. One of them, whom I was taken to meet after a performance of Tennessee Williams's *You Touched Me*, invited me to stay in his family's apartment. His only major Broadway appearance so far had been as one of the Lunts' sons in Robert Sherwood's play about occupied Norway, *There Shall Be No Night*, but his name was becoming known to insiders: it was Montgomery Clift.

Monty was surely the outstanding American discovery of recent years. As our friendship grew, I came to respect the extraordinary insight and enthusiasm which he turned upon the American theatre. I always felt apprehensive for him. He loved the theatre passionately. He was a poet, and his feverish pitch of exaltation reached out towards impending catastrophe. Many of the ideas which, for better or worse, I hold on the American theatre were formed from our endless talks and grew from our enthusiastic disputes.

Monty fitted in with the obsessed and neurotic writings of Tennessee Williams, who is perhaps the greatest American dramatist of my generation and whose early plays, such as *The Glass Menagerie* and *A Streetcar Named Desire*, were works shot with a curious beauty and simplicity. The decadent characters of his later plays, drawn to the precipice of perilous and extreme situations, were inflated to exaggerated proportions by a neurotic urge for outrage. But he has always remained a master of his craft.

1. Noël Coward in Switzerland (1970)

2. William Armstrong (Liverpool, 1939)

3. The author as an ensign in the Coldstream Guards (1940)

4 (*above*). Gertrude Lawrence and Laurence Olivier with the author at *The Way Back* (1949)

5 (*top right*). Michael Redgrave and friend in *Dead of Night* (1945)

6 (*below*). Alfred Lunt and Lynn Fontanne at Genessee, Wisconsin (1945)

7 (*bottom right*). Freddie Lonsdale (1935)

8. Ivor Novello with Dorothy Batley in *The Rat* (1922)

10 (*below*). The author and Phyllis Monkman in Ivor Novello's *We Proudly Present* (1947)

9. C. B. Cochran in his office (1948)

For Peter.
from his friend
a very old party.

11 (above).
W. Somerset
Maugham (1944)

From Peter
Thursday May 15th
1950
I confirm our
deal. That I am
to play Gaumorance
for you.

Either in England
or New York.
Ever
really
A E Matthews

12. A. E. Matthews's
contract with the
author for *The Gay
Invalid* (1951)

Not all the talent on Broadway then was young or American. Throughout the 1930s and the war years New York had become a haven for writers, artists and intellectuals who had fled before the advance of Hitler's legions to the refuge of the New World. The flower of Europe's theatre between the wars—German, Austrian, Czech, Hungarian—could be found crammed together within a few blocks of Manhattan, struggling to put down roots in that tough alien soil. Brecht was translating his *Galileo* for a production with Charles Laughton. Kurt Weill, his musical partner of *The Threepenny Opera* days, had scored two Broadway hits, *Lady in the Dark* and *One Touch of Venus*. In the season just ended Piscator had directed an undistinguished comedy; the Hungarian dramatist Bush-Fekete had adapted Franz Werfel's *Embezzled Heaven* for Ethel Barrymore; Elisabeth Bergner had appeared in a thriller, Katina Paxinou in a comedy about Polish immigrants, and the great Viennese star, Mady Christians, in a sentimental piece called *I Remember Mama*, in which she played Marlon Brando's mother. Finally, to make them all feel at home, Jan Kiepura and Marta Eggerth were singing *The Merry Widow* at the vast City Center, a production which they were to repeat for me at the Palace Theatre in London in 1955. In New York beat the vigorous pulse of world theatre.

Alongside these refugee enclaves there existed a colony of British exiles. Most of its company were elderly writers and actors who had contributed to the war by keeping the Union Jack flying in New York, while leaving scarce rations and accommodation for younger folk at home. That at least was their explanation, though it was not hard to feel that their spiritual residence had become New York as much as London. Most belonged to the age when American theatre had been the western terminus of a busy transatlantic traffic in glossy international star vehicles. The majority of them—including Cedric Hardwicke, Edmund Gwenn, Dame May Whitty, Nigel Bruce and Clifton Webb—seemed delighted to see me. 'After all, we were all one family and we have been through a lot together,' Edmund Gwenn informed me. 'We met every Sunday to discuss "war strategy".' They opened their arms to me as one of them, a new member of the club, if slightly late in putting in an appearance.

As a group they are embalmed for eternity in Evelyn Waugh's *The Loved One*. They clung together like the civilians of an Indian

E

frontier garrison, organizing charity matches and 'Bundles for Britain' benefits; and meeting for 'community tune-ins' to the B.B.C. in one another's apartments. It told something of the quality of their transplanted lives that among the lions of their circle was my friend Michael Arlen.

Twenty years before, this man, whose Hawes & Curtis backless waistcoats had aroused great envy in Noël Coward, published his sensational bestseller, *The Green Hat*, which brought him a bright yellow Rolls-Royce and a reputed £120,000. When its heroine, the gay, dreadful and intense Iris Storm, her green hat shading eyes like 'two spoonfuls of Mediterranean blue in the early morning of a bright day', swept into the society of the 1920s, Arlen followed in her wake. The story of her appalling life and her eventual self-sacrifice for love, as she drove her shining Hispano into her favourite tree, catapulted the author from his little flat in Shepherds Market into the high society he described. Noël Coward has recalled meeting him soon after his success, 'the odour of recent shabbiness lingering in his nostrils'.

Now—with the 'Bright Young People' a thing of the past— he had become a sort of elder statesman of the dinner table, never committing the indiscretion of writing anything more. But he still boasted the profile of an old-fashioned Monte Carlo roué, still fitted his long cigarette-holder with mentholated cigarettes shipped by a tobacconist in Notting Hill Gate, still turned lavender epigrams which one might hear coming ten minutes ahead but could not help admiring for their antique polish. His exotic aura made his mannerisms forgivable, even attractive. His talent, he made you feel, was a kind of youthful accident. Here, at last, he was able to practise his true profession —that of the perpetual cosmopolitan guest.

In the 1920s his Armenian extraction had, he claimed, given him objectivity in observing 'these charming people', but now he had lost his way in the modern world. He would sit lonely, isolated, elegant, brought alive by the mention of Tallulah Bankhead, Lady Howe or Noël. 'Occasionally', he would say, 'I see someone who remembers me, but these visits are like angels—short, far between and empty.' It was a £200 cheque from Arlen that had enabled Noël Coward to put on *The Vortex*. This not only gave Noël the break which was to launch his career, but provided Arlen with a memory that he fondly cherished.

When he spoke of it his face went as white with excitement as when, after the first night, he had said to Noël, 'I'd have been so proud, so *very* proud if I had written it.' In later years he never went to a play or read a book.

How happy Michael Arlen would have been now to have seen *The Green Hat*, and his earlier novel *The London Venture*, reissued, and his play *Lilli Christina* presented with great success on television during 1968. He was a sweet sort of eccentric, and anybody who cared to take the trouble loved him.

We are told by Robert Conquest in his book *The Great Terror* that Stalin was deeply affected by his second wife Nadehda's death: 'He felt it for the rest of his life. Blaming it on enemies, and on Michael Arlen, whose book, *The Green Hat*, she had been reading at the time...' This account is substantiated in Svetlana Alliluyeva's reminiscences of her father, *20 Letters to a Friend*. If only Michael Arlen could have known that *The Green Hat* had had a direct bearing on the course of history he would have died a happy man.

An even grander carnivore of the colony was Somerset Maugham, to whom his nephew Robin Maugham, the distinguished novelist and playwright, had given me a letter of introduction when I first arrived in New York. With him I struck up an illuminating, if uneasy, friendship.

After the rigours of the evacuation from the Riviera in 1940, an episode to which Maugham still referred with considerable asperity, he had been sent—largely, he told me, at the instance of Duff Cooper—to America as a sort of unofficial ambassador of good will. However unexpected the selection may seem—for the quality of good will does not leap obviously to mind in connection with that analyst of the human condition—there he was, almost as large as life, a resident of the Plaza since before Pearl Harbor, full of strictures upon the tactlessness of the English in their social dealings with Americans and irradiating the homespun scene with a glacial geniality which, if it chilled my heart, seemed to pass in New York for real love of his fellow creatures within the Western Hemisphere.

'Our sad lack of hospitality to American troops in England', he said, across an expanse of expensive roses in his bijou penthouse, 'does not enhance our popularity. They feel, in the light of their own lavish hospitality to English visitors to this country, that no one in England can be bothered with them.'

As he spoke, I could not help thinking of all those English families who had given hospitality to the American forces. And those girls too who had given birth to little half-American remembrances of our reserve and lack of hospitality. What more could England do, I wondered?

'That is why', he continued, 'I am so careful, however intolerable it may be, to be polite to all the strangers who pester me and intrude on my privacy. Many total strangers ring me up on the pretext that they have met a great friend of mine whom I wouldn't have heard of, and say they are dying to meet me. So I have them up, give them a drink, and then, to get rid of them, finally announce that I have a pressing engagement and that they will have to excuse me. After all, that was the job I was sent over by Duff Cooper for in 1940, and although officially my job is at an end, I do consider that it is the job of every English visitor to this country to put themselves out in an effort to re-adjust this prevalent American conception of the average Englishman. We are hated for our reserve, our shyness, which they put down to coldness and bad manners. I am about the only resident Englishman here', he went on, pouring me out a dry Martini, 'who has scrupulously and successfully avoided giving offence. But it is amazing how stupid and tactless some of our prominent citizens have been. Before we adjourn for dinner let me give you two words of advice for your trip here—never criticize an American to his face, unless it's to rave about something, and never call an American by his surname if he's already calling you by your Christian name—which he will do automatically.'

He employed no secretary. Knowing the persistence of American lion-hunters, I asked Maugham during dinner how he warded off their assaults. Surely every time the telephone rang he was at somebody's mercy? He nodded. 'The real problem is, they don't take "no" for an answer. One man rang me up to read me a poem he had just written. I told him I was just going out; he inquired if he could come the following day. I explained that I was to be out of town; but nothing would deter him. Finally, in desperation, I said, "But I don't want to hear your poem, sir." There was a dreadful pause; then the voice said,

"Oh, go to hell."' Maugham sighed. 'Just the sort of incident I'd do much to avoid.'

Maugham approximated in few ways to my youthful conceptions of him. As a boy I had yearned to meet him, imagining a character who, beneath an affectation of cynicism, would show in his daily commerce with others a profound understanding and a sublime compassion for all their secret aspirations and disappointed hopes. Not a bit of it. I had often remarked casually, without particularly registering the observation, that many a writer who shows in his books an exquisite sensibility for human feelings turns out on acquaintance to be an emotional bulldozer, quite insensitive to the mental climate in which he moves. It would be wrong to accuse Maugham of precisely this sort of obtuseness. The fact is that when you had got to know him, you came to realize that he was not the great philosophic, compassionate analyst of mankind that, for instance, Flaubert or Dostoyevsky was. He was certainly an analyst, but an analyst exclusively concerned with human frailties; confronted with virtues, his retorts and refineries ceased to operate.

His manner was a strange amalgam of chilling sarcasm and pedantic harshness; beneath the metallic rhythm of his conversation I detected a hint of unexpected ribaldry in the close embrace of primness. The eyes carried a look half-candid, half-veiled, and the finely chiselled face suggested a mandarin who had got little comfort from his experience or years. A profound melancholy seemed to lurk beneath the ironic crust, a deep and exacerbated grudge against his personal defeat by life. I often wondered if he had ever known the happiness which comes from genuine affection, and, if not, whether fame had proved a pitifully inadequate substitute. As I later discovered, he robbed any relationship of grace, affection and the excitement of discovery almost as a psychological reflex.

Fortunately the exaggerated patriotism of the expatriate English was almost equalled by the Anglophilia of many New Yorkers. Among the most enthusiastic was Sam Behrman, who, it will be remembered, had given me the British rights to his successful Broadway adaptation of *Jacobowsky and the Colonel* by Franz Werfel, whom Behrman had called the leading creative genius to come out of Central Europe. Like *Jacobowsky and the Colonel*, some of

Behrman's most successful plays had been adaptations, such as *Amphitryon '38* after Giraudoux, written for and played by the Lunts.

Sam Behrman is a doyen of the *New Yorker*, for which he has written since 1927 and in which his books *Duveen*, *Portrait of Max* and *The Worcester Account* all first appeared. He is, I think, the greatest wit I have met. Small, bald and exquisitely civilized, with the beaming innocence of a business-suited Buddha, he possesses a kind of Oriental delicacy both in humour and sensibility which, while making him marvellous, lovable company, has also turned him into a sort of recluse. He slips in and out of life, seemingly unable to face the results of his experiments, which, as far as one could judge, have always been successful. Behrman was to act as my counsellor through the labyrinth of New York.

During the 1920s he had been a founder member in New York, with Robert Sherwood, Maxwell Anderson and Elmer Rice, of the Playwrights Company. This was an enterprise that had started with high hopes. Its opening production, Sherwood's *Abraham in Illinois*, was a huge success. But owing to the company's ruling that every play written by any of their members must be produced, the productions often proved disastrous. This was certainly so with the closing production, Sherwood's *The Rugged Path* (a title which caused Behrman sad amusement).

I had gone to Washington to see this production in the hope that it might be a possibility for London. While there I met Spencer Tracy, for whom the play had been specially written. Tracy was a dynamic and adaptable actor, but there was little he could do for this intractable battlefield epic. I went round to his dressing-room with Robert Sherwood, and he seemed pleased to see a visitor. When I started to deliver the old dressing-room platitudes he stopped me dead. 'I'm not interested,' he said. 'Tell me about yourself—sit down and have a drink.' He then proceeded to concentrate all his attention on me. He had a magnificent head and his eyes reflected a curious mixture of confusion and rapture, but there was something deeply disturbing about the whole interview. My eloquence at this exacting moment was vibrant. I never stopped talking, giving him a whole history of the war, as Bob Sherwood glared down at me with a melancholy expression of dying chivalry.

Then I suddenly realized that Tracy was not listening. He was staring me straight in the face, but with the expression of some-one half-mortgaged. He was bored to tears, and I brought my story of the battles of Italy to a full stop. It was only when I got up that he came to life. I eased myself out of his dressing-room amid a profusion of grateful thanks.

Sherwood himself was a very shy man, enormously conscious of his height but full of humour and splendid fun. He was the top-paid writer in Hollywood, but had been extremely careless with his money. Behrman told me of a lunch he had with Sherwood just after he found that all his earnings had been embezzled by his broker. Sherwood had handed over all his income to the broker, never asking any questions. 'How could you do that, Bob, without ever asking to see what stocks he had bought for you—how could you do that?' And Bob had replied, 'He was so boring that I avoided him.'

Behrman had originally worked as publicity officer for the theatrical producer Jed Harris, a saturnine autocrat whose hold over his subordinates' lives extended to ringing them up, with scathing commands or upbraidings, at all hours of the day and night. The experience had marked Behrman for life. He later went to Hollywood, where he wrote four of Garbo's scripts, including *Queen Christina*.

For Behrman, Hollywood always conjures up a certain incident that he can never forget. One day he had had an appointment with a great friend, a director of Metro-Goldwyn-Mayer, and walked into his office to wait for him and sat down at his desk. He saw in front of him a heap of yellow paper headed 'Artists Available'. From idle curiosity he thumbed through several pages, and came across the name Scott Fitzgerald. His heart stopped. It was well known throughout the studio that only those on the 'Artists Unavailable' list were to be employed. Everyone on the 'Available' list stood in the death-cell, with no means of reprieve. 'This was one of my saddest and most poignant experiences,' Behrman told me.

The three or four days which I and Behrman spent together on tour with *Dunnigan's Daughter*—the new play that he offered me for London—have never ceased to be a rich topic for conversation between us. His director on the tour was a dark, solicitous young man named Elia Kazan. At the time I had barely heard of him. Sam told me he had first seen him in Clifford Odets's *Waiting for Lefty* in the 1935 production by the Group Theater. 'He is an extraordinarily brilliant man. He is a wonderful actor and is marvellously talented as a director—especially in plays which depend on violence. When he is dealing with a play which does not rely on violence, which depends on subtlety of characterization, on grace of dialogue, and on nicety of inflection in the different actors, he is quite lost. He has tried several of those plays, but they are in a language he does not understand.'

I found Kazan to have an irresistible charm. He was small and bow-legged — a physical insignificance of which I felt he was very conscious, but which he made up for with the stature of his vitality. It is this compelling vitality and resilience which have obviously sustained his extraordinary career as actor, director, novelist and, most notably, film-producer. Like a pocket version of Goethe's universal man, he has surmounted every difficulty. Born in Constantinople of an Armenian family, he later emigrated to America, where he spent six years as an actor with the Group Theater before starting to direct on Broadway. In 1947 he was co-founder of the Actors' Studio Theater, from which he took the actors Marlon Brando and James Dean for his memorable films, *On the Waterfront* and *East of Eden*.

The story goes that on his arrival in Hollywood a senior studio executive had suggested that Kazan should change his name to the more acceptable 'Cézanne'. When Kazan pointed out that this was the name of a rather well-known painter, he was told: 'You make just one good picture, and nobody will even remember the other guy.'

While Sam Behrman wrestled invisibly in hotel rooms with the recalcitrant second act of the play, I was free to discover the splendours of the early New England autumn—the red and golds which lent an almost Technicolor unreality to the wooded hills, the leafy villages of white-frame houses where old ladies rocked on their piazzas, calling the latest gossip to each other under yellowing lime trees. I was also introduced to the New England cuisine, in particular to its superb lobsters, shrimps and tiny crabs, which, caught between the casting off of one shell and the growth of another, are fried in batter or breadcrumbs to make one of the tenderest, most delicious sea-foods in the world.

As the tour went on, it became increasingly clear that *Dunnigan's Daughter* was a problem script. Though this production was the main pretext of my trip, I had hopes of finding other plays to take back to London with me. So, venturing even farther into the American hinterland, I took up the most dazzling of the invitations which I had brought with me from England: to go deep into the Middle West to stay in Genesee, Wisconsin, with the stars for whom Behrman, Coward and Robert Sherwood had written some of their greatest hits—Alfred Lunt and Lynn Fontanne.

My contact with them had come through Graham Robertson, for whom they were the only living deities worthy of the same degree of worship that he had offered the theatrical Olympians of his youth. They had been brought to Witley by his friends the Hamish Hamiltons; through the same kindly friends I had met them in 1944 when they were playing *There Shall Be No Night* at the Aldwych. In their suite at the Savoy I had spent an evening dining with them in the company of three future friends—John Gielgud, Edward Molyneux and Cecil Beaton—so enchanted an evening that I could remember little of it save the luminous serenity of our hostess and the paradoxical surprises of our host. I had believed it axiomatic that great actresses must be difficult. Here was one whose transparent goodness shone forth from candid eyes, a lovely smile and an unexpected schoolgirl laugh. I had assumed that the leading English-speaking actor of sophisticated comedy must be himself a *boulevardier*, aloof and blasé, yet my first impression of Alfred Lunt was of a huge, handsome collie who at any moment might sweep some delicate piece of Meissen off the table with his shaggy, faithful tail.

I came away feeling I had been a tongue-tied bore. Astonishingly, Lynn wrote a few days later to Graham Robertson that 'We have met Peter, and both of us are in love with him.' We met again regularly, their growing friendship a thread of brightness through the darkest days of the flying-bombs. Now I was on my way to stay with them, boarding the night train for Chicago at Grand Central.

Arriving at ten o'clock in the morning, I telephoned Lynn and was informed by her distant, crystal voice that Alfred was even then standing by for my arrival at the station at Milwaukee. He had four more hours to wait; not until two o'clock in the afternoon did acres of brightly coloured billboards—showing lovely giantesses with implausibly slim waists hoisting tankards of

Schlitz's lager in their rosy hands—slide past my window and
signal my arrival in the brewing-capital of the United States. But
the vigorous delight of Alfred's welcome was almost embarrassing
as he bore me off by the arm to his Cadillac.

We whirled out of Milwaukee into a lean, haggard landscape
which stretched to infinity, its only vertical feature a cat's-cradle
of power lines marching towards the horizon. A cluster of anonymous houses rose out of the plain: Genesee, where lanky figures
lounging against the corner of a drug store came to sudden life,
saluting Alfred in his vast black Cadillac. Then we turned into a
drive flanked by scraggy woods, at the end of which sprawled an
amiable confusion of white clapboard and green shutters, looking
rather like a golf-club or, as Alfred suggested, a two-star country
hotel. As we pulled up in the courtyard, a pony-tailed teenager in
elegant blue jeans flung herself out of the house and into my arms,
bubbling 'Darling! Darling! Darling!' It was Lynn, perennially
radiant; and in her 'darlings', utterly remote from the empty
cries of the theatre dressing-room, was a welcome which, for the
first time since I landed in New York, gave me the secure strength
which comes of knowing yourself surrounded and protected by
love.

This was the beginning of ten perfect days, lifted out of the
vulgar stresses of ordinary life into a gay serenity which brought
to mind the golden leisure of Turgenev's country gentry, talking
for weeks on end with unflagging vigour in their faded manor-
houses. Not that there was anything faded about the gleaming
woodwork and bright, tight-buttoned Victorian sofas of the
Lunts' home, whose apparent haphazardness concealed all the
cunning apparatus of American comfort and the busy schedule of
a working farm. While Alfred pursued his stern round of morning
labours, coaxing eggs from chickens more temperamental than
any West End star and delivering them to the near-by Cow &
Gate factory along with more and more milk for more and more
babies, Lynn and I would stroll over the wild piece of scrubland
known to the family as 'Lynn's Proper', laughing and talking
about everything under the sun.

Returning for lunch, we would find Alfred in the kitchen,
planning the meal like a general plotting a momentous offensive.
At table he would preside anxiously over the outcome of each
elaborate strategy, watching us to see the effect of a cream soup

or an omelette. Success elated him; anything less than ecstasy on our part would sink him into a dejection far lower, I am sure, than any consciousness that he had given (if he ever has) a bad performance in the theatre. Lynn played up valiantly to his dazzling culinary displays, and in return he would lead the conversation round from the most improbable starting-points to the one dish at which she was his peer. 'Do you', he would suddenly ask, in the midst of an animated discussion on Sartre or the relative virtues of artificial manures, 'care for trifle?' If you said 'Yes' his face would light in a smile of triumph, while Lynn visibly had to restrain herself from clapping hands. 'There you are, Lynn, this is your moment,' he would exclaim. 'All my life I've failed to make a decent trifle. But Lynn's—ah, there's a masterpiece!' By which time Lynn would be sitting with pencil poised over her diary. 'Now,' she would ask, 'which day shall be trifle day?'

Idyllic as such domesticities were, I could not help wondering whether the bleak, half-broken landscape of Wisconsin could hold the Lunts for long after their glories in New York and London. Once, as if he guessed my thoughts, Alfred broke out suddenly with 'Oh, we've been so happy down here. I've never been so happy in my life! I get up at six in the morning, work right through the day round the farm, and go to bed every evening at nine. I'm blissfully, but blissfully happy; and the awful thing is, I dread going back to the stage. I never want to act any more. After all, what's the point? I've had more than my full share of it. I think happiness such as I have at the moment much more important.'

One evening he broke his routine for a special occasion. It was the reopening of the local pub, the Walkyshaw Liquor Bar, on the return from the wars of its owner, Stag. 'It's a great event, you know,' said Alfred .'Stag would certainly appreciate it if you and I dropped in.' That was the plan—an evening of male carousing. But Lynn, lounging in a dazzling black-and-white silk pyjama suit, put a spoke in that wheel.

Alfred drew her into whispered conference outside the door. Clearly he was preoccupied by the possible effect of her pyjama suit in a rural Middle Western saloon. However, the whispered conference ended in the only way possible, with Lynn smiling and triumphant.

Of course when we reached the Walkyshaw Liquor Bar it

showed no vestige of the temple of gaudy Western sin these
hesitations had led me to expect and the villagers were delighted
to see the Lunts, clearly accepting them as friends and neighbours;
not for their theatrical prestige, but as successful, unobtrusive
and likeable members of the agricultural community.

The evening flew. It seemed only minutes after our arrival
when Alfred came up, showing all the symptoms of train fever.
'It's terrible,' he said, displaying his watch agitatedly. 'Ten
o'clock—half an hour over my bedtime. I must get back at once.'
We said good night and set off on the dark walk back to the farm.
The night was clear, the sky a prairie of stars. Alfred remarked
how much bigger and brighter the stars in the Mid-Western sky
seem than elsewhere. 'I think', pronounced Lynn, 'that they hang
lower in this part of the country.'

We stopped in our tracks, mouths open in astonishment.
Then Lynn saw the grave fatuity of her remark. She began to
gurgle with laughter. We caught it from her. 'My God,' cried
Alfred, 'that's your best so far!' We stood there in the enormous,
friendly night, doubled up by a helpless contagion of laughter,
choking and wiping our eyes. The stars seemed to grow larger
as we stood there. It was one of those rare moments when one
recognizes an indescribable happiness as it occurs.

Too soon it was the eve of my departure. Alfred had gone to
bed punctually. I sat at Lynn's feet in the softly lit drawing-room,
talking over my theatrical future with her. 'Is there any way I can
help?' she asked. 'Anyone whose influence I could help mobilize
for you?' There were few people in the American theatre whose
good will could have been more helpful to me. We ran through a
list of playwrights, and reached the name of John Van Druten,
whose *Voice of the Turtle* was then a smash hit on Broadway.
After the early English success of *Young Woodley* he had found
London unreceptive to the light comedy which was his real
talent and had emigrated to Broadway, where it flowered
brilliantly. 'Of course John will help you,' cried Lynn; 'he's
such a dear person.' Immediately she wrote to him about me in
terms of the warmest generosity.

I left for New York the next morning, travelling through deep
snow. Winter was coming and we had to return to work in hand:
I to my quest for plays, Lynn and Alfred to prepare Terence
Rattigan's *Love in Idleness*, which was produced in America as

O Mistress Mine. But I went with a sense of emptiness, wondering whether I should ever recapture, on their rare visits to Europe or mine to America, the intimacy of that short stay, the impetuous affection which had drawn me into the personal torrent of their lives.

More than once, I am proud to say, I have. When my son was born in 1949, for instance, Lynn wrote:

> I have taken far too long to thank you for the lovely photograph. It is difficult to believe that you, Peter, are the father of that darling little wax doll, and still more so that your wife is the mother. It seems only a matter of sex that decides which is the baby ...
>
> We are taking a long vacation so that Alfred can have a real rest to buoy himself up for the coming production. The plans are to give it a three-week try-out and then come into New York in November. Do be there, both of you, it would be a lovely warm feeling to know you were out in front.

Eighteen months later, at the time of Ivor Novello's death, shared emotion about him prompted her to write again: a long letter which went on to give a fascinating, tragi-comic description of the hazards of touring on the American 'road', surpassing in its rigours even those of our more compact provincial circuits. Their company had suffered a robbery in Hartford, Connecticut, an armed hold-up in Boston, blizzards in Pittsburgh and consequent delays which forced them to open in Detroit without scenery or costumes. In the Mid-West they met sleet, ice-storms and a railway strike which drove them on to the frozen highways in trucks and buses; in Philadelphia both stars came down with flu, and in Portland, Maine, descending the steps of their hotel, Lynn caught her heel in the hem of her skirt and fell, breaking her arm.

> I have been thinking of you a great deal ... and some of the mysteries of how you wash your hand and dry it, and how you are able to bath and dress yourself—a lot of this has been cleared up. I have found such ways and means. There is one pippin of an act that I do with a wash-glove, which I soap and then fasten to the towel-rack. By dint of a lot of twisting

and acrobatic movements, I manage to wash and dry my uninjured arm ... I had to write to you because I know how much it would amuse you to see me finding my way in a one-armed world.

Once back in New York, however, I was pursuing my most urgent objective: to try and coax a play out of the most legendary of the playwrights of that cosmopolitan world of theatre. My friend Adrianne Allen had sent a letter of introduction for me to Frederick Lonsdale and I was eagerly awaiting a reply. It was not long in coming. One day, towards the end of the hot weather, he asked me to lunch in the expensive intimacy of the Colony Restaurant. I found before me a figure who bore about him no recognizable signs of the theatre, but might rather have been a successful bloodstock breeder, the sort of person who never misses the Newmarket Sales. As celebrities around us chattered and screamed and sent notes to their most feared columnists, I came straight to the point of our meeting. He was, I think, vaguely flattered by the directness of my approach, perhaps even touched by my having travelled so far to seek a play from him. At all events, far from snubbing me, he confessed that he did indeed have an embryonic idea in mind. If necessary, he added, warming to the thought, he could begin working on it straight away.

'I never work out anything in advance; I just write a couple of pages every day, and see what happens. If you really want me to write a play, why not drop in every morning at ten o'clock, and I will read you what I have written. And now, let's talk about something else. I've always thought the theatre stinks.'

Freddy Lonsdale stood out startlingly from the throng around us. The son of a tobacconist in St Helier, Jersey, he seemed, in his daughter's words, 'a villainous and undisciplined child'. Constantly refusing to go to school, he was as a result almost entirely without education and totally lacking in taste and culture. Yet he spoke with the accent and manner of a man educated at Eton and Oxford. For the rest of our luncheon he talked evocatively of his great days in the London of the 1920s when the opening of a new Lonsdale comedy was an event of far greater importance than, for instance, an unsuccessful *Putsch* in Munich by a ridiculous band of cranks who called themselves National Socialists.

He had in his time been a friend of most of the names that

glittered in the gossip columns and enemy of many; denounced as a social and political menace to their class, ordered out of their houses by some of the most elegant. Yet, although he did not forfeit his integrity, he seldom lost such friendships for good. In the end they would be won round by his cool charm— 'maddening, but irresistible', as his friend Cary Grant once described it to me, recognizing him as a perennial, crotchety, not entirely responsible rebel.

Perhaps it was this shared combination of toughness and sentiment, as well as the international freemasonry of horsiness, which provided the basis for Freddy's curious intimacy with the sports journalist and short-story writer Damon Runyon. It must have been a bond deeper than conventional communication, for Runyon had been left virtually speechless by an operation for cancer of the throat and was forced to converse by means of laboriously scribbled notes. In spite of this handicap he never failed to project his satirical wit and passion. Freddy showed himself at his best in the exquisite daily encounters as he conducted this painfully lopsided dialogue with the dying creator of Harry the Horse, Nathan Detroit, Nicely-Nicely Johnson and the other brilliant Bronx caricatures from his short stories which were to come to life on the stage in *Guys and Dolls*.

I remember so many pleasures when lunching or dining with Freddie in the exotic surroundings of the Colony—a world of legendary names from my gallery of schoolboy infatuations. Freddie led me round the tables introducing me to them all, rather like a soured *maître d'hôtel* recommending a new *plat de jour* to a clientele over-used to a menu of each other's reputations. I dined with the ageless Anita Loos, with her sleek black bob and face like a Japanese mask looking as she had twenty years earlier when she wrote *Gentlemen Prefer Blondes*, and with Norma Shearer, Metro-Goldwyn-Mayer's queen of the 1930s, luscious and incredible as some enormous tea-rose; exchanged notes over coffee with Damon Runyon; got hopelessly lost with Fred Astaire during a rainstorm in the small hours in the streets of the 70s; and fell in love with the incomparable Gertrude Lawrence, who later confirmed my opinion of *The Gay Pavilion* in her husband Richard Aldrich's production at Cape Cod.

The play progressed even more slowly than Freddy had warned me. Morning after morning I would turn up at his apartment to be regaled by brilliant talk of anything but the work in hand, of plans for the future and how he would never again write about dukes. His plays *The Last of Mrs Cheyney*, *On Approval* and *The High Road* had surfeited the public with dukes. As the public had never met a duke, he said, they once thought that dukes really talked like that in real life. Now they did not care any more about how dukes talked.

'Dukes', he added, 'are finished, as finished as infidelity;' in future he would write about ordinary people or perverts. A page or two at a time, he delivered to me the script of what subsequently came to be played under the title of *But For the Grace of God*. I found that presented in it were one duke, one infidelity and one pervert.

In the course of these mornings I got to know Freddy well and became extremely devoted to him. He was a difficult, paradoxical fellow—almost the embodiment of his own paradoxical dialogue. He was both cynic and sentimentalist, the one I suppose acting as a shell to protect the other. Presumably this was the link between the hoary inanities of his libretto for *The Maid of the Mountains*—the original success of which had launched him in 1917 into a social world utterly remote from that tobacconist's shop in Jersey—and the smart cruelties of *On Approval*. The bandit camp and the ducal grange were both dream-lands, ministering to the discontent of those who had given up hoping for romance to arrive with the 9.15. But mingled with his infatuation for the coldly glittering world of dukes was the intimate asperity of one who had observed it first from below, as from among its servants.

He was, of course, witty, yet it was generally wit of a rather old-fashioned, considered kind; he was not often attracted to the spontaneous sally, but once I asked him whether he liked New York. He turned to observe some workmen, glorying in the infernal racket of their pneumatic drills; 'I would', he said, 'if they'd finish it.'

Meanwhile I still had to secure a complete last act. Christmas was approaching and I could not long delay returning to London. Freddy was past the hurdle of his second-act curtain, but there was still a major scene missing from his third act. 'Don't worry, old boy,' he reassured me, brushing aside my fears, 'it'll be on the next boat. Or better still, I'll give it to Billy Rootes to bring

13 (*inset*). Rosario and Antonio (Madrid, 1951)

14. Roland Petit and Colette Marchand in *Carmen* (1953)

15 (*top left*). Jean Babilée in Cocteau's *Jeune Homme et la Mort* (1956)

16 (*above*). Martha Graham in *Cave of Heart* (1954)

17 (*bottom left*). The Moisseyev Russ Dance Company in *Football* (1955)

18 (*below*). Jerome Robbins—*Ballets: U.S* (1959)

19 (*below*). Chekhov reading *The Seagull* with the original Moscow Art Theatre company (1898)

20 (*top right*). Alexei Gribov as Firs in Chekhov's *The Cherry Orchard* (1958)

21 (*bottom left*). Angelina Stepanova as Arkadina in Chekhov's *The Seagull* (1970)

22 (*bottom right*). The Moscow Art Theatre's production of Gogol's *Dead Souls* (1964)

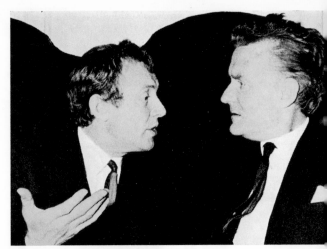

23. The author with Inno-kenti Smoktunovsky (1966)

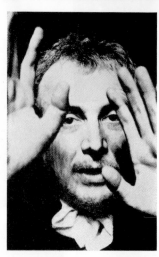

24. Smoktunovsky as Prince Mishkin in the Leningrad Gorky Theatre's production of *The Idiot* (1966)

25. The author with members of the Habimah Theatre, Tel Aviv (1964)

over—he's flying next week.' My anxieties were not wholly allayed, but I could stay no longer.

It had been a visit of great pleasure and varied success. America as a whole had enthralled me; the expedition to the Lunts in Genesee remained in the memory as one of those rare moments of happiness fully enjoyed. I had actually acquired a play, or at least most of a play. On the other hand, *Dunnigan's Daughter*, which Sam Behrman had so generously offered me, seemed to me at the try-out to be a trifle too confused for a London public. Lynn Fontanne's intervention with John Van Druten had had immediate effect. He was nothing but friendliness and charm; with rare kindness he offered me the English rights of his new work, *The Mermaids Singing*. But unfortunately he became dissatisfied with it. It possessed moments of great wit and poetry, but it lacked the compactness of his other plays; and he was therefore unwilling, he said, to let London see it in its present shape.

So, by the time I was once again on shipboard, I had one play and at least the hope of others to follow. I somehow knew I would always cherish this, my first encounter with the great romance that is America. As I peered over the side, the choppy waves, under a crescent moon, crashed and overturned into each other like good-hearted Christmas pedestrians on a last-minute buying spree on Fifth Avenue. I felt strangely excited—as though the curtain had just come down on Gogol's stunning *coup de théâtre* in *The Government Inspector*—the comedy was over and the drama had begun.

5
The West End — Lonsdale, Novello, Maugham, Coward

From my earliest youth there had been four names in the theatre which fascinated me: Lonsdale, Novello, Maugham and Coward. Now, on my return from America, a series of partly fortuitous circumstances thrust me successively into close association with each of them. I had, of course, in a sense arrived towards the end of the party. Lonsdale and Coward had known their first glory in the 1920s and 1930s. One of the curious effects of war is to leave one conscious of time passing for oneself while convinced that it has stopped for everybody else. This phenomenon is probably the consequence of society disintegrating, of people becoming lost to sight, so that one retains an earlier image of them. I was now far from being the schoolboy of 1937. Yet I assumed that the world in which my four heroes once reigned had not changed at all! I never doubted that the Lonsdale great houses still stood where champagne and epigrams flowed in erotic confusion, that Coward was still the ordained interpreter of the age's restless genius.

My first difficulty came with the arrival — at least two months later than promised — of the final pages of Frederick Lonsdale's *But For the Grace of God.* I was swollen with pride and joy at receiving the play at last, but a problem at once presented itself. The play's setting, the very nature of its plot, demanded actors who could not merely play ladies and gentlemen, but who could also convince an audience of a society where reputations could be besmirched; where a name could matter sufficiently for the subject to dread blackmail — 'superb beings of aristocratic style', as Freddy called them. None of his plays, Lonsdale once admitted to me, could have succeeded without the fastidious touch brought to them by such actors as Gerald du Maurier, Ronald Squire, A. E. Matthews and Gladys Cooper. In the hands of these 'superb beings' his plays exuded a sense of good breeding as strong as anything to be found in the stalls opposite them. But in the West End of 1946, where I began casting his new comedy, it was almost impossible to find young players with any comprehension of the 'aristocratic style'.

This is a style which has been much admired in the European theatre. It was a heritage which stemmed from Charles Hawtrey and continued through Ronald Squire and Rex Harrison. Rex Harrison, a great actor on many levels, told me that seeing du Maurier play 'gave you the feeling that he was just there. It was impossible to detect what he did.' As a young actor Rex had acted with A. E. Matthews in *Short Story* by Robert Morley, and every night he would stand in the wings to watch and learn the marvellous timing as Matty played like a Wimbledon champion. Sometimes Matty could be off-form, netting the ball, so to speak, but he was always a master of comedy. 'He was also, as you know,' Rex told me, 'a master of improvisation.'

I was once surprised to encounter this style of acting in the leading actor of a musical play in Budapest: a veteran with three Stalin Awards. I asked the two custodians who accompanied me —it was the eve of the tragic Hungarian revolution—if I might possibly meet him. They took me back-stage to his dressing-room. When I said how much I admired his performance he was moved to tears. He told me how before the war he had made frequent visits to London, where his daughter had married a station-master and where he had studied the London theatre and had seen 'those two actors who influenced the whole of my life'—A. E. Matthews and Ronnie Squire.

On returning to London I told Matty and Ronnie how their art had percolated as far as Hungary. Matty was overjoyed, but Ronnie thought I was making the whole thing up.

It was the style, at least, of their generation which I needed for the success of *But For the Grace of God*. But here another shock awaited me. For months the script circulated from one star name to the next. Some returned it unread. On every hand they said that Lonsdale was finished—a forgotten name from an outmoded past. Those who overcame their prejudices sufficiently to read it politely tore it to shreds. It was antiquated, limping, disagreeable, and—worst of all, they said—unfunny. When *The Last of Mrs Cheyney* had been produced in London in 1925, stars had literally fought to appear in it. Twenty-one years later I might have been trying to persuade them to play in some archaic problem-drama by Henry Arthur Jones.

Lonsdale plays never read well. There is a vast disparity between the effect of his lines when read and when spoken. This had mattered little in the great days, when it was enough for them to be written by Lonsdale and spoken by du Maurier or Squire, but in 1946 it mattered a great deal. The war was still supposed to have ushered in the Age of the Common Man. No one dreamed of a day, not far off, when the doings of dukes and debutantes, the rich and super-rich would be devoured even more avidly in gossip columns than in Lonsdale's prime.

Fortunately one of the great personalities who had mastered the Lonsdale manner, A. E. Matthews, survived and was willing to play for me. I approached him with some trepidation for the part of the duke. I had never met Matty before, but I knew him as a giant among actors and had heard stories of his free way with authors' dialogue. One, told by Lonsdale himself, concerned the New York production of his comedy *Spring Cleaning*. Matty had a line which ran: 'With a charm of manner, there's a hell of a lot of fun to be had in cathedral towns.' At rehearsals Matty kept omitting the initial clause, and Freddy prompted him from the stalls: 'With a charm of manner, Matty.' The third time this happened, Matty strode inexplicably from the stage and out of the theatre. Freddy followed him to one of his favourite haunts, where he found him glowering to himself, and read him the full line. 'Oh,' said Matty, jumping up, 'I thought you were criticizing my acting.'

Matty was an extremely lovable man, whose friendship carried with it a wonderful working association. He had the appearance of being a man of fifty, in the prime of life. We knew he was much older than that, but the truth did not reach us until one day in 1946 I was hailed in the Garrick Club by Seymour Hicks. 'Matty's eighty today,' he said, 'so don't, for God's sake, forget the cake!'

I was to find in Matty many of the same qualities which were so endearing in Freddy. They both belonged to the same theatrical generation and had made their way up from similar origins. When Freddy was helping in his father's tobacco-shop in Jersey, Matty worked as a young clerk on a high stool in a London office. In fact Matty had come from a famous family of clowns. His uncle, Thomas Matthews, was an assistant to Grimaldi, the greatest of all pantomime clowns.

As a boy earning ten shillings a week in the most sordid conditions, his background sounds like an episode from *Nicholas Nickleby* or *David Copperfield*. In his admirable autobiography, *Matty*, written with the aid of his old friend Joc Orton, he tells how, walking home late one night, instead of going down Holborn and Oxford Street he had turned up past old Newgate prison to Ludgate Circus, and then on down the Strand. He stood outside the Lyceum Theatre, looking at the playbills pasted up outside: Henry Irving in *The Lyons Mail*. 'It was incredible to think', he writes, 'that this great actor had actually been an inefficient office boy like myself!'

However, both Freddy and Matty had knocked around the world, acquiring a sophistication which did not trouble to conceal a basic ignorance of, and indifference to, the Arts (with a capital 'A'). Both cultivated the dress and habits of eccentric country aristocrats; I always see Matty in a patched tweed coat, suggesting the twenty-sixth in a line of rather rum earls whose family principle is never to come to London except for the Eton and Harrow match.

That was also rather the impression Freddy gave when he landed at Southampton a few weeks later, returning to England for the first time since the war—nominally to direct his play for me. I went down to Southampton to meet him; it was a great comfort to me to encounter once again the red face, the inevitable white socks and white muffler, and the Olympian contempt for the theatre.

His daughter Frances Donaldson describes in her biography (*Freddy Lonsdale*) how Freddy had developed a reputation for an unpredictable and senseless temper. However, she says, 'Mr Daubeny had the grace to hero-worship him, and, as a consequence, managed him better than anyone else.'

Like the clubman who despised any club which would have him for a member, Freddy scorned the medium in which he excelled, making you feel that theatrical success was a matter of casual hocus-pocus. In our subsequent weeks of rehearsal I began to suspect he might be right. He would stroll in at any unpredictable hour, sit down beside Matty and start gossiping about the good old days at the Garrick Club, apparently without bothering to notice what was happening on stage. When he found time to look up, he conducted the actors through a fastidious process of elimination, rather like a connoisseur turning over and rejecting the trash in an antique shop, steadily moving towards the objects of real worth. Every now and again he would pounce on something he did not like. An admonitory finger would caress the fruity nose and out would come a suggestion which, if caustic, was always directly to the point.

However unconventional the method, the result was alchemy. In some ways, as its critics pointed out, *But For the Grace of God* was an old-fashioned play, with a touch of 1880s melodrama under its fashionable jokes. A young wife is slightly unfaithful during her husband's absence at the war. She is blackmailed by her scapegrace brother-in-law, who is then murdered by her amiable American light-of-love only a few hours before the husband's return to the Scottish baronial home.

The first act, which set the scene and relationships, was creakingly mechanical. In incompetent hands the whole production might have seemed intolerably artificial. But it was all transformed by a superlative cast. Nothing but the best would do for Freddy. The part of Matty's wife, though admirably drawn, was a comparatively small one. I suggested Mary Jerrold for it. We should never get her, Lonsdale was sure, to play so insignificant a role; but if we did, he added, it would make the play. For the sake of A. E. Matthews she readily agreed, and her performance was to be one of our main delights.

Freddy was mainly worried about the difficult part of the young husband, who appeared for only ten minutes at the end. This was eventually perfectly performed by Robert Douglas with such a style that it earned him a Hollywood contract. He wanted a huge salary for this rather small part. The budget could not afford it, but the problem was swiftly solved by the author. 'Don't worry, I'll pay the difference. Let's get the damn thing on.' And 'the damn thing' went on without the difference being paid—except by me!

Michael Gough, as the brother-in-law, gave us another outstanding performance in an extraordinary study in villainy and perversion which made him a star overnight. His playing culminated at the end of the second act in a disastrous fight with the American lover, played by Hugh McDermott, and in a broken neck. I imported into the theatre the good-natured middle-weight champion Vince Hawkins to teach and produce the combatants. Though Gough and McDermott were hurt several times during the run of the play, the result was acclaimed as one of the most realistic stage-fights ever seen on the London stage. The whole cast of *But For the Grace of God* was splendid, but, for me, it will always be Matty's performance as the duke that made the play a unique experience.

But For the Grace of God opened after an encouraging provincial try-out at the St James's Theatre on September 3rd, 1946. It ran for seven months, well into the coldest winter for years, and then, in spite of fuel shortages, floods and deepening post-war austerity, for another three or four months touring the provinces. Perhaps the austerity in fact helped. Audiences seemed to find a positive comfort in escaping into Lonsdale's eternal pre-war world.

During the run of the play I made friends with a young actor in the cast who was to play a curiously important part in my life. His name was Tony Forwood. His unvarying affability towards everyone always reminded me of a great blond horse in a sunny meadow, nosing towards you for a piece of sugar. One day he asked me if I would see a young friend of his who had had very little luck in the theatre, and to please Tony I told him that certainly I would see him, but at the moment I was not casting any play.

When I met him in Tony's dressing-room I gathered that he was a young out-of-work actor doing some scene-painting at the Queen's Theatre, and that his theatrical experience was practically nil. He made no impression on me at all, except that his face, with its Spanish black eyes, reminded me of Eddie Cantor.

Towards the end of the run of *But for the Grace of God*, John Sutro, the film producer, rang me up one day to tell me of a company stranded at the New Lindsay Theatre in Notting Hill with little to their name but a play called *Power Without Glory*. The backers who leased this little playhouse—one of the best experimental laboratories for the theatre in London—had apparently disappeared and the modest enterprise was paralysed. Saddest of all, the play was, in Sutro's estimation, of unusual brilliance, by an unknown young playwright called Michael Clayton Hutton.

I felt no immediate desire to become involved in this situation and had no great wish to see the play. But John Sutro was persistent, laying siege to my telephone till I gave in. Very well, I would go and see the play. 'How much', I asked, 'would it cost to put on?' 'Two hundred and fifty pounds.' Before setting forth I made out a cheque for that amount. It was the line of least resistance. I felt too much of a coward to pass a death-sentence upon these young actors, whose whole future might well depend on outside good will. Little did I suspect at the time how much it did. As I set out for Notting Hill I felt I was committing a folly.

The tiny theatre seemed no bigger than a potting-shed. Immediately I entered I could feel it vibrating with nervous tension. A few figures lounging in the auditorium leaped the few feet on to the stage and took up their positions, for all the world like members of an orchestra waiting, fiddles and trumpets raised, for the first flick of the conductor's baton. At once the adventure, hitherto ridiculous, took on pathos and significance. The characters were set against a background of cockney attitudes and brutal humour which possessed real drama and plausibility and began to engage my interest. All the names of the actors were unfamiliar: Kenneth More, Mary Horne, Dandy Nichols, Maureen Pook (later, at Noël Coward's insistence, to change her surname to Pryor).

Suddenly there rushed on to the stage a breathless figure, half choking with emotion: a slight, dark youth, radiating a curious, almost hypnotic power; every movement, every inflection of his voice, uncannily suggesting the poetry of the gutter, of a lost soul. Beyond any doubt, here was an actor of the first quality. It turned out to be the young man with whom I had been so unimpressed shortly before and his name was Dirk Bogarde. As I handed my cheque to the director, Chloë Gibson, I felt that on the strength of Bogarde's performance alone it would be money well spent.

During the course of the run Dirk and I became great friends. Just as youth turns to maturity for dependence, interpretation and hope, as I had done to Maugham, Coward, Lonsdale and Novello, so he turned to me. Every day we either saw each other or spoke on the telephone. We often went home to my father and mother's house at Churt. We planned a trip to New York. We spent some happy week-ends at Tony Forwood's aunt's in

Bournemouth. Perhaps Dirk was holding on to me as his only straw. After the closing of the play at the New Lindsay the actors were out of work, but, like the crew of a sinking ship, they stood together, waiting in hope for a boat to carry them to the West End. During the melancholy interim Dirk suggested one day at Churt that we sign a contract. But twenty pounds a week for any work that might turn up, films, television or theatre, was in that situation more than I could afford. No managers or West End theatres had shown the slightest interest. Only my melancholy cheque for two hundred and fifty pounds had carried this small enterprise on a two weeks' cruise.

No one is interested in what happens on board ship so long as the captain brings you into port. For the first time in my life I felt deeply needed and, in consequence, deeply committed. It is only in realizing that one means something to others that it is possible to feel there is both point and purpose to existence. Often in the night the telephone would ring. It would always be Dirk, even if we had just left each other after dinner, asking how I was, and adding the inevitable words, 'Any news?' I imagined him as the spokesman of a stranded ship's company in a Somerset Maugham novelette—and something about it all made me feel uneasy.

Even now I still recall the vivid emotions of those challenging days with nostalgia. The terror, expectation and disappointment will always be with me. I remember my casual pride when, in answer to the interminable inquiry, I was able to answer, 'It's all fixed.' This was my proudest theatrical moment.

On the night before the play opened at the Fortune Theatre I invited Noël Coward to the dress rehearsal. He sat through it with tears in his eyes. He was profoundly moved, and his enthusiasm touched me deeply. 'This', he whispered, 'is absolutely wonderful. We must make it an enormous success.' As he was anxious to help the play in any practical way I could suggest, I asked if he would give us an appreciation which we could advertise on posters all over London. He immediately agreed, and wrote on a postcard: 'Anyone in London who really cares for vital, true and exciting acting must see *Power Without Glory*—a most moving and finely written play and on all counts an enthralling evening in the theatre.'

Power Without Glory was acclaimed by the press as a minor

masterpiece. They described it as 'a tense and remarkable play' (*Daily Express*), 'a beautiful job of precise playwriting' (*Daily Mail*) and 'a play of cracking nerves and tense emotion which deserves to do well' (*Daily Telegraph*).

However, despite powerful support from many quarters, including A. T. Smith, the owner of the New Lindsay Theatre, and the renewed enthusiasm of the critics, *Power Without Glory* persistently lost money. We were nevertheless able to keep it going for a limited run of eight weeks. At first, moreover, we were hopeful that our losses would be recouped from other quarters. John C. Wilson acquired the play for America and several substantial film offers turned up. Alas! *Power Without Glory* flopped on the other side of the Atlantic. I was obliged, therefore, to write the venture off as an 'artistic' flutter, a gesture which, I hoped, had brought pleasure to the public. Certainly some good had come of it. It had apparently at least given the author a start along the road to success. The director of the production, Chloë Gibson, had proved her worth and as a result she was in 1949 to direct a very successful play for me, *The Late Edwina Black*. In varying degrees the talents of Dirk Bogarde and his fellow actors had caught the attention of the public. As for me, I lost £6,000.

At the conclusion of the run Noël Coward popped the whole of my cast into his new production, *Peace in Our Time*, with the exception of Dirk Bogarde, who by this time had been signed on by Rank and was already embarking upon his film career.

In 1949 I presented another outstanding young actor, Richard Attenborough, in a production of an American play, *Home of the Brave* by Arthur Laurents—a terrifying study in war-time psychiatry. Feeling the title was unsuitable, I had retitled it *The Way Back* and I presented it at the Westminster Theatre with Arthur Hill and Stanley Maxted in the main supporting roles.

On the eve of the first World Theatre Season in March 1964, Dickie Attenborough wrote me a letter which I shall always treasure, to acknowledge, as he said, his 'own personal debt of gratitude':

I remember so well when in 1949 you asked me to play in *The Way Back*. I was totally bowled over by Arthur Laurents's writing and I couldn't believe that anyone would consider

me as a possibility for such a play. Having worked solely in
the cinema since leaving the Air Force, I had, of necessity,
become tagged with a 'film star' label, the result of which
was that it was very difficult to be taken seriously as an actor.
That you should have done so, resulting in the offer to play
'Coney', is something that I shall remember with profound
gratitude all my life. You allowed me to re-establish myself
as a theatre actor and, if this had not happened, much of the
work that I have had the opportunity to participate in
subsequently might never have come my way.

This production was therefore a milestone in the career of an
actor whose imagination over the years has developed new aspects
of theatre and cinema experience. In 1969 his dynamic direction
of the film version of Joan Littlewood's original Theatre Workshop production of *Oh What a Lovely War!* brought him international fame.

Power Without Glory was still running when I became involved
with another production by one of my pre-war idols. Three years
earlier, on my first night home in London from North Africa, I
had looked around my cheerless bedroom and decided that not
even the bangs, whines and whistles of the air raid in progress
outside would keep me from seeking out what vestiges remained
of the glamorous life I had tasted so briefly before joining up. I
hurried round to the Savoy Grill, where the first person I set
eyes on was Ivor Novello.

It is easier to make an aphorism about a man than to understand him, but in the case of Ivor Novello aphorism and understanding went hand in hand. Ivor was pleased with life. He took
it as it came and enjoyed every minute of it. Through this
pleasure he possessed the unique gift of attracting the friendship
and confidence of anyone he met. He seemed to like everyone,
which made some people suspect he liked no one. But he was
deeply perceptive and sensitive, as I was to find out again and
again.

Ivor Novello had been the most famous of our early film stars
and the most popular figure in the British theatre. His flat in the
Aldwych above the Strand Theatre, where he lived for forty
years, possessed a creaking little lift like an erratic yo-yo which
perilously transported you up and down; and there, during the

First World War, the theatre had come to greet him when he was on leave. Fay Compton, Beatrice Lillie, Gertrude Lawrence, Leslie Henson, Noël Coward, Robert Andrews, Seymour Hicks, Phyllis and Zena Dare, Phyllis Monkman, Henry Kendall, Jack Buchanan, Sir Edward Marsh—thirty years later many of these well-known figures were still entering the lift.

In 1915, when he was twenty-one, he was in the Royal Naval Air Service and already the composer of a song, 'Keep the Home Fires Burning', then echoing all over the world and eventually to become part of English tradition: Ivor himself gave a fascinating insight into the sources of his inspiration in an article he wrote for the magazine *Band Wagon* in 1949:

> I was brought up on the classics, nurtured as a chorister with dollops of Bach, Beethoven, Haydn, Handel, Mozart, Byrd, Purcell, Gibbons. Now, with the exception of Mozart's opera, I can't bear any of them. To me they are too full of form and lacking in emotion. At this moment I can positively hear gnashing of teeth and bellows of rage from classical music-lovers. 'Who does he think *he* is?' I can hear them say.
>
> Perhaps as a reaction from my severely classical musical boyhood, I swung clean over to the romantics, and my present preferences run from Mendelssohn onwards; with anything before his time, barring a few exceptions, I am out of musical sympathy ...
>
> Of course I like the Strauss's, Lehar, Fall and Kalman. Of the English musicians my favourite is Elgar, to whose veneration I have become a late convert. I like Bliss—his piano concerto particularly—William Walton, Addinsell, and Edward German.
>
> To which school of British musicians my own humble efforts belong is difficult to say. Viewed dispassionately, I am sort of betwixt and between; if there was a hymn that was neither ancient nor modern, it would be me.
>
> I started writing very young. My first song was published when I was only fifteen, and at twenty I wrote 'Keep the Home Fires Burning', a song that became a best seller all over the world, and is still remembered. Many moons have passed since that first war marching-song was written, but essen-

tially my music remains the same, simple, emotional, and directed unashamedly towards the heart. I make no apologies for that. I repeat, I like that sort of music, and I am convinced the British public like it, too.

Ivor Novello will always be remembered as an English musical legend, which began with *Glamorous Night* and continued with *The Dancing Years, Crest of the Wave* and *King's Rhapsody*, one of the most colossal stage successes in history. Starting its career in 1939, it ran almost continuously in London and the provinces for nearly ten years. *Perchance to Dream* was another Novello triumph. It was spectacular, colourful and tuneful, with its lilting songs like the famous 'We'll Gather Lilacs', and was the ideal mass entertainment for the post-war years of peace and adjustment. It is amusing that 'We'll Gather Lilacs' was first suggested to him by his great friends Alfred Lunt and Lynn Fontanne, who had so admired his lilac trees while staying with him at Redroofs in 1944.

One day in 1947 towards the end of the London run of *But for the Grace of God* Ivor rang me up and asked me down to Redroofs to receive 'a great surprise'. I went down and received from Ivor, as he lay in his vast bed, just what I had expected—the play he had promised to write for me. It was not until I was in the train on my way back to London that I got a chance to look at it.

Leaving aside any estimate of his musical fantasies, nobody with any instinct for the theatre could deny that Ivor had showed at times a vivid talent for 'straight' comedy. His *The Truth Game, I Lived with You* and *Fresh Fields* had been delightful. I was naturally flattered that I should now be the subject of a new play from his hand.

But as I began to read *We Proudly Present* enthusiasm and pleasure drained away. The play dealt with the varied and ludicrous fortunes of two stage-struck amateurs, fresh out of the army, who go into theatrical management. They are blessed with a spirited and resourceful secretary, and a ripe bitch of a leading lady to plague them. There is also an imperious handful of a Viennese soprano to increase their discomforts. They start as highbrow idealists putting on an 'advanced' play, and in the end are reduced to transforming it into a successful farce. Here and there were amusing moments, and plenty of good fun, if of a somewhat narrow parochial kind. But the writing lacked style and wit. Inevitably one was forced to compare it to that brilliant *coup de théâtre*, Coward's *Present Laughter*, which showed an exotic and fascinating attitude of mind, a private vision of the theatrical mentality. Beside it Ivor's effort seemed poor and flat.

However, there could be no question of not putting it on. Not only had Ivor written it specially for me, but it purported to be based on my own experiences. Moreover, being delighted with it, he was convinced that he was doing me a good turn by slipping into my hands a really big potential money-spinner. Perhaps, I told myself, fighting back dismay, it might get by, if carefully and cleverly cast.

In this, at least, the gods were with us. The vital part of the fallen star turned secretary had been specially written by Ivor for Phyllis Monkman, still as full of vitality and *gaminerie* as when she had won the admiration of my father and all his generation. There was only one actress, I felt, who could give full value to the part of the leading lady—Ena Burrill. Luckily we were able to engage her too, while Irene Handl fitted admirably into the part of the Viennese star. The presence of Mary Jerrold in the cast, the third play she had done for me, seemed to be a guarantee of good luck, and Peter Graves and Tony Forwood at first played the two idealistic simpletons. Later, when Forwood was obliged to leave the cast, I took over my own part, and woke up to find the press fascinated by the novelty of a theatrical manager caricaturing himself.

Under the witty direction of Max Adrian, and with the accomplished assistance of the Misses Monkman, Jerrold, Burrill and Handl, the play began to take on unexpected life at rehearsals. When it opened at the Duke of York's Theatre on May 5th, 1947, my early fears were confounded by an excellent press. Of course the critics tended on the whole to recognize the thing as no more than a trifle, but they admired the artful contrivance of it and went into ecstasies over the performances of the four female stars. If the piece did not turn out to be the money-spinner of Ivor's vision, it certainly did far better than I had ever hoped. In the course of the five-month London run it kept its head above water, then went on a successful tour with Phyllis Monkman and myself as co-stars, and ultimately enjoyed adequate production by many leading repertory companies.

The only other person who appeared to feel about it as I had on a first reading was Noël Coward. 'I should not have minded losing my arm,' he lectured, wagging his finger at me amid the din of a cocktail party, 'but I should mind, desperately, losing my integrity.' His disapproval shook me; but despite the embarrassments of production, I knew that *We Proudly Present* had turned out to be an experience I would not have missed for the world. It brought me into close working contact with Ivor; and the more I saw of him, the greater became my admiration.

He was, I realized for the first time, naturally lazy; yet suddenly a childlike enthusiasm would galvanize him into fabulous activity. He was totally devoid of conceit or pretension where his work was concerned, and would willingly rewrite any scene which bothered Max Adrian or myself. His maxim always was, 'Let's try it and see how it goes.'

Easy though he was in ordinary relationships, he would suddenly become transformed into a conscientious disciplinarian if ever he came to think that the public was not being fairly treated. In his view, the theatre demanded and merited a treatment by the players just as reverent as the Church requires of a priest.

One day he brought this sense of disciplined reverence violently home to me. My part in the play called for me at one moment to yell furiously at the majestic Miss Burrill 'Get out of the theatre!' Suddenly I remembered the absurdity of my last appearance on the stage with her, at Liverpool in Willie Armstrong's company. Then her massive charms had awaited seduction on a hard-worked sofa; now, queenly in a picture hat, she stood before me like a public monument to the last garden before Judgment Day. It is almost impossible to convey on paper the precise cause of helpless laughter; of laughter from the stomach. Rarely does real wit set one laughing so; generally it is some ridiculous fancy that hardly bears repeating. On this occasion, for the silliest reason, I was overcome all at once, helplessly, hysterically, by the giggles. I was powerless to stop, and the malady, instead of burning itself out, in turn infected almost the entire cast.

Between the matinée and evening performance I hurried into Hyde Park, hoping to overcome among its moulting, melancholy plane trees my mounting convulsion of what had long ceased to be laughter and was becoming a kind of nausea. The dingy autumnal flora seemed to sober me, and, steeling myself, I returned to the theatre determined to perform honourably. Yet the moment Miss Burrill's picture hat confronted me again, my reflexes mutinied. Hysteria rose again in a great wave, bursting from me and engulfing the cast until Phyllis Monkman, Irene Handl and even the imperturbable Mary Jerrold became helpless. The malady spread to the audience. Some of them began to giggle uncomfortably. Fortunately it was not long until the end of the play, and the curtain mercifully fell upon my ignominy.

I had been nursing my disgrace in my dressing-room for only a few minutes when I was summoned to the telephone. For fifteen minutes a furious gentleman from Streatham harangued me on my monstrous conduct, demanding his money back and threatening a personal protest to Ivor Novello. His anger was nothing to Ivor's at a special rehearsal he called for the entire company at ten o'clock the following morning. 'You've failed me disgracefully,' he pronounced, stony, grey-faced and remote as I had never seen him. 'I'm bitterly disappointed in you. You have let the public down badly. We will go through the play from beginning to end with a fresh and sharply focused vision.' He drilled us like a sorrowing chaplain with a class of backward candidates for confirmation, and as he laboured to restore order and seriousness my sympathy went out to him. He would rather have died than betray himself as we had done on a stage. That evening I played with the solemnity of a Scots sabbath; had Miss Burrill's hat suddenly doubled in size, like Alice's mushroom, it would have drawn not a quiver from me. For reward, we saw the frown erased from Ivor's face, to be replaced by his customary radiantly forgiving smile.

Ivor never diminished what one admired and never failed to pick out some seed of quality that had been neglected and unperceived. When I told him that I had not seen Flora Robson in *Black Chiffon*, he dragged me to a matinée the same day. In revealing her fine art, it was as though he had been struck by blinding light on the road to Damascus. Our meeting afterwards with this wonderful actress was to result in three important productions. Two of these came some years later, in 1959: *The Aspern Papers*, in which she gave a memorable performance as Miss Tina (the production also including the fine art of Beatrice

Lehmann and Michael Redgrave, who was responsible for this beautiful adaptation of Henry James's story); and Ibsen's *Ghosts*, with Donald Wolfit and Ronald Lewis. But first, in 1956, came *The House by the Lake* by my friend Hugh Mills, in which Andrew Cruikshank also played a leading part. This was my greatest commercial success, but it was only by accident that its run was not concluded after two weeks.

I was motoring down to Oxford for the week-end with my wife, knowing that *The House by the Lake* was going badly. Business at the theatre was minimal and I was convinced that we had a flop. Through my mind flashed Jack Buchanan's warning, 'Pocket your pride and save your losses,' and when we saw a telephone box I stopped the car. I had decided to take his advice and ring the manager of the Duke of York's Theatre to instruct him to put up the notice. With a heavy heart I popped in the money and waited, feeling terrible. I was letting down a brilliant cast, and I had not consulted either the author or John Fernald, the director.

Hugh Mills had written a successful comedy called *Laughter in Court* which Cochran had presented with Ronald Squire and Yvonne Arnaud just before Mills was incarcerated in a concentration camp in Paris. After the war he returned to London and wrote two or three fairly successful comedies, but when I had read this detective drama I immediately sensed a big commercial success. I felt desperately ashamed of what I was about to do, since I felt his whole life depended on it.

I tried three times to get through to the theatre, but again luck stepped in and averted a calamity by blocking the line to London. After several attempts I gave up. Later that night I met Hugh by chance, who joyfully told me we had played to a nearly full house. This we continued to do for two years. The call-box had turned into an alchemist's cell.

Of all the many people who promised help in those early days, Ivor Novello was one of the few who actually held to his promise. He did this not only be writing me a new play, but, the previous year, by involving me in a revival of Somerset Maugham's *Our Betters*, presented at the Playhouse by the two of us with Ivor putting up all the money. There was a beautiful performance by Dorothy Dickson, finely supported by Cathleen Nesbitt and Max

Adrian, who also directed admirably, and a dazzling decor by Cecil Beaton. The production was not a success, but it may have been partly responsible for an invitation from Somerset Maugham the following year to spend a holiday at the Villa Mauresque, his home on the Riviera. I leaped at the chance of pursuing the friendship begun so tentatively in New York. In the cold and exhaustion of a bitter winter of austerity, I looked forward to the luxury of the sun and the relaxation of his hospitality. But my stay with him was not the glimpse of the golden world of the elegant and sophisticated life of *Our Betters* that seemed to have vanished from Europe.

I remember a feeling of disappointment upon entering the house. It seemed dark, dull and lifeless. We crossed a small marble hall leading into a large salon. On the right was the dining-room, decorated by several portraits of ladies by that most anaemic of French painters, Marie Laurencin. Opposite the dining-room was a curling staircase which led to the bedrooms.

After lunch Maugham suggested a siesta, and Alan Searle, his secretary, showed me to a comfortable double bedroom with a large mirror in the adjoining bathroom. Alan, with his gentle good humour, bade me rest well and remarked that I must be careful because the mirror in the bathroom was double-sided.

When I came down Maugham suggested a walk with Alan and himself along the *corniche*. We went a short distance and as we turned the corner of the road a car roared by, loaded with a holidaying family and a perambulator strapped to the roof. 'That's what you'll be doing a year from now,' commented Maugham, chuckling and slipping his hand into mine. I had just become engaged to be married and had broken the news on my arrival. There was something faintly suggestive in his tone of voice, and in a reflex I pulled my hand away. I immediately sensed that I had done something foolish and gave him an uneasy smile. It was met by a face of freezing scorn and hostility. The walk continued in ominous silence. It had started to rain.

On that first evening I sat on my bed in misery. I felt the same element of corrosive malaise and sensual disquiet which Pinter was later to commercialize like a patent cough-mixture. Diderot remarked to Voltaire that he was like an old haunted castle which was falling into ruins, inhabited by an ancient sorcerer. Now, sitting in this house shrouded in a ghostly downpour, I felt the sorcerer at work. I looked despairingly at the mirrors and listened for sounds, feeling numb with apprehension. I suppose I should have fled then, but the vague hope of healing the wound I had done his vanity kept me.

From then on the week was pure disaster. At dinner, and every subsequent meal, Maugham made desultory conversation, but with an icy, withering malice, bitingly disparaging of anything I had done in the theatre and scornfully implying that I was incapable of doing better. A failure to reply brought silences which fell even more glacially.

One day a young man, who like myself had been introduced to Maugham by his nephew Robin, came to lunch. As we sat in the salon awaiting his arrival, I sensed a particularly bad atmosphere. The young man was nervous and received no succour, except from Alan Searle, who made a great effort without losing his sense of control or humour.

Lunch was announced and we followed Maugham into the dining-room. After what seemed an endless silence, Maugham adjusted himself like some predatory animal about to crush his victim before devouring him. He settled his beak into his helpless guest. 'Why', he said to the young man, stuttering badly, 'did you come to the South of France?' There was just the sound of the rain filling in the gaps as the vulture poised for the kill. 'I felt I wanted to come when you wrote that marvellous play about the South of France,' the young man eventually replied. This was followed by total silence. 'But', Maugham then continued, focusing on his target, 'I have never written a play about the South of France.' The young man looked at me in desperation. 'Didn't you write about it in *Lady Frederick*,' I chirped up gallantly, sensing immediate but inevitable disaster. Maugham took no notice, and after one or two further munches of *bœuf à la mode* he reconsidered his young guest, who was on the point of expiry. 'If you have come (stammer) to the South of France because (stammer) I mentioned it in a play, I feel (stammer followed by gulp) very sorry for you.'

The meal proceeded in silence except for the sound of the rain. Maugham finally rose from the table and disappeared from the room. Left alone, the young man and I stared at each other in utter helplessness. 'It really is wretched weather, isn't it?' he said finally. 'Yes,' I replied, 'but there's a lovely swimming-pool. Would you like to come and see it?' 'Yes, that would be marvellous.' We got our macintoshes and, through the rain, made our way to the pool. 'It's jolly nice, isn't it?' 'Yes, jolly.' We stared at the water. 'Gosh, I must be going. I'd better go and say goodbye.' We returned very slowly to the house, where he bade farewell to his host, who gave him a chilly nod. As the front door closed behind him, Maugham gave a sort of spit into the air like a witch and accompanied it with the most ungracious exclamation I have ever heard. 'That little Welsh tyke will never come here again.'

A year later the young man was found drowned in his bath at Albany.

For the remainder of my stay the rain continued and the atmosphere grew even more strained. To make matters worse, I had developed the unmistakable symptoms of a sore throat. When I told Alan I felt feverish he showed consternation, but not for me. 'For God's sake don't tell Willie,' he said; 'he can't stand anyone being ill. If you can't hide it, keep out of his way as much as you can.' Feeling close to death, I retired to my room nursing my inflamed throat and wondering how high my temperature must be: 105? 106? I felt like a prisoner; no one suggested that I should go out, or indeed any other activity. Each time I presented myself for one of those inevitable meals—to ask for a tray in my room would have revealed my illness—Maugham met me with total indifference, the most offensive of all weapons. There seemed nothing to do but go on as I had begun, pretending nothing had happened; and it was in the same way, still trying to pretend under the hooded stare of those cold, savagely hurt old eyes, that I miserably made my escape.

The trouble is, possibly, that there was too little reverence in Maugham's character; and where it occurred, it was reverence for the very things which, in such plays as *Our Betters*, he affects to despise—the smart world, its intrigues and gossip. Surely one of the saddest social processes in England is that by which writers, and sometimes politicians, even those of the Left, make their names by railing at the Establishment; and then, becoming sought after, are clasped to the bosom of high society to be finally killed by its embrace. Snobbery is at best, of course, a romantic impulse. It is the enjoyment of boredom in distinguished company. As such, it is almost a Christian virtue, eminently defensible. Maugham was certainly conscious of it in other people. He was a craftsman of acute intelligence. He was, however, also a person who always seemed, to me at least, to be constantly engaged in a bitter war with his own ethos.

I have often thought about that visit, and I am sure that a relationship with Maugham at that time of his life was impossible for anyone. It was as though the countenance of glossy illusion in Gerald Kelly's famous portrait and the core of reality so disturbingly revealed by Graham Sutherland had collided head-on and only a nasty accident remained. This was the Pirandellian conundrum.

Two years later, in 1949, I successfully revived Noël Coward's play, *Fallen Angels*. One night, at the height of the run, I invited Maugham, who was on one of his visits to England, to come and see the show. We arranged to meet at the Savoy Grill afterwards. When he met me in the foyer, I noticed that his face was white and set. I felt immediately that my fresh hopes of establishing some kind of contact with him had been absurdly misplaced. We went in silence to our table. 'The dinner's on me,' he said, his voice strained and hostile. I pointed out that he had agreed to be my guest. His face took on a furious life. 'After the insult you've subjected me to this evening,' he said, 'I never want to see or speak to you again.'

However, twenty years later we *were* to meet again in the same restaurant, and perhaps then, and only then, I perceived some sad fading flicker of fellow-feeling behind Maugham's impenetrable character. He looked very frail. After a life of lasting confusion he seemed to have taken a final inventory of himself. I approached the table with more fear than I ever displayed on a battlefield. He looked up at me like an amiable old toad. We indulged in light social exchange as though nothing had happened. He asked where I was living. I told him and said, 'You must come and see us.' He replied, 'I should like that,' and went on with his meal. I left the Savoy feeling much happier.

Soon after my return from my visit to Somerset Maugham in France there burst about me the one big rumpus of my career to date. Ironically enough, the row was with a personage who has always been an inspiration to me — Noël Coward — and centred on the very same production that later, as I have described, gave Maugham such erratic grounds to turn on me—*Fallen Angels*.

This early comedy of Noël's is about two flibbertigibbet London wives who drink themselves almost into a state of paralysis while waiting for the arrival of the Frenchman who had loved them both years before. Today its chief effect is one of innocence, faintly scented with mothballs; but in the 1920s it delighted and shocked the West End, earning the accolade of denunciation as near-pornography by a bishop. As a result of its success in revival, the managers of the provincial tour approached Hermione Gingold and Hermione Baddeley with the proposal that their production should come into London, with the two Hermiones playing the leads.

As it happened, Hermione Baddeley was under contract to me at the time, while Gingold was discussing with me a possible production of Giraudoux's *The Madwoman of Chaillot*. They asked my advice, which was that while the idea seemed to possess a promising glint of humour, I doubted whether Noël would ever agree to a casting which inevitably implied a guying of his play. You could hardly entrust such material to a pair of female clowns as practised as Gingold and Baddeley, I felt, and hope for it to come out anywhere near 'straight'. I was astonished, therefore, when spending a night at Noël's house at St Margaret's Bay to discover that he enthusiastically approved the casting of the two Hermiones. He went further. He would not consent, he said categorically, to a London production of *Fallen Angels* with any other actresses.

Next the two touring managers asked me to handle in conjunction with themselves the London presentation of the play. My successful run of the efficient little thriller, *The Late Edwina Black*, was due to end shortly at the Ambassadors. This charming theatre is ideally suited to intimate comedy, and the touring managers suggested that I should follow *Edwina Black* with *Fallen Angels*.

Before committing myself I had a serious consultation with Gingold, who had returned the day before from America. Unlike Baddeley, who generously clasps the world to her bosom and lets anything drop inside, Gingold is gifted with theatrical shrewdness and tactful cunning. Consequently I attach great value to her opinion. Could Noël, I asked her, be really serious in advocating such casting? With her and Baddeley, the play could only become a travesty of itself. I had no wish to incur the wrath of a friend and benefactor.

'Serious?' she cried. 'Of course he's serious. Why, only the other day he cabled me in New York, imploring me, literally imploring me, to play the part of Julia. But I want to play Jane. Here's what I answered.' She handed me the text of her cable. Absent-mindedly I put it in my pocket. I have it in front of me as I write: 'DARLING QUITE AGREE JULIA IS PIVOT BUT DONT SEE MYSELF PIVOTING THE OTHER LADY IS IN MY MIND MUCH FUNNIER STOP RESPECT FOR YOUR JUDGMENT UNCHANGED AS ALWAYS BUT MY HEAD IS THAT OF A PIG MUCH LOVE BOODLES.'

My qualms allayed, I let the play go into rehearsal. One day I went to the theatre to see how the performance was shaping. I was horrified by what I found. Baddeley was playing absolutely 'straight', with a sort of awed gentility. It was in disastrous conflict with Gingold's satire. At the end of the rehearsal, having consulted the director, Willard Stoker, I decided to speak seriously to them. I warned them that unless the play was given the full value of their personalities it wouldn't run three nights. The production could only succeed if it became a burlesque of a 'period' piece.

Baddeley put up a brisk defence. She was, she claimed, playing as Noël would want. In that case, I asked, why had Noël insisted on Gingold—who could not after all alter her style and personality? It was for Baddeley then to match her manner with Gingold's. Both actresses saw the justice of my attitude.

When Noël arrived in Plymouth to see the play before our London opening, he was in excellent spirits. At the sight of my insistently 'sporting' tweeds, he asked if I had left my horse in the hall! I was delighted. In this mood, I felt, he should take the evening very well.

Casually he inquired how the play was going. On its own level, I answered, it was tremendous fun. 'On its own level? That sounds rather ominous.' He could hardly, I pointed out, expect a realistic interpretation. No doubt he would accept it as he had Tallulah Bankhead's satirical fooling when *Private Lives* had been recently revived in New York.

His faint apprehension seemed to turn into tolerant amusement.

He told us how one night during the original run of *Fallen Angels* he had been horrified by Tallulah's antics. Afterwards he had torn her to shreds, at the same time imploring her to return to the admirable performance that she had given on the first night. He might, she had retorted hotly, say what he liked about her present way of playing. For her part, she infinitely preferred it. Moreover—and this to her seemed to clinch the matter—the Milford Havens, who had been in the theatre on the previous evening, also infinitely preferred it.

'Thereupon', Noël added, 'I left the theatre in a rage and sat down and wrote a letter to the press, agreeing with everything the critics had said about the vulgarity of Tallulah's playing. In consequence we didn't speak for three years.'

When we arrived, the curtain was already up and a packed theatre was roaring with pleasure at Noël's *Fumed Oak*, which we were doing as a curtain-raiser. Gingold as the grandmother found unexpected treasures of *double entendres* in an apparently innocent text. But, studying the Master's face, I saw that he did not share the ribald merriment which brayed around him. I decided not to go near him at the interval. Instinct told me that a storm was brewing, but I saw no reason to precipitate its outburst.

There was no avoiding his rendezvous with the cast on the stage after the final rapturous curtain. When I got there I found Noël standing in the middle of the set, his face flushed and tense, an apprehensive company round him. Only Hermione Baddeley wore her habitual look of sublime, feckless complacence.

'Tell us the worst, Noël darling,' she purred in a baby voice. Noël swung into withering action. 'The worst? The whole evening was bloody from beginning to end! You all ought to be deeply ashamed of yourselves.'

Gingold cut his outburst short. It might, she suggested with assumed indifference, be as well to continue the post-mortem elsewhere, not in front of the stage-hands. Like children told to play 'consequences' we crowded into Baddeley's dressing-room.

A moment's lull; then Noël rounded on Baddeley. 'Would you mind telling me why you commit such a gross indecency by playing it as you do?' 'Well,' she wailed, 'I didn't ever want to play it like that. But I was told to.' 'Told to? And who told you?' 'Well,' she hesitated; 'Peter told me to.'

At once I became the storm centre. I braced myself.

'How dare you ... ' he began; but Baddeley, realizing the terribly vulnerable position into which she had put me, attempted to shoot me a lifeline.

'Lizzie Lezard told me too.' (Poor Lizzie, with his passion for the theatre, had gallantly committed a few pennies to the enterprise.)

Noël swung back to her. 'And who the hell is Lizzie Lizzard?' Dimly Baddeley saw that her shot had gone wide. Hopefully she fired again.

'And Willard Stoker—the director.'

'Well then, the director's sacked. Never, *never*, NEVER—' But I was no longer listening to the spate of angry words; I felt tired. Now, probably, Noël would not speak to *me* for three years. If that happened it was just bad luck. I could not see how the play could be expected to attract a West End audience in the late 'forties unless it was played in the manner which had aroused such spleen in Noël. Needless to say, the production *was* a great success in London. Noël was not there to see it. He had sailed with his grievance to Jamaica.

My devoted respect for Noël was far too deep to allow a real rift in our friendship. I felt, as most people do, that Noël Coward has always been in our presence. For three generations he has epitomized three words: sophistication—the art which transforms the mundane into the stylish; wit—the capacity to say sparkling things in an amusing and unexpected way; and glamour—the ability to create around oneself a magical spell.

On December 16th, 1969, Noël Coward celebrated his seventieth birthday. London rose to this great event with television programmes, a film festival, a banquet at the Savoy and a midnight gala. It was the greatest acclaim for any theatrical figure in his or our lifetime. In the New Year's Honours List he received a knighthood, and London rejoiced with him in this belated recognition.

Shortly before these celebrations my wife and I had spent an enchanted week with Noël at Les Avants, his home in Switzerland, where the spirit of the past was recaptured as we listened to records of Noël's songs. He was the perfect host, surrounding us by warmth and by evidence that 'The Master's' wit lived on. His contribution to the theatre is unique. Perhaps John Osborne expressed it as well as anyone could when he wrote that 'Noël Coward, like Miss Dietrich, is his own invention and contribution to this century. Anyone who cannot see that should keep well away from the theatre.'

The idea for my next production came from one of my frequent visits to see the productions of the Birmingham Repertory Company, which under the direction of Sir Barry Jackson became the best company of its kind in the country. One evening in January 1950 I learned on arriving in Birmingham that we were to go forthwith to the company's current production, *The Gay Invalid.* I learned too, almost with dismay, that this was an adaptation of Molière's *Le Malade imaginaire.* I had seen several Molière productions in English; they had invariably opened up for me prospects of abysmal, prodigious boredom.

Molière is obviously one of the greatest comic geniuses the stage has ever known, and the debt of our English playwrights to him is not one that any sane man would attempt to assess. Without Molière, could the Jonsonian 'Comedy of Humours' have ever been changed so gloriously into the 'Comedy of Manners'? Congreve's Millamant, for instance, in *The Way of the World*—perhaps the most enchanting heroine ever imagined—is the glittering cousin of *Les Précieuses ridicules.* When she talks of how she uses her love-letters for curl-papers, and gets tolerable results only from those tributes written in verse; when her maid says '... but when your Ladyship pins it up with poetry, it sits so pleasant next day as anything, and is so pure and crisp', it is the spirit of Molière talking, a spirit distorted, even perhaps refined, by the peculiarities of the English genius, but Molière nevertheless. When Molière remains the inspiration and the remote ideal of our comic writers there is no end to the benefit; but when he is brought bodily into our theatres it generally ends in tears.

It will always remain a hazard to present in English even his most superb plays. *Le Malade imaginaire* is far from being one of these. Indeed, it is not strictly a play at all in the sense that *Tartuffe* and *Le Misanthrope* are. True, it guys quack doctors and credulous patients; but it is not the slashing, sustained attack upon a social evil which Molière was wont to give his public in his great days. Rather it is the lament of a man who is at the end of his tether and knows it. Two years before he wrote *Le Malade*, Molière was warned by his devoted friend Boileau that he would wear himself out with writing and acting at the same time. But the great man would not listen. He felt himself to be an actor as well as dramatist, and it is probable that we shall never see his great roles interpreted with such authority as he gave to them. The price he paid was disastrously dear: his life became beset with doctors, and the fun of *Le Malade* is tempered by an odd sort of melancholy, as if he knew all along that he must die after the third performance.

Yet, perhaps to take his mind off bodily frailties, he decked out the slight comedy with a whole series of ballets, mimes and choruses, so that at times it became far less 'straight' theatre than a *divertissement* designed to welcome Louis XIV home from a victorious campaign in the Low Countries. The machinations of Lully, who had been piqued at not being invited to write the music for *Le Malade*, may have prevented its performance at Versailles. It remains, however, the lightest mixture of comedy and mime, designed to amuse a tired monarch without putting him too much under the obligation of thought.

It was precisely this element in the Birmingham production which gave me a shock of pleasant surprise, so that by the time the evening was over all my caution and most of my critical faculties were agreeably atrophied. Against my better judgment, I could think of nothing but a London production. It was essential, I felt, here if anywhere, to cast against type. The part of the invalid could reach its full stature only on the shoulders of that style of comic playing, apparently effortless but infinitely contrived, which Charles Hawtrey had brought to perfection. My thoughts naturally turned to A. E. Matthews and Ronald Squire.

The story of *Le Malade imaginaire* turns upon the wiles of an unscrupulous doctor, who profitably fools a rich and simple old hypochondriac. But it would have taken a major feat of the imagination to conceive of Ronald Squire ever being fooled by anyone.

Matthews, on the other hand, always brought to mind those kindly, modest and slightly eccentric country gentlemen who, on repeated occasions in English history, have borne every sort of injustice and hoodwinking just so far and no further and have turned to rend their enemies. He is in the tradition of that famous Victorian, the Duke of Devonshire, who used to say he would rather see his pigs win first prize at Skipton Fair than get the Garter.

It was in just such a shape as this that I envisaged the character of *Le Malade*. Immediately after the Birmingham performance I therefore sent a cable to New York, where Matthews was appearing in *The Chiltern Hundreds*. In it I suggested that his chance of entering the classical field under the banner of Molière had at last come round. Knowing Matty's contempt for the classics—his views on Shakespeare were vigorously irreverent—I had no great hope of his being particularly fired by the idea. Back, however, came a reply that was at once characteristic and unexpectedly genial: 'NEVER HEARD OF THE FELLA WILL DO ANYTHING YOU SUGGEST.'

I was now quite ready to let the problem of casting rest until Matty's return from New York. Meanwhile I turned my attention to other aspects of the project. It obviously called for an inspired director, but such paragons are rare; indeed, the shortage of first-class directors was one of the most serious problems with which the theatre had to contend at that time. The director of a play had assumed an importance comparable to that of the director of a film. This was a comparatively modern development. For all the lavishness and the polish of their productions, how much direction in the modern sense of the word did Tree or Alexander give? Certainly in Shaw's criticisms the emphasis is focused upon plays and players, rarely upon direction. As far as I know, it was Reinhardt who was the first director to achieve international fame.

In Birmingham, in this same production of *Le Malade*, I had been very much impressed by the work of a young director called Michael Langham, then not yet known in London except by name. On a difficult stage he had invested the production with style and a suitable nobility; by his mimes and music he had emphasized those garments of fantasy in which Molière had wrapped his grim, sardonic theme; and he had evoked a world of illusion admirably suited, I thought, to the temper of a London public at a moment when it had little reason to be in love with reality. I resolved to make the experiment of offering him the direction. To my delight he accepted.

Next came the question of designer. A modern director, however admirable, unless he is working only within the relatively stylized bounds of a drawing-room comedy, can be hamstrung by an unimaginative designer. Now, for the first time in my short career as manager, I was about to launch a production which stood urgently in need of sensitive and inspired art direction. I was therefore forced to take stock of the designers upon whom a manager in this country might call. On the whole my stock-taking filled me rather with respect than hope.

At that time English stage design at its best was still founded on pastiche. We were haunted by the Augustan Age, the pediment, the urn. Excellent ghosts to be haunted by, no doubt, but I wanted to see an escape out of the museum library, into a field of pure invention unfenced by any suspicion of the antiquarian.

After due reflection on the alternatives it was to Oliver Messel that I turned to add his magic touch to the new production. I have always felt an unbounded admiration for his personality and his work. He is above all things a serious craftsman; not merely the scribbler of a few pretty drawings which are subsequently botched by incompetent hands during the process of translating them into full-sized scenery, but one who follows every design through the laborious stages from sketch to fully dressed achievement. He is one of the few designers too who really understand the characteristics of the materials in which they work, who know instinctively, for instance, how a certain velvet or silk will fall. His wit, his sense of colour and his sense of style have placed him on a plane where, since the death of Rex Whistler, he reigns in solitude.

Alas! as usual, he was not free; but, as a friend, he took the liveliest interest in my venture and was rich in advice. I could not, he said, commit myself into better hands than those of Paul Shelving, who had designed the set for the Birmingham production. Having made a great reputation for his work in the London theatre, Shelving had for some years been resident designer at Birmingham, and I had greatly admired the invention and ingenuity of his designs for *Le Malade*. So I was content to accept Oliver's opinion.

One day shortly afterwards I went to lunch with the Cochrans. I arrived to find Evelyn Cochran alone; C. B. had been detained at the office. I mentioned to Evelyn a rumour I had heard that

Elisabeth Bergner was in England, staying at the Ritz. Evelyn's admiration for Elisabeth Bergner was no less deep than C. B.'s, and although she refused to believe that Bergner could be capable of coming to London without letting them know, the rumour surprised, hurt and amused her all at once. My suggestion that I should ring up the Ritz to find out one way or the other immediately caught her fancy.

I got through, asked the operator for Miss Bergner, and the next moment a hoarsely languorous purr greeted me. I handed the telephone to Evelyn, who had become thoroughly confused by the whole affair. She began a conversation with Bergner, and in the course of it told her who I was. 'He's a great admirer of yours, and wants to find a play for you.' She thrust the telephone back into my hands, and I found myself asking Bergner if indeed she would care to play for me. 'Well, why not? Find a play, and I will do it.'

A couple of nights later I was asked to dinner to meet her at Jan van Loewen's, the agent who represented her in England. It is an ordeal to get to know some great artist whom one has admired since childhood. It rarely happens that one likes them immediately; luckily it happened to me on this occasion.

We talked until late about plays. Just before I left I asked Bergner, 'Why don't you play Toinette in *Le Malade* to A. E. Matthews's Argan?' She seemed taken by the idea. 'How funny you should suggest that! I've played it twice before: first as a girl of fourteen, then later under Reinhardt at Salzburg. I admire Mr Matthews so very much, but my part hardly exists.' I assured her that the part of Toinette could easily be built up, and as a matter of policy I suggested that her re-introduction to London under the cloak of Matthews's popularity would be no bad thing, since the press was still far from friendly to her.

Even before the part was 'blown up' she seemed to me to be the ideal casting for the part of Toinette, that *gamine* debunker who keeps the flag of sense flying in the heavy medicated air of Argan's sick-room, and who by her very pertness confounds the quacks with their pompous Latin formulae. I believed that the combination of her and Matthews would prove irresistible at the box-office.

As I grew to know Bergner I became fascinated by the odd and often charming quirks of her character. She clung to the

habit, for instance, of wrapping herself in mystery. It is a habit
largely abandoned now. The bomb-blast of war, so to speak,
tore away our façades; the social revolution that still continues
and our present fear of annihilation have left little time for
concealment. But for Bergner the habit of making a mystery of
her slightest action, her slightest movement, remained an essential
part of the fantasy of existence. It was this impulse, rather than
any wish to hurt, which had prevented her from telling the
Cochrans of her presence in London.

Many great actresses live in and through their imaginations.
By some subjective process they turn the joys, sorrows and
adventures of other people into their own. Bergner possessed
that faculty to an almost alarming degree; she lived, suffered,
rejoiced in a world where fact and make-believe were so inextricably mingled that it was often impossible to determine where
one ended and the other began. Once, for instance, during the
rehearsals of *The Gay Invalid* she came to me with her great eyes
full of anguish and almost slipping off her face: certain members
of my theatre, she assured me, were against her, were her enemies;
the management as a whole did not love her; I must immediately
sack the lot or she could not continue to rehearse. I refused to
take this drastic step; she spent the evening in close communion
with the Sermon on the Mount, until, convinced that the meek are
blessed, she capitulated, and I became light-hearted once again.

By October 1950 we were ready to begin rehearsals and were
to open in Manchester on November 6th. In the adaptation by
Sir Barry Jackson of *Le Malade*, Argan had been rechristened
Crank, and in place of the interminable choruses and ballets in
honour of Louis XIV, Walter Gore had devised a series of mimes
to be executed outside Crank's house by a troupe of strolling
Italian comedians.

All seemed set for a successful production; but from the very
first days of rehearsal, a *Pech*, a hoodoo, a jinx appeared to brood
over the venture. Bergner arrived a week late for rehearsals,
flying back from a triumphant tour of *The Two Mrs Carrolls* in
Australia and admitting that she had hardly read the script. This
naturally upset the company and put Michael Langham on an
aggressive sort of defensive.

Too late did I discover what his methods of direction, admirable results though they had achieved, were likely to provoke

on this occasion. Langham worked to a meticulous pattern of pre-conceived mechanics. This technique is generally useful and effective in repertory, or with malleable young players. But Bergner and Matthews were artists of impulse whose work only attained its vitality through a sort of spontaneous combustion. The very first morning of rehearsal Langham drove Bergner into a jungle of mechanics; she remained attentive and uncomplaining but it was clear that a functional strait-jacket suited her no better than it did Matthews.

Soon the whole production was in serious jeopardy. Bergner had been reduced to trying to follow like an automaton; Matthews was making no progress towards learning his lines. He was in fact scared stiff; every time he spoke, he was interrupted by some instruction on where to move. I had the greatest respect for Michael Langham. Unfortunately, on this occasion at least, he showed no personal flair in his dealings with his actors. Under pressure from me he modified his methods, but still the weeks went by without the production taking shape.

I suggested to Matthews that he should take a few days off and in the quiet of his country cottage relax and concentrate upon learning his lines. The strain of a long important role, and a method of direction utterly alien to him, had already affected him physically; he could not sleep, he ran a high temperature, and the doctor forbade him to rehearse for a week.

Bergner strove on valiantly, and Matthews returned a few days before the Manchester opening, still too confused to be able to rehearse without his book. I tried to hide my forebodings behind a cheerful façade. I assured Bergner that Matthews was a first-night actor; once facing an audience in Manchester, I said, he would pull the trick out of the bag. It was hard on the rest of the company. Argan–Crank was, after all, the corner-stone of the whole structure; with Matthews so shaky neither style nor timing was possible.

On the train to Manchester Bergner and Matthews travelled together. She was tireless in her attentions to him, going over and over their scenes in the hope that his confidence might be restored in the course of that five-hour journey. Yet at the Opera House that same evening Matthews begged to be excused the dress rehearsal. If he could sit in the stalls and see the whole production from outside, he said, it would help him enormously to assess the complete picture. In reality, of course, it was a last despairing effort to recover his bearings.

I do not want to dwell on the painful and melancholy experience of the opening. Matthews's nerve went entirely and he lost what little grip of his lines he had ever achieved. Elisabeth Bergner's performance, on the other hand, was a *tour de force*. She animated and supported Matthews throughout the evening. She was facing an English audience for the first time in fifteen years, an audience which, the press had warned her, was unlikely to be sympathetic; she had also to manipulate the countless strings which gave Argan life. If the evening was not a triumph, at least she saved it from utter disaster.

Matthews played the following evening's performance, but the strain was evidently too much. I told him to go home, to rest, not worry, and to return as soon as he felt better. That evening he asked me to put on the company notice-board the following message:

> To one of the most loving and loyal companies I have ever been associated with: This is to say, with the greatest regret, that I am forced to forsake you. Throughout my three attempts to play Mr Crank you carried me through; that I appreciate most sincerely, but, my friends, for the sake of you all I decided to listen to my doctor's orders for the very first time in my life. The three performances I attempted have shaken me to such an extent that I had to give in. I am told that Mister Molière survived three performances of this play and died during the fourth. Being a coward, I dare not risk a similar fate, so I thank you, everyone of you, and God bless you.   MATTY

Terribly shaken, and upset, he went home and set to work doggedly on his part. Meanwhile, by dint of nightly playing, the production was beginning to acquire some sort of polish, while Bergner's example had kept our spirits high.

She had always persisted in the belief that provided Matthews recovered he would be preferable to any other actor in the role of *Le Malade*. She was prepared to take a gamble, as indeed I was, on his return; but she made one stipulation—I must take over direction of the whole production. In the end I agreed to direct all Bergner's scenes with Matthews, which were in fact the main scenes of the play, while the ballet and mime sequences I would leave in the capable hands of Walter Gore. I explained the situation to Michael Langham; naturally his pride suffered an unpleasant blow, but, far from being obstructive, he behaved with the greatest magnanimity.

At Oxford, Matthews returned officially and gave an excellent performance. He had made a brilliant come-back, no mean achievement for a man in his eighties whose whole acting habits had been disturbed. Thenceforward, during all the weeks at Eastbourne, Malvern and Croydon, I was rehearsing Matthews and Bergner, Harriette Johns, Tod Slaughter and Michael Shepley.

Now the whole company was co-operating with an almost schoolboy enthusiasm, contributing ideas and an heroic effort, and all the while Matthews's performance was gathering authority and momentum; the general playing of the company had attained a high quality, while at moments Bergner achieved flashes of exquisite poetry. Yet bad luck still dogged our endeavours. Leslie Bridgewater, who had composed a charming score for the production, had fallen backwards into the orchestra pit after a performance and fractured his neck. And worse was yet to come.

Throughout the whole of this production, C. B. Cochran had allied himself in spirit to the venture. His love for Elisabeth and his friendship for me had made him, to use his own words, as concerned as though it were his own production. Wherever I was, he would ring me at least twice a week to discuss in detail everything that I had been worrying about and, all through, his wise and wonderful counsel helped me to persevere over a very difficult task. But on the day of the opening performance at the Garrick Theatre Evelyn telephoned my wife to say that that morning he had badly scalded himself in his bath and that they would both be unable to attend the first night with us. It was not until later in the day, just before the curtain rose, that I learned of the appalling effects of this accident, and how his life hung in the balance. He died within a week of the London opening.

My chief pleasure of friendship with Cochran during his last years had been to bask in the afterglow of his greatness, encouraging him to pile reminiscence upon fantastic reminiscence. When he started talking, before one's startled gaze lumbered the legendary Hackenschmidt fresh from throwing the Big Turk;

the Dollies and their collies tripped across the stage of the Winter Garden again, squeaking in surprisingly little voices some nonsense or other from beneath enormous fur-swathed toques. Sacha Guitry and Yvonne Printemps were flirting again, and flirting with artistry such as we shall rarely see in the theatre of this serious age. It was of Sacha Guitry that Cockie was talking the last time I saw him, a few days before his accident. The sudden entry of Evelyn into the room had inspired a story I had never heard before. 'My favourite story of Sacha', said Cockie, 'concerns Evelyn. When we were over in Paris recently, Sacha called on us at our hotel. This flamboyant genius, with his thick white hair, ruddy complexion and unlimited confidence in his own attraction, looked perfectly magnificent.' 'Oh Sacha,' Evelyn said, greeting him, 'how like your father Lucien you look.' 'How funny you should say that,' Sacha replied; 'this morning as I was shaving I glanced in the mirror and said, "Oh Papa! What a handsome man you are!" '

Cochran's death was followed a few weeks later by another irreparable loss. On his way back from Jamaica Ivor Novello fell ill with a severe attack of influenza. While he was recuperating before rejoining *King's Rhapsody*, he telephoned to say that the only visit he was paying to the theatre was to *The Gay Invalid*. He sat in a box with Phyllis Monkman and enjoyed every minute of it; it was, he told me, something he would have been very proud to put on himself. At one point in the performance, however, he began to feel ill, and sent for a brandy. He recovered in due course, and the incident did not seem to have spoiled his pleasure. Indeed, a few weeks later, when I told him that business was disappointing and that we might be forced to close, he offered me additional capital to keep it on, so great was his belief in its ultimate success. Three days later he was dead.

As I thought of Ivor, I realized that he possessed one of the most precious among human qualities, reasonableness. He enjoyed a serene, incorruptible gift of simplicity and of loving-kindness; but at the same time was innocent of affectation and full of fun. That gay and apparently careless manner hid acute powers of observation, and a secret and impenetrable citadel of reserve.

The Gay Invalid had opened in London at the Garrick Theatre on January 24th, 1951. It had received a good reception from its audience, but the critics on the whole were lukewarm. Most

of them assumed that a full-length Molière satire had been cut in
the adaptation to make room for superfluous miming and ballet.
'Ballet dancers keep prancing in,' they complained; 'there is too
much tinkling music'; '... decked out with music and mime ... ';
'not so much a version of the French as diversion in English'.
Diversion? Is not that what Molière was aiming at?

The adventure into Molière had proved an exciting experience.
I should have hated to have missed a single rise or fall of that
giddy wheel of fortune on which we had ridden so perilously,
and at times tragically, and which was to pitch me into the world
of the dance.

6

The World of the Dance

During the production of *The Gay Invalid* the world of the dance had come to fascinate me. Walter Gore's mimes had perhaps been the most satisfactory element in the Molière production. Strongly influenced by Massine and Ashton, Gore had been the mainstay of the Ballet Rambert, both as choreographer and dancer. His hair was corn-coloured, his nose appeared to mock the heavens, his eyes sparkled with mischief, and he had a lively personality which made it impossible to ignore him on or off the stage. He was like a Harlequin let loose in ballet—and it was this role which he danced in *The Gay Invalid*. Watching him work out choreographically the patterns which we had been discussing five minutes before was an infinite stimulus to the imagination.

In 1950 Cochran had sent on to me a letter that Vita Sackville-West had written to him:

Dear Sir Charles,

I was so glad to hear that you were interested in Antonio, the dancer I saw in Madrid. I have no hesitation in saying that he is really a great dancer and actor, and as you know the Spaniards are extremely fastidious about the technique of dancing and he has their entire approval. I am afraid I don't know what his surname is but he dances with his sister as *Antonio and Rosario* at the Fontalba Theatre in Madrid, which address would certainly find them. They have been to America and I do feel a definite effort ought to be made to bring them to London.

Yours sincerely,
V. SACKVILLE-WEST

This had stirred up a dream that had been lying comatose in the recesses of my mind. Now, in the spring of 1951, after *The Gay Invalid* had closed down I found myself free to think of these two Andalusians, Rosario and Antonio, whose dancing was earning for them a prodigious reputation on the Continent as well as in Spain itself. Cochran, who after all had brought the incomparable Argentina to this country, had communicated to me something of his passion for Spanish dancing; indeed, for some time he had been planning to bring Rosario and Antonio to London himself.

I resolved to go in search of them to Spain, a country which had always attracted me, and invited Simon Harcourt-Smith to accompany my wife and myself. His knowledge of the country would I knew be an enormous asset. And so one fine April morning we set forth by car towards Madrid, and we hoped towards a meeting with Antonio.

Arriving in Madrid we began a fruitless search. Antonio had last been heard of dancing in Seville, at the *Feria*; he was supposed to be off to Cairo, to perform at some party in connection with King Farouk's wedding. Perhaps he had already left? Who knew? Perhaps in a few weeks' time one would be able to contact him.

I can imagine few capitals where waiting could be more agreeable than Madrid in the spring, when the Buen Retiro gardens blaze with the white candles of the chestnut-trees glowing above statues of former Spanish kings, not one of whom the Civil War had left with a whole nose. A delicate scent of daffodils and frying crayfish pervades the streets; the drains have not then begun to declare their presence, and bull-fighting is just getting into its stride.

But alas! we were in no position to while away a few dreamlike weeks until somehow, somewhere, we might come across Antonio. The worries and the urgencies that flog men along the streets of London or New York may well appear grotesquely unreal in Madrid. Yet the fact remained that I was caught in an intricate network of agreements and commitments; if I could not find Antonio now, if I could not bring him to London by June, I might not be able to bring him at all in 1951, and the whole project which I had in mind for a season of international ballet at the Cambridge Theatre might well remain no more than a dream.

Finally we ran to ground Antonio's manager and we were able to arrange a meeting with Antonio for that afternoon. It took place in Antonio's flat near the Prado, amid innumerable photographs of Hollywood beauties, Joan Fontaine and Gene Tierney and I don't know who else, all dripping charm and passionate dedications.

Antonio came into the room, with a smile almost too intensely radiant for comfort, and walking delicately, like an Arab stallion. We made good progress, although the final negotiations could only be conducted with Antonio's representatives in Paris. Still, it was settled in principle that he would come to dance in London early in June.

We returned the following evening to a cocktail party given by Antonio before he flew off to the royal wedding in Egypt. As he moved among the chattering crowd of his guests, I took the opportunity to observe closely this slight exquisite who had risen from obscurity to be the highest-paid dancer in the world, and, much more important, to enjoy in Spain itself such popular adulation as was normally reserved only for the great bull-fighters like Belmonte or Ortega.

With his partner Rosario he had been dancing for nearly a quarter of a century. Antonio told me how they made their first public appearance in a couple of silent films in 1927, when their pay was no more than a box of sweets. They had been trained by that great master of the Spanish dance, Realito, and were beginning to make a name for themselves when the Civil War broke out in 1936. In company with the best of the Spanish dancers then in the capital they fled to Buenos Aires. They were dancing in some provincial South American theatre when Toscanini, who was on a concert tour in those parts, saw them and was entranced. It was Toscanini's influence, more than anything else, which got them their first engagement in a New York night-club, and it was in America that the foundations of their success were laid. When Spaniards at home heard of it they were incredulous and suspicious, knowing how easily America corrupts artists—particularly Spanish artists, with their fatal national desire to please and to do what is expected of them.

Yet, to the astonishment of Spain, Rosario and Antonio returned home with comparatively few meretricious tricks to set against their brilliant traditional artistry. They conquered the Spanish public as they had conquered the American; Antonio now enjoyed in his country a princely prestige. In 1951 Franco awarded him the Cross of Queen Isabella the Catholic, 'for services to art'.

They had danced briefly at the Edinburgh Festival of 1950; but London was the one capital of any consequence in the world that had not yet seen them. As Antonio picked his way fastidiously through the crowd of his friends (reminding me more than ever of an Arab stallion with every movement), I wondered how London audiences would take to him.

Rosario and Antonio opened in London at the Cambridge Theatre on June 14th, 1951. There was no company in the true sense of the word: only Rosario and Antonio themselves, three guitarists, a *flamenco* singer, and two pianists who accompanied some of the less specifically Andalusian dances, and in the intervals between the dancing played the rich melodies of Granados, Albéniz and Falla.

For any manager, even one of the most sluggish sensibility, the first part of a first night is always a nightmare. The audience seems to expend all its amiability and energy on recognizing the great and being recognized in turn; by the time the curtain rises no emotion, one feels, can be left in it but spleen and fatigue. In the case of Rosario and Antonio I had been well depressed beforehand by the misgivings of most of my friends in the theatre.

When the curtain rose, Rosario and Antonio opened in an admirable if unspectacular *pas de deux* that discreetly embodied many of the classic steps of *baile hondo*. Rosario's mustard-coloured dress looked austere against a plain grey curtain; the tide of sympathy was, I felt, flowing away from the stage and the performers; the audience was giving them nothing save, at best, polite indifference. The next number succeeded little better. Then Rosario danced a brilliant *jota*, which was to be followed by Antonio in his famous *zapateado*. If that did not move the house, then nothing would. I sat in my box, tense, as the curtain revealed Antonio in a circle of light, erect, immobile, in his flashing blue costume. Here was the moment of crisis; if he failed to subdue the audience with this piece of virtuosity, then the evening was lost, the whole venture best forgotten.

The *zapateado*, I should explain for the benefit of those who have never seen Antonio dance it, is a sort of Andalusian version of a 'soft-shoe' routine, but infinitely more dramatic, more complicated and more brilliant than any picture that that phrase may evoke of a top-hatted dancer, stick under arm, pattering through an old-fashioned cabaret. As, with eyes aflame and head thrown back, the dancer moves backwards and forwards, the drumming feet and extreme muscular control seem to hold the concentrated essence of all *flamenco*.

Antonio is not only a great technician who can project a dazzling charm across the orchestra pit; when he dances the *zapateado* he performs one of the greatest miracles in contemporary show business. The success of this kind of dancing depends in a large measure upon lashing together audience and dancer by a cord of sympathy, which is then twisted and twisted till the tension grows almost unbearable and the fall of the curtain is like the cut of a knife. This was how it happened on the first night. One moment the audience was nothing but phlegmatic lines of white shirt-fronts and bare shoulders, the next it had suddenly become a part of the show; the superficial defences of English reserve had crumbled, and the essential romanticism of our national character, with its curiously accurate instinct for good dancing, was uppermost, excessive frigidity giving way to an almost extravagant enthusiasm. The house rocked and shook with cheers from that moment on, in what was one of the most extraordinary evenings I can remember. The audience were soon according to the accompanying guitarists an acclamation only a fraction less tumultuous than that with which they called Rosario and Antonio back before the curtain again and again. This time Spanish dancing had certainly made history in the English theatre.

Business was slack for the first few days. There was barely a notice in the daily press. Peter Williams, a great connoisseur of the dance, whose friendship I have enjoyed for many years, wrote a rave notice for the *Daily Mail*. The following morning we found it had been cut out. On Sunday, however, after a week of anguish we were suddenly assailed with glowing praise. In the *Sunday Times* Cyril Beaumont wrote an ecstatic notice, while Richard Buckle, who had long proclaimed Antonio's genius, wrote in the *Observer*: 'It would be a pity if London theatre-goers missed the chance of boasting to their grandchildren that they had seen the greatest male dancer of the day.'

These notices, and the report of what had happened at the first night, which by this time had circulated throughout the West End, turned the tide. From the following Monday we were playing to packed houses. Then, just when I thought I could allow myself the luxury of relaxing for a moment, I was brutally reminded that the manager's profession is fraught with incalculable hazards. One night my wife and I were watching Antonio dance his *Bailes Boleros* when an ankle collapsed without warning under him with a great crack that sounded like a pistol-shot.

A gasp went up from the audience as he limped off stage. I quickly went in search of Cyril Tanner, the theatre manager, and found him congratulating himself and his colleagues that we were all set for a triumphant season. As I approached those smiling faces, I saw all at once the real absurdity of the theatrical profession. Here I was, unavoidably the bringer of evil tidings, the wiper away of gaiety; how crazy any of us were to pin our fortunes to the proper functioning of a dancer's body, a fragile structure of blood and bone, any part of which could go wrong at any moment.

I told Cyril Tanner to go behind and see whether Antonio was still able to dance, and then waited anxiously. A few moments dragged by, as long, it seemed, as a whole day of frustration, before Cyril Tanner came back. His countenance exuded reassurance. 'I think it's going to be all right,' he said. 'Through a miracle we got hold of a masseur who was just over the way at the Saville. No bones broken, he thinks; he's strapped up the ankle. Antonio's going on again.' Rosario and the guitarists had been continuing with the performance; when Antonio appeared it was as though nothing at all had happened. I marvelled at Antonio's resilience, for I knew he must be in great pain. I steeled myself, however, for the consequences which were bound to develop.

They had, indeed, done so by the time I reached Antonio's hotel next morning. He was lying in bed, looking very black. The masseur of the previous evening stared at the injured ankle with canine dejection. Antonio looked at me reproachfully. 'I shall be off for several days,' he said. 'There's nothing to be done.' 'That's right,' mumbled the masseur gloomily; 'terrible state the gentleman's in.'

Antonio smiled gratefully at him. At that moment the door opened and in walked a breezy young hotel manager, with another gentleman whom he introduced as the hotel's public relations officer. With an admirable show of solicitude he explained that he had heard how Antonio had suffered an accident. How was he? I saw through their ghoulish errand, however. I was resolved that they should not make publicity for their hotel out of my worries, and when Antonio showed signs of growing expansive I quickly shut him and them up.

At that moment the telephone rang. It was Richard Buckle. He suggested that I should immediately submit Antonio's ankle for the inspection of the renowned Miss Sparger. That remarkably dexterous lady supervised and guarded the precious ankles of the Royal Ballet. He would arrange an appointment forthwith, and accompany us into the wilds of Baron's Court for the consultation. Dicky felt certain that Miss Sparger, if anyone, would have Antonio dancing by the evening.

When I announced the plan and Dicky's hopes to Antonio his face only grew a trifle blacker. With the masseur's fumbling help, I somehow got Antonio dressed and into the hired car where a bland Dicky Buckle was waiting for us. Antonio's spirits seemed to rise slightly when he saw that the car was a vast Rolls-Royce limousine. 'You have a fine car, Peter,' he said, smiling at me for the first time that day. I did not disillusion him.

We seemed to travel for miles. One almost expected to smell the sea. Then, somewhere near St Paul's School, the car halted before a small house built of angry red stone. Miss Sparger appeared, benign, unruffled, and took in the situation at a glance. We helped Antonio out and into the little house. The black look was returning to his face. 'Wait till he gets inside,' Dicky whispered; 'he's obviously expecting something that looks like an operating theatre on the movies!'

Nothing looked less like a clinic, however, than the tidy austere room where Miss Sparger worked her miracles. No gleaming switchboards, but a tired old sofa and a chipped sun-lamp. 'In Spain', Antonio grumbled, 'we have all the latest equipment.' Miss Sparger took no notice. 'Sit down there, and I'll get you right in no time.'

I looked nervously at Dicky, wondering whether he had, in fact, brought us to the right place. But already Miss Sparger's fingers were delicately exploring the swollen ankle. 'I shall not dance for another week,' Antonio said with a groan.

'Nonsense!' Miss Sparger looked almost severe. 'You'll dance tonight. Why, I had Mr Anton Dolin here once with a broken ankle, and I got *him* on the same night. Nothing broken here.'

And in fact she did. After an hour's manipulation of the ankle,

Antonio could walk, albeit painfully. We could not yet be sure, however, that we would not have to cancel the evening's performance until we had fortified ourselves with a radiograph. By that stage it was nearly six o'clock, and a frantic theatre had never been off the telephone.

In the event all was well, and thereafter Rosario and Antonio played without further dramas to packed and thundering houses, whose appetite for encores became insatiable. It was almost impossible to keep admirers from obstructing the side gangways, even though we extended the season for an extra two weeks.

Although I presented Antonio many times in London, I found that one could never really become very close to him. You could only be an accomplice. Artistic collaboration is non-existent. Lunch or dinner with Antonio can be most engaging. He is usually intoxicated with his own conversational *bonhomie*, and he chatters away as busily as a castanet, with the hint of a lisp like the whisper of a flute. But at other times 'he is as grand as Doomsday and as grave', surrounded by his train of court parasites hovering like languid smoke.

The success of Rosario and Antonio's visit gave me the confidence necessary to face the risks of continuing at the Cambridge Theatre with a season of international dance companies, which was to last without interruption for a year—my first prolonged season of visiting foreign productions. From June 14th, 1951, to June 14th, 1952, I presented nine sparkling world companies: Rosario and Antonio, the Ballets des Champs-Élysées, Pilar Lopez, the Grand Ballet du Marquis de Cuevas, Mrinalini Sarabhai and her Hindu Ballet, a return visit of Rosario and Antonio, Katherine Dunham, Carmen Amaya, and the Yugoslav State Company. Little did I think then that by mid-1954, three years after my début as an impresario of dancing, I would be giving my twenty-fifth London dance presentation. The company which followed Rosario and Antonio at the Cambridge in August 1951 more than fulfilled the hopes I had for my first season. This was the Ballets des Champs-Élysées, the most stimulating independent development in ballet in the previous decade in France.

Over the next five years I was to work in close association and friendship with Roland Petit, and I brought his work to London on six occasions. When his Ballets des Champs-Élysées, with which he had made his first appearance in London some years earlier, came over for my Cambridge season, Petit had, in fact, already moved on to form his new company, the Ballets de Paris de Roland Petit. This company I presented twice in my 1953-4 season at the Stoll Theatre, and again with continued success at the Palace Theatre in May 1956. I was also to include in my Stoll season in 1954 a visit from the company of Petit's early partner and collaborator, Janine Charrat, and in 1960 another production of Roland's at the Royalty Theatre with Zizi Jeanmaire.

This series of visits represented the genius of Roland Petit—at once a superb dancer and a unique choreographer—besides presenting a synthesis of design, music and talent not seen in London since Diaghilev. Aiming at immediacy and simplicity, Petit scorned classical ballet. 'Covent Garden bores me and Balanchine is dreadful. The old tradition of dancing is like a corset for a woman. She must wear it, but what a relief to get out of it. I may do a classical ballet one day—in my way!'

The Ballets des Champs-Élysées was the first flowering of pure French ballet since the romantic era of the nineteenth century. It began with a performance on a winter's evening of 1944. A small group of dancers at the Théâtre Sarah Bernhardt gave six concert performances with hired costumes, no scenery and a piano on a bare stage. This had been organized by Irene Lidova, the photographer and ballet historian. The company were all under twenty. They included Jean Babilée, Colette Marchand, Janine Charrat, Zizi Jeanmaire and Roland Petit. They were determined, fearless, exultant and defiant. It was just after the Liberation, and the Parisians felt that they were opening their windows on a vision of a brave new world.

The triumph of these recitals enthused two older men, veterans of the ballet—Boris Kochno, Diaghilev's private secretary and author of several of his scenarios, and Christian Bérard, the painter, whose delicate theatrical overtones transfigured reality into his own world of enchantment. They were both inspired to form a company around these very young dancers. The birth of the Ballets des Champs-Élysées took place at the Théâtre des Champs-Élysées on March 5th, 1945. Roland Petit, aged twenty, produced a minor work of art with *Les Forains* which was to make him famous overnight. With its exquisite decor by Bérard and haunting score by Henri Sauguet, it was the story of a wandering circus, which sets up its booths in front of a small uninterested group of spectators, from whom there is little response. The performance peters out, and the performers gather up their props and disconsolately drift on to their next pitch. With this ballet Roland was to arouse the interest of a remarkable entourage of designers, composers, writers and poets—including André Derain, Leoni Fini, Darius Milhaud, Jean Cocteau, Jean Anouilh, Jacques Prévert, Henri Sauguet, Jean Dutilleux and Igor Stravinsky.

During a short season sponsored by his father at the Théâtre Sarah Bernhardt, Petit was to choreograph another work of art, Jacques Prévert's *Le Rendezvous*, with its romantic score by Kosma (which included the melody *Autumn Leaves*), and its photographic montage by Brassai. Picasso painted the dropcloth, which lent it an added quality of excitement. It was a sad gutter-poem about the inhabitants of Montmartre. The characterization and choreography were as vital and individual as a French film of the Paris underworld.

Roland now had his first permanent theatre. Kochno became the artistic director, Lidova the general secretary and Roland the *maître de ballet*. His body was tall, thin and sharp as a knife. With his black curly hair, pale face and long, admirably shaped legs he had a vivid, individual personality. This impatient and angry young man of ballet was self-educated through his passion for cinema, magazines and jazz.

Throughout our association I saw that his diffident, sardonic bearing contained a spirit of animal restlessness and devouring insatiability. He had to attend to every small detail himself. His eyes, dark and hectic in a wax mask of pale asceticism, could turn from summer to winter without moving a muscle. He could be tender and he could be malicious. He had a genius for the unexpected and, like Colette's *Chéri*, he was someone who attracted love and sometimes trouble. He also had great sweetness and wisdom, and I became very fond of him.

My relationship with Roland started with a blazing row over the eternal problem of choice and length of programme. 'You still hate me,' he told me once with childish glee; 'that's wonderful. You were starting to get like every other manager—like a sort of head-waiter.'

During the three years that he was with the Théâtre des

Champs-Élysées Roland choreographed and staged Jean Cocteau's brilliant creation *Le Jeune Homme et la Mort*, which was to bring international fame to the great dancer Jean Babilée. This ballet is a deeply poignant tragedy which unfolds in the cluttered claustrophobia of an artist's studio. The young artist impatiently awaits the arrival of his girl friend. They chase each other through the encumbrance of furniture, frames, tables and paintings. Her seductive indifference drives him mad and the young painter hangs himself. The walls of the studio fade away to reveal the rooftops of Paris. The Eiffel Tower shines like a beacon, and the spirit of death appears in the form of the young girl. She places her mask over the face of her lover and draws him away across the rooftops of Paris. Nathalie Philippart, who is married to Babilée, played the girl. They were both to appear in these roles in my season with the Janine Charrat Ballet at the Stoll Theatre in April 1954.

Babilée is the kind of artist who can seldom be imitated in the roles he creates. A dancer of electric personality, he has a quality of perfection which seems at times almost reckless. Short and thickset, his high cheekbones, expressive eyes and powerful limbs give him an air of animal grace and romantic virility. In December 1953 he had replaced Roland Petit in *Le Loup* at the Stoll Theatre and had also given, with Violette Verdy, a magnificent display of classical dancing in 'The Bluebird'. During the dress rehearsal of the latter I was sitting in the stalls with Marie Rambert, whose enthusiasm and spiritual vitality have always been a wonderful source of encouragement to me. Babilée appeared before us holding Violette Verdy above him like a pillow of feathers. He held her helpless above the orchestra pit for a moment, then slowly retreated to the back of the stage. He put his delicate partner down, signalled to the orchestra, and walked through the *pas de deux* with disdainful indifference. This represented a temperamental protest that came from a deeply erratic personality often difficult to control. I asked Mim Rambert whether I should dare to let him dance the following night; she said that it was worth taking a chance! And indeed his performance was magnificent.

Petit had created the role of the wolf in *Le Loup* and had danced it with Violette Verdy during the company's first visit to the Stoll earlier the same year. Babilée's interpretation was less savage than Roland's, but was deeply touching in the smooth and

powerful sense of animal seduction that it evoked. The story by
Anouilh tells of a young bride deserted on her wedding-day by
her bridegroom, who has run away with a gypsy. She is made to
believe that her groom has been changed into a wolf, and elopes
into the forest with him. When the wolf is unmasked and hunted
down, she dies with it. The forest, a superb creation in Carzou's
design, had a density and fluorescence through which the muted
colours of the pursuers rippled like stained-glass windows in
changing lights.

Another wonderful role which Roland created was that of Don
José in his *Carmen*, to which he brought the full fierce, seductive
emotion of Prosper Mérimée's novelettish tale. His lithe and
glowering performance was a masterpiece of portraiture, his acting revealing with flashing inspiration a young man possessed by
his fatal love for a gypsy girl. Against Bizet's haunting music and
the glowing decor of Antoni Clavé, Roland Petit and Colette
Marchand, who played Carmen, brought to ballet the pulsating
heat and violent passion of great theatre. For me *Carmen*, *Le Loup*
and *Les Forains* will always be Roland's greatest works. In them
he gathered together in full strength all the forces of music, dance
and drama.

As well as Carmen, Colette Marchand danced the main role in
the slick, fast and acrobatic *Ciné-Bijou*, a kind of musical satire on
the Hollywood gangster era, and in *Deuil en vingt-quatre heures*, an
equally frivolous concoction, with absurdities of situation and
comic mime in the great French tradition. But perhaps the most
intriguing addition to the repertoire in this visit of August 1953
was *The Lady in the Ice*, conceived and designed by that visionary
genius Orson Welles, which gave both Roland and myself a lot
of delightful trouble.

At the Palace Theatre in 1956 Zizi Jeanmaire danced *Carmen*
with Petit, while an exciting addition to the programme was *His-
toire Policière* by Georges Simenon, with Buzz Miller, and designs
by the artist Bernard Buffet. In 1960 Zizi Jeanmaire returned with
her own revue, which I presented as the opening production at
the new Royalty Theatre in Kingsway. This included the world
première of Roland Petit's version of *Rain* by Somerset Maugham,
in which Zizi's individual singing pulsated to the deafening blast
of Michel Legrand's Concert Orchestra.

The public came to know Petit as the *enfant terrible* of ballet.

He is the poet of modern dance, an innovator and a romantic.

After this close association with Roland, which lasted well over five years, he himself summed up his feelings in a letter he wrote me:

> You were a slave driver and a monster, but always so attractive and so wonderful. You have a wonderful wife, always a generous welcome, but suddenly when there is something you don't like, you become a stone, a sort of Dr Jekyll and Mr Hyde.
>
> We have had a wonderful association, and now London is the only place I could live, if I'm not living in Paris. It is the only place I could work because I have had a great start here with you, and each time I come back I will always have the feeling I am home and that time is the same. My friends will always be there.

The Ballets des Champs-Élysées were succeeded at the Cambridge (on September 6th, 1951) by the Pilar Lopez Ballet, which we had met in Madrid a few months before. With her sister, the late Argentinita, Pilar Lopez has been, one may fairly say, the main inspiration of the modern renaissance in Spanish dancing. It was Argentinita who first brought Spanish dancing into the theatre, and Pilar Lopez has shown with her Ballet Espagnol that she has inherited her sister's ability, and can continue her work. If she and her company could not, to some tastes at least, offer quite the excitement and the breathless poetry which we had come to expect from Antonio, it was, on the other hand, a full company, not merely two dancers stretching their prodigious talent to fill a whole evening.

Pilar Lopez and her husband, the musician Tomas Ríos, stayed with us for the duration of their London run. Apart from the pleasure of watching her dance, it was very agreeable to sup with them after their show, to come to know that remarkable woman, to talk with her of García Lorca, whom she had known intimately, while the candles gleamed and from my gramophone across the hall came the strains of some Spanish record which Tomas Ríos had brought with him. Great artists are rarely free from foibles, and those are not necessarily pleasant ones. But in Pilar's character one could detect none of the jealousies, sulks and overwhelming vanities which I had reluctantly come to accept as the inseparable companions of talent. Instead, she possesses the largeness of view, the compassion and humour of someone who has never allowed the circumstances of her life to divorce her from all contact with her native soil.

There followed an invasion of Spanish dancing, most of which I presented. One of the most outstanding companies consisted of the great gypsy dancer Carmen Amaya and her family. They were the vital embodiment of gypsy *flamenco*. For Cocteau Amaya was like 'hail beating down on window panes, the cry of a swallow, a black cigar smoked by a brooding woman, the thunder of applause'.

On October 8th the Grand Ballet du Marquis de Cuevas followed Pilar Lopez to the Cambridge. This company was a descendant of the Ballet de Monte Carlo, gallantly formed by the late Colonel de Basil from the debris left after the death of Diaghilev, to whose inspiration we owe the ballet as an accepted part of our cultural life. The company was fortunate enough to enjoy the protection and wise direction of the Marquis de Cuevas. The Marquis belonged to an ancient line of European nobility, but his background was entirely American. Having been born in Chile of a Spanish father and a Danish mother, he married Margaret Strong, grand-daughter of John D. Rockefeller, and became an American citizen.

He was a genius flawed by fatuity. Yet, as he undulated into a room, his elderly but spritely frame lightly encased in brilliant blue, his presence enhanced by six white yapping Pekineses, he seemed to be stepping straight out of the pages of Proust. He reminded me of Daudet's wonderful description of Robert de Montesquieu, the model for Proust's Baron de Charlus: 'He would burst into the shrill laughter of a hysterical woman, then suddenly, as though seized with remorse, he'd clap his hand over his mouth and rear back until his inexplicable glee was controlled—as though he was coming through laughing gas.'

When I presented his company in London I came to know him well, and later, whenever I was in Paris, I would call to see him. For me his technique of presentation was always the same. First he showered me with a torrent of indiscreet confidences; then, darting about like a goldfish in a bowl, he spoke with quivering passion of how he had been robbed, cheated and broken by the 'cut-throats' of the theatre. In the same breath he diluted the acid with the treacle of sentimental eulogy as he spoke of his intercourse with the eminent, for whom he enjoyed an insatiable passion. Next he involved me in a rapid questionnaire which he answered himself, and finally, utterly exhausted by his recitative of man's venality, he collapsed like an accordion among the ornate clutter of his drawing-room and said, 'Now tell me about so and so.'

Thanks to his generosity and vision, the Ballet du Marquis de Cuevas had become the foremost unsubsidized company in the world, with a well-trained *corps de ballet*, two admirable *danseuses* of American-Indian descent—Hightower and Tallchief—a young dancer of dazzling virtuosity—Serge Golovine—and undoubtedly the finest romantic *danseur* of the time—Skibine, a pupil of Massine. The Marquis was clearly able to pay high salaries and attract some of the world's most brilliant dancers. London audiences were later to see the great Markova dancing in his production of *Giselle*, when I brought his company back for a season at the Stoll Theatre in 1954.

Skibine's great powers were exhibited to perfection in an entrancing work of Balachine, all too rarely seen here, *Night-Shadow (La Somnambule)*. I know of few creations which more perfectly evoke the spirit of the 1830s than this remarkable ballet, with its decor by Delfau that seems to be made out of hopeless moonlight, and the almost consumptive gaiety of the round dance at the beginning.

At the end of the Cuevas season I was given the chance of bringing to the Cambridge from India the company of Mrinalini Sarabhai and her partner, the great dancer Panniker. Their formalized language of hand-gestures had a graphic beauty, as they depicted swimming fish, horned beasts and bees taking nectar from the lotus. The part of the Prince in their Fish-Princess ballet was taken by Panniker. I would go far to see again his performance in *Man*, the Indian equivalent of 'All the world's a stage'. It depicted the cycle of human life from womb to grave. I shall always be haunted by the poignancy of the moment when Panniker, representing the new-born child, gazes for the first time in a pool of water. There, to his delight, he sees himself. The brilliant smile which suddenly invaded his face may belong rather to the world of drama than of ballet.

Later I had the opportunity of presenting my friend Ram Gopal in London. Since these visits to London in the early 1950s there has been a great resurgence in Indian dance. Gopal had presented a blend of at least four major dance-styles: the *Kathakali* and the *Bharapanatyan* from southern India, the *Katsha* and the *Manipuri* from the north and east. He placed Indian dance within the framework of Western classical ballet and presented ensemble dancing, more easily appreciated than the filigree cut by the individual Indian dancer. India's independence has brought about the discovery of a number of excellent dancers who have presented a style more intrinsic and organic than the hybrid forms of Ram Gopal. Gopal's function, however, was invaluable in that he presented Indian dancing to the West at a time when most Indian arts were unknown outside India, and prepared the way for more specialized companies in future years.

Following in the wake of such dancers as Ram Gopal, Uday Shankar, Balasaraswati, Mrinalini Sarabhai and Shanta Rao, was the appearance of Kama Dev at the Round House in May, 1970. Dev sustained long, hypnotic passages of pure or descriptive dance with his range and technique; he projected a new language. Later the same year Indian dance reached the height of popularity in England with a successful visit to Sadler's Wells of the Kathakali, the dance troupe from Kerala. Based on stories from Hindu epics, the Kathakali dance dramas with their elaborate costumes and spectacular make-up invoked the ritual splendour of Oriental mysticism, reminiscent of both Nō and Kabuki. With their stylized action and ornate *mudras* (symbolic hand-gestures) these classical Indian dancers from southern India entranced their audience.

Among the many other folk-dance companies that I brought to London, one that made a memorable impression was the Yugoslav National State Dance Company. This title made it sound like a band of factory folk-singers, and I rechristened the enterprise *Slavonik Rhapsody* to give it the proper flavour. *Slavonik Rhapsody* provided an exciting and stirring experience. The music, a haunting web of intricate melodies and rhythms, was often breathtaking, and the performers, dressed in rich peasant costumes, had brilliant attack.

Lord Beaverbrook had been curiously interested in the visit of the Yugoslavs. He had questioned me, made a note on his pad, and promised to pay a visit to the Cambridge Theatre. His interest had resulted in a rave notice in the *Evening Standard* and something equally glowing in the *Sunday Express*. Then, with his customary expansive generosity, he invited me to take the whole company down to his country house, Cherkley, in Surrey. It was an exciting idea. But I soon realized that my grateful acceptance had committed me to an unpredictable adventure in which a focus had to be resolved between political, social and production pitfalls. With Iron Curtain companies one has to take all the precautions of an animal-trainer in a circus.

The invitation, with its obscure promise of delight, was received by the company with tremulous excitement, but by the Yugoslav authorities with wariness. 'The Ambassador will have to be consulted,' I was informed, but fortunately this was merely a formality. I received an acceptance from the Embassy and the expedition was put under way.

The Sunday of the visit dawned with the panic of bad weather. As we motored to Cherkley for luncheon ahead of the company, the sky was a mottled leaden grey. On our arrival I was instantly removed by Lord Beaverbrook for urgent consultation. He was anxious that nothing should be left to chance. Beaverbrook was not a conversationalist, nor did he suffer from loquacity or small talk. With the precision of a trench raid, he could shoot intimidating missiles at his guests. 'What do you think of so and so?' he would demand. Your reply had to be swift and sure, aimed back like a bullet. You replied 'awful' or 'marvellous', and in counter-attack you could be warmly applauded. Hesitation rendered you an immediate casualty.

After lunch that Sunday Dicky Buckle and I followed him into the drawing-room to make an 'appreciation' of the situation. The room was large, about forty feet long by twenty feet across, with French windows giving on to a gravelled path with stone steps leading down to a huge lawn, which was where the performance was designed to take place. The sofas and chairs had been pushed back to one end of the room, leaving an empty space for the dancers. This was to be their stage if it rained. Lord Beaverbrook seemed entirely satisfied. He settled himself down on one of the chairs in the centre of the room, like a genial sphinx of mottled Indian hue who has camped out in every storm, and invited fate to do its worst. The floor was covered with carpet. Even if the dancers could be manœuvred within this confined area, the carpet was out of the question except for a Chinese tumbling act.

Somewhat apprehensively I raised this delicate problem. 'Nothing must interfere with the show. No need to worry,' replied Lord Beaverbrook to my query. 'Raymond,' he bawled, and Raymond and Albert and several others filed into the room like an execution squad. They awaited the order to fire. 'Take up the carpet,' said Lord Beaverbrook, as naturally as if he were saying, 'Pull down the blinds,' and the majestic pile was ripped away. In its place a polished parquet surface, as slippery as a sheet of ice, confronted us.

'There you are,' said Lord Beaverbrook, peering at his reflection in the polished surface; 'that looks fine.' I glanced hopelessly at Dicky. This floor would need a ton of resin to make it safe. And when you are having a performance on a dry lawn, nobody thinks of resin. Dicky had a brainwave—talcum powder. Lord Beaverbrook was delighted. 'Raid the bedrooms and remove all talcum powder.'

Raymond shot out of the room like a commando in search of gelignite. A few minutes later, dozens of tins of scented talcum powder seemed to appear from nowhere. 'You take the Chanel,' said Raymond, thrusting a tin at me and handing a similar preparation of Morny to Dicky Buckle, while Albert and others proceeded to create a highly scented snowstorm which covered the parquet floor with a light feathery gauze.

Throughout this and all subsequent proceedings Lord Beaverbrook, with his stubborn and ageless charm, dominated the room in his new role of showman. Surveying the decaying panorama of his setting, his face was lit with huge grins of abandoned mischief. He seemed well satisfied with the sweet-scented disorder, by now luring some of his other guests into the room.

Robert Sherwood, the American dramatist, went into a dangerous palais glide and landed on his back. Lord Grantly sniffed with disgust, was overpowered by the fumes and retired in a volley of oaths. Covered with a handkerchief, his face reappeared round the door. 'My mother always told me that if you have a sticky ballroom the best way of producing an animated surface is to treat it with talcum powder and get everyone sliding round. This is what you've done and you've made a frightful bloomer, Peter.' 'Nothing succeeds,' as Wilde said, 'like excess.'

But it was too late for criticism. Something excessive was needed. Then I had my brainwave. 'I think a little sawdust—lightly blended'—and with his ability to digest any new experience and then tell you what it is all about, Lord Beaverbrook was ready to take charge. I think if I had suggested a bulldozer he would have agreed.

Raymond was dispatched to the sawmills for bags of sawdust. Fresh recruits stood by for their delivery. Within a short space two bags of sawdust were emptied on the floor, which trembled and shuddered to the martial stamping of a dozen boots. The slaughter gathered momentum, and after a few minutes the whole place looked like a ploughed field under fire. 'This', I said to Raymond, 'doesn't seem to work either, and the floor is ruined.' 'I couldn't agree with you more,' poor Raymond hissed back. 'It will take at least six months to put right.'

The arrival of the company put a halt to our activities. Lord Beaverbrook gave them a wonderful welcome, displaying his impulsive geniality and making them feel immediately at home. This time there was none of that furtive restlessness and gnawing irritability that the representatives of certain Iron Curtain countries seem to carry around with them. They entered the large hall with the wonderment of shy children entering a fairy palace haloed by legend. All my fears vanished in a flash. After a huge tea, the dancers explored the house and gardens with simple, beaming faces. The sky was dark and threatening and a thunderstorm seemed imminent. Instead of organizing swimming, Lord Beaverbrook decided to entertain them in the cinema which he used for his guests after dinner, always keeping a close secret the film he was going to show. They were both dancing pictures this time: the first a film of Spanish *flamenco* with Massine's lightning satire and Toumanova's Fabergé glamour; the second a fantasy with Gene Kelly crooning and dancing over the Paris rooftops. It was a careful selection which enchanted and flattered his guests.

I slipped out towards the end of the film to accompany Madame Skovran, the Yugoslav *maîtresse de ballet*, on a tour of inspection. Even she, usually burning with bright ideas, stopped dead when we entered the drawing-room, like someone caught in an ambush. 'This', she said, 'is absolutely impossible.' Suddenly she brightened. 'Maybe it would still be possible. We have got some resin—let us get to work with it.' Once again, exhilarated by despair, the activity started, as resin was pounded into the floor.

Madame Skovran moved over the battlefield with the pallor of a
martyr, knowing that the honour of her country was at stake.
And then a miracle happened—the sun burst through the clouds.
In a moment the homicidal gaiety of our indoor pranks was forgotten. An hour later, with the unsophisticated abandon of a
happy boy, Lord Beaverbrook proudly led his guests on to a
rose-scented English lawn to witness a Balkan dance-drama that
held all the suspense of a stage thriller.

An hour flew past with a dazzling vision of beauty, reflecting
all the history, sentiments and regrets of another world. The
green lawn on that summer's evening was transmuted into wild
mountain settings, where Macedonian outlaws triumphantly
waged battle against the Turks. The dancers were carried away
and the audience captivated. When the performance was over,
Lord Beaverbrook rose for his speech. It was very short. 'The
men—God damn them—the women—God bless them!' There
were shouts of triumph and delight. As the buses rolled away
down the drive and out of sight, Lord Beaverbrook turned to
me. 'Thank you', he said, 'for a perfect day.'

Earlier in 1952 at the Cambridge Theatre I had presented an
altogether different treatment of folk-dance in the person of
Katherine Dunham. This forty-year-old woman M.A. of Chicago
University, anthropologist, choreographer, poet, producer and
painter, had dished up the fastest, most colourful and stimulating
entertainment in the world. She had turned dances inspired by
Brazilian, African and American Negro folk-lore and ritual into a
highly theatrical art of her own, ranging from the urgent primitive barbarism of sacrificial rites to the delicate Brazilian wit of the
elegant *Choros* and Latin American quadrilles. I was electrified
when I first saw her dance at the Prince of Wales in 1949, and I
had paid the show at least a dozen visits. For long afterwards I
had been haunted by the throbbing animal frenzy of the dancers
in the *Shango*, the ritual dance that is performed in Trinidad on
the 'sacrifice of the white cock' to the furious accompaniment of
deafening drums; by Dunham's perfect ballet *L'Ag'ya*, which
unfolds the story of an eighteenth-century Martinique beauty who
fell under the influence of a love charm stolen from the King of
the Zombies, and the ensuing destruction of the spell by the
violence of a fight to the death between her two lovers, brilliantly

danced by Vanoye Aikens and Wilbert Bradley; by the impeccable satire of the honky-tonk rhythms of Harlem; and by the irresistible *Batucada*, in which a flirtatious woman becomes entwined in the coils of a fisherman's rope.

I had had to fight a long and bitter battle to bring her back to London under my banner, and in the flush of victory I rashly undertook to make myself responsible for her company for eight months. Dunham's seasons at the Cambridge began in a blaze of glory. I was confident she could easily play there to capacity for twelve weeks, and provincial theatres were clamouring for her.

However, some weeks after the brilliant send-off, Miss Dunham seemed to be growing perceptibly larger—which, to say the least, was some cause for alarm. On February 6th her stage-designer husband John Pratt entered my office, like a messenger in a Shakespearean play, with the astonishing words: 'Katherine Dunham is unable to dance. She has just been taken to a nursing-home to have a baby.' I realized that there was nothing to be done; we should have to close the show.

Two hours later came the news of the untimely death of King George VI. All theatres closed down that night, but reopened the following evening—with one exception: the Cambridge. I was in an appalling quandary. We could do nothing but maintain our period of mourning beyond the prescribed time. This lone, prolonged closure for a few days in excess of the other theatres was immediately heralded as a great patriotic gesture, but if the Cambridge Theatre had to remain in mourning longer than the Monday following, the true explanation would have to come out. As it was, baffled reporters demanded to know why we alone remained closed for four days; they even inquired if I had any special Court connections that could justify such a fine and noble gesture. On the contrary, beyond the imperious Miss Dunham I had no royal connection. Then nature came to the rescue. That evening, incredibly, Miss Dunham was dancing again; and the sad secret of her miscarriage was kept from the press.

In 1953 I presented a provincial tour of the American National Ballet Theater, which had given birth to an American tradition of dance and was notable for its choreography by Agnes de Mille and Jerome Robbins with such ballets as Aaron Copland's *Rodeo* and Leonard Bernstein's *Fancy Free*. These ballets were a revelation to the provincial public. Their idiom was familiar to film fans, but now they were interpreted by classically trained dancers. To many people it was a renaissance in ballet and the beginning of a new form of art.

The next year, 1954, I brought Martha Graham on her first visit to London. There is in Martha Graham something puritanical. She comes from a family of New England Presbyterians, and from her father, who was a neurologist, she acquired a deep instinct for the motivation of human behaviour which she applied to her researches into the psychological, mystical and sociological aspects of dance. She sought to introduce a new social significance into the medium, developing a new technique of movement with a rhythmic co-ordination of muscular control and breathing. She has had a great influence on American dance training, and her method, which is entirely her own, produced a wonderful team of self-controlled dancers of unmatched tautness and grace. In America she inspired a popular cult, and was undoubtedly an influence on Agnes de Mille, Anthony Tudor and Jerome Robbins. The abstract beauty of her techniques, with their repertoire of esoteric gesture and flat-footed movement broken by sudden side-kicks, made me feel at first as though I were watching the spasms of lunatics in some modern Bedlam. It seemed to represent an experience which, at its best, was too difficult to respond to. And, alas, she played to almost empty houses during that first season at the Saville Theatre. But on every return visit she has made the house has been sold out. 'For my dance,' she told me once, 'I seek to express life in a moment of evolution—a human being in crisis, at the cross-roads. The story is not important, but the cross-roads is.'

Martha Graham's great contribution to the dance is a revolutionary extension of the range of movement commonly allowed in ballet, yet she can also be telling in repose—standing or sitting on the stage, she can convey an eternity of tragedy by the position of a hand or the tilt of her head. There is no doubt that she has had a profound influence on the dance in America.

The two seasons of Jerome Robbins's Ballets: U.S.A. were to be my two final dance presentations in that decade from 1951 to 1961. The first, in 1959, hit London like a hurricane. This pre-eminent of all theatrical choreographers had already directed *West Side Story*, which was to re-orientate the American musical.

I had seen his extraordinary work at Spoleto, and decided to bring his company to London, where he presented some of his finest works, *Interplay*, *Fanfare*, *Pied Piper*, *Afternoon of a Faun* and *Age of Anxiety*.

I found Robbins uneasy to work with. He is small and sparse, and everything about him is neat and hard-compressed, austere and dignified. His great dark eyes burn from a face of ascetic disdain. Robbins, unlike Petit, is never in tumult. He has an infinitely discriminating intelligence, mathematical common sense: a man enriched with culture, a sense of humour and a marvellous smile.

In his youth he admired the writings of Thomas Wolfe, but now he found he was influenced by Dostoyevsky; by certain types of play like Gelber's *The Connection*; by directors like Tyrone Guthrie and Joan Littlewood; and by the film art of Antonioni. Orson Welles he sees as the greatest unrecognized influence in the American theatre. 'But now', he said, 'I am turning towards the East, towards the ritualistic culture of Japan.'

At rehearsals, to all except his dancers, he is unapproachable. Like a monk who has locked himself in and lost the key, he retreats into his cell of inaccessibility. On the day of an opening he can be found in the theatre at five o'clock in the morning, smouldering through a battery of lights and brightly painted backcloths. He talks without emotion, as though absorbed beyond feelings, and when he says nothing the theatre radiates an invisible, noiseless energy. His dancers and actors love and fear him. They will down tools, whatever they happen to be doing, and follow him whenever he cares to pipe a tune. 'I know I demand a lot—I am tough. I can only be bothered with people who want to extend themselves, who are reaching for more, but I drive only as far as their limitations allow.' There is nothing in life more difficult to achieve than simplicity. Robbins is a simple man, simple in speech and manner, a man of integrity and native genius. He never exaggerates. He is not a passing adornment, and his influence has been felt throughout the whole world of contemporary dance, from the musical to the classical ballet. He is outside all conventional assessment: too mutable to set down on paper; too restless to catch for a portrait; too mobile for anyone to guess what road he is going to take next.

For myself, I should like to think that the programmes of

ballet and folk-dance which I was able to present in London
during those years had at least some significance and influence on
the course which dance was to take in Britain in the future.
Richard Buckle in fact wrote this summary:

In Autumn 1946 I asked Elsa Brunelleschi to write a piece
for my ballet magazine about Spanish dancers in London.
The point of this was that there had been so few that they
could be covered in a space of a short article. Argentina and
Argentinita were golden memories, and there had been no
Spanish dancers on the London stage for years. Now, after a
breathless decade of Peter Daubeny's activities, we have not
only become quite knowledgeable *aficionados* of the Spanish
dance, quite picky and choosy, but we are on the way to
becoming well versed in the dance of a great many other
countries as well. Ballet from France is one thing, modern
dance from America is another; but when it comes to troupes
from India, Russia, Yugoslavia, Georgia, Africa and China,
we are really becoming very sophisticated indeed. There is
absolutely no question but that today London is the capital of
the dance world; and this is not just because of the Royal
Ballet, Ballet Rambert and Festival Ballet, but because we as
an audience have had our experience enlarged and our sensibilities deepened by seeing dancers in so many styles and from
so many lands. That we should have had this life-enhancing
experience has been largely due to one man, Peter Daubeny.
How surprised he and I should have been that warm hazy
day on 4 September, 1943, as we landed on the beach at
Salerno, to know of all the exotic companies that he would
bring to London — and which I should write about in the
Sunday papers!

Meanwhile my involvement in dance had pointed me in a new
direction. I had found on the Continent, in Asia and in America a
remarkable wealth of talent for which there was not only a keen
and eager public, but an actual need. There was so much to be
learned from foreign companies, so much that could be done to
help break down the isolationism which had for too long dominated the British theatre.

Theodore Komisarjevsky wrote in his book *Myself and the
Theatre* that Diaghilev had achieved brilliant results with his

Ballets Russes, 'because he sought and found inspiration not from a narrow "national" outlook, but from the four corners of the world.' I wondered if this principle could be applied to the theatre. I felt I should like to have a shot.

PART TWO

26 (*above*). Cléo de Mérode (1890)

27 (*right*). Roger Planchon, director of the Théâtre de la Cité, Villeurbanne, Lyons (1969)

28 (*below*). Edwige Feuillère and Jean-Louis Barrault in Claudel's *Partage de Midi* (1968)

29 (*top left*). Madeleine Rena in Billetdoux's *Il Faut Pas* *Par Les Nuages*—Théâtre France (1968)

30 (*above*). La Comédie-Fr. çaise: Jacques Charon a Robert Hirsch in Moliè *Amphitryon*, directed by J Meyer (Paris, 1957)

31. Sacha Guitry in his stud 18 Avenue Élisée Reclus (19

32. Maurice Chevalier (1962)

33. Vittorio Gassman in
Visconti's production
of Alfieri's *Oreste* (1948)

The author with Peppino de
ppo and Federico Fellini at a
earsal of *Metamorphoses of a*
dering Minstrel (1964)

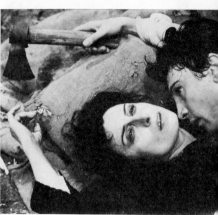

36 (*above*). Anna Magnani and Osvaldo Ruggieri in Verga's *La Lupa* (1969)

35 (*left*). The Compagnia Dei Giovani: Valli, Albani, De Lullo and Falk (Palermo, 1963)

37. The chorus of blind musicians from Giuseppe Patroni Griffi's production of *Naples by Night, Naples by Day*—Rome Stabile Theatre (1968)

7

Discovering the Russian and Israeli Theatre

The lonely airstrip crouched in the long grass and dandelions, bordered by a few Nissen huts. It was Stansted Airport, as it was then, before the British Airports Authority had developed it as a fairly presentable overspill for Gatwick and Heathrow, and before any nation-wide row had broken over the possibility of their making it the third London airport. I had driven there with my wife on a bright Sunday morning in the spring of 1958, along leafy highways that cut through the ancient forest of Epping. The isolated airstrip, remaining practically as it had been when abandoned by the U.S. Air Force, seemed an unlikely setting for an event which represented the culmination of several years of frustrating struggle on my part and one of the most significant events in the post-war British theatre: the arrival on English soil of the Moscow Art Theatre, the first Russian theatre company ever to visit these islands.

On the way we had passed the column of pilgrims organized by Paul Scofield and Diana Wynyard to greet the honoured visitors, and who included John Neville with a party of twenty-one from the Old Vic. But Mr Malik, the Soviet Ambassador, was there ahead of us. When I met him he was surveying the scene with sharp hostility. 'What is this place?' he demanded. 'It is an insult.'

Gazing at the long grass, dandelions and Nissen huts pressed about so closely by rural Essex, I could only agree. The TU 104 in which the company was flying from Moscow had been forbidden to land in all its glory at Heathrow because, the officials said, it would be too noisy. Quite what political motivation there may have been behind this we shall never know, but *The Times Educational Supplement* in a leader called it 'a puny and ridiculous pretext' put up by the Government. Hence, in any case, our gathering at Stansted on that spring morning.

The welcoming party gradually formed themselves into desolate groups awaiting the plane, which was due at midday. But at half past one Paul Scofield rushed into the Nissen hut to say that the jet had not yet even left Copenhagen. As John Neville and his party sadly returned for a dress rehearsal in London, Diana Wynyard told me that she had forgotten every word of her speech in Russian, which she had spent all night rehearsing. The delay was ruining her nerves.

We found some tables and chairs and I moved an increasingly irate Mr Malik on to the grass, fortified by Christopher Mayhew, the M.P. who was Chairman of the Soviet Relations Committee of the British Council, and a bottle of whisky to face this fraught atmosphere for another three dragging hours. Suddenly, at five o'clock, there was a roar overhead and the silver-grey TU 104 streaked through the evening sunshine. The misery was over and pandemonium had arrived.

As the plane landed, a crowd of four hundred actors, officials, reporters and sightseers crashed through the police cordon, throwing paper streamers and shouting 'Dobro pozhalovat'. I rushed to our car, while a crocodile of vehicles, including two yellow trucks, three fire engines and a mysterious open boat trailed by Theatre Workshop, streamed across the tarmac. Even as the whole procession came to a full stop at one end of the runway, the jet stopped at the other. Helpfully, and hopefully, the plane moved towards us. But fiasco remained the order of the day. The airport officials failed to produce a flight of steps high enough to reach the airliner's doors. The company of sixty peered at us unsmilingly in astonishment. Finally my wife and I managed to board the plane, and we entered a vast cabin of Victorian-style brass, blue grey leather and neat little curtains. We were greeted affectionately by Solodovnikov, the administrator of the Moscow Art Theatre, who handed me a letter of greeting from Madame Olga Knipper-Chekhova, Chekhov's ninety-year-old widow.

In it she wrote:

Dear Mr Daubeny,

I want to take this opportunity of saying how very glad I am that the Moscow Art Theatre—beloved of my late husband—is at last making an official visit to England, and that it has been chosen to make the sixtieth anniversary of the company a Chekhov season. I must tell all my friends in England that I am a little sad that I cannot come to London with my company, but I feel that I am really too old to travel any more. It has always been a great source of happiness to me that my husband's plays have been so very popular in England, and I am very moved that this honour—and with his own company—should have been made to his memory.

The company eventually disembarked to be showered with kisses, wilting flowers, paper streamers and fragments of speeches. The long afternoon wait was soon forgotten. Someone pushed me forward to make a speech, but the occasion was too much for me. 'Thank you so very much for coming,' I gulped with choking emotion.

Swiftly encircled by Embassy officials, the members of the company boarded two buses and were swirled off to the Prince of Wales Hotel in Kensington. The Moscow Art Theatre had arrived in England on the sixtieth anniversary of its founding.

Paul Scofield was later to write his own account of the fraught scene of their arrival, recalling this event as the most historic in our last hundred years of theatre:

It was a very bright May day in 1958, and we had all come out to the little grassy airport of Stansted in Essex, a large, mainly young, group of actors and actresses from many London theatres and companies, in order to see the members of the Moscow Art Theatre set foot on English soil for the first time. It was the year of their own sixtieth anniversary as a company. Diana Wynyard and I were there to speak the first words of welcome to them. And, as we waited, we remembered a similar occasion, two years earlier, when we were part of the first English Shakespeare company to arrive and play in Moscow.

Our plane had descended through a light flurry of November snow, out of the evening half-darkness on to a landing-strip that was blazing with light. The light was concentrated entirely on to our plane, and as we blinked through the windows we were aware of a silent mass of people just beyond its radius. We emerged on to the gang-plank, and silently the mass swept forward, carrying flowers and pressing closely and softly around us with such open and clearly felt expressions of emotion that all formal greetings were swept aside. Talk burst out of the silence, there seemed no need for personal introductions, we were theatre people among theatre people, and with tears and flowers and a lot of laughing we were all carried off to our hotel.

And now we stood on the grass at Stansted Airport, not an official reception committee, but a group of actors very conscious of all that the Moscow Art Theatre traditions had done to influence our own attitudes in the theatre and somehow envisaging the approaching plane as containing some magic that we all wanted to share.

The plane landed and down they came, familiar faces to me and Diana and others who were in Moscow in 1955, Stepanova, Tarasova, Vassilye Orlov, Belokurov, Galya the wardrobe mistress, round and beaming, Popov the carpenter ...

The rest is theatre history, their season of plays at Sadler's Wells Theatre presented by Peter Daubeny contained performances of Chekhov of a depth and density and liveliness that cannot be forgotten. As for the airport meetings, slender details though they are, I'd like to think they can happen again.

As we drove back to London, I was able to look back over the previous four years: the months of waiting, calamities and problems which had at times reduced me to utter despair at the prospect of the task I had undertaken.

Any period of negotiation with a company is like a seasonal flirtation, and my affair with the Moscow Art had all started a long time ago. My ambition had always been to bring to London this particular company, the most famous in the world and a foundation-stone of modern European theatre. But it had seemed a hopeless quest.

Firstly, the Russians were not used to private impresarios. They believed that the theatre was not the concern of a private individual, but the responsibility of the Government. No Russian company had ever visited London. The Russian Embassy regarded the whole idea as a caprice, and battened down their hatches. It was to them an eccentric excursion, and they were not disposed to engage in letters or meetings. Yet while they passed me round like a tailor's dummy, I hung over them like a relentless and gloomy cloud.

When everything else had failed I turned for help to my great friend from Eighth Army days, Christopher Soames, then Winston Churchill's personal private secretary, who plunged into the drama with a demonic urgency. Revealing the instinctive sense of showmanship which had nearly lured him into the theatre during our long discussions on the eve of the Italian campaign, he rang a senior official in the Russian Embassy and achieved in two minutes what I had been attempting for two years. He arranged for the First Secretary at the Embassy to call on my wife and myself.

As we waited one morning for his arrival, like conspirators in a James Bond novel, for the first time I had a real feeling that something exciting might happen. The black car duly drew up outside our house, and then a sallow-faced man with a Victorian air of gravity was standing in hat and coat in our drawing-room. He removed his hat, but clung to his overcoat. Feverishly, like a despairing lover, I tried to nurse at least a glint of hope out of the wary doubts which he expressed in a languid monotone. He stayed only a few minutes, accepted a vodka, replaced his hat, and departed as mysteriously as he had come. Then, unexpectedly, there was a stir of activity. The Embassy had become more yielding. I received an invitation to call. With great friendliness they advised me to ally myself temporarily with the Society for Cultural Relations, just then planning to bring the first-ever Russian company to London—the Moscow State Dance Company, the Beryozka. Accordingly, in a crumbling office in North London early in 1954, I met Pat Sloane, who conducted his business with an almost militant fervour, emphasized, it seemed, by his uncanny resemblance to Stalin, whose portrait towered above his desk.

Our association was not a happy one, but from it I managed to get four wonderful companies to London. This was my first experience of the complicated dealings with Russian cultural authorities in years to come. The Beryozka ('Little Birch Tree') company was a folklore group of forty young ladies whom Cochran would have been delighted to have taken on as his own. With some trepidation I flew to Amsterdam for their first performance outside the Iron Curtain. Their extraordinary display of dancing and singing was full of an infinite sadness and haunting passion. The sensuous strains of the balalaika and accordion soared like birds on the wing to express that spirit of underlying poignancy and sudden joy so characteristic of the dancing of every Russian company. Through all the music of Russian and Slovak folklore runs a plaintiveness and lyricism that breaks down all reserves.

But the general effect was of a concert in a village hall. As each number came to a full stop, a queen conductress issued information at great length on the next.

I was alarmed at the thought of bringing the production in this state to London, but realized that I had to have the support of the Anglo-Soviet Society. I therefore arranged a very straight talk with their representatives over a very expensive lunch. If it was to succeed with the London public, I said, it had to be presented with the pace, fluency and lighting of a revue. They acquiesced. Then I had to confront Nadezhda Nadezhdina, who had created the company and who was a figure of enormous regal dignity and spiritual serenity, formerly a famous ballerina and now married to a senior cultural official. Expansive and full of kindly humour, she reminded me of Queen Salote of Tonga. Her name could be translated, fittingly, as 'hope and hope again'.

Returning to London, I worked on the production with Robert Nesbitt, who had generously agreed to lend it his unique flair. This was exciting for me because I had admired his genius in the world of revue and musical comedy ever since seeing his first stage show, *Ballyhoo Revue*, during my schooldays. I had gone up to London to the dentist, taken the afternoon off to go to this daring revue, and on my return to prep school this had so shocked my French teacher that she refused to speak to me for a year.

Nadezhda Nadezhdina was thrilled with the result of Robert Nesbitt's work. We became friends, and Mr Orvid, her husband, who was a senior official at the Ministry of Culture, became an ally in my mission to bring the Moscow Art Theatre to England.

The press and public were enthusiastic over the Beryozka. The Stoll Theatre was sold out and people were surprised to find that the girls were not only Russian, but human. They wore lipstick and nail-varnish, ate bacon and eggs for breakfast, and returned to Moscow with nearly half a ton of presents. The Stoll audiences loved them for their charm and feminity, and above all for their dancing. Gliding effortlessly across the stage in their long flame-coloured shirts as if on castors, they created an astonishing range of beautiful, vibrant and deceptively simple patterns.

This was the first of many memorable visits from Russian dance companies which were to allow British audiences to see some of the greatest dancing of our time.

The fervent Mr Sloane now approached me with another venture—the Obraztsov puppets, to be presented at the London Casino in July 1954. Sergei Obraztsov's Moscow State Puppet Theatre is the only puppet company in the world that can compete with the Japanese Bunraku. It is a puppet theatre so unbelievably skilful that one wonders whether these are really puppets at all.

Obraztsov is an immensely likable man, full of charm and exuberance. His importance as an artist gives him total freedom of expression in the creation of an extraordinary work of art. He had given up painting to become an actor, and as a member of the 'Lysistrata' troupe, he had appeared on Broadway in the early 1920s. 'I had always dreamt of puppets since I was very young, and I wanted them to create their own parts in their own plays as we do in life. Some of the plays were created by the best playwrights. Moscow had no puppet theatre and I formed mine in 1931.' His puppet theatre now has a repertoire of forty different plays, and he employs a staff of two hundred and fifteen.

No one who saw them could ever forget Mlle du Beast with her performing poodles, or the magician who plucks handkerchiefs from the air and chickens from top-hats with a carefree abandon. Obraztsov's puppets dive, skate, play football, sail and even circle a horizontal bar. Yet it is a display not only of skill of manipulation and presentation, but of sensibility and, above all, vitality. As John Gunther has written in *Inside Russia Today*, 'Obraztsov's theater has more life in it than most live theaters.'

Only one small problem arose in the presentation of this company—the two-foot-high puppets, unlike those I had seen in Sicily, unlike the Japanese Bunraku, were operated from below by long sticks. So as not to spoil the effect, no seats except the stalls could be used. The circle had to remain closed throughout the whole triumphant run.

Suddenly, in the mid 1950s, a wealth of Russian culture exploded upon London. Apart from many individual distinguished musicians, there followed the Cossack Dancers, the Moisseyev and the Red Army Choir. The cracks in the Iron Curtain had widened, and Russia was beginning to reveal herself.

In 1955 the British Council rang me one day with the news

that the Russian fleet had arrived in Portsmouth. This was a historic occasion, and as a token of friendship the Russian Navy had asked if they could entertain London. Would I be able to arrange a theatre and present them the following Sunday? It was then already Friday, but impulsively I agreed. With the help of Claude Langdon I obtained the Empress Hall. The B.B.C. announced the event on the nine o'clock news, and by the following morning the box office was under bombardment from a frenzied crowd. I waited anxiously to greet the advance party.

We had only twenty-four hours in which to organize, edit, cut, amplify and adapt their entire performance. I asked Peter Ustinov to compère the show, which he practically took over. Lord Fraser of the Fleet was to give the big diplomatic hello. The Empress Hall meanwhile was sold out.

In taking on the Russians I had hardly contemplated being responsible for the welfare of their entire fleet. But when the bus-loads of sailors arrived the following day, they demanded ten pounds a head before singing a note or moving a muscle. I was left with a debt of nearly a thousand pounds which took me six months to recover, and then only after two Labour M.P.s had put down a motion of protest in the House of Commons.

Events such as this will clearly confirm that I had served a melancholy apprenticeship in the field of Russian culture. But, as the Russians had promised, I was shortly to be rewarded. In August 1957 Mr Orvid invited me to Moscow to discuss a contract for a forthcoming visit of the Moscow Art Theatre under my personal management.

'I should like to have lived and died in Paris,' wrote the poet Mayakovsky, 'if there were not a universe called Moscow.' My own first visit was not so encouraging. We stayed at a small hotel, the Europa, close to Red Square. Before the Revolution it had been a first-class hotel, but now its atmosphere was corroded and musty. The interior decoration and furniture had remained untouched since the events of 1917 swept away its clientele. The telephone refused to function, a silent wireless stared at us in challenging silence and the bath-plug was missing. The dingy corridors, along which Isadora Duncan had once floated, now swarmed with Chinese athletes, strictly surveyed by grim ladies who sat like custodians in a museum, keeping a strict check on

keys and the moral discipline on each floor. In the strictly utili-
tarian foyer below, crowds of visitors, victims of the shortage of
hotel accommodation, struggled to obtain the few rooms available.

The following morning I took a taxi to the Ministry of Culture.
We drove along streets which, though crowded, were strangely
silent; no horns sounded in Moscow and aeroplanes were forbidden to fly overhead. On street corners men gathered to read
Pravda or to drink vodka from paper cups. Our interpreter was a
young male student, friendly, sensitive and extremely tactful. I
asked him if we could drive round Red Square. This vast open
space, where pageantry and death are so closely intermingled, is
bordered on one side by the Italian-built walls of the Kremlin,
which brood all over Moscow. On the north side, however, the
arena's devouring menace is relieved by the magical architectural
fantasy of St Basil's, whose architects Ivan IV ('The Terrible')
rewarded with the removal of their eyeballs, lest any other autocrat might conceive a desire for a similar toy.

Many other palatial relics of the Imperial dynasties remain elsewhere in Moscow. The Bolshoi Theatre (literally, 'the grand
theatre') glows with classical grace both inside and out. Here
beauty and discipline create that spellbinding effect which has
produced the best dancers in the world, the prize possession of a
country where dancers are adored and idolized like football
teams or pop stars, not only in Moscow but in every one of the
forty-five cities that possess their own ballet troupe.

At the Ministry of Culture I began to discover for the first time
the difficulties of working with the Russians, for whom, it has
been said, the word 'now' means 'tomorrow', and 'tomorrow'
'never'. However, despite difficulties and after four days of daily
meetings, Mr Solodovnikov, the administrator of the Moscow
Art Theatre, signed the contract—it was as unforgettable a
moment as that endless day at Stansted.

'There you are,' he said, as we sat at a small desk in a bare
office of the Ministry of Culture, 'it's yours.' For the first time I
saw his eyes twinkle behind the thick lenses of his glasses. The
last formidable obstacle in a five-year assault had been overcome.
As Solodovnikov produced a bottle of vodka, we toasted the
Moscow Art Theatre and drank to mutual success. Then I rushed
out of the building to join my wife at the hotel and tell her the
joyous news.

That day we lunched with the British Ambassador at the Embassy. This was housed in the former palace of the sugar millionaire Haritonenko. Before 1917 the house had been the scene of some of Moscow's greatest social evenings: dinners which were followed by entertainments, dancing or rides through the deserted streets in fast troikas. All the furnishings in the house remain as they were then, Gorky having urged Lenin to preserve Russia's treasures and buildings. 'Every stone you take', he wrote, 'is part of our heritage.' The Bolsheviks had sold the palace to the British Government in 1930.

All the Haritonenko family had disappeared during the revolutionary years, except for a daughter. From the bed-sitting-room in Rome where she lived, she had demanded payment for the sale of her family property from the British Foreign Office.

It was not only the old social order which suffered in the aftermath of revolution. At first, in the general ferment of ideas, the arts had seemed to be flourishing, springing anarchically like plants in a desert after a rare fall of rain. A new *avant-garde* arose in every field of art technique. Painting evolved constructivism, and in literature poets like Mayakovsky sublimated revolutionary ideals, and indulged in a long-suppressed but acute sense of social satire and iconoclasm. From the films of Eisenstein and Pudovkin a whole new concept of cinema emerged, confidently using startling techniques which have never been surpassed, even in that highly sophisticated medium. The situation was the same in the theatre. Stanislavsky was still at the height of his inspiration, and directors like Vsevolod Meyerhold, who had started his career as an actor with the Moscow Art Theatre and who founded the Theatre of the Revolution, took his work even further forward in productions and techniques which left the rest of the world far behind. But few of the participants in that unique but brief and ill-fated cultural renaissance were to survive the dark years of the 1930s, and the rule of the secret police was in time to crush almost every manifestation of individual achievement. The theatre was attacked as savagely as any of the arts, though the Moscow Art Theatre survived—some feel at the expense of becoming, as it were, a sort of museum relic during this period. Meyerhold's theatre, however, was dissolved in 1938, even though he was usually considered a good Communist. In June 1939, when he was invited to attend a conference of theatrical directors in Moscow, he chose to address them in these terms:

> Without art, there is no theatre! Go visiting the theatres of Moscow. Look at their drab and boring presentations that resemble one another and are in each case worse than the others ... Everything is gloomily well regulated, averagely mathematical, stupefying and murderous in its lack of talent. Is that your aim? If it is—oh! you have done something monstrous! ... In hunting down formalism you have eliminated art.

This courageous gesture had its inevitable outcome. Two nights later he was taken from his flat to disappear into the maw of the labour camps, where it is believed he perished in about 1942.

Taking a wider view of the history of the Russian theatre, however, we find that it was not in fact until the second half of the seventeenth century that the first official theatre became established during the reign of the Tsar Alexis Michaelovich.

One day, shortly after the death of his first wife, Alexis had called unexpectedly on a personal friend, Artainov Matveyev, and had met his adopted daughter, Natalya Naryshkina. Matveyev was not only highly cultured, possessing a magnificent library and being a writer on his own account, but also maintained a small theatre in his house together with a troupe of actors to act in it. He had seen Natalya one day when driving through the village of Kirikov: a beautiful child crying by the road. Discovering that she was an orphan, he and his Scottish wife agreed to adopt her. When later the Tsar Alexis met her, he became entranced by her and shortly afterwards she became the Tsarina. It was for her pleasure that he had started the first theatre in Russia: a theatre which was to be further encouraged by their son, Peter the Great.

During his reign, Peter the Great opened in Red Square the first public theatre in Russia, to house a company of German actors he had hired from Danzig. It was he who Europeanized Russia. Breaking with a tradition-bound past, as Stanislavsky put it, he 'flung wide the gates of Russia to the advance of Western Europe'. Noblemen now began to travel; they hired French tutors for their sons and later sent them to European universities. The result was an influx of new culture into Russia, Germany proving influential and several *commedia dell'arte* troupes visiting the country. But it was French culture which dominated Moscow throughout the eighteenth century. French became the language of the aristocracy, French actors the masters on stage—a vogue that was to continue until the end of the nineteenth century. Indeed, Lucien Guitry achieved some of his greatest successes in Russia, and his son Sacha was born in St Petersburg.

The founding of the Imperial Theatre in Moscow in 1756, and of others elsewhere in Russia, gave impetus to the slow growth of an indigenous theatre. Russian plays remained only false imitations of the works of Shakespeare, Molière, Racine or Corneille brought by the foreign companies, but already a growing number of talented Russian actors and actresses was emerging both in tragedy and comedy. It was not until the middle of the nineteenth century, however, that the skills of actors were matched by those of playwrights when there appeared a writer of great talent and originality, Alexander Ostrovsky, whose works were to achieve international acclaim and whose most famous play, *The Storm*, was first produced in 1859.

Thirty-eight years after that first performance, Stanislavsky's Moscow Art Theatre created a revolution of a kind as shattering in its own sphere as that later one of 1917 was to be for world politics. The company had been founded after an all-night conversation between Stanislavsky and Nemirovich-Danchenko on June 21st, 1897, and its impact was momentous and world-wide. With its fifth production, Chekhov's *The Seagull* in 1898, the seal had been set on its success.

In Stanislavsky's own words from his classic work, *My Life in Art*,

> The founding of our new Moscow Art and Popular Theatre was in the nature of a revolution. We protested against the customary manner of acting, against theatricality, against bathos, against declamation, against overacting, against the bad manner of production, against the habitual scenery, against the star system which spoiled the ensemble, against the light and farcical repertoire which was being cultivated on the Russian stage at the time.

Acting as it had been known until then, with its exaggerated and repetitive mannerisms and its idealization of life, became totally changed. Suddenly its aim was an imitation of life itself, with all its imperfections, vulgarities and pauses. When I talked to Zavadsky, the director of the Mossoviet Theatre, who had himself worked closely with Stanislavsky from 1915, he told me how Stanislavsky had tried 'to penetrate the soul of the Russian man, to understand his conflict with reality, make him appear as himself. Every role, however small, was important.' 'There are no small parts,' Stanislavsky and Danchenko agreed, 'there are only small actors.'

Stanislavsky would research each detail of costume and setting and rehearse his company at length, placing a painstaking concentration on each individual detail of characterization, every movement, every gesture. 'Do not imagine', he wrote to a young student, 'that theatrical laurels are to be won without real work.' His rehearsals were long and arduous. Before their first production, *Tsar Feodor Ivanovich*, the company had met on 74 occasions, rehearsing for a total of 244 hours.

The Seagull was the Moscow Art Theatre's first production of Chekhov and made Chekhov's name as a dramatist. After the disastrous reception the play had received when first performed—exactly two years earlier to the day—on October 17th, 1896, in Leningrad at the Alexandrinsky Imperial Theatre, Nemirovich-Danchenko had persuaded Chekhov to allow the Moscow Art Theatre to stage it anew.

Chekhov's plays were ideally suited to the style of the Moscow Art Theatre, whose growth he had watched with interest and loving care. His wife, Olga Knipper, a member of the company, would write to him from Moscow to Yalta, where he lived in self-imposed exile, to tell him of the news of 'the new theatrical venture so close to your heart'. He in turn wrote of the countryside, the flowers and trees of his garden, the building of his cottage. 'If I were to give up literature and become a gardener just now it would be a very good thing, for it would add ten years to my life.'

In a centennial edition of Chekhov memoirs published in 1960 by the Moscow Foreign Languages Publishing House Maxim Gorky, Chekhov's friend and admirer, writes in an essay of this strong feeling for nature in Chekhov's work.

Reading the works of Chekhov makes one feel as if it were a sad day in late autumn, when the air is transparent, the bare trees stand out in bold relief against the sky, the houses are huddled together, and people are dim and dreamy. Everything is so strange, so lonely, motionless, powerless. The remote distances are blue and void, merging with the pale sky, breaking a dreary cold on the half-frozen mud. But the mind of the author, like the autumn sunshine, lights up the rutty roads, the crooked streets, the dirty, cramped houses ...

Gorky also spoke of the man himself.

A subtle mockery almost always twinkled in his grey mournful eyes, but occasionally these eyes would become cold, keen, harsh, and at such moments a hard note would creep into the smooth, cordial tones of his voice, and then I felt that this modest, kindly man could stand up against any hostile force, stand up firmly, without knuckling under to it.

Chekhov had revealed to Gorky his own feelings about the Russian character when he said:

The Russian is a strange being. He is like a sieve, he can hold nothing for long. In his youth he crams himself eagerly with everything that comes his way, and by the time he is thirty nothing is left of it all but a heap of colourless rubbish. If one wants to lead a good life, a human life, one must work. Work with love and with faith. And we don't know how to do that in our country. After building two or three decent houses, an architect sits down to play cards for the rest of his life, or hangs about the backstage of a theatre. As soon as a doctor acquires a practice he stops keeping up with science, ... and by the age of forty is firmly convinced that all diseases are caused by colds ... An actor who has performed two or three parts with fair success, no longer learns his parts, but puts on a top hat and considers himself a genius ... What an absurd clumsy country our Russia is!

The Stanislavsky theatrical revolution could not long be contained within one theatre or one city. The warnings of Chekhov's sister quickly proved ill-founded. 'You must be crazy,' she had cried when she first saw the filthy Hermitage Theatre. 'Who do you imagine will come to this dirty theatre to see unknown people?' During those early days following the October Revolution, the theatre was sent on a lengthy European tour. 'If there is a theatre from the past which must be saved and preserved at whatever cost', wrote Lenin, 'it is, of course, the Moscow Art Theatre.'

It was in 1922 that Michel Saint-Denis met Stanislavsky in Paris, when the audiences were packing the huge Théâtre des Champs-Élysées each evening to see the Moscow Art Theatre. 'Stanislavsky was then at his best,' he says. 'All the famous names were still in the company, and the Russian Revolution was only five years old.' Yet though we in England had experienced the influence of Stanislavsky through other companies and other eyes, there had never been any opportunity to see the real thing—the Moscow Art Theatre itself. The company's tours had never extended across the Channel. Now finally, exactly sixty years after the company's founding, the chance had arisen.

Returning to London as I thought in triumph, I found, however, that my difficulties had only just begun. Having signed a contract which would involve me in bankruptcy if the season failed, it seemed impossible to find a theatre. Our get-out (that is to say, the money required to be taken at the box office if weekly expenditure is to be covered) was over £6,000 a week.

The then Chancellor of the Exchequer, Peter Thorneycroft, advised me not to undertake the presentation without official backing. 'Only the two countries will benefit—no one cares a fig for you,' he told me. It was then that the British Council kindly used their influence to make Sadler's Wells Theatre available by moving out an already scheduled production. For services rendered, they insisted that they should appear beside my name as co-presenters of the season, refusing, however, to share any of the financial risk. Many of my friends regarded the venture as pure folly. Over dinner one night Peter Cadbury, the head of Keith Prowse, told me he felt dubious about selling more than ten pounds' worth of stalls.

Yet when the box office opened, six weeks before the company's arrival, a miracle seemed to take place. The theatre was besieged and crowds patiently queued all day. Then disaster struck again. The London bus drivers went on strike and rendered Sadler's Wells almost inaccessible.

But still the audiences came. Despite all gloomy prognostications, bus strikes, official apathy and a legion of financial worries, the

Sadler's Wells season was a sell-out. After the triumphant first night, Mme Tarasova, the leading lady, sent Mme Knipper-Chekhova a telegram telling her how well the British public had received *The Cherry Orchard*. All the British theatre stars assembled for a party on stage added their signatures to her message: IT WENT LIKE A DREAM I THINK YOU AND YOUR HUSBAND WOULD HAVE BEEN PROUD OUR LOVING WISHES.

Certainly the performance that evening *was* dreamlike. For me and several thousand others a new dimension was brought into the theatre. The Moscow Art Theatre had shown us in *The Cherry Orchard* a young, vigorous Chekhov rather than the spiritless, defeated author of the traditional English approach. Here was a supreme art of acting based on a microscopically detailed knowledge of human experience.

The weeks the company spent in Britain were crowded with extraordinary incidents. Each morning at half past ten a meeting of the company's *collectif* was called at the hotel. I was present at all the daily meetings of this small parliament which controlled the affairs of the company. Performances, food, entertainment, complaints, requests and everything on their consciences were deeply probed and analysed with the gravity of a Cabinet meeting. I watched their verbal conjuring with fascination.

Though its members were full of humour and kindness, the company as a whole seemed like spoilt children whose rich parents had made them invulnerable to the authority of new masters. Our attitude towards each other, though mutually indulgent, could also be equally unyielding.

On the eve of their departure for London, the British Ambassador in Moscow had given them a farewell party. Only a handful had turned up. Later, when I asked two of the leading actors to my house for lunch, they sent two understudies. Furious, I refused to attend the *collectif* on the following morning. The First Secretary and Press Attaché hurried round to explain that my invitation had been accepted in the spirit of the company. It did not matter whether the individuals themselves could come as long as their representatives attended. I demanded a written apology. To my surprise it was delivered the same afternoon.

Though, as artists, they worked with that selflessness and harmony that comes when man regards the theatre as the very

38. The author with Turi Ferro (Catania, 1969)

The Daily Mirror

THE MORNING JOURNAL WITH THE SECOND LARGEST NET SALE

No. 1979.   Registered at the G. P. O. as a Newspaper.   TUESDAY, MARCH 1, 1910   One Halfpenny.

CHILDREN OF THE SICILIAN ACTORS NOW PLAYING IN LONDON IMITATE THEIR PARENTS ON THE STAGE.

39 (*insert*). Umberto Spadaro, Turi Ferro and his son, Guglielmo, in Pirandello's *Liolà* (London, Catania Stabile Theatre, 1970)

40. Umberto Spadaro as a child with the Grasso Troupe (London, 1910)

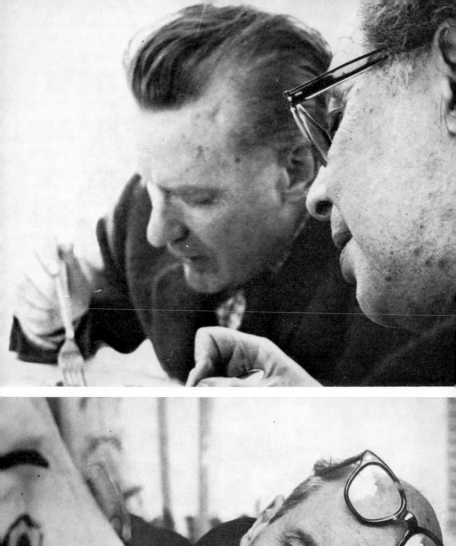

op left). The author with Karolos
n (Athens, 1965)

ottom left). Yannis Tsarouchis at
on one of his masks for *The Birds*
eek Art Theatre (1964)

bove). Erwin Piscator, director of
Volksbühne, Berlin

right). Helene Weigel and Bertolt
t in Marx Engels Square, Berlin
)

elow). A design by Karl von Appen
3recht's *Mother Courage*—given to
uthor by Helene Weigel during the
ner Ensemble's season in London
)

46 (*left*). The author with Martin Held (*far left*) and other members of the Schiller-Theater in front of the Kaiser Wilhelm Memorial Church, West Berlin (1963)

47 (*above*). Samuel Beckett working with Martin Held on his play, *Krapp's Last Tape*, at the Schiller-Theater (1969)

48 (*bottom left*). Erwin Axer, director of the Polish Contemporary Theatre, Warsaw (1964)

49 (*below*). Adam Hanuszkiewicz, director of the Polish Popular Theatre, and the novelist, Roman Bratny, with the author on a visit to the Warsaw Ghetto (1965)

breath of life itself, as individuals they were as consistently unpredictable as their interpreters were unreliable.

But a sense of humour ironed out many difficulties. One day a member of the company took an English electrician to a pub called the Empress of Russia. When he returned to the hotel he was intercepted by members of the *collectif* and ordered to return to Russia. He replied that this might be an ideal situation for him. He was grossly overworked and they were welcome to get on without him. 'I can't see what all the fuss is about,' he counterattacked. 'If you complain about my going to the Empress of Russia, why are we all staying at the Prince of Wales?' The *collectif* saw the point.

The Moscow Art Theatre presented three Chekhov plays during its weeks in London—*The Three Sisters*, *The Cherry Orchard* and *Uncle Vanya*—as well as a new Russian play by Leonid Rakhmanov, *The Troubled Past*. But it was the Chekhov plays which caused the greatest interest, for they made us all wonder whether we had ever really known Chekhov at all. Chekhov was now revealed to us as one of the world's most profoundly humorous dramatists, his sense of the comic and absurd taking on redoubled importance through his gentle expression of the tragic undertones of his characters' lives.

I brought the Moscow Art Theatre back to London with *The Seagull* to end the 1970 World Theatre Season, and this was their first new production of the play since Stanislavsky's historic one. Boris Livanov's production was a semi-successful and controversial attempt to break away from Stanislavsky's suffocating naturalism, which had so upset Chekhov. Stanislavsky had seen *The Seagull* as a tragedy of frustration which was invoked by the curious sounds of crickets, barking dogs, distant thunder and moody silences. Chekhov saw that his characters could be both sympathetic and comic. This eluded Stanislavsky. Livanov's new approach in many ways went to the other extreme. He certainly captured the comedy, but his production, set in semi-abstract settings and punctuated by passages of Scriabin, lacked that feeling of sympathy which is essential to Chekhov. His stylized theatricality, at times almost melodramatic, also contained in certain scenes the subtle mixture of pathos and humour which smoulders uneasily in the texture of Chekhov's plays. This production, which completed the quartet of Chekhov's plays that I

L

had brought to London (*The Three Sisters, Uncle Vanya* and *The Cherry Orchard* being the others) was equally historic in the performance of I. P. Miroshnichenko as Masha and A. I. Stepanova as Madame Arkadina, and above all in revealing new possibilities in the interpretation of the play.

When Chekhov proclaimed through Konstantin in *The Seagull* that 'we need new forms, and if they are not here, then nothing is needed', this was some sort of dream which *he* never championed. At no time did Chekhov come forward as a practical exponent of new forms, either in dispute, in conversation or in any article. That is why the Moscow Art Theatre is Russia. Livanov's production, it must be said, *was* a bold attempt to transfuse new ideas and forms into the work of the Moscow Art Theatre, and whatever the overall success of his *Seagull*, this was certainly an exciting and fascinating innovation.

The Moscow Art Theatre's first visit in 1958 had been a triumph, and the Russians were overjoyed with their success. Touched by our reception, they showered us with medals. One day, when I took Rex Harrison to a matinée, the director of *The Three Sisters* discovered that he had run out of medals, and I hastily offered him one of mine. This was duly pinned on to Rex's chest with all the ornate ceremony of a Buckingham Palace investiture. Rex was profoundly touched.

For many of the company the climax of their visit was their meeting with Charlie Chaplin. Tarasova said that just the fact of meeting him would have made their visit worth while. He was their idol—a legendary figure to meet in the flesh.

I asked him to come and see the company after a performance of *The Cherry Orchard*. As we went through the pass-door and on to the stage, an extraordinary sight met us: the whole Moscow Art Theatre assembled, roaring and stamping like a crowd of football fans. Chaplin was deeply moved. With tears in his eyes, he told them, 'This has been the most wonderful evening of my life.' Then he described how he had started his career just up the road at the Collins Music Hall at a few shillings a week. 'I wheeled a barrow across the stage dressed as an old tramp. I was allowed three minutes, but by the end of the first week it took me twenty to cross the stage.' Then, turning to Gribov, a sturdy man of fifty who had played the old retainer Firs, he asked him, 'How long do you take?' 'Half an hour,' Gribov replied. 'There you are,' said Chaplin delightedly, 'I was practising the art of Stanislavsky before you were born!' For days after, the company could talk of nothing else but Chaplin's visit. How excited they were, they told me, to be able to return to Russia and tell their friends that they had been admired by the great Charlie Chaplin.

When we left the theatre together Chaplin said, 'Let's continue this marvellous Russian evening. We'll go to the Savoy and have a supper of cavier and vodka.' In the early hours of the morning he remarked how tired I looked. Indeed I felt completely worn out. 'Come and stay with me,' he said. 'What you need is the peace of my garden and my beautiful trees.' But before I could accept his offer I had to go off to Paris to prepare for the Moscow Art Theatre's season there. Little did I know what disasters awaited me.

Before the company flew to France, the final night of their Sadler's Wells season formed a tumultuous farewell. When the last curtain fell, both audience and actors sensed that it was a moment in history. They took call after call, and then began to applaud the audience. Solodovnikov and I went on stage together. 'This is a sad moment,' I told the audience and company. 'This is the last of the shining Moscow nights with which the Moscow Art Theatre has celebrated its diamond jubilee in London. Their acting has been a source of inspiration to the whole of our theatre profession and also to the general audience. We shall always remember the quality of their acting, its passion for truth and simple observation which has miraculously transcended the language barrier. I do want to thank this wonderful company for its co-operation, its friendliness, its humility. It has been a joy to work with them.'

Playing with superb consistency, the Russians repeated their London triumph at the Théâtre des Nations in Paris, easily winning the hearts of the audience and the plaudits of the critics. I had expected this success, but what I had not and could not have anticipated was the note of discord which began to creep into our back-stage relationship.

For all the problems of London, as we had grown to understand each other we had established a hectic but happy atmosphere of trust and good will. In Paris this was quickly dissolved into suspicion and unease. The actors seemed suddenly subjected to a nerve-fraying political surveillance. With prominent French

Communists regarding the company as within their personal charge, we entered a world which jealously guarded its secrets and emotions. This development, combined with an administrative quarrel with the Théâtre des Nations, formed a sad end to an exciting adventure.

The next visit by the Moscow Art Theatre took place in 1964, when they participated in the first World Theatre Season. The season was launched that year to celebrate the four hundredth anniversary of Shakespeare's birth, though I had been discussing the possibility of a World Theatre Season with Peter Hall in 1962. The Royal Shakespeare Company's policy of touring for about ten weeks in each year had made the Aldwych Theatre an obvious venue, and supported by the enthusiasm of the Royal Shakespeare Company's publicity director, John Goodwin, we decided to launch the first World Theatre Season with seven of the world's greatest companies. Pre-eminent amongst these was the Moscow Art Theatre which included in its repertoire a sensational dramatization of Gogol's *Dead Souls*. This play had been first produced at the Moscow Art Theatre in 1932, eighty years after the death of its author, who never fully recovered from the uproar caused by his play *The Government Inspector*.

Also in 1966 I presented as a part of the third World Theatre Season the Leningrad Gorky Theatre in two plays: an adaptation of Dostoyevsky's *The Idiot* and the delightfully folkloric *Grandma, Uncle Iliko, Hilarion and I*. To make arrangements for this visit I had gone to Leningrad in November 1965. In his office Georgyi Tovstonogov, the great director of the Leningrad Gorky and adaptor of *The Idiot*, introduced me for the first time to Innokenti Smoktunovsky, who played the part of Prince Mishkin in *The Idiot*, and whose name was already familiar to Western audiences from his performance of the title-role in Grigori Kozintzev's remarkable film version of *Hamlet*, first shown in London in 1964. I shall always remember this first meeting. Tovstonogov was dark and nervous. Conversation with him creaked like an old sofa, while Smoktunovsky observed me, watchful and silent. I was conscious of being examined by his large, pale blue eyes. There was a long pause; then he said, 'I have been watching you, and I shall give an imitation of you.' He proceeded to do a terribly funny imitation. It broke the ice, and was typical of his capacity for making the drabbest people and the dullest events gay and amusing.

Smoktunovsky, who was born in Siberia, is, in my opinion, among the world's greatest actors. At the time we met, six years had passed since he had last played Mishkin. 'My approach to the role remains the same,' he said to me, 'but my own capacities are different now. My performance is more restrained, but I hope it's a little deeper. Perhaps I've become wiser.' His performance certainly carried a shock effect, for he played it with an intensity and truth that I have never before experienced. It was the most totally absorbing and convincing performance that I had ever seen on any stage.

Smoktunovsky's performance established him as an actor of world stature. In his portrayal of this dangerously innocent holy fool there was a double quality in his acting, projected through his immaculate sense of timing, which allowed his reactions and speeches to appear either deliberate or those of a mind diseased. There was about his performance a glowering intensity and watchful expectancy—was he saint or epileptic simpleton? The trance-like, semi-mystic quality of his acting gave a lingering ambiguity to his portrayal which haunted both the play and the audience. He called upon the repose and economy of a great and unique actor.

The Leningrad Gorky Theatre itself is the oldest Soviet theatre, having opened its doors, with Schiller's *Don Carlos*, in 1919 on the site of an old private theatre of 1879. Like the Moscow Art Theatre, it now bears the title 'Academic' and ranks with that theatre as the greatest in Russia today.

In spite of the absurd diplomatic obstacles, the ideological misunderstandings, the frustrations and panics in which my associations with the Russians involved me during the years from 1954, it was all made more than worth while by the warmth of human contact which I discovered in that often baffling and contradictory phenomenon, the Russian character. An entire hidden continent of subtle emotion and a wonderful passion lie concealed beneath the bureaucratic stereotypes and the weight of twentieth-century history. In bringing their productions to the West, it has been possible to show others something of that character, to illuminate a dark area with understanding and enthusiasm.

While in 1917 a fierce civil war was raging in Russia, a new studio was started under Stanislavsky. Epidemics and hunger spared no region, and fear and anguish gripped every heart. It was in these conditions that a group of fewer than ten people gathered one day in a little house not far from the Kremlin, in order to dedicate their efforts and whole existence to the foundation of a new theatre. The members of the group were Jews and their aim was to create a Jewish Hebrew theatre in Moscow. Never before had such a thing happened in all the long history of the Jewish people.

The birth of the 'Habimah' was revolutionary, a unique creation, the beginning of a new history. In order to grasp to the full the kind of atmosphere which prevailed at the Habimah Hall at the dress-rehearsal of their first performance in October 1918, it is enough to recall this testimony from the diary of the late actor and director, B. Chemerinsky:

> ... Young men and women wearing boots and thick woollens rushed from the top of the stairs so as to secure a seat. The hall was packed and many had to sit on the carpet. All of a sudden, complete silence ... 'He is coming.'
>
> When an old, distinguished man came smiling into the hall, everybody rose to their feet. He sat down at his little table in the corner and we all sat down after him. The most absolute quiet reigned. The words passed with difficulty through the heavy lips but, gradually, syllables became words and the words clear sentences. We drank his words and took some rapid notes. 'The stage is a magic seat which does not allow its occupant to lie. Only the true artist may appear upon the stage.'
>
> He talked at length of the truth of art and quoted examples. 'The actor must constantly recreate his character. He must prepare for it methodically and faithfully ... ' And Stanislavsky went on to describe in detail what the actor was to do and think, at every instant, from the moment he left his home to the moment he went on stage, passing through the dressing-room.
>
> Stanislavsky talked thus for five consecutive hours. He had started at ten o'clock in the morning, and when afternoon came, we felt somewhat tired, but he was as fresh and fit as ever, and his style as faultless.

Not only did Stanislavsky fight for its rights until the Habimah was promoted to the rank of State Academic Theatre, but he also gave it his most brilliant pupil, the Armenian Vakhtangov, as director. Vakhtangov took the company in hand and strove to strip it of Stanislavsky's tendency towards sloganism. The greatest creation of that period, and one may perhaps call it an 'immortal creation', was, and remains, *The Dybbuk*. Vakhtangov died a few days after the first night at the age of thirty-nine, and since then the Habimah has lit more than a thousand candles to his memory, one at each performance of *The Dybbuk*, whether in Russia, Europe, America or Israel.

The Habimah remained an active force in Russia until 1926, when the Government department in charge of fighting Jewish culture closed the theatre. Maxim Gorky, who was obsessed by the Habimah, and Kamenev, the Commissar of Education (later shot by Stalin), failed to save it. In 1926, like the Wandering Jew, Habimah took to the road. It is now Israel's National Theatre.

A few months before bringing *The Dybbuk* to London for the World Theatre Season in 1965, I had visited Tel Aviv to see the company at work. Everything in Israel is unexpected: the Germanic thoroughness of its immigration officials, the wall of tropical rain, an obsession with social courtesy, even the fact that I once came near to drowning off the beach near my hotel. Our first conference with the Habimah was brisk and businesslike, but one big issue was raised by the Israelis. Flattered though they were to receive an invitation to London, they wondered if it might be a mistake to bring *The Dybbuk*, though they knew the play was the jewel of their repertoire. It took almost the whole of my stay to demonstrate why I wanted this play, and for me, on my part, to realize the basis of their concern.

They felt that the picture of Jewish tradition which *The Dybbuk* presents might give English audiences a totally false idea of their new nation. It was certainly a play of exorcism, madness and synagogues. But, as the company admitted, *The Dybbuk* and the world it portrays are far from dead, and to prove it they took me to a synagogue, very much like the one portrayed in the play, in the old quarter of Jerusalem. Here the elders, with their staring eyes, waxen faces and black coils of hair, which fell beneath a species of black Victorian top-hat, sang a blessing. Then, resuming their study of the prophets, they retracted into a compulsive trance, rocking backwards and forwards in rhythmic meditation. As one of the actors told me, 'Their laws are ruthlessly biblical in the cruellest sense and ridiculous in the comic sense.' These *are* the characters of *The Dybbuk*.

I even encountered this Hebrew-praying and Yiddish-speaking community—who practise their faith and live in a medieval world seemingly so out of tune with the reality of present-day Israel—in a personal confrontation. These extreme sects run against the stream and are sometimes openly hostile to the State. Such was their intolerance that when, innocently, I took out a small cross that I had just bought near Calvary, I had to be hustled out by Maier Asher, the *Daily Telegraph*'s correspondent in Israel, for fear of causing a minor riot.

The following day, when I met one of Israel's leading poets, Yal Gouri, he commented as we drove towards Jerusalem's border, 'Israel is a country that is so small on the map that its name has to be written on water. Yet we are an island surrounded almost completely by land.' We neared the border, stopped the car and stood staring at sandbags and gun-turrets, a Berlin-like wall a stone's throw away. He pointed across the barrier. 'There is the road to Bethlehem. I am sorry the first time you see it it is across barbed wire.'

I remember one evening discussing the background to the Jewish tradition of theatre with Yehudi Menuhin. It had always seemed amazing to me that, until the advent of the Habimah in Moscow, the Jew had never portrayed himself in the flesh and had never satirized or caricatured himself. He had left this to the outside world, which had cast him in a variety of unflattering roles. 'I always find it is a pity that he left this task to others,' said Yehudi, 'but now there's a Habimah, and in its wake a great number of new theatres are emerging.'

But the Habimah—and Israel's other old theatre, the Ohel, founded in 1925—were not Israeli theatres; they remained strictly under Russian expressionist influence. This was not the case with the Cameri Theatre, which I brought to London for the 1967 World Theatre Season, in—fittingly—the first Israeli musical, *King Solomon and the Cobbler*, originally written in German by Samuel Gronemann. In flavour it recalled the spirit of The Arabian Nights, and perhaps the play's highlight was the double performance by Illy Gorlitzky as Solomon and his cobbler.

When I had visited Israel to sound out the Cameri Theatre, I had dined one evening with Iesaja Weinberg, its director, and we had discussed the growth of a new and genuinely Israeli theatre. 'What happened', he told me, 'was that after a certain period of time, the younger generation, the Israeli youth who were born in Israel and were educated in Israel, suddenly began to feel that this old theatre in its spirit, in its style, in its plays, belonged somehow more to the exiles than to their new surroundings in Israel, and the result was the creation of a new theatre, the Cameri, in 1944.'

United by an aggressive patriotism, Israel had absorbed an enormous number of different Jewish cultures without developing any distinctive culture of its own. Now, finally, Israel had its own theatre, created in Israel by the new Israelis. The Cameri had brought to audiences throughout Israel two vital elements hitherto lacking from all Hebrew-speaking theatres—the ability to express itself in everyday Hebrew with the accent of the generation born in the country and the ability to play in a modern style.

8

France from Molière to Chevalier

I do not think I had ever grasped the enormous ramified unity of
the French theatre until I started negotiations to present the
Comédie-Française in London. No city in the world offers such
exquisite theatrical pleasures, nor leaves one so eager for more, as
Paris. The very heartbeat of that great city is reflected in the
wealth and variety of the French theatre. The venture, I knew, was
a bold one. It was like, in effect, attempting to borrow what
James Agate rightly described as one of civilization's most
treasured possessions. One might as lightly have tried to hire the
Taj Mahal for display at Battersea Fun Fair as seek to uproot the
prestigious company of Molière. There, beside the gardens laid
out by Richelieu, stood the most famous theatre in the world,
rich in three centuries of stage history, the embodiment of a
culture refined to perfection by generations of actors and actresses,
each adding to it in the way that a colony of tiny animals in the
sea gradually builds up a magnificent and dazzling coral reef.

My notion of bringing to London the 'Maison de Molière' was
to prove no simple cultural transfer. What I had not anticipated
was how many other roots would need to be disturbed, how
many strings would need to be pulled, how many laboriously
created connections with the French stage would require exploitation.

My adventure began in the summer of 1958. Having successfully presented the Moscow Art Theatre in London, I had taken
the company to Paris, where they repeated their London triumph.
As I described in the last chapter, behind the scenes all was not
happy. In delivering the Russians into the hands of the Théâtre
des Nations at the Théâtre Sarah Bernhardt, I discovered that
I had committed a grave tactical error. The contribution of
the Théâtre des Nations to world culture represents a unique
achievement, but on this occasion their prodigal generosity in
distributing free seats was threatening the economics of the

entire season. All my representations were ignored. Arguments blossomed into flaming rows, and I found myself forced into a squalid round of threats and recriminations with the director-general of the theatre, Monsieur Julien, *Légion d'honneur*, C.B.E.

Like some ripe Victorian *maître d'hôtel*, Monsieur Julien glowed all over the place with euphoric courtliness. One felt that, with his vital gift for smiling intimacy and ceremonious panache, he would have been able to extract the top secrets of every nation, had he had a mind to. But personally I could extract nothing from him whatever.

I was finally driven to put my complaints to a senior official at the Quai d'Orsay; he listened gravely but expressed regret. He was powerless to intervene in a dispute between myself and the Théâtre des Nations. Would I, though, be interested in a counter-proposal? Would I, suggested the minister, accept the offer of a London visit early next year by the Comédie-Française?

I was overjoyed. The difficulties of the Russian visit to Paris were instantly transformed into an opportunity for fulfilling one of my most cherished ambitions. Since the days of Molière, its founder, the Comédie-Française has been at once the glory and the despair of the French theatre. When André Gide, asked who was the best French poet of the nineteenth century, replied, 'Victor Hugo, hélas', he expressed something similar to the contemporary opinion of the Comédie-Française, the oldest theatre in Europe. Like the Académie Française, it is violently criticized by each generation. Yet almost every great French actor has been associated with it at some time in his or her career. It has become, to use Jean-Louis Barrault's words, 'a filter that lets nothing through ... Its judgment is implacable.' But such notable individualists as Jean-Louis Barrault, Madeleine Renaud, Edwige Feuillère and the great tragedienne Marie Bell have all in fact managed to slip through the filter to form their own companies.

While three hundred years of tradition can be a disadvantage, they can also be a strength. The history of the Comédie-Française is like a roll-call of the history of French dramatic art. If Molière, Corneille and Racine are among the authors it regularly presents, so too are those arch-*boulevardiers* Courteline, Feydeau and Sacha Guitry. This baffling institution is something more than a theatre, something more than an exclusive club and something only slightly less than a religion. And like a religion it continues to hold within its gilded chains even those who have rebelled against it, so that it has had to define the nature of their rebellion as a dogma defines a heresy.

Delighted by my unexpectedly successful talk with the Minister of Culture, I took an affectionate farewell of the Russians and flew off to make arrangements for other visiting companies to appear in my forthcoming season at the Princes Theatre. Some weeks later, returning from Berlin, I broke my journey in Paris, unaccountably disturbed by premonitions that something had gone wrong with the arrangements for the Comédie-Française. The moment I reached my hotel I telephoned London. My worst fears were confirmed. During my absence the entire deal had fallen through.

I caught the next plane to London and drove straight to the French Embassy. There I was informed that all my plans had been cancelled by the French authorities. Another impresario had gone over my head and offered the company at least £2,000 more than the offer we had agreed upon. To raise my original offer would have meant financial disaster, and the Embassy, on whose kindness and support I had come to rely, was unable to help further.

I returned to Paris the same evening. There I found the doors of the Quai d'Orsay barred to me. Letters and telephone calls were ignored. But by now my desire to bring the Comédie-Française to London had become an obsession. I was determined not to return without them; to pull every string, bring every ounce of pressure to bear, use every friendship and connection I had built up over the years with the great names of the French stage.

Returning to my hotel, which overlooked the Jardin du Palais-Royal and faced the Comédie-Française, I found a message from Jean-Louis Barrault asking me to see him immediately at the Théâtre du Palais-Royal, the most romantic of the small theatres of Paris. I arrived there, three blocks away, at seven thirty, and Barrault was on the stage darting about the set with supple grace. His mobile, aquiline face was afire with ecstasy and frustration. As a single concession to theatricality he wore draped around his shoulders a small fringed shawl made of fine coffee-coloured wool. The moment he saw me, he leapt into the stalls like the horse in his very first mime. I was carried back to the pale, love-lorn harlequin of those marvellous mime sequences in Carné's *Les Enfants du paradis*.

Alas, I knew that, for personal reasons, he was not at that time in a position to use his influence on my behalf with the theatrical Establishment and I realized it was hardly the time or the place to engage him in my troubles. But he sensed that something was wrong; immediately he tried to cheer me up by invoking memories of his and Madeleine Renaud's 1956 season in London. We recalled his visit to Prince Charles and his friends, to whom he gave an exhibition of his famous mime of a man riding a horse in a circus ring.

In the midst of mutual effusions Barrault was called back to the stage, extracting a promise that, if I were to find myself in further difficulties, I would call on him again.

Later that evening, badly in need of a laugh, I drifted into the Comédie-Française itself to see a performance of *Le Dindon*, Feydeau's farce of vintage quality, played at breakneck speed, in which beds are swopped as often as French Governments were before de Gaulle. The anguish of Robert Hirsch as the lover, totally incapacitated by a night of debauch, when the irresistible Micheline Boudet, the woman he has always longed for, suddenly arrives to fulfil his desires but finds herself unable to arouse a flicker of excitement, was the funniest piece of acting I had ever seen in my life.

Another friend to whom I could turn was the actress who had shared with Barrault his triumph in Claudel's *Partage de midi*, and whose beauty had persuaded the dramatist to allow the play's performance after a forty-year restriction—Edwige Feuillère.

She received me in her flat near the Eiffel Tower with the exquisite, tremulous sympathy which has put her among the finest romantic actresses. As she listened to the plaintive account of my frustrated mission, her luminous concern seemed on the brink of tears. She appeared almost as moved as she had been in London on the first night of my presentation of *La Dame aux camélias* in 1955, when she had stood clutching the curtain, still shaken and disarranged by Marguerite's death-scene, while stalls and gallery rose in homage to her. Afterwards she told me, 'I have never had such stage-fright in all my life.'

Fear, indeed, is the key to Feuillère's psychology. She is afraid of everything: of crowds, machinery, movement, of her own emotions even. She is afraid 'not of being weak'—she knows that she is—'but of showing it'. More and more, as time goes by, her love of passing incognito, her passion for solitude, for concealing herself behind her dark glasses, remind one of Garbo. She is plagued by insomnia. She suffers in cities—her favourite hiding-place is a small family *pension* on a fjord near Bergen in Norway. The real Edwige bears no resemblance to the superbly poised Feuillère that the world knows.

In 1937 she first played the role with which she will always be identified: Dumas *fils*'s tragic courtesan, Marguerite Gautier, in *La Dame aux camélias*. It was a role Bernhardt had made peculiarly her own; to a generation still living, it was inseparably connected with that dead-white, blazing face, throaty voice and wiry, electric hair. Playing it totally differently, with a softness and desperation all her own, Feuillère claimed it afresh for herself. When I brought her to London in the part in 1955, the critics, with one exception, had hailed her as the Marguerite of our times.

The exception came in a review by John Barber, then critic of the *Daily Express*, who wrote ' ... but in the vital scenes of the play the actress muted herself down too much, as if afraid of the theatrical effects. And she was too *refined*.' I immediately rang Lord Beaverbrook, who gave me *carte blanche* to reply, 'as long as you go for Barber'. My reply to the review had run as follows: 'John Barber complains of the manner in which Mlle Feuillère interprets the principal role in *La Dame aux camélias*—Marguerite Gautier. Here is a prostitute. In England we think of street-walkers, but Mr Barber seems to have forgotten that throughout French history there have been social ranks among prostitutes. Remember Du Barry, La Païva and Mlle Mérode?'

The term *demi-mondaine* (a word invented by Alexandre Dumas *fils* as the title of a play he wrote in 1855) or *grande cocotte* designated a world of kept women with establishments furnished with staff and a carriage in which to drive in the 'Bois'. But many *demi-mondaines* were faithful to one protector, or at least to one at a time, and some even married into the nobility, such as Jane de Tourbay, who died Comtesse de Loynes. Many had *salons* which were frequented by the most eminent men of the day. But the word 'prostitute' implied brothels, street trading and melodramatic infamy, just as it does today.

I had no sense of running into danger by replying to Barber's peevish review, but my reference to Cléo de Mérode was most unfortunate. Out of the blue, a letter soon arrived from the *Daily Express*'s legal department enclosing the translation of a letter which they had received.

Sir,

I was stupefied to see your article which appeared on September 20th, 1955, in the *Daily Express* under the signature of Mr Peter Daubeny, who has not hesitated to say of me that I was neither more nor less than a prostitute.

I have no need to tell you the pain that this has caused me, seeing that my life has always been dedicated to dancing, and only to dancing, and that no one has ever had any doubt of the perfect dignity of my life. It would be extremely painful to take proceedings to obtain reparation for the damage, which is considerable, or the moral pain that the article in question has been causing me.

I do not know which decision I shall make in this respect, but I rely absolutely on you from now on, to insert a correction in your newspaper, which seems to me to be at least the first step towards the reparation to which the unqualified levity of your correspondent entitles me.

The letter was signed 'CLÉO DE MÉRODE'.

There crept over me a terrible feeling of doom as I envisaged a £50,000 libel suit. In consternation I rang the legal department and spoke to the manager. I explained that it was quite impossible that this lady, who in 1890 had been voted Beauty Queen of Paris, was still alive. We mutually agreed that this must either be a hoax, or her daughter. To further reassure myself, I telephoned an old friend, the eighty-year-old Baroness de Stoeckl, who in her book *Not All Vanity* has proved herself the the historian of the elegant wits and *grandes horizontales* of the *fin de siècle*. She seemed indignant at my query. 'Alive? Absolutely out of the question!' she said with an energy that withered further inquiry.

But alive she proved to be, and Jacques Charon, who frequently saw her, spoke of her ravishing beauty and saintly dignity. She was ninety. As Colette said in her dedication to her in *La Chatte*, 'To Cléo de Mérode who defies time.'

She had certainly been one of the greatest professional beauties of her period, but might claim with justice that she had never been either a *grande cocotte* or a *demi-mondaine*. She had danced at the Opéra, where Leopold II of the Belgians fell under her spell. He offered her a house in Brussels and a villa in Ostend. She declined both. But this did not prevent her name being linked with his, as he advertised the secret of his infatuation and earned himself the lifelong nickname of 'Cléopold'.

The *Daily Express* quickly published an apology to the outraged lady. I wrote a reply to her letter with the help of the late Gilbert Harding, who took a benevolent interest in my predicament. Gilbert, who always proved a marvellous friend, was a superb, classical crank. Like Johnson, whom he must have resembled in many ways, he stood up for the rights of self-assertion and rudeness. He lost no time in taking up my cause. The letter we wrote together expressed my belief that Mlle de Mérode had been, in all probability, a legendary, or at any rate long-dead, *demi-mondaine* in the distant days of the Duc de Praslin.

We all held our breath. Cléo de Mérode behaved like a great lady and dropped the case, which could have won her a fortune. It proved to me, however, that in answering a critic one only wades into deeper water. While Barber's judgment may have been wrong, my reaction was nearly catastrophic.

To my everlasting regret, though Jacques Charon promised to take me to tea with her, Cléo de Mérode and I were never to meet.

Two years later I persuaded Edwige Feuillère back to London for a season which included not only her former success but also Henry Becque's *La Parisienne*, a melodrama of the 1880s, and Racine's *Phèdre*. As Phèdre she was magnificently moving, a figure of sumptuous passion in her sombre crimson robe. But perhaps she lacked the ferocity of the true Racinian tragic heroine. Her Phèdre was all woman, yearning, quivering, strangled with her own shame; never the sexless Medusa of pure violence who, from the closing snare of tragedy, flies with blind horrific recklessness at the face of doom.

While I have called Edwige Feuillère our finest romantic actress, for me the greatest tragedienne of our time is Marie Bell, whom I presented also in *Phèdre* at the Savoy in 1960 in a season of Racine which also included *Bérénice* and *Britannicus*. Where Edwige is all feminine timidity, Marie has the daredevil abandon of a racing motorist. 'In this business', she once told me, 'you can't afford to be cautious.' This was an understatement, on or off stage.

Marie Bell could say with Madame Defarge of *A Tale of Two Cities*, 'Tell Wind and Fire where to stop, but don't tell me.' Her private life is as highly coloured a mixture of impersonations as her public one. She will slap on a wig and tiara for dinner with the Duke and Duchess of Windsor; crouch at your feet for a fireside chat with the gypsy intensity of Carmen Amaya; sit by a friend's sick-bed all night, holding her hand like Florence Nightingale; roar off to the Quai d'Orsay on ministerial affairs like a human canonball; rumba all night with the tireless verve of Mistinguett; and turn up to rehearsals at ten the next morning in jeans and a sweater. 'If I stopped, I should no longer be an actress,' she admits. No wonder that, in her sixties, she could pass for a vigorous forty-year-old.

During the Occupation she worked for the Resistance, concealing Frenchmen and Allied servicemen in her flat in the Champs-Élysées, while at night she played at the Comédie-Française. One day the worst happened: she was arrested and taken to Gestapo headquarters in the Avénue Foch, where she was confronted with one of the forged passports used by her escape-contacts and told she would be deported for subversive activities. 'I decided to strike first,' she says. Rising with all the dignity of Racine's barbarian queen in *Bérénice*, she launched into a tirade of condemnation. With no weapon but the powerful passion of her voice—a passion which had moved her great admirer Claudel to write of her, 'Toutes les cloches dans le ciel/ Carillonnent à l'appel/Triomphal de Marie Bell,'—she fixed the Gestapo deputy-chief with the eye of one 'loosed out of hell to speak of horrors', rolling forth words of thunder and passion. 'Would you, as a loyal German patriot, have behaved differently?' she ended ringingly, and sank back exhausted into her chair, awaiting sentence. The Gestapo chief sat stunned, staring at her for several minutes, 'quite drained of colour', she says. Finally he spoke. 'Thank you, Madame Bell, you may go now,' he said faintly, and she swept majestically through the door which he held open for her.

Racine is perhaps the most difficult French author to play on the English stage. Even in French, as Barrault once put it, he

M

confronts the actor with as many problems as there are dials in the cockpit of an airliner; in translation the exclusive French qualities of his alexandrines—the ripple of their poetic cadence, firmly pointed but never emphasized, the diamond flash of their taut imagery—vanish as do the savours of those delicate *vins du pays*, faultless at home but impossible to ship abroad.

For this reason Racine has never been popular in London. But Marie Bell's Savoy season was a triumph which broke all box-office records. Alan Pryce-Jones wrote in the *Observer*, 'She makes of her tragedy what it should be: a stain on the air, a word cut into the calm perfection of Poussin—like antiquity.'

For Marie Bell herself the high point of her London visit was not the critics' warm reception or the enthusiasm of the packed houses. One morning she rang me up, carolling with joy over a letter she had received. 'It's my paratrooper; he turned up to see *Phèdre*, with no idea that it was me he would see again. I hid him for several days. Now he knows who I am.' It must have been a fantastic shock for the man she had helped to escape fifteen years before when the bejewelled hand which presaged Phèdre's blood-curdling appearance, clutching the cavernous entrance of the tunnel, turned out to belong to his Paris landlady. But the following evening, when we asked him round for a drink on the stage, he arrived with roses, champagne and a face shining with love.

While I can think of no ally I would rather have than Marie Bell in a desperate, last-ditch stand against overwhelming odds, at this stage in my predicament my immediate need was for con-solation and a restored confidence. For these I turned to Edwige Feuillère, who supplied them beautifully. No doubt Marie Bell would have descended on the Quai d'Orsay like a fury to rage through its corridors, and have emerged in due course with an agreement duly signed and witnessed and slightly spattered with blood. Edwige, on the other hand, had a gift for healing concern. She listened to me with a luminous melancholy that seemed to take every trouble on herself. Gently she promised to do every-thing in her power to help to take the Comédie-Française to London. I left her feeling strengthened and hopeful, and went in search of the next friend whose help and influence I hoped to engage.

This was Jean Vilar, whose dark, austere strength seemed a

perfect complement to Feuillère's sympathy. I had first presented his Théâtre National Populaire in London in the spring of 1956. Vilar holds a special position between the studio theatre, to whose tradition Barrault is the unique heir, and the theatre of the boulevards. In 1951 he created a whole new province of French theatre by taking over the T.N.P., then languishing for lack of financial support in the vast Palais de Chaillot, and building it into a genuinely popular theatre of the classics. He slashed traditional seat prices, reducing the best to ten shillings, the cheapest to two; introduced a repertoire of plays ranging from Molière to Brecht; chose new stars—Maria Casares, Gérard Philipe—whose reputations had been made in the cinema; attracted audiences who had probably never set foot in a legitimate theatre; put on talks, seminars and concerts, all combined with stage performances and dances in a 'T.N.P. week-end' whose tickets the poorest student could afford. He took 'theatre to the masses' with a vengeance.

Vilar is an inspired director, whose productions combine a classical emphasis on voice and the studio theatre's simplicity of design with an earthy, popular naturalism which reflects his own personal vision. Stripping the stage at the Palais de Chaillot of footlights and battens, he extended it into the audience to create a flexible platform for experimental productions which would involve their viewers as intimately as music-hall. On seeing his work for the first time I had been struck by the daring way in which he used space, limiting it by means of lighting. Scenery was for him only a background. His costumes, generally designed by painters, not by stage designers, built up the actor's image by means of strong blocks of colour without unnecessary details. He made considerable use of music and sound. The nearest English equivalents to Vilar's productions were, I suppose, Joan Littlewood's early re-interpretations of the classics at her Theatre Workshop in Stratford East; but the strength of Vilar's work lies in his emotional stability, his quiet non-French sense of order.

His Roman face, waxen and detached, with diffident eyes and sarcastic mouth, gives no hint of the theatrical visionary behind it. He dresses like an undertaker on holiday—the only time I have ever seen him moderately animated was when I hustled him off in London to be measured by my tailor for a new suit. Now, quietly smoking one of his innumerable pipes, he listened gravely to my troubles, now and then jotting down a note. His brain moving swiftly behind the impassive mask, he went straight for practical measures; he would bring my case to the attention of the National Theatre Committee of Finance. Unsmilingly, he added that he would back me to the hilt. Such behaviour was typical of him, both in its absence of fuss and in its practicality, which took friendship for granted. I imagine it may be this unsentimental directness which so endears him to the young, such as those who, until 1968, flocked from all over Europe to participate in the courses he held each summer at the Avignon Drama Festival, where dialogue between Vilar, actors, directors and audiences ran on much the same lines as did his T.N.P. week-ends during the 1950s.

Roger Planchon's Théâtre de la Cité from Villeurbanne, a huge industrial suburb of Lyons, has done much to continue the work which Jean Vilar began, and I presented this dynamic company in the 1969 World Theatre Season, in Racine's *Bérénice* and Molière's *Georges Dandin*.

During the several days I spent at Villeurbanne watching Planchon at work, we discussed his career and his aims at length. He had embarked on what seemed the foolhardy venture of setting up his own theatre in Lyons where there was little to encourage him. Only two or three thousand people out of a population of nearly a million ever went to the theatre, and when they did it was to see second-hand touring productions of the big commercial successes from Paris. In his first theatre—a tiny place seating only a hundred or so—he aimed to establish a regular and clearly defined repertory. He tried to reach people who never ordinarily went to the theatre, to turn the privilege of a small minority into the privilege of all. Needless to say, he enticed very few of the working people he was after. Yet the working-class percentage of his audiences is the highest in France—and to have brought this about in the unpromising grimness of an industrial city like Lyons is a rare achievement.

The French reputation of the Théâtre de la Cité rests chiefly on Planchon's interest in contemporary problems. He has concentrated on Brecht, O'Casey, Marlowe—authors whose plays cannot be regarded as 'easy' for an audience not over-endowed with culture. He argues that it is not difficult to attract large audiences for the classics. People have heard of Shakespeare and Molière, and they are the dramatists who fill the theatre more completely than any modern writer. But Planchon sticks resolutely to his ideal.

Planchon confessed to me that he would have preferred to bring over some of the contemporary plays on social and political subjects for which his company is celebrated. But I felt that everything in his production of *Bérénice* reflected the methods he uses. The cast was very young, with the Emperor Titus played by a film star, Sami Frey. As many as four out of the six weeks' rehearsal were spent in reading the text, discussing it, commenting and criticizing. In his insistence on the text and its interpretation Planchon is a true follower of Antoine, whom he so much admires. His production of *Bérénice* brought out an important motive in the plot: the cruelty which people inflict on each other. The result was a complete success. Despite early fears about what an English audience would make of it, the first-night reception endorsed the line he had followed. And even those to whom the French ideal will always remain alien paid handsome tribute to its grave nobility.

From Vilar's apartment I returned to my hotel. The mass of the Comédie-Française still faced me across the Palais-Royal gardens, proud, blank and tauntingly impregnable. At the desk I found an invitation to supper with yet another friend and his wife. My spirits, raised by my visits to Edwige Feuillère and Jean Vilar, soared. If there was one man in Paris who had sufficient influence and detachment to help me concretely, it would be Pierre Fresnay.

It is difficult for an Englishman to understand the prestige Fresnay holds in France. He is an actor who, for many years now, has appeared chiefly in boulevard comedies designed to show off the virtuosity and charm of his wife, Yvonne Printemps. Partly his success lies in a triumph of art over material, and many regard him as the finest actor in the French theatre; partly it lies in the public's recognition in him of a peculiar unworldliness and concern for the human race which places him far above the petty egotism of boulevard acting. There is about him an almost medieval air of saintliness and scholarship, and his admirers rightly identify him with the monastic values and inner humility he illuminated so masterfully in his film biography of St Vincent de Paul, *Monsieur Vincent*. Once, jammed in a box with a French family, I watched Fresnay perform a scene of highly suggestive bedroom comedy. Suddenly the mother turned sharply in the box to admonish her children. 'Vous savez', she hissed severely, 'qu'il est très haut spirituellement!'

But, apart from his own qualities, Fresnay also enjoys the benefit of the utterly different regard in which the boulevard theatre is held in France. In England we have finally accepted Wilde as a classic, but there was a tremor of outrage when the National Theatre, by including *Hay Fever* in its repertoire, laid claim to a similar status for Noël Coward. In Paris the theatre of the boulevards has at its best always held a kind of parity with the classic and studio theatres. Its finest fruits are recognized as masterpieces in their genre. Its most notable actors, like the Orleanist branch of the Bourbon family, have all the prestige of a twin royal line of descent. Fresnay is the descendant who wears the crown left vacant by that Louis XIV of the boulevard, Sacha Guitry. And he even implemented his symbolic right by marrying Yvonne Printemps, Sacha's former wife.

Meeting Yvonne was like meeting stage history personified. She had become a star at twelve, and had surprised Paris audiences with her powers of mime and satirical fooling in Guitry's *La Revue de printemps* by appearing in quick succession as the Prince of Wales, Diana de Poitiers, half of the Dolly Sisters, Yvette Guilbert and that bejewelled *cocotte*, La Païva. Half a century later she remained an idol of the French theatre. But it was a very different Yvonne from the sophisticated waif who had wrung the hearts of a generation of Londoners with her broken English and singing of 'I'll Follow my Secret Heart' in Coward's *Conversation Piece*. Her personality was to Pierre's as the North Pole is to the South. Whether gossiping about mutual friends or maliciously taking off mannerisms of her great contemporaries, Yvonne reveals herself as one of nature's clowns. In her mimicry all the shallows of theatrical superficiality and human hypocrisy stand unveiled; not with cruelty but with a subtle, pungent sense of fun.

'To be a great artist', she argued, 'you must also be a clown. Bernhardt was the greatest of all. You must never be afraid of having to do anything. Blacken your teeth, pull your hair over your face, laugh like a hyena. Lynn Fontanne shied away from the grotesqueries of *Auprès de ma blonde*, and lost the impact of the part. Feuillère, in a film we did together, was horrified to see me laugh like a fishwife. She told me that I should only laugh with my eyes, keep my face still and make a sound like a horse neighing; otherwise my face would be ruined by lines.' She laughed first in the manner prescribed, then with the Hogarthian gusto against which she had been warned.

We continued laughing together until midnight. Then, with concerned faces, they listened to my third repetition of my troubles that evening. Fresnay's eyes darkened with distress as I told him that all would be lost if the Minister at the Quai d'Orsay stuck to his refusal even to see me. 'Don't worry,' he said quietly, 'you will see him tomorrow. I will arrange it.' The gentle confidence of his words stayed with me as I retraced my footsteps through the haunted arcades of the Palais-Royal gardens. I was still full of doubts, but now at least hopeful.

The next morning I was summoned to the Quai d'Orsay at noon. The Minister had agreed only to see me, but I presented myself at his office resolved to stay there until either matters were decided in my favour or else I was removed bodily from the building. It was nearly two o'clock when, under my own propulsion, I hurtled out of the front door to join Edwige Feuillère, who had been waiting for an hour at a near-by restaurant. Over lunch I was too emotional to eat but, as I told her, my troubles were over. The Comédie-Française were finally and irrevocably committed to come to London under my management.

Four months later, on March 17th, 1959, the company triumphantly opened at the Princes Theatre, in the presence of the Queen Mother and Princess Margaret. The play was Feydeau's *Le Dindon*, directed by Jean Meyer, a great director who shortly afterwards withdrew from the great national institution to create his own theatre in Paris, the Théâtre Michel, and to direct the Théâtre des Célestins in Lyons. His vivid humour and touching awareness of life, with its half-tones and complexities, enabled him to be equally at ease with de Montherlant or Feydeau. There had been considerable controversy in France about the house of Molière mounting the bedroom scamperings of *La Belle Époque*'s most accomplished farce-maker on the same stage as Corneille and Racine. The London success of *Le Dindon* crowned the Feydeau revival with respectability. When the Comédie-Française returned for the first World Theatre Season at the Aldwych in 1964 they brought with them *Un Fil à la patte*, directed by Jacques Charon. It was a continuation of the success which had begun with a production of *Occupe-toi d'Amélie*, which the Barrault–Renaud Company had brought to the Palace Theatre for me in 1956. Two years later Charon was invited to stage *A Flea in her Ear* for the National Theatre. It was not an easy assignment. English actors had yet to adapt themselves fully to the peculiarly French wit, speed and artificiality of Feydeau. But Charon worked miracles, and that production has remained one of the National Theatre's finest.

I took a special pleasure in the triumph of *Le Dindon*. Feydeau has always seemed to me the incarnation of the greatest period of the French Theatre. Only a man who had plunged through that whirlwind of *La Belle Époque* to a stillness of his own at its centre could have transformed it so utterly into a new, purely theatrical creation. Cocteau once told me how he used to see Feydeau leaving Maxim's in the early hours of the morning, the collar of his coat turned up imposingly, his bowler hat balanced over a tiny face with eyes that peered out through narrow slits; in his flabby hand a huge cigar which he would lift to his thin mouth. From Maxim's he would wander through Paris until morning, cane in hand, from café to café, by a curious roundabout route which eventually brought him back to the Hôtel Terminus, where he lived. 'Often,' Cocteau said, 'I went with him to the newspaper stall at the Gare St-Lazare, where he would stand talking until dawn. When accosted by the streetwalkers he would twitch his aquiline nose and reply, 'But I'm not bored, *chère Mademoiselle*,' and on he would go, oblivious of time passing, until with an incredulous look he saw the sun rising over Montmartre. 'Good heavens,' he said to a passer-by, 'is that the dawn?' 'I don't know,' came the answer. 'I'm a stranger in these parts myself, Monsieur.'

Feydeau's success had not been immediate even in France. Sacha Guitry once told me how, at the first night of an early play which was booed, Feydeau rushed down the aisle and joined the booers. When a friend asked why, he replied, 'This way I can't hear them.' But at the opening night of *Champignol malgré lui*, according to a prominent critic of the time, 'The public was so worn and exhausted with laughter that they could hardly stand it. The hysterics which took hold of the audience were so loud that nobody could hear what the actors were saying. The act was done in pantomime.' From then on, Feydeau was often hailed as France's greatest comic playwright after Molière.

As I watched the London audience convulsed with laughter at *Le Dindon*, I felt the occasion was in a sense a climax of my long exploration of the French theatre. Besides epitomizing *La Belle Époque*, Feydeau gathered together all the traditions of the French stage. His plays are classical in construction. Their plots, machine-turned with impeccable precision, carry the action forward like lightning. Each word is exactly placed and carries vital consequences. 'I always start from real life,' he explained; 'one fact—which has to be discovered—crops up to disrupt the normal order of events as they would logically have occurred. I amplify this single incident. If you compare the construction of a play with the building of a pyramid, you shouldn't start from the base so as to arrive at the summit, as people have done up to now. I turn the pyramid upside down: I start from the summit and widen the debate!'

Feydeau 'acted' all the different parts while writing his plays. When he created a main character who was utterly absurd, he took care to 'pair' him with a secondary character who was even madder, so as to make the first character seem almost normal by comparison. His famous witticisms were entirely spontaneous and arose naturally from the dialogue. He scorned authors who wrote a whole scene for the sake of ending with a powerful *mot*. All preparation, he declared, meant the death of wit.

Feydeau's plays demand, in their frank artifice, the athletic miming and team-work of an ensemble theatre. In high style and sophistication they reflect the comedy of the boulevards. And in their broad, superb vulgarity they belong also to the tradition of music-hall, the last refuge of the great clowns.

My first direct contact with the French theatre had come through Michel Saint-Denis, before the war, after the fourth triumphal visit to London of his troupe, La Compagnie des Quinze, which Bronson Albery and Charles Laughton had presented in André Obey's *Don Juan*.

Saint-Denis had begun his career at the tiny Théâtre du Vieux-Colombier, launched in 1913 by his uncle, Antoine's successor,

Jacques Copeau. Copeau's influence in France and, through Michel Saint-Denis, in Britain cannot be underestimated.

Copeau fervently believed in the power of the word. He had begun life as a drama critic, and after crossing the footlights he was determined to adhere strictly to his principle. His dream was of a literary theatre, strictly opposed to commercialism, the cult of the star and any unnecessary distracting realism. Avoiding the then contemporary fetish for elaboration, he stripped the stage of its heavy decor, using, as in the Japanese Nō drama, a semi-permanent setting without any proscenium arch. Sets were simplified to the point of symbolism.

His 1911 production of Dostoyevsky's *The Brothers Karamazov* brought immediate fame to the actor Charles Dullin. In spite of his poor physique and undistinguished features, this reluctant lawyer turned actor became one of Copeau's most brilliant discoveries. His Harpagon in Copeau's production of *L'Avare* was a superbly Molièresque creation, and for the next thirty years he continued to confirm his teacher's faith in him. Another recruit was a young man who, while recently qualified as a pharmaceutical chemist, implored Copeau to engage him. Gaunt, lugubrious, with jerky diction and legs always a trifle too long, he played Aguecheek in *Twelfth Night* and delighted audiences at the Vieux-Colombier with his gawky version of what was for Parisians the outlandish poetry of Shakespeare. His name was Louis Jouvet.

Saint-Denis had worked with his uncle from the opening of the Vieux-Colombier until being conscripted in 1916. Copeau trained all his actors and actresses in the simple, sparing style which his productions demanded. Clowning, mime and improvisation were important here, since he aimed at restoring the magic and suggestion of Nō as opposed to 'the logic that has taken the poetry out of our Western theatre'. Here indeed was a counter-revolution against the massive, concrete literalism of Reinhardt's more spectacular productions, though, like Reinhardt, Copeau sought that rhythmic unity which is the essence of art. 'Copeau', wrote Dullin, 'has cleansed the stage; he has brought back the predominance of mind over machine and of true culture over literary veneer.'

'It was very romantic,' Saint-Denis told me. 'It was a small theatre, with four hundred seats. First of all I was the secretary to the management, then I became an administrator, and gradually I was transferred to the stage, during the four years I worked there. I eventually became a producer, Jouvet having left, and in some ways I replaced him, directing the rehearsals and sometimes acting.'

They were touring America when Saint-Denis was called up. At that time the company was facing a hard struggle to make ends meet, and in the end was obliged to put on a different play each week. In 1924, back home in France, Copeau decided that they needed 'to renew contact with the soil' and left for Burgundy with a group of his students. There the 'Copiaux', as they had become known, wandered through the countryside acting in village squares and inns, travelling during both summer and winter in a cart loaded with props and costumes. 'They could act as they had in school, using mime and improvisations,' Saint-Denis told me, 'as they were unable to do with actors in Paris, or with the majority of actors.'

After six years in Burgundy, Copeau felt tired and ill. He wanted to hand over the reins. 'It was then', says Saint-Denis, 'that I founded the collaboration between an author and fifteen determined actors.' The reputation of Saint-Denis's team was quickly established, in Paris and elsewhere. Certainly London had never seen the like of the harmony they achieved. They brought something new into the theatre—the art of ensemble playing against an anti-realistic background. Although Saint-Denis's English production of Obey's *Noah* with John Gielgud three years later failed to achieve the rich fulfilment of his French productions, the London Theatre School was greeted with enormous professional enthusiasm.

Saint-Denis offered a salutary shake-up, but whether his methods were entirely suited to the English temperament I was never sure. There seemed to be too little communication between master and pupil, but George Devine became his devoted follower, and Gielgud, Olivier, Byam Shaw and Fernald were all deeply influenced by his teaching. Laurence Olivier, who played in the Old Vic *Macbeth* which he staged before the war, and who was instrumental in setting up the Old Vic School, which Saint-Denis ran until 1952, summed him up to perfection: 'You either believed in him or you didn't, but something told you instinctively that you had better do so if you were to get any good out of him. This resulted in a kind of enslavement which, though not

at all disagreeable, was apt to make you feel like a donkey enticed by a carrot at every mile-post, along a road which kept re-
appearing ahead of you just when you thought you'd come to the
end of it.' But he was always equable and persuasive; and it was
his quiet, reticent individuality which dominated our pre-war
impulse towards a group theatre, bringing into the English
theatre of the 1930s a new faith born of Copeau's ardent revolution in Europe.

The greatest disciple of Copeau and the French studio theatre
was, I suppose, Jean-Louis Barrault, whom I several times
brought to London with his wife Madeleine Renaud. Barrault had
trained with Charles Dullin in the 1930s. His first appearance on
the stage was playing a part of one of the servants in Jules
Romains's translation of Ben Jonson's *Volpone* on his twenty-
first birthday. He remained with Dullin at the Théâtre de l'Atelier
for several years and his studying of the art of mime under
Decroux was to lead to a production of a mime play based on
William Faulkner's novel *As I Lay Dying*. When he took over
Dullin's Atelier in 1939 he brought to the theatre a new sense of
life. One of his earliest productions was *La Faim*, adapted from
Hunger, the novel by the Norwegian writer Knut Hamsun.
Hamsun's preoccupation with the situation of the individual and
his relation to society gave Barrault an opportunity for a vivid
portrayal of the loneliness of a starving man in the heart of a
great city. Simone de Beauvoir in her book *The Prime of Life* has
written an absorbing account of this production:

> In this play, dialogue was only of secondary importance,
> and often replaced by the montage technique known as
> *fatrasie*, a new device with which Barrault achieved some
> excellent effects; but his own favourite mode of expression
> was mime. Though a pupil of Decroux, who had devoted
> his whole life to reviving the art of mime, Barrault did not
> regard it as an adequate independent medium, preferring to
> use its resources as an adjunct to the development of the
> drama. He could not resist the temptation to introduce
> several bravura touches into *Hunger*: at one point, for in-
> stance, he climbed an imaginary staircase by 'marking time',
> an exercise which stuck out from the over-all pattern of
> the production and disrupted its rhythm. I was far more

appreciative of those moments when gesture per se became a genuine mode of dramatic self-expression. There was one scene conducted wholly in dumb show, where the hero, through sheer physical debility, failed to possess the woman he desired: this was as strikingly successful, and though daring contained not the slightest hint of coarseness.

During the Occupation years, 1940 to 1944, Barrault worked under Copeau himself, now general administrator of the Comédie-Française. Before the war he had contributed several engaging cameo parts to films, but it was his role as Baptiste Deburau, the mime in Marcel Carné's *Les Enfants du paradis* in 1944, that introduced him to an audience far wider than that of the Parisian theatre and won him international fame. His gaunt white features, dark tragic eyes and stylized, almost choreographic acting set the seal on a film already distinguished for the purity of its photography and direction and for the evocative dialogue by the poet Jacques Prévert. This success may have given him the confidence to break with the Comédie-Française. With a starting capital of only a thousand pounds, he and Madeleine Renaud, now his wife, launched their own company at the Théâtre Marigny. For the next ten years Paris, watching sceptically but with greedy curiosity to see how they would fare, was astounded and confounded by the brilliance of his productions.

The Marigny became the most exciting theatre in the city. Within the course of a decade it accommodated nearly fifty plays—works by Shakespeare, Marivaux, Claudel, Salacrou, Vauthier, Christopher Fry, adaptations from Kafka and Faulkner, and a veritable Pleiad of other stimulating, provocative authors. Inevitably they made as many enemies as friends for Barrault and his wife. Often criticized for changing his style of production with each new subject, Barrault refused to shy away from the most directly uncompromising line. His aim was a theatre which would go beyond the superficialities of style to rest upon movement, rhythm and intonation. His production of Christopher Fry's *A Sleep of Prisoners* in 1955 held the shades of a nightmare which few of those who saw it would ever forget. In the years following the war he brought a renewed prestige to the French progressive theatre and, incidentally, gave me some of the most exciting theatre of my life.

Neither he nor Madeleine Renaud is content to rest on past laurels. For Barrault the theatre is 'first and foremost an art of motion'; 'Everything must always be wiped out, forgotten, so that we can start again. It is a permanent revolution. There lies its passionately interesting side. Every day we must be born again. There's the rule.' In 1956 his company was again on the move. Owing to back-stage politics and misunderstandings they had lost the Marigny and were 'homeless rogues and vagabonds tramping the world', as Barrault put it. They set off on a long world tour, beginning with the season at the Palace Theatre when I presented my two-year programme of foreign companies.

It was entirely due to Barrault that the epic verse-drama of that fiercely Catholic poet, Paul Claudel, became familiar to modern audiences. Claudel and Barrault met at Brangues in 1936, an event which is important in the annals of French theatre. It signalled the start of a unique collaboration between an author and a director. 'Our conversations together', Barrault said, 'proved that we spoke the same language—right from the start.' From his work with Antonin Artaud in the short-lived *Théâtre de la cruauté* Barrault had learned the principles of total theatre, a combination of acting, film, music and mime. Claudel held to the same ideal of a theatrical totality which could represent every facet of creation: inner and outer, legend and dream.

In 1959, when André Malraux offered Barrault the Odéon, which had been rechristened the Théâtre de France, it was an offer both marvellous and dangerous, but impossible to refuse. 'The aim of the Odéon', its first director, Poupart-Dorfeuille, stated in 1795, 'is to foster a new generation of actors and to inspire not only those who interpret great works but comic and tragic poets as well. In short, it plans to give fresh life to all those who can add lustre to the French theatre.' When the theatre was officially renamed, Barrault commented, 'These words sound as appropriate today as they did in 1795.' In the nine years of his occupancy Barrault built the Théâtre de France into a great national treasure equal to, and at times surpassing, the Comédie-Française. But in 1968 a revolution of the same kind which had given birth to the Odéon ended his directorship. In the student riots of May 15th a crowd from the Boulevard Saint-Michel invaded the theatre. Barrault tried to reason with the students and begged them to let his season continue, but they jeered him off the stage. Theatrical circles in Paris believed that Barrault tried to please both Government and students and succeeded only in offending everyone. Others believed that he was the helpless victim of a Government still living in fear of a student rebellion. The consequences were disastrous for both sides. Malraux dismissed the man whose achievement had been one of the glories of his Ministry of Culture. Barrault, however, is too generous to bear a grudge. He accepted his dismissal as part of the perpetual revolution which art must always be for him. 'According to Aeschylus,' he once wrote, 'destiny is the result of three forces: the situation of the past, the cross-roads of the future and the opportunity of choice. It is this last point that makes us all free men.' In a telegram to me in the autumn of 1968, he ended, 'L'AVENIR EST À NOUS LOVE JEAN-LOUIS.'

Salacrou once summed Jean-Louis up. 'Barrault is not an actor, he is a bomb ... I shall never be able to visualize him outside the theatre—in common daylight he seems to vanish. He once told me he intended dying in the theatre, like Molière and Jouvet ... "It is the only place where I find life glorious." '

Paris today has its equivalent to off-Broadway, or off-off-Broadway. It was, for example, at the Théâtre de la Huchette, in the Quartier Latin, that Ionesco was discovered seventeen years ago, since when his words have been performed there continuously. The *avant-garde* tradition continues in the numerous small fifty- to hundred-seater theatres that have grown up on the Rive Gauche, in Montparnasse—in small side-streets, basements and cafés— presenting a varied and exciting repertoire of Arrabal, Gatti, Duras, Obaldia, Adamov and of new, young authors of the most experimental *avant-garde*. The French theatrical tradition of the Theatres of Cruelty and Absurdity and their modern counterparts in the writings of Genet, Ionesco and Beckett have offered daunting challenges to the theatregoer, and in my 1960 production of Billetdoux's *Tchin-tchin* I offered London audiences an opportunity to see another leading modern French author.

Billetdoux's theatrical metaphors are both revealing and perplexing. I saw him playing the lead in *Tchin-tchin* at a tiny theatre in Paris with Katherina Renn. It was a comedy with sharp, sad overtones about alcoholism, and took its title from the drinking salutation. Its leading character is an Italian-born industrialist,

Cesareo Grimaldi, become a naturalized Frenchman as well as an alcoholic, because 'drink makes the colours brighter.' He encounters in a Paris tea-room an Englishwoman, Pamela Puffy-Picq, who is married to a French doctor. Their respective spouses are having a love affair, which we see through the eyes of the prim Englishwoman and the volatile Cesareo. They thus meet in a common bond of despair. The play had a peculiarly individual flavour, and the comedy lay in what these absurd opposites could make of each other.

I bought the play, and sent it to Laurence Olivier and Celia Johnson. Celia accepted the part of Mrs Puffy-Picq, and from Larry at Morecambe, where he was shooting the film of *The Entertainer*, I received a rude postcard of 'Mother's posterior appearing from the brine' with the words 'Chin-Chin from us and bottoms up from Mum'; the outlook seemed bright.

One evening Larry came to tell me that he was attracted but absolutely confused by the play. Realizing that a wonderful opportunity was slipping through my fingers, I analysed, clarified, elucidated and edited in my enthusiasm to reinforce the waning interest of Britain's greatest actor. Two hours later he said, 'You can sell anybody anything, and in principle I should like to do it.'

I then had to go abroad for a week, though I asked him before he left not to see the French version, which he agreed. But with George Devine he at once flew to Paris to stay with a mutual friend, Ginette Spannier. On my return to London he telephoned me to say that we had made a big mistake. He was appalled at the arty little theatre, the performances of the actors and his own indiscretion in ever having played around with the idea. I said I disagreed with him, but entirely understood.

The play then travelled on a curious journey from Vittorio Gassman to Pierre Fresnay, Peter Sellers, James Mason and Orson Welles, my old friend of the Ballet Petit days, from whom it received immediate attention.

Welles had no criticism of the play beyond objecting to the name 'Mrs Puffy-Picq'. He signed to direct and play Grimaldi, but later discovered that he was unable to fulfil his contract because of a change of date over the theatre, which was my fault. Ironically, the ideal casting lived in London just round the corner from me in Wilton Street—Anthony Quayle. With characteristic generosity he said that he would love to do it, although he was diffident about playing the part.

Tony Quayle is without doubt one of England's best actors. His unique achievement was his eight years as director of the then called Shakespeare Memorial Theatre at Stratford-upon-Avon. 'Stratford', he told me, 'had got to be made into the foremost theatre of Shakespeare in England and thereby, it seemed to me, in the world.' Over the course of these eight years he attained this objective, and the productions at Stratford with Laurence Olivier, Vivien Leigh, Michael Redgrave, Ralph Richardson, John Gielgud, Peggy Ashcroft and Edith Evans became landmarks in the British theatre. When, in 1960, Peter Hall took over the company's direction from Glen Byam Shaw, he further extended the quality and range of the Royal Shakespeare Company's work and founded their London base at the Aldwych Theatre — this in turn was to house the World Theatre Seasons, which Peter, with his constantly innovating genius, did so much to establish.

My account of the French theatre would be incomplete without the two greatest legends of the Paris boulevards: Sacha Guitry and Maurice Chevalier.

The late Sacha Guitry was without doubt the most universal and colourful figure in the French theatre in the twentieth century. It was in 1953 that I made the first of a series of trips to Paris to try and persuade him to come to London for a season. Twenty years had gone by since his divorce from Yvonne Printemps and her remarriage to Pierre Fresnay, but I had an impression that even then he was still a man trying to hide a crippling shock, and lost without her in a wilderness of bitter-sweet memories. Yet nothing had impaired his art as an actor: off stage or on, he remained the most flawless comedian I have ever seen, and trying to get him to London was both a baffling and a stimulating experience.

Like a king importuned by a courtier for some favour, Guitry dallied, temporized, ignored my messages or graciously returned irrelevant ones, avoiding any reference to the question I so urgently wished him to answer. It was Coronation year, and hotel accommodation was at a premium in London, though my friend Mr Hofflin of the Savoy answered my tentative inquiry with a magnificent response, 'Tell Monsieur Guitry his suite is ready for him at any time—we are waiting for him to come home.' Finally I sent off a telegram: 'LONDON'S CORONATION PLANS INCOMPLETE WITHOUT AUTHORITIES KNOWING EXACT DATE OF YOUR OPENING IN JUNE AND THE PLAYS YOU WILL PERFORM', and followed it closely in person to that unique house in the Avénue Élisée-Reclus which, like a miniature Versailles, housed the treasures and memories of a dynasty of French theatre.

From the softly lit circular hall a curving staircase of marble and wrought iron led upwards, with arrogant theatricality, to Guitry's famous gallery. There an array of portraits stood like a guard of honour before an audience chamber. I stopped before Oswald Birley's portrait of Lucien Guitry, France's greatest actor of the *fin de siècle*. It was a likeness which caught the hypnotic quality of his legend, explaining his famous remark: 'You can call yourself an actor when you have made yourself understood by three people in the audience—the man who cannot see, the man who cannot hear, and the man who can see and hear but not understand your language.'

Suddenly, as if the legend had come to life, his son advanced towards me, hands outstretched in greeting, with the ease and nobility of a practised eighteenth-century courtier. Here was the sixty-five-year-old legend of the French theatre in person. I saw the massive build, the thinning shock of white hair above the leonine mask, the poised demeanour, and those compelling eyes, inquisitive, penetrating yet curiously modest—the eyes of one attracted yet surprised by life.

Sacha Guitry loved London, where he and his father had been acclaimed several times under Cochran's management. From his father he had inherited a fascination for odd clothes. With his bangles and beads, his bottle-green suits and his green crocodile shoes, he might have been the precursor of Chelsea's King's Road set. I asked him why he dressed in that eloquent way. 'We cannot be trapped by the conventions of a period. Everyone needs colour, exhilaration and a new sense of time. It is a means of losing yourself in someone else's identity—very restful.'

Not only did Sacha own one of the finest autograph collections in existence, including letters by Mozart, La Fontaine and Mirabeau, but he had also acquired a vast array of objects. The illuminated glass cabinets in his gallery contained such bizarre items as milk-bowls moulded from the breasts of Marie Antoinette, Flaubert's ring and dressing-gown, Napoleon's hat, Clemenceau's gloves and scarf, Robespierre's waistcoat, some withered flowers picked by Napoleon, and a telescope which the Emperor had once owned. Although his display cases took up most of the floor, Tanagra statuettes, Greek sculptures, Ming china and ceramics were scattered around on stands and plinths. The only remaining space would have been on the walls, except that these too were covered with his famous collection of pictures.

We became close friends and I discovered in him an undercurrent of extreme poignancy and even despair. He was now an aged and embittered man who would never really recover from the shock of his disgrace and the injustice of the treatment he had received after the liberation of France when he had been accused of collaboration with the Germans. Regret had taken the place of dreams. He was full of confusions and complexities. He lived in a world where he had to learn to make peace with humiliation.

Yet during hours of his enchanting talk I came to know as if in the flesh such past celebrities as the politician Clemenceau; the painter Renoir; the actor Raimu; Alfred Jarry, creator of the monstrous 'Ubu'; the composer Oscar Straus; those irrepressible writers Jules Renard, Alfred Capus and Tristan Bernard. He evoked clearly Sarah Bernhardt in the sunset splendour of her glory. Acting her, he brought her to life in the room where we spoke, and made redundant those old cylinders and scratched gramophone records which are all that survive of her vanished magic and which so utterly fail to preserve the beauty of a voice that cast a spell on all who heard it.

Sarah Bernhardt always gave one piece of advice to the young actors who surrounded her—to take Lucien Guitry as their model. He was, she said, the last of the giants, and they should study him closely in every detail of his performance. Sacha had written the last play in which she planned to appear. It was called *Un Sujet de roman*, and offered Sarah a magnificent part as the ambitious wife of an ailing novelist (this part played by Lucien Guitry) determined to gain for herself the meretricious fame which he, having the scruples of an honest writer, had always shunned. She delivered her main speech at rehearsal with monumental power, and a long silence followed in the empty theatre. Lucien could not take up his cue. He was weeping at the achievement of this great actress who, at nearly eighty years of age, had lost nothing in her skill to create overwhelming emotion. On the night of the dress rehearsal she collapsed. The gravity of her illness made it necessary to replace her, yet, determined to play to the last, she lay at home in bed and, as Lucien acted out the drama in the distant theatre, declaimed the speeches she would have delivered on the stage. Not even Sarah could long repel the advance of illness and decay. She sat already like a ghost, wearing a dress of pink Venetian velvet which Sacha had given her, calmly issuing instructions on the management of her funeral while journalists waited below for the inevitable news like hovering vultures.

'You know that my father built this house in 1910?' Sacha remarked. Once upon a time he met a famous fortune-teller. 'Shall I ever be rich?' Lucien demanded. 'Rich?' she echoed. 'Never, but I see an exquisite house—small, but perfect!' From that moment, obsessed by this idea, he accepted whatever part he was offered, with one mirage-like view in mind—his small, perfect house. Twice Lucien endured the horrors of seasickness for twenty-one days on a boat to South America, to act in twenty different plays. With the profits of the first tour he bought the land; with the profits of the second, a year later, he built the house. When the Brazilian Ambassador came to lunch with him, he cheerfully greeted him with 'Vous étes ici chez vous.'

During his father's life the salon we were standing in then had been, in Sacha's words, 'like the Louvre'. Pink marble, a huge Gobelin tapestry which he used as a backcloth for his production of *Le Misanthrope* and a portrait of the Grand Monarch dominated the room. Lucien filled his house with priceless pictures and Louis XIV furniture; he loved it like a woman—passionately, every day adorning, decorating and improving her just a bit more. After Lucien Guitry's death in 1925 Sacha had transformed the interior and lived in grand style with the aid of a liveried staff, a giant Cadillac and a chauffeur. Sacha smiled reminiscently and drew me by the arm to a window.

'I myself have lived here for twenty-six years, yet do you know an extraordinary thing? The first time I saw this house I was walking with a friend over there in the gardens opposite. I asked him if he knew who lived here. "Your father," he replied. He and I hadn't spoken to each other for ten years.'

In 1905 Sacha had become a small-part actor in his father's

theatre, using a pseudonym until he might prove himself worthy of the Guitry name. Proud of his costume as Paris in *La Belle Hélène*, he went to be photographed in it, forgot the time, and turned up late for a performance without his wig. When his father posted his name on the call-board with a stiff fine, he flung out of the theatre in a rage. It took thirteen years to heal the breach, and it reduced Sacha to such financial straits that he was forced to sell caricatures.

Clearly Guitry's arrest for collaboration was still a bitter subject, but I took the plunge and asked him what it had been like in prison. 'Uncomfortable,' he replied with hollow cheerfulness, 'but otherwise not bad at all. After all, most of the best people were there—the best artists, soldiers, ministers and writers. If you wanted to meet such people, you had to go to jail.'

A band of guerrillas had hauled him from his house and marched him through the streets of Paris at the point of a tommy-gun. On the way a hysterical woman had rushed at him and torn from his lapel the rosette of the Legion of Honour. Guitry kept his dignity. 'Madame,' he said, 'as you did not give it to me, you cannot take it away.' When he reached the prison a revolver was placed at his head, and he was pushed into a cell and the door slammed. 'I awaited the final curtain of this tragi-farce. Instead, my captor produced a dirty scrap of paper from his trouser pocket and demanded my autograph! Later, when I demanded to see on what charges I had been arrested, they looked up my file and produced a sheet of paper headed "Public Rumour". I remarked to the magistrate in charge of my case that if posterity should ever look him up in the French Encyclopedia, they would find him not under his own name, but under mine!'

When Sacha was finally brought before the board of inquiry after detention in a concentration camp, his accusers claimed that his plays were saturated with German propaganda. A detailed analysis of the three plays he had produced during the Occupation proved this to be ridiculous, but he was returned to prison. On August 8th, 1947, after an interview with the *juge d'instruction*, Sacha was at last cleared of the charges against him.

That had been the bleakest of autumns in a career spanning fifty years and a hundred and twenty-six plays—longer, if you included his debut as a tiny pierrot in a pantomime performed at the Imperial Palace in St Petersburg before Tsar Alexander III.

Perhaps that beginning, and his father's friendship with the famous clown Dourov, had given him his lifelong feeling for the poetic melancholy of the clown's art and the inspiration for one of his best plays, *Deburau*. Within ten years of his quarrel with his father he had built up a second 'Guitry' legend, as the most popular actor-playwright in Paris and one who was referred to as the 'Molière de nos jours'. The quarrel ended when Lucien Guitry, paying for his seat like an ordinary spectator, came to a performance of *Deburau* and sent his son an invitation to lunch next day. As they rose from the table, Lucien said, 'Write me a play, quickly.' In five days Sacha, for once not tongue in cheek, wrote the five acts of another of his best dramas, *Pasteur*.

He had first astonished Paris in 1905 with *Nono*, which without doubt was a very modern play compared with the lumbering pace at which boulevard comedy was then played. He remained a man before his time, and his friendship with Jarry, Antoine and Cocteau placed him in the forefront of the *avant-garde*. Jean Cocteau adored him. 'Sacha', he would say, 'was my youth.' Sacha's description of Jarry's room, a disused livery stable, could be a reproduction of a set for *Ubu Roi*: ' ... four walls, a roof of doubtful waterproof-tightness, and no flooring, only beaten earth. The door, which had no lock, swung to and fro and did not reach the ground. Inside there was a commode—which was scarcely commodious since it had neither top, nor drawers, nor bottom. His desk was a plank laid across two clothes-horses. His bed was a pallet covered with old clothes, beneath which he slid to sleep at night. His bicycle hung from the ceiling by a cord and pulley. "Otherwise the rats would eat my tyres," he explained.' Antoine, the father of Naturalism, became an intimate admirer of Guitry, and when he was at the Odéon Theatre told him to write a three-act play, which 'I will take unseen.'

Doubtless the comparison of Sacha with Molière was exaggerated, but certainly each must rank as the chief exponent of the comedy of manners of his generation, and each wrote with the practised speed of the actor-manager. Sacha's mind achieved exquisite results by inspired industry (he disapproved of any rest). If his art as an actor, playwright and wit stopped short of genius, it contained a tenderness, gaiety and poetic melancholy that gives us a unique view of the whole world.

His private life compared divertingly with Molière's. Both

men drew their wives from a circle of actresses, and used them not only as leading ladies but as characters in their plays. It was Lana Marconi who was his wife when I knew him. 'The others have been my wives,' Sacha told me, 'but she will be my widow.'

Looking back to my Coronation Season of 1953 at the Winter Garden Theatre, it is impossible to remember what Sacha's play *Écoutez bien messieurs* was all about. The first act was virtually a monologue, delivered by Guitry in a set copied from one of the rooms in his Paris house. The other two seemed equally a one-man feat of pure, personal virtuosity, a juggling-act of sparkling epigrams. 'His play', wrote Richard Buckle, 'was a perfect vehicle for his perfect performance; in fact the production was an illustration of my ideal collaboration between actor and author ... In his inflections of voice and deftness of gesture, Guitry seemed to embody the art of the old Italian comedians, refined by the subtlety of France.' 'What a lesson in acting!' A. E. Matthews wrote to me. 'I am thankful to have lived to see him.'

Sacha had an impulsive generosity. One night during the run I asked him for one of his caricatures as a memento of his visit to London. Two days later, while lunching at the Savoy, he handed me a thick parcel. I was already thanking him for the caricature when I noticed something very different in the parcel. 'You've made a mistake,' I said, gazing at the most beautiful Bonington I had ever seen. 'Not at all,' he replied. 'Bonington is a better artist than me, and my father gave it to me. I want you to have it.'

On a recent visit to Paris I was drawn once again to the site of that *pavillon* in the Avénue Élisée-Reclus to which all Paris had come during the years of his and his father's success. Of the house nothing remained. In its place stood a hideous chromium-plated block of flats designed specially, so it seemed, for the world of Jacques Tati in his film *Mon Oncle*. Only the bust of Lucien Guitry still stood staring into the Champ-de-Mars like the figure-head of a man-of-war. 'Thank God', I thought, as I walked sadly away, 'that he can't see what has been going on behind his back.'

Maurice Chevalier has been king for nearly seventy years of the French music-hall, and for the last twenty the friend whom I have been most proud to claim in France. I met him first lunching with C. B. Cochran just after the war, when Chevalier was making a triumphant return to London. Our conversation was shy and awkward. I managed to say how long it had been my ambition to present him in England. Ten years later the great opportunity came, and with it the chance to know him intimately—not just the legend of innumerable newspaper biographies, in which imagination—much of it Maurice's—has played as great a part as fact, but the man himself, his philosophy and inner resources, and the strength which has enabled him to deploy his talents for so long and in such a way that they never lost their power or freshness.

Maurice is one of the most fascinating people I have ever encountered. Not the least of his mysterious charms is the secret by which he has held the affection of the public for so many years in so many countries. In age, as in youth, he exudes the joy of living.

Maurice has always been, in every sense, a member of the working class. He rose from the gutters of Paris, in the suburb of Ménilmontant. His father, a house-painter, deserted his mother and the three surviving children of the ten she had borne him when Maurice was eight. The mother, frail with child-bearing, eked out a few sous making lace, but the family often went hungry. Maurice was sent to an institution which could at least provide him with two meals a day. He had endured it for two years; then, with his brother Paul, he left school to become, for a time, a circus acrobat. After this he worked as a clerk; mended fuses; made drawing-pins. Meanwhile a new dream replaced the 'Big Top' for him. 'I chose to be an entertainer. I did not have much of an advantage. Just a red-nosed kid, who had what they called a nice face.' At twelve, a precocious small boy with a large head, he sang and cracked jokes in cafés, amusing the audiences excruciatingly with the vulgarities and obscene gestures he copied from the adult comedians. 'In spite of their mockery, I knew that they liked me. That was all I wanted to know.' He rose to better-class halls, learning as he went that the sort of humour that delighted Ménilmontant, such as donning female underwear while singing a comic song, did not succeed with middle-class audiences. At last he found himself in the back row of the chorus at the Parisienne, the greatest music-hall of the boulevards. Earning enough to buy himself some new clothes, he indulged a taste for everything that was loud and solid—thick plaids of feverish patterns, soles half an inch thick, coats square and padded in the American style. His appearance earned the ridicule of friends and gave him a permanent inferiority-complex.

Even now he still enjoys solid shoes and heavy clothes for walking. 'When you have been poor, you get a kick out of them till your last day.'

He was dressed like that when he was taken round to the near-by Eldorado to meet its star, Mistinguett. 'A great timid chap, his broad shoulders fitting awkwardly into his coat,' she said later of him, and she recalled how he blushed and stammered, trying to pay her compliments which she turned with a word of friendly patronage. That was all, but it was enough to stir interest in the woman, and to rouse romantic adoration in the boy. She recognized him as one of her own class: starting as a flower-girl, she had also worked hard since childhood with no backing but her own talent. She held out a helping hand by offering him a part opposite her in a comedy number she was to play in the Folies Bergère of 1910. They had to waltz crazily round and round, whirling the furniture along with them, until, tangled in the stage carpet of coconut matting, they rolled over and over together. It was there, rolled together in that strip of coconut matting, that their great partnership started with a kiss. 'To me,' Mistinguett said in her old age, frail as a dyed and withered feather, 'that strip of matting seems just as beautiful as any setting for *Tristan and Isolde*. We no longer met as Chevalier and Mistinguett, but as the young Paris apprentice and flower-girl, both speechless.'

She made Maurice a *jeune premier*, and as her partner he achieved a premature reputation. He found it precarious and somewhat humiliating to owe his budding popularity to her, however, and made jealous scenes. In 1913, when he was twenty-five, he was called up. Within a year, war broke out, and he was wounded and captured in his first battle. During two years in prison-camp he learned English from a fellow prisoner, anticipating astutely that it would open doors to him in England and America. In 1916 he was repatriated, and returned to the stage. Though suffering physically and mentally from the after-effects of internment, he opened again at the Folies opposite Mistinguett. She remained attached to him. But this time it was he who was the star, the idol of Paris: the grinning young man with the big ears whose matter-of-fact cheekiness provided a link with reality between the audiences and the gorgeous spectacular numbers, with their dazzling settings, jewels, plumes, and exquisitely undressed girls. The thirst for spectacle had suddenly come into fashion with the war, as if in answer to an unspoken craving by men facing death to cram all the colour and beauty they could into the short time remaining to them.

The new strain put on the relationship with Mistinguett was resolved by an invitation to Maurice from the American star Elsie Janis, who wanted him to partner her in the London revue *Hello America*. From then on Maurice's career soared upwards, in 1927 inevitably leading him to Hollywood. Equally inevitably, Hollywood had to find him a label. 'In Paris they said I was "sympathique". But the thing that sold me in America was a word I had never heard—charm. It stuck like sticking-plaster and I couldn't get anybody to take it off. The image was created—everyone talked of my charm, and the women poured in!'

Those nostalgic films of the 1930s, *The Love Parade*, *The Smiling Lieutenant*, *The Merry Widow*, all with Jeannette Mac-Donald, made him world-famous. Eventually he asked for the singer Grace Moore as his co-star. She was not regarded as a sufficiently big name. A year or two later, she blossomed sensationally in *One Night of Love*, and invited Chevalier to star opposite her. But her studio insisted on giving her top billing, and Maurice would not give way, much as he liked and admired her. Deciding that he would rather play top of the bill at the Montparnasse Casino for one hundred francs a day than second at the Palace, New York, for a thousand dollars, he packed up and left Hollywood. He was just forty-six. Years later he summed up Hollywood for me in two words: 'Crazy and dangerous. I hated every second of it.' In Hollywood the cheery cock-robin vitality and benevolence of his stage personality had given way to a shy, sensitive, curiously unworldly man, who had to teach himself everything he knew, and who still continued to consume learning.

When the great moment arrived for me to realize my dreams of presenting Maurice in London, I was convalescing in Brighton after a serious illness. It was in fact the beginning of a tumour on my brain. The letters that Maurice wrote were not only a comfort to me, but revealed clearly the character which lay behind the shy reserve I had seen at that lunch seven years before:

Of course your letter is a 'choc'—but we must not listen to our sensibility and—in a good old English way—we simply have to face it. You won't be with us, but we will all work our best so that a radiance gets into your blood. You are an exceptional person—Peter—and exceptional things have to happen to you. That is the price. I leave today for Stockholm to try out my new English material. Pray for your old soldier and friend,   MAURICE

Outside your family, I am the one of whom [sic] misses you more because I feel certain that seeing each other more than before would have been strengthening and entertaining—for both of us—but life decides and we just do our best—and our best is to bring you proud and happy thoughts while you wait for health. Bless you, you are a fine Peter,   MAURICE

After the first night he wrote:

... after a charming supper at your home. Your wife was more than ever sweet and lovely. We drank to you—we thought and talked about you—and in spite of your being in Brighton—you were all over the place in our hearts.

I remember an October evening in 1954 when I sat in the Théâtre des Champs-Élysées. Maurice was giving the first of what turned out to be a number of farewell performances to his public. His goodbye was not only to the generation who had, so to speak, grown up with him, but also to the new youthful public who saw a new Chevalier—a philosophic statesman—yet adored him no less fervently than their parents. Fourteen years later, Maurice, aged eighty, had conquered another generation, and in October 1968 he gave yet another final performance. 'The great success that you have given me', he told the audience at the crowded final matinée, 'has touched me greatly and I will never forget this, my last appearance on the stage. I have wanted these twenty-one performances to be given in homage to Paris. To the Paris where I was born. I began my career in a music-hall in Ménilmontant, I ended here in this beautiful Théâtre des Champs-Élysées, after sixty-eight years of good and loyal service—and it is good that it should be so. I could go on. But I do not wish to end my career, like so many sad examples that I know, in disaster. Besides I shall not be leaving you completely; cinema and television will still keep me occupied, this time at home. The word "adieu" is too sad. I will just say "au revoir" with all my heart.'

9

'Naked Masks'—Italy and Sicily

The Italian theatre sometimes seems like a cauldron bubbling endlessly with private dramas and public feuds in the tradition of the Renaissance. There is thunder in the air and an assassin waits at every corner. If you belong to no camp, you are like a *condottiere* circulating around the *piazza* between cliques with mobile anonymity until you get an arrow in the back, or receive the patronage of some great name in return for your exclusive loyalty.

This conspiratorial atmosphere came again to the front of Italian artistic consciousness when Rome became the 'Hollywood of the Tiber'. The people of Italy paid tribute at the feet of Rossellini, de Sica, Visconti, Zeffirelli, Pasolini, Antonioni and Fellini, who, in Renaissance tradition, held separate and competitive courts, supported by noble scions of the great aristocratic families, and who, becoming as involved in theatre as in film, turned the Italian theatre into a director's theatre.

Before the 1960s England knew relatively little about the Italian theatre. Apart from Pirandello, who takes his place with Chekhov as one of the central forces of dramatic literature, only a scattering of names—including the romantic antique D'Annunzio, as well as such figures as Visconti and Zeffirelli, famous for their film and opera productions, and perhaps the Piccolo Teatro of Milan as being linked with the *commedia dell'arte* tradition—were in any way familiar.

In fact the Italian theatre contains two separate constitutional streams: the *stabile* companies, subsidized by the city, and the *giro*, or touring, companies. The *stabile* theatres, which are now to be found along the whole length of Italy's backbone from Milan, Rome (spasmodically), Genoa, Turin, Bologna, Trieste, and Florence, receive state as well as city aid, but rarely move from the city that sponsors them. The *giro* theatres are state-aided only and have a volatile history; touring companies headed by Vittorio Gassman, Albertazzi and Anna Proclemer, Eduardo de Filippo, to mention only a few, have sprung up and withered away.

During the 1930s there was also a tradition for two or three stars to organize themselves under a good director and produce high-grade productions of famous plays. These *compagnie a mattadore* (star companies) were thrown together by exceptional actors like Duse, Salvini, Emma and Irma Gramatica, and the great Sicilian comic Angelo Musco: stars in the line of such nineteenth-century actor-managers as Kean and Macready.

In Italy there are independent productions and nearly all plays are subsidized. This relative paucity of the Italian theatre, compared to that of France and Germany, is due both to geography and to the make-up of the population. Neither Rome nor Milan has any equivalent to Broadway. The theatre-going public is small. Most plays—except the great companies—run for little more than a few weeks, and in attempts to repair their expenses and enhance their renown both *stabile* and *giro* can find themselves doing the same play in the same city. Competition is fierce and the balance uneasy; as when the leading *giro* director, Visconti, temporarily turned *stabile* in 1964. He persuaded the Stoppa-Morelli company and the Compagnia dei Giovani into joining his massive Free Theatre Group in Rome, but personal conflicts disintegrated the group and nothing was ever staged.

Competition between *giro* and *stabile* has in fact been most bitter between the two leaders, Visconti and Strehler; but they remain, with their acerbic contrasts of viewpoint, the two master-minds of the Italian Theatre, and their tentacles embrace it entirely.

Between 1964 and 1970 no less than six leading Italian companies and artists came to London for the World Theatre Season: Peppino de Filippo, the Giovani, the Piccolo, the Rome Stabile, Anna Magnani, and the Catania Stabile from Sicily. In 1963, when I had already discussed with Peter Hall the possibility of presenting a season of international drama, with the help of John Francis Lane I brought Vittorio Gassman to the Aldwych to perform *The Heroes*. John's energy and versatility make him a stimulating and instructive companion to the Italian scene, and I have always valued his eclectic knowledge and lively mind.

In this try-out year for the World Theatre Season I presented two other successful productions at the Aldwych besides Gassman's *The Heroes:* Micheál Mac Liammóir's *The Importance of Being Oscar* and a new programme, *I Must be Talking to my Friends.*

Gassman is an extraordinary figure. His first star performance came when he played for the Italian National Basketball Team, and his athletic grace and beauty—attributes much venerated by the Italian—provided a springboard to his becoming the most popular star in Italy. In 1943 he became a professional actor, and from 1944 he played with a number of major Italian companies. He soon worked under Visconti, who was the first director to impose some discipline on his style, and when in 1948-9 he rejoined Visconti, he swept through a season of Caldwell, Cocteau, Shakespeare and Tennessee Williams, a season that also included Alfieri's *Oreste,* which, like Magnani's *La Lupa,* became his *cavallo di battaglio* (party-piece). By 1949 he was moving easily between high drama, comic impersonation and poetic lyricism, and in 1952 he created the Italian Art Theatre, which he directed with Luigi Squarzina, presenting a complete version of Shakespeare's *Hamlet* in which he himself took the lead, catching the hearts of the Italian public.

Gassman not only became 'fashionable' as an actor, but he also made the theatre fashionable. Then a highly successful television series, *Il Mattadore,* made him a national hero. He was known to every Italian man, woman and child as the 'Mattadore', an Italian word for one who likes to show off a bit too much. Yet his reputation as a *mattadore,* confirmed by a film in which he played a dozen roles, left Gassman dissatisfied with his achievements. Above all he felt that the theatre was never merely a question of being in vogue or of playing the *mattadore.*

His film career continued in Hollywood, where he married Shelley Winters (who always talks about him with devotion in spite of their divorce) and made several pictures, including a wonderful portrayal of Anatole Kuragin in *War and Peace.* He became, and remains, Italy's top cinema actor—although his image has never seemed to me to work so well on celluloid as in the theatre, where he can respond to a live audience—and by 1959 was ready for the next move. He had always dreamt of an educational, mobile and popular theatre—'something like a travelling circus'—and in 1960 he inaugurated the Teatro

Popolare Italiano, building the largest mobile theatre in the world, set up in a vast field in the Villa Borghese gardens in Rome.

It consisted of a steel semicircle covered by an immense canvas, all of which was to be erected in twenty-four hours by forty specialized workmen, the whole structure being kept in place by nine thousand bolts.

This 'Moby Dick', as the press soon nicknamed it, was so solidly built that the cost of moving it became too high. So it was abandoned, and for three years, in circus tents, on platforms, in hangars, in ancient arenas and modern cinemas, and in public squares up and down Italy, he fought the Italian Government's apathy towards the arts. Like Jean Vilar's Théâtre National Populaire there were meetings, lectures, discussions and recitals of drama and poetry.

With this People's Theatre Gassman seemed to have found a new faith in the theatre. He was no longer the romantic actor-manager dedicated to the classics and his own flamboyant private life, a role that he played so well in his Sartre–Dumas *Kean*. With his 'recital' productions he had created a new audience, drawn from the people rather than the sophisticated theatregoers of Milan and Rome. He had offered them a conception that embraced Aeschylus and the medieval mystery play, Alfieri and Shakespeare, but which also up-dated his repertory to give a vision of our own age, the problems and passions of Italy in the mid twentieth century. His idealism in fact led him to Sicily to work for a year with Danilo Dolci—the man whom Aldous Huxley called 'the ideal twentieth-century saint'.

I met Vittorio Gassman when I was in Venice with my wife enjoying a six-day holiday. Mrs Claude Vincent, a loyal fan of his and a sincere *aficionada* of Italian theatre—with a manner towards the world which was slightly apologetic owing to physical incapacities which involved semi-paralysis and partial blindness—put me in touch with him. When we arrived at our hotel I was delighted and astonished to find a note from him with the words: 'Please ring me at the Excelsior. I should love to be the first person to show you Venice.'

When I arrived at the Excelsior on the lido he was sitting in a chair by the sea. As he leapt up to greet me I saw at once why Italy should be at his feet. He had the beauty of a Roman athlete: a mixture of virile grace and delicate stature. His features showed a classic Roman perfection. Our conversation lasted for three hours, and by the end of it he had arranged to take us across to the city in his private motor-boat.

We sped across the lagoon, the unsuspected glories of the floating city of Venice lying before us. He knew his way around the city as a caretaker knows his way around a block of flats; but a caretaker persistently followed by all the occupants. Clusters of fans followed us everywhere.

The Heroes, which he brought to London in May 1963 as one of the precursors to the World Theatre Seasons, was an astonishing anthology piece. It drew its material from a repertoire of authors stretching from Aeschylus to Brecht, including Seneca, Plautus, Alfieri, Dumas and Pirandello, and incorporating material from *Waste*, the third volume of Danilo Dolci's famous survey of the poverty and suffering of present-day Sicily. His collaborator in preparing the programme was Pasolini, the poet and film director, a leading Italian left-wing intellectual who — some would say ironically — directed what was probably the most convincing and moving portrayal ever of Christ on the screen in his film of *The Gospel According to St Matthew*. Pasolini had worked twice before with Gassman in preparing modern productions of the *Oresteia* of Aeschylus and the *Miles Gloriosus* of Plautus, and extracts from both these appeared in *The Heroes*. The objective, in Pasolini's words, was to communicate 'the whole mystique of the theatre'; the effect was mercurial and challenging.

For the triumphant first night I had invited many of England's leading stars: John Gielgud came straight off a plane from the United States, Laurence Olivier hobbled in from the Brighton train with terrible gout, Paul Scofield travelled in specially from the country. The ovation Gassman received was a truly heroic and spontaneous tribute and he wrote of the evening later as 'the greatest in my life'.

Pasolini has called him Italy's 'foremost actor, the incomparable speaker of the richest Italian poets, who yet seems more often at home with the common characters who speak our equivalent of cockney'. The terrific impact that he made on London prepared the way not only for the World Theatre concept as a whole, but also for the overall panorama of Italian theatre which the seasons were to include.

There is a strong tradition of improvisation in the Italian theatre, which springs up from the origins of *commedia dell'arte* and which also shows itself in creative Italian cinema, most outstandingly in the films of Federico Fellini. In 1963 the *Sunday Telegraph* sent me to Italy to interview Fellini, and I spent four days with him on the set of the film that was to become known as *8½*.

I found myself entering the lobby of a five-star de luxe hotel, the inmates being from every walk of life and seeming to have settled into an apocalyptic limbo. A cardinal, resplendent in his robes, gently and mockingly rocked to and fro in the entrance hall; a Roman senator in a long white toga was mounting the broad sweep of staircase, watched by a handsome grey-haired man with a polite but tortured smile; a night-club entertainer strolled across the acres of floor space in tails, his face gaunt with a clown's make-up. I felt suddenly in a state of suspension between sleeping and waking, and it took the sudden appearance of Fellini himself, striding towards me with an expansive greeting, to reorientate myself to reality.

I was immediately struck by his eyes, perhaps, after Picasso's, the most remarkable eyes of the century; they seem to search into every unsuspected corridor of a man's soul, probing with insight, understanding and compassion. He moved with a subtle energy, conducting me through his 'hotel' — a set for a film that had no script, where the contracted stars had no idea of the roles they were to play, and where not even the producer had the faintest idea of what was going to go on the celluloid.

I asked whether it might be fitting to put as a theme those lines of Dante's *Divine Comedy* which read: 'In the middle of one's life one finds oneself alone in a dark wood...' He looked out beyond me at the great hotel that he had called into being to help him to understand his life. 'Yes,' he admitted, 'that is the theme. The theme is a man in the middle of his life, lost in the wood.'

Fellini was born on January 20th, 1920, in Rimini. As a boy he fell in love with the circus; at nine he was bullied by the priests at a boarding school; at twelve his first confession was greeted by the priest with a blow on the head; and at fifteen he fell in love for the first time. 'She was a girl called Bianca,' he said. 'She looked like Barbara Stanwyck.'

At sixteen he started his first career as a caricaturist — 'A Hungarian beach artist gave me the idea and I sold them to the tourists'—and at eighteen he was sent off to Rome by his parents to study law. But he wanted to become a journalist, though the only job he could find was editing the love-letters in a women's magazine. 'I had to compose the questions and answers as nobody sent in any letters for advice.'

The turning-point of his life came when Fellini saw Aldo Fabrizzi at the Giovinelli Theatre. He went backstage to meet him, told him he wanted to write an article about him, and instead found himself writing sketches for him. He joined Fabrizzi's company, toured provincial Italy, lodging in filthy digs but discovering how laughter could be born amidst rags and gloom. After various adventures escaping the Fascist police, he returned to Rome in 1943, started selling stories and drawings to magazines, and married the enchanting actress Giulietta Masina.

With no money and few prospects, in 1944, outside the Quirinale Hotel, he ran into a drunken Englishman. 'We decided to sell caricatures of British soldiers for cigarettes and white bread. This gave me the idea of setting up a caricature shop in the Via Nazionale selling cartoon postcards to British soldiers. I called it the Funny Face Shop.' One day he recognized Rossellini peering into the shop window. Rossellini entered the shop and asked him to do him a favour. 'He wanted me to ask Fabrizzi to play the part of Don Morosini, the priest shot by the Germans. Fabrizzi agreed.' This film was to be combined with another documentary about the cunning of the urchins during the German occupation and was to announce the birth of the new Italian realistic cinema; it was called *Rome, Open City*, and Fellini was part-author of the script.

Next he worked on the story and script of Rossellini's *Paisà*, for which he was also assistant director. 'Rossellini and I became great friends. We travelled the length and breadth of Italy, passing through that terrible inferno that was Naples in 1945. It was only then that I knew that my vocation was the cinema.'

After directing his famous comic film *The White Sheik*, which satirized the romantic Italian photo-comics, he wrote the story of *La Strada* for his wife. Unable to interest a producer, he succeeded in selling the idea of *I Vitelloni*. 'In those days', he said, 'it had a success comparable with *La Dolce Vita*.' Despite the resounding success, he still encountered the same difficulties when he once again proposed *La Strada*, but after a great struggle he had his way. The film triumphed at Venice, and Fellini and his wife achieved international fame. Yet his next film was to prove harder to mount than any of the others. At last the fifteenth producer he had approached, Dino de Laurentis, agreed to present *The Nights of Cabiria*. Then, despite two Oscars and film festival awards, Fellini faced the same stubborn resistance from producers when he proposed making *La Dolce Vita*, a film that became one of the greatest successes of all time.

Primarily, Fellini is not concerned with any message, social or religious. He can make piercing social comment, for his canvas is large, and he raises religious and theological issues because he is concerned with what ultimately concerns us all: what to believe. Above all he is that rare thing, a creative artist who sees, and presents everything that he sees, no matter how tawdry or savage. And everything he sees is transmuted into the visual poetry of a man who can see beauty in the midst of degradation. Fellini does not hate the sin and love the sinner; his secret is, he loves the sinner and *understands* the sin. In a man who deals with people this quality is called sanctity; in an artist it is called genius. And that is why to so many people Fellini has seemed to be a little of both.

It was Fellini who was anxious for me to meet Peppino de Filippo, of whom he wrote, 'I love Peppino, his theatre, his plays and the atmosphere of childish expectation which stirs the audience when he is about to make his entrance. I think the people of any country in the world would love and understand him, because of the joy he gives and the truth he shows over and over again.'

I saw Peppino's *Metamorphoses of a Wandering Minstrel* in Paris in 1963, the same year that I met Fellini. For his performance Peppino won the Young Critics' Award. There was so much improvisation that the French management was obliged to suppress the simultaneous translation over the headphones, since it would have been quite impossible to keep up with the Italians along the by-ways where their unbounded comic imagination and high spirits led them. Nineteenth-century-style gongs, played by a jaunty orchestra before tatty, red-plush curtains and even tattier scenery, accompanied the high jinks, characterized by the

marvellous costumes (designed by Franco Laurenti), the red
noses, the painted faces and the outsize bosoms. Behind it all,
keeping the ball rolling without once letting up, was Peppino,
the master of mime.

The *Metamorphoses* are taken from the libretto of a sixteenth-
century farce that was still being played as it was played eighty
years ago—and with the same design of sets. Originally the
commedia dell'arte ('of the profession') was improvised, but it had
developed its own discipline and its own scripts. It used masks
mainly, but not invariably. The actors took a simple plot, and
through rigorous rehearsals arrived at the final play (*spettacolo*).
Their technique was to embellish the rough scenario with their
improvised business, or *lazzi*, as it was called, and indeed still is,
by Italian comedians.

The elements are sentiment but not sentimentality, music, and
invariably a strong infusion of buffoonery. The proceedings may
be broken down into a stock pattern: the prologue, the plot, the
display of feminine appeal, the dialogues with their intricate
punning and word-play, the series of practical jokes, the blend
of fooling and fantasy, the plight of the lovers, the denouement
through tricks reminiscent of the history of farce from Plautus
to the Crazy Gang, and the musical finale—in the *Metamorphoses*
a tarantella. The characters are also 'stock': the Pulcinella, the
Arlecchino, the Brighella, the Capitano, the Dottore, and so
forth.

The time inevitably came when the great dramatists wrote
scenarios with fixed dialogues, even the *lazzi* being described in
the stage directions; all of it had to be repeated identically at
every performance, and much of the spontaneous originality of
the *commedia* companies became lost. But the comedy of improvisation was far from being lost for ever. It had been kept alive
over the centuries in various parts of Italy, and particularly in
Naples. Today, in our age of high-powered technological
entertainment, it still exists as a driving-force in the theatre, and
even in the Italian cinema.

Like Joan Littlewood, Peppino encourages his actors to
improvise; his plays, like the films of Fellini, develop during
rehearsal. This secret lies behind their dazzling, impeccable
timing. It is a miracle of subconscious exactitude; the stammers
are counted, the signs calculated. A year after seeing his Paris

production I was with him in Rome preparing for the 1964 World Theatre Season. On my way to meet him I stood by the Trinità dei Monti in the liquid heat of an August afternoon. The dome of St Peter's was shimmering under a veil of red and blue. Here was the eternal city, bathed in a haze caught midway between earth and sky—the Roman light, which is like no other. Leaning over the top parapet, I remembered Zola's words: 'Il y faut monter par un escalier interminable, et de là-haut on possède Rome entière d'un régard, comme si en enlargissant les bras, on allait la prendre toute.' I also thought of that multitude of great talents from Goethe to Gogol, from Macaulay to Ibsen and Henry James, who had associated themselves with the city. Their ecstatic voices still come together in a collage of international sentiments; I had no idea that so powerful and agreeable an excitement was to be found in the world. Rome projects an emotion seductive beyond all resistance. The moonlight there can seem more illuminating than the day.

I walked slowly down the Spanish Steps, past the amorous couples, the predatory photographers, the pimps and the loitering students and tourists, to the flower stalls facing Bernini's marvellous boat-shaped fountain crammed with flesh-and-blood passengers seeking the refuge of its waters to soothe their tired feet. The English tea-rooms, once owned by the Misses Babbington, were to the right; to the left was the small house in which Keats had lived and died, and where I was to spend many happy hours browsing in the small library.

The scene could have changed very little since Dickens wrote *Pictures from Italy* a century before. In our own time Tennessee Williams may have invented his Mrs Stone, watching from a *palazzo* balcony for her stealthy assassin below, but Dickens had seen the very man a hundred years earlier: 'The *dolce far niente* model, looking out of the corners of his eyes which are just visible beneath his broad slouched hat. This is the assassin mode.' Rome is eternal; only youth passes.

The sun beat down. The maze of little streets, narrow and smelling of cats, pasta and an odd scent compounded of snuff, incense and unwashed parts of the body, led to the Piazza di Spagna, which I crossed before entering the famous Greco Café, where Peppino and Laura Stainton were waiting among the ghosts of Byron, Dickens, Thackeray, Schiller and Browning.

Fellini once said to me that going to see Peppino on stage was not like going to the theatre at all—'It is as if we have been invited to dinner in a family where things end badly and instead of eating you have to witness a quarrel and are obliged to take part in it.' My personal meeting with him ended well, but hardly began happily. Neither of us could speak the other's language, and my dear Italian friend, Laura del Bono Stainton, whose unselfish and devoted work has been invaluable to me in sustaining the vitality of the Italian Theatre in London, for once failed to bring us together in spite of her great linguistic gifts.

Peppino himself recorded his reactions, which I received from him in translation, in the *Messagero* some time later.

'I had the pleasure of meeting Mr Daubeny personally on the day that it occurred to him to bring me to London to act at the Aldwych. I must confess that seeing him for the first time, I had the impression that nothing would come of it, because I suddenly became aware of how in certain ways our characters—apart from the difference in nationality—seemed so similar. He was headstrong; I was the same. He tenacious, and so firm in his proposals; I also. I, like him, running on; both ready to reject each other ... Physically, I didn't have a good impression. I was aware of a head too small in proportion to the tall and bony figure, of narrow and slightly hunched shoulders, small, round, clear eyes, a pale face, a well-made nose—but too small—a thin sharp mouth, and when he spoke he hardly moved his lips ... it was difficult to trace his teeth. With straight hair, shaven, blondish and unkempt, gradually balding, he wore an old-fashioned and crushed suit, a light shirt, rather crumpled, and a scruffily done-up tie.

Happily this melancholy portraiture went on to improve beyond recognition:

Things didn't turn out as I had imagined. I very soon realized that before me sat a man who was intelligent and lovable in every respect. In fact it occurred to me that Mr Daubeny did a great deal in showing me his admiration and sympathy. I rapidly came to do likewise ... and noticed in those small, round, clear eyes a horde of ideas, wisdom and loyalty. We both took the necessary steps to smooth things towards the signing of an agreement as soon as possible, and this actually came about after several months. The consequence of our fortunate and happy encounter is noted in the history of the theatre.

For my part, as I had shaken hands with this small, dapper-looking man, bespectacled, short and rather severe, the image of a bank manager had shot through my mind. In our meetings in real life we tend so often to impersonate ourselves as well as others. We cast ourselves in the ephemeral images of the passing scene. But Peppino, as I was to discover, wore his mask on stage —he later confessed that his trouble was 'I can't act off the stage. I just have to be myself'—and his obvious, slightly testy sincerity prevented me from putting on mine. It was an amusing situation. But a developing understanding grew from a combination of impulse, gesture and facial expression, which, being unpremeditated, created a true relationship without the sometimes false coinage of words which can bounce back like dud cheques. Together we created a language where the expression of mime revealed a practical reality, and the fact that I was performing with one of the masters of the *commedia dell'arte* made it a memorable experience.

One of Peppino's most fascinating stories needed the services of Laura Stainton, as Peppino told me of his first encounter with Luigi Pirandello in Naples in 1932. Pirandello came back-stage after seeing the de Filippo company. 'He sat quietly in my dressing-room, analysing not only the character I had been playing, but also my own personality and the process of my emergence from the one and my resumption of the other.'

Peppino had then invited Pirandello to the traditional Nativity play given in Naples every Christmas Eve and produced and performed by the local people. Pirandello was delighted. 'When we arrived', Peppino said, 'the noise was deafening. I forced my way through the crowd, and Pirandello was pushed from side to side like a football. As the time for the performance approached, the noise became intolerable. Every incident was an excuse for a fusillade of balls of paper, potatoes, rotten tomatoes —even shoes.' But no one in that audience knew that the little man with his Mephistophelean moustache and pointed beard was not the quiet solicitor's clerk he seemed, but the greatest playwright alive. 'I asked Pirandello if he wanted to leave. No—he was finding it most interesting. Suddenly something wet descended from the gods and landed on top of his shiny bald head. Furious, I took my friend's arm and fought a way out. "Good gracious!" he said, "that was nothing. I'm used to that kind of pandemonium—although I must say I think that's the first time anyone has ever spat on top of my head!" A great cresendo of booing rocked the house; we rushed back and peered through a crack in the door—the curtain had gone up, and so had Gabriel. There he was, dangling in mid air, one moment going up a foot or so, the next dropping down again. It looked as though the Devil was on one end of the rope, and poor Gabriel's feet never touched the ground. "Just like one of my own first nights," said Pirandello.'

I began to feel closer to Peppino as Laura Stainton told me something of his life, of his early years with the Molinari company, and of the romantic family made up of his sister Titina, his brother Eduardo and himself, who were the most famous trio in Italy. Their productions at the small Neapolitan theatre achieved great popularity and had a close affinity with *commedia dell'arte*, but in 1945 the brothers split, and Titina joined Eduardo's company. Eduardo became one of the more important writers of contemporary Italian theatre, and has been identified as a dominating force in the confusion that reigned during the 1940s and 1950s. With their commitment to radical socialism, his plays express a depth of power and humanity. There is also something of Pirandello in the mood and expression of his writing, and his style is reminiscent of the dialect play by Pirandello called *Liolà*, which I presented with the Catania Stabile Theatre at the World Theatre Season in 1970. (It was when Peppino had played in the original production of this play, with the author directing, that the two men had become so close.) In Athens I had already seen an exquisite production of Eduardo's *Quesi fantasasmi* (*The Ghosts*) done by Koun's Art Theatre, and in Europe I tracked down three others, *Le voci di dentro* (*The Inner Voices*), *La paura numerouno* (*The Number One Fear*), and *Filumena Marturano* (*Marriage—Italian Style*).

John Francis Lane took me to see Eduardo in his small apartment in the chic Parioli district of Rome, where he lived surrounded by china plates, cups and saucers. He presented a melancholy, detached figure who seemed, like so many great actors, to have become a victim of his own comic inventiveness, which had drawn him subconsciously into the miseries of life. He seemed far more interested in his collection of English bone china than any visit to London. While courteous and full of grace, he gave the impression that life had become a boring habit. From his great career of the past he had nothing to recapture, and from the future nothing to expect. I left this kindly, inscrutable and unsmiling host among his glittering display of porcelain.

In Rome Eduardo de Filippo can still fill the theatres, and today Peppino's appearances on the stage, television and films have made him the best-known and best-loved comic actor in Italy. My preparations to bring him to London, however, were far from plain sailing. Nothing seemed to go right, and after one particularly ragged and disturbing rehearsal, which looked rather like a game of tennis with sodden balls, I told Peppino that the cast were simply not good enough to take to the Aldwych. He told me to mind my own business. He was absolutely resolute, and said he would take the whole production to London at his own expense. I became desolate. Our tempers rose, and only the gentle wisdom of John Francis Lane, who intervened with the grace of a surf-rider jumping from one giant wave to another, prevented disaster. During the dress rehearsal I sat with Fellini and his wife, Giulietta Masina, who both left before the end because, as he told a friend later, he felt so sorry for me. But on the opening night in London a total metamorphosis had taken place. Peppino triumphed.

During the quicksands of my Peppino adventures, I caught a glimpse of the epoch of the great Duse in the person of the renowned actress Emma Gramatica, who was reputed to have been born in one of her own prop baskets. One afternoon in Rome after rehearsals Laura asked Peppino and me to go and see her. Peppino smouldered about this suggestion, but an invitation to meet Italy's theatrical legend was not to be missed, and I pushed him grumbling into a taxi.

Emma Gramatica had been born in 1875. She had been able to act in German and Spanish besides Italian, and was famous for her interpretations of the women in Ibsen, Pirandello and, especially, Shaw. Now she was a very old lady, small, curiously wistful and frail. In the company of her ex-manager and his friend, she greeted us like a young child, with cakes and tea, in a small flat decorated from top to bottom with her collection of china, photographs, medals and trophies representing an era of past glories. She still showed great vitality and those inner reserves of strength which old people preserve for special occasions; everybody knew and adored her, but Rome was hardly a city to strengthen the wavering thread of old age. She was deeply honoured that Peppino should have called on her, and to me she talked excellent English. Then, after an enormous tea, her two old gentlemen all the while peering in and out of the 'parlour' like aged spaniels, she invited herself to do a small recitation. Her confidence and authority were magnetic. She slipped from Shelley to Shakespeare, improving on both with miraculous self-confidence as though she were reciting a single piece:

> Hail to thee, blithe Spirit! Bird thou never wert
> Come day come dawn
> Love and favours pass through the roughest day
> As London Bridge saw great flakes of white falling.

One afternoon after our tea-party I wandered into the small hall. There was a loud hiss, and her manager's head popped out of his bedroom and sharply beckoned me with a flick of his head. I walked four yards and entered his bedroom. The great impresario looked very excited. He held up his finger for caution, declaring in a tremulous whisper that he had found 'it', and then proceeded to read me a beautiful letter from the great Madame Patti, which expressed all the stifled and pent-up emotions that had furnished his whole existence for many years. It seemed a sort of appeal for recognition of the fact that he existed at all. He replaced the frail enclosure that looked like green lace, and put it away in a drawer with tears in his eyes. I felt deeply touched. I had been read a romantic letter from an opera singer, and the scene itself might have come straight from Henry James.

Emma Gramatica in fact appeared for the last time in the Giovani production of *The Aspern Papers*, in which she played the hundred-year-old Miss Bordereau. Rossella Falk told me that she had been marvellous in the part in which Beatrice Lehmann had scored such a triumph in the London production.

When Miss Bordereau discovers that her hidden letters — letters from a great and long-dead poet — have been stolen, she falls to the ground. Beatrice Lehmann gave an exquisite performance, contriving a fall as memorable as that of Edwige Feuillère in *La Dame aux camélias*, and I asked her how she did it. 'One day during rehearsals I saw Madame Bussy — the widow of Simon Bussy, the painter — fall backwards to the earth when she thought there was a chair behind her. She was over ninety. She fell slowly, gently, inevitably, like a dry twig fluttering down off a tree. She looked like a little heap of dust. I practised alone and I think I got it — as near as makes no odds.'

I do not quite know what Emma Gramatica did about that scene, but I do know from Rossella Falk that the grand old actress had a habit of falling asleep, and would have to be carted in her wheel-chair behind a screen for a good snooze until her next dialogue. 'Once', Rossella told me, 'she was wheeled out for some dialogue with me. I was sitting on the sofa, and she was next to me in her wheel-chair. In the middle of my speech I noticed she was fast asleep, so, without giving anything away, I thumped the side of the sofa with all my force. She woke up and reprimanded me sharply: "Don't make such a noise!" '

Rossella Falk was herself one of the founder members of the Compagnia dei Giovani, the others being Giorgio de Lullo, Romolo Valli, Elsa Albani, Tino Buazelli and Annemarie Guornieri. They had originally come together in 1954 with the backing of the Milan theatre proprietor, Renigio Paone, and they came to the World Theatre Season two years running in 1965 and 1966.

Vittorio de Sica said of the Giovani, 'They call themselves the young ones, but they are now fully grown up. Signorina Falk is now la Signora Falk. With their enthusiasm, their spirit of enterprise and their open-mindedness they have remained young, definitely the young ones.' I first saw them perform in Sicily in the company of Peppino, Laura and John Francis Lane. In the golden haze of that magical island I felt that Pirandello had been revealed to me for the first time through the perfection of this unique ensemble and the inspiration of de Lullo, its great director.

Rossella Falk is today one of Italy's greatest stars. She has the stature, gestures and voice of a tragic heroine. Yet, at the same time, her attributes include a profound spontaneity and sense of ease that helps to bring the theatre into closer contact with every-day life. Fellini once said to me, 'She holds the attention almost like a beautiful striptease artist with a series of pure movements, by mime, without speaking. And she communicates so much joy in being on the stage that she makes one want to jump on to the stage and keep her company.' When she first came to London with the Giovani in the 1965 World Theatre Season the critics were ecstatic, one of them writing of her as 'a kind of jet-age Garbo, a female Olivier.' But Garbo was never so vivacious nor so heartbroken, never so real nor so seemingly intelligent. Rossella uses emotion with the indiscriminate violence of a flame-thrower, and stillness with breathless grace. In comedy she presents another mask that mixes eroticism and laughter into a wickedness of which only the innocent are capable. She had seemed the very incarnation of Fabbri's heroine in *La Bugiarda*, the play which had so scandalized conservative Catholic circles in Rome. In the same season she also appeared in *Six Characters in Search of an Author* in a production which revealed the heart of Pirandello's genius. Another revelation for me on that first visit in 1965 was Romolo Valli, and as I became aware of the warmth of his performances, and of his huge compassion for human weaknesses, he seemed to me to rank among the greatest come-dians of the world.

Giorgio de Lullo, the director, had a charming rambling villa on the Via Appia, and on my frequent visits the Giovani and I would sit around a little white table in the greenness of the garden talking. Seeing the company together I began to realize that they do not do Pirandello just because he is Pirandello, Italy's modern master, but also because his obsession with 'naked masks' is their own. They are trying to come to understand themselves. They have that splendid human modesty tinged with vanity that is the essence of theatrical magic.

Watching de Lullo, I saw why it had to be an Italian, Pirandello, who raised the question of the true nature of identity and of the line of division between reality and fiction. Giorgio's groomed, slightly fatigued good looks, his hands in a perpetual arabesque of explanation, suggested more a tired prince shrugging off a disastrous loss at the casino than a great director expanding the ideas behind one of his theatrical triumphs. Fabbri once told me that he had never met, in a world accustomed to diplomacy and refined duplicity like that of the theatre, a man more genuine than Giorgio de Lullo. 'He is genuine to the point of being himself sometimes defenceless. The risk is that he may lose himself at any moment by obeying his inner spontaneity and discretion.'

Six Characters returned to the Aldwych in 1966, and de Lullo's productions of this and *The Rules of the Game* were startling. The designs by Pier Luigi Pizzi added a unique sophistication and glamour to the productions and, in *Six Characters*, reflected de Lullo's emphasis on the timelessness of this fairy-tale of sorrowful creatures searching for their own identity, by rejecting the idea of setting the play, as is usually done, in the period in which it was written. De Lullo saw 'the search' as wholly acceptable, as a dramatic and poetic event unrelated to any specific time. 'This', de Lullo declared, 'is surely why Pirandello adopted the make-believe of stage rehearsal—a fiction which makes it posssible to free the characters from the limitations of their historically defined costumes and return them to the naked text.'

Our conversations always seemed to centre around Pirandello and the company's relationship to his work. 'Each one of us', wrote Pirandello, 'believes himself to be one, but that is a false assumption. Each one of us is so many, so many—as many as are all the potentialities of being that are in us ... We ourselves know only part of ourselves, and that in all likelihood the least significant.'

In contrast to his approach to *Six Characters*, de Lullo kept *The Rules of the Game* closely linked with the time when Pirandello created the play. In 1918 the playwright had not yet abandoned naturalistic theatre; the story of *The Rules of the Game* even re-echoes the classic situation of the husband–wife–lover triangle. 'The play's originality', said Giorgio, 'lies not in the plot but in its development, its language and the reactions of the characters. It becomes necessary to create unmistakably the climate in which Leone, his wife Silia and her lover gradually bring their love to a climax.'

After their second season in Britain the Giovani wrote me a letter about how they felt about London and their success:

One of the reasons we find it so fascinating to act on the Aldwych stage is that it gives us the opportunity to compete with the best theatrical groups in the world. But this experience had one further meaning for us: it gave us the sense of a great *meeting*—the meeting with the London audience at the very moment when the most noble aspirations of British culture and theatre aim at a new and more efficient dialogue among theatres and cultures in the rest of Europe.

It is universally known that peace and liberty depend chiefly on the meeting of different peoples and cultures, and on their mutual understanding. We are proud to feel that we have personally been eager witnesses and passionate participators ... We are sure that actors, directors, managers and technicians from all over the world have enjoyed this same feeling during the years that the World Theatre Season has taken place ...

Perhaps they felt that the end was near, because in February 1970, after sixteen great years, they admitted that they could no longer go on. Their last season had produced a deficit of thirty million or forty million lire, far more than they could afford. Rising costs had been mainly responsible, since all wages had gone up by an average of 13 per cent over twelve months, and they had been unable to increase their receipts in proportion, mainly because of the Byzantine laws under which the theatre operates in Italy. According to law, the take is immediately reduced by 35 per cent to pay for taxes, workers' welfare organizations, authors' royalties, theatre rent and sundry other items. Provided a list of complicated conditions is met, the Government will later return some of this money—an arrangement invented by the Fascists to ensure good political behaviour from theatrical companies. But any rebate is only a small percentage of the money originally deducted, and is further reduced by being paid indirectly through a state bank, where it incurs heavy interest. As a result, the greatest *giro* that Italy had ever known had reached the verge of collapse.

Carlo Goldoni, the eighteenth-century dramatist, had his roots in the *commedia dell'arte* tradition, but tempered his art with the sophistication of Molière. This combination was depicted in Giorgio Strehler's beautiful production of Goldoni's *The Servant of Two Masters*, which the Piccolo Theatre of Milan brought to

the World Theatre Season in 1967. The chief fascination of the
play lies in the character of Arlecchino, the servant of the title.
Ferruccio Soleri, who took the part, is the heir of Marcello
Moretti, the greatest Harlequin of the century, and he triumphantly demonstrated his right to his inheritance. His dazzling
acrobatic and juggling skills displayed in the scene where the
servant has to keep two meals going simultaneously were
irresistible. This role is as important to an Italian actor as Hamlet
is to one in England. Not until Robert Hirsch in *Les Fourberies de
Scapin* and the electrifying Jiří Hrzán in the Činoherní Klub of
Prague's production of Alena Vostra's *Whose Turn Next?* — cor-
nered by the enemy and diving at the floor boards as though they
were water — did I see anything like it again.

Giorgio Strehler himself is an austere, almost mystical, figure
who has been deified by the post-war generation of Italian actors.
All his productions carry his individual stamp, the Milanese
having nicknamed him the Toscanini of the theatre from the way
he builds his plays into equivalents of symphonies. Rightly he
claims to be the creative interpreter, and with each production
something new, however familiar its basis, is revealed. His great
rival is Luchino Visconti, and their epic differences are a part of
modern theatrical legend. Strehler has explained that for him the
aim of Italian theatre is not so much to stage perfect productions
as to create lasting organizations to promote the theatre as an
institution. Thus he believes in a theatrical community developing
through a *stabile* municipal theatre.

His genius as a director has chiefly been associated with two
authors, Goldoni and Brecht, and his stagings of the German
dramatist's work, particularly his *Galileo*, are among his most
notable achievements. Hélène Weigel said that Brecht himself so
respected Strehler that he considered the Piccolo production of
The Threepenny Opera to be better than that of the Berliner
Ensemble.

In recent years Strehler has shown signs of an aesthetic crisis.
He expressed this vividly and effectively in a staging of Pirandello's
unfinished symbolic work, which I saw in Milan, *The Giants of the
Mountains*. Strehler imagined a finale illustrating the words with
which Pirandello's son Stefano summed up how the play was to
end. I had plans to bring this production to London, but the
Aldwych proscenium was too small for the massive iron curtain

which, in Strehler's conception, came creaking down to crush the symbolic cart on which the travelling actors performed.

The year after I brought the Piccolo to London, Strehler resigned to form a company of his own on a private management basis in co-operation with his actors and technicians. For some time he had confessed to feeling stifled by the bureaucracy and political wrangling that went on in Milan between the city and the Piccolo. Then, after a year of private management, during which he staged Peter Weiss's *The Song of the Lusitanian Bogey* he returned to the helm of a public theatre, as artistic director of the Rome Stabile, a post from which he has since in turn resigned.

The Rome Stabile is one of the youngest of Italy's civic theatres. During its five years under the artistic direction of Vito Pandolfi its most highly acclaimed presentation was Giuseppe Patroni Griffi's production of *Naples by Night, Naples by Day*, which came to the Aldwych in 1968. This production was designed by Scarfiotti, whose beautiful craftmanship caught the odours of the Neapolitan gutter and the cruel lustre of an effete aristocracy. Griffi had taken two plays by the Neapolitan actor-writer Raffaele Viviani, and made a composite and exquisite entertainment which offered a musical pastiche of Neapolitan life in the 1920s and gave poignant expression to the values of resignation in the philosophy of Naples and its people.

When I met Griffi at the Rome Stabile Theatre he told me about Viviani, who had been the son of a theatre manager and had made his stage debut, as the de Filippos had done before him, acting in Naples as a child. The death of his father had forced him to join touring companies throughout Italy, making him a star of the music-hall during the years around the First World War. As a result of the war his type of music-hall satire had to be modified, and so he came to write longer sketches that eventually turned into plays. During the Fascist period his work became more and more lyrical and less attached to the reality of the day. After the Second World War, hampered by ill health, he was forced to retire from acting and died in March 1950.

Griffi felt a deep attraction to Viviani. 'I recognize the way he feels his characters. He was a vaudeville player, and so he wrote for actors who can juggle, play instruments, sing and so on. Viviani's work arose from experience which was fundamental for him: that of the café concert, of the theatre, which was then

50 (*left*). Ladislav Pesek in the Czech National Theatre's production of *The Insect Play*, designed by Josef Svoboda (1966)

51 (*above*). Ladislav Fialka of the Theatre on the Balustrade billed outside the Aldwych Theatre (1967)

52 (*below*). The author with the actor, Vaclav Sloup (*second from left*), director Jan Grossman (*second from right*) and other members of the Theatre on the Balustrade (Prague, 1966)

55 (right). The author with the playwright, Alena
Vostrá, in the courtyard of Hradčany Castle, Prague
(1969)

54 (below). The author with members of the Činoherní
Klub of Prague (London, 1970)

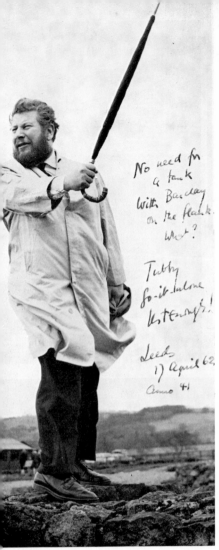

Peter Ustinov (1962)

top right). A design by Micheál Mac Liam-
: for a character from an O'Casey play

right). Cyril Cusack in *The Shaughraun*—
cy Theatre (1968)

59 (*above*). Max von Sydow as Faust and Toivo Pawlo as Mephistopheles in Bergman's production of *Urfaust* (1959)

60 (*right*). The author with Ingmar Bergman (Stockholm, 1968)

61 (*below*). The Chinese Classical Theatre from Formosa (1957)

called *Varietà*, like your music-hall. The very structure of the "variety show" helped Viviani to leap beyond the clichés which then paralysed the Italian theatre: aestheticism and Ibsenism.' Griffi had approached Viviani as a classical author whom the audience knew intimately. 'Not so as to bring to life a vocabulary and context which are old,' he assured me, 'but to give life through a modern artistic approach using formal disposition of today's art.'

Griffi is one of Italy's leading playwrights and the author and the director of the distinguished film *Il Mare*, which was, in his own words, 'totally concerned with visual images', and which starred the brilliant young actor Dino Mele. His play *Metti, Una Sera a Cena* (*One Evening at Dinner*) was one of the most successful of de Lullo's last productions for the Compagnia dei Giovani, and has since become a record-breaking film directed by Griffi himself.

Griffi told me that one of the reasons why most young writers turn to the cinema rather than to the stage is that it just is not possible to make money as a writer for the theatre, and it is rare for a play to sell to the cinema on a profitable basis, as often happens in America or Britain. It is even rarer for a successful playwright to be called in to write a film script. This is because in Italian cinema the 'author' is usually the director.

The spoken word in Italy does not correspond exactly with the written language. Playwrights have had to choose between the dramatic literature (Betti, Fabbri) and the limited, if realistic, dialects of Goldoni and de Filippo. Griffi has broken completely with literary tradition in reproducing the speech of 'the ordinary people'. He has used the slang and catch-phrases of Italian youth, and the young people going to the theatre have recognized themselves in his productions. He represents, in fact, a leading spokesman for the post-war generation of his country, applying the cinema technique of neo-realism to the stage. Originally from Naples, when he came to Rome in 1945 he brought with him the words of bars, the small apartments and the crumbling *palazzi*. 'My theme', says Griffi, 'is love. My plays are completely autobiographical, but none of them are true.'

The 1969 World Theatre Season welcomed another Italian play, *La Lupa*. The writer, Giovanni Verga, had something in common with Viviani in that he turned to his native part of Italy for his inspiration—in his case Sicily, while in Viviani's case it was Naples. His novels were admired, and some were translated, by D. H. Lawrence; his most popular plays were *Cavalleria Rusticana*, which was adapted for the libretto of Mascagni's opera, and *La Lupa*.

Verga was a forerunner of the world of Pirandello. Born in Catania in 1840, he aspired to become a writer. Unable to fulfil his ambitions in the backward Sicilian society, Verga, like others before and after him, had to go to the mainland of Italy to find a background and atmosphere suitable for his development as a writer.

La Lupa was based on a true incident—an actual sexual crime committed in Sicily at the end of the nineteenth century. The middle-aged 'La Lupa' falls in love with a young man, Nanni Lasca, who rejects her and marries her daughter, but not before submitting to seduction by his mother-in-law to be! Insanely jealous, she returns and ruins her daughter's household, eventually driving Nanni to take up an axe to kill her as the curtain falls. Verga concentrated within simple outlines on the inward intensity, the storm of conflicting passions and emotions. Magnani in an interview said that the play was 'not old-fashioned. Women have not changed. Maybe now they do not get themselves killed—they say "Who cares?" Darling, when a woman is really in love nowadays in that kind of situation she will have exactly those same instinctive reactions that are shown on the stage.'

After its original opening in 1965 in Florence at the Maggio Musicale, *La Lupa* had been seen in Russia, Austria, Switzerland and France.

I first saw the production in Paris, Magnani giving a performance which left a smouldering memory, like smoke in damp air which returns as soon as you try to push it away. At the time I thought that her portrayal must sweep the world in agony and wonder, and that this production must be seen in London. But it was an elusive phenomenon, difficult to pin down. It fell within the *mattadore* tradition, being built around a great star, Magnani. But unlike most *mattadore* or star companies, it featured exceptionally good supporting actors and a fine production from Franco Zeffirelli. However, either the cast was not available; or Magnani was ready to perform, but at the last moment a film intervened; and so it went on. Then in 1968, when I was with de Lullo in Turin, I had several calls from a young impresario called Fontana, who told me that Anna Magnani was now ready to do the play in England. I discussed it with the Giovani, and then flew to Rome to meet her in a great state of nerves.

Magnani had begun her career in night-clubs and touring companies in 1934. In 1946 she was in *Rome, Open City*, her partnership with Roberto Rossellini continuing with *The Human Voice* and *The Miracle*, though it was to break down when Rossellini chose Ingrid Bergman to star in *Stromboli*. Magnani at once set up a rival company, producing a film called *Volcano* on a similar theme and beating Rossellini by several months. In 1955 she won an Academy Award for *The Rose Tattoo*, which Tennessee Williams wrote specially for her. Through these performances she had created an imperishable living myth, like a much-loved public monument which people knew about but rarely saw. 'She's wonderful,' people would say in England. 'What have you seen her in?' you might ask. 'I can't remember, but she's marvellous.' She was, both on and off the stage, the complete incarnation of the epithets she has gathered throughout her long career: earthy, explosive, volcanic, primitive, full-blooded.

I met her in the dramatic setting of the Palazzo Altieri, of which she occupied a whole floor. Fontana and I waited for her in a small salon of great taste and vitality, and suddenly she made a superb entrance into the room with her jet black hair and her great smouldering eyes, and wearing a voluminous negligée. Her face, I saw, was fine and classical, a mask of cool serenity and gentle composure. But as she moved across the room to offer a drink, I sensed within her a power of energy and hectic obsession balanced by a feeling of insecurity — the qualities which had made her into a great artist. Behind the regal effect I was to discover an enormous simplicity and humour. She might have been a great comedienne, but, she told me, while she would love to play comedy, Tennessee Williams, Pasolini and Fellini invariably wrote tragic parts for her, seeming to see her tragically.

Magnani avoids too many social demands and loves her home by the sea, where she does everything for herself — housework, cooking and gardening. She has green fingers with flowers, like a healer's touch, and it is this 'healer's touch' — communication — that she can share with any audience in the world.

La Lupa was one of Zeffirelli's best productions. He began his career as an assistant director to Visconti on one of Magnani's most famous films, *Bellissima*, following this with productions at La Scala, the Metropolitan Opera and Covent Garden. He achieved fame in England with his historic production of *Romeo and Juliet* at the Old Vic with Judi Dench and John Stride, later directing and designing the colourful and controversial *Much Ado about Nothing* for the National Theatre. In Verga's play he concentrated on catching a true naturalistic style and avoiding all melodramatic effects. He re-created the pressure of Verga's intense realism in a stark and brooding production without falling back on his more obvious, some would say saccharine, skills.

I learnt through the 'intimate sources' so rampant in the Rome theatre that Zeffirelli was infuriated because I had brought the Giovani company to London twice. However, in spite of this indication of the minefield of gossip and intrigue which I was traversing, there were no difficulties. Zeffirelli was in fact re-covering from the facial injuries he had received in a car crash with Gina Lollobrigida. The play was re-produced with tre-mendous skill and self-control by my friend Pasqualino Pennarola, who rode the storm as steadfast as a lighthouse and, showing extraordinary perseverance, brought the production to London. Zeffirelli was also in London during the *La Lupa* run to visit his doctor, but though he was spotted sampling the night-life, he did not venture near his 'family' at the Aldwych.

The preparations were fraught with chaos. Magnani was suffering from a cold; the scenery had been lost in transit, and then would not fit on to the Aldwych stage; and the dress rehearsal had continued to half past seven of the morning preceding the first night. The curtain went up twenty-five minutes late, to rows of impatient critics, increasingly embarrassed ambassadors, and a furious gallery. Magnani's unfamiliarity with the Aldwych acoustics caused an impassioned cry of 'Voce!' from the back stalls, her voice at the beginning being barely audible to half the house. But, as the action proceeded, Magnani, as the middle-aged she-wolf of the title, began with a subdued and calculated brutality to manipulate the young couple, her daughter and son-in-law, becoming the personification of venomous, corrosive passion.

Throughout she maintained a supreme balance between proud manipulation, cringing despair and self-torment. As she bent down to snatch up a discarded shawl and shake the dust and straw from it, her fiery eyes, hunched shoulders and stooped head expressed a blazing mixture of impatience and loathing. Her carefully controlled range of a few sudden gestures — grabbing a local village gossip by the scruff of the neck and contemptuously throwing a mug of water full in his face — were sudden wild flashes, illuminating the great force of her characterization and emerging from a strange, sombre inner concentration and growing sense of malaise. Every detail of her performance, from the long, anguished stares to the slight nervous quiver of the hands and a slow, deliberate feeling of her forehead, built up to a veritable *tour de force*. Osvaldo Ruggieri as Nanni gave a moving portrayal of a village peasant caught in the storm of passions, and Manuela Andrei, as La Lupa's daughter, was tragic in her poignant anguish.

At the finish the applause was tumultuous, the audience rising to its feet cheering. Flowers were flung on to the stage with, for the English, an untypical lack of reserve. Magnani had triumphed.

As J. W. Lambert said in the *Sunday Times*, 'This is theatre, and drama, as most people still understand it — reaching us, even teaching us, imaginatively, through the concentrated representation of recognizable human beings, in a given place at a given time: about them all the accretions of sensibility and circumstance that author's, actor's and audience's knowledge and insight can bring to bear.'

La Lupa broke all box-office records for a World Theatre Season production. In it Magnani created a furore which amounted to the greatest personal and box-office success of any of the foreign seasons I have presented. It played to standing-room business, and at each performance long queues of disappointed theatregoers had to be turned away. If I had to state which I thought were the two greatest performances to have been seen at a World Theatre Season, I should unhesitatingly say that of Magnani in *La Lupa*, and that of Smoktunovsky in *The Idiot*.

The 1970 World Theatre Season followed on *La Lupa*, the play of an ex-patriate Sicilian, with the work of the most famous Sicilian company, the Catania Stabile Theatre.

No island is more magical in its history, architecture and archaeological treasures than Sicily; but the history of Sicilian drama is more difficult to trace, even though the theatre must have existed there in some form or another since the emergence of ancient Greek comedy, such as that of the Syracuse-born dramatist Epicharmus, who in the fifth century evidently exerted great influence over the development of the Sicilian-Greek comedy. Sicily is also the country of heroic folk-puppets, relics of the age of chivalry, which are fashioned in minute detail with their armour and finely worked costumes. One of the greatest living puppet masters is Emmanuele Macri, who runs the Mariano Pennisi Theatre in Acireale. His puppets have toured the world and have something in common with the Bunraku. Standing approximately three feet high and each weighing forty-five pounds, they are manipulated by rods from above. Macri, using three assistants, narrates the legendary scenes.

Although popular in Italy, the marionette has achieved its height of perfection in Sicily. In addition to the fury of shining knights re-enacting ancient battle-scenes, a lot of the stock characters, plots and mannerisms of these puppet shows are drawn from the *commedia dell'arte*.

As the opponents clash, the atmosphere is made almost unbearable by the accompanying rhythm of the operator's stamping foot. In the slack periods the barrel organ rumbles continuously with a musical buoyancy that fills the silent gaps for the enthralled audience.

Most of their stories can be traced back to specific literary works. The best-loved of them are those based on the Charlemagne saga, and Macri has 347 separate playlets in this series, from the birth of the great Charles to the death of the nearly invincible Paladin Roland at the Battle of Roncesvalles in A.D. 778. Other plays about Roland come from Ariosto's *Orlando Furioso*, and there are Crusader stories from Tasso's *Jerusalem Liberated*. But the tradition has been handed down not by the literary-minded but by the common people, through their itinerant story-telling singers, the *cantastorie*, who can be traced back at least to the fourteenth century, and who still exist today. Proud, defiant of time and eternally noble, the heroic folk-puppets of Sicily still fight their wonderful battles. Jets rumble above their ancient island, television and the movies entice their traditional audiences away, the modern world ignores them but heedlessly they continue telling their tales of a time when simple courage and steadfast virtue were all that counted.

The puppet theatre understandably became the training-ground of the itinerant actors, strolling players and touring companies before 1880, and those two great, legendary actors Grasso — who himself began as a puppeteer in his father's theatre — and Musco acknowledged it as the foundation of modern Sicilian drama, which emerged with Verga's play *Cavalleria Rusticana* together with the work of Capuana, Martoglio ('Sicily's Goldoni') and Pirandello. The rich Sicilian language, with its Greek, Spanish, French, Arabic, Byzantine and Latin assimilations, has flowered as vernacular literature for nearly a thousand years. Its vibrancy and raciness have given it a pagan earthiness much removed in sound from Italian, and the great expert G. A. Borgese, in extolling the beauty of expressiveness of Sicilian, has likened it to 'the sound of ancient Greek with its deep gutturals, reminiscent of the Arabs'. For Pirandello, Sicilian was not a dialect but an independent language, and he insisted with some justification that the hero of a play situated in Sicily, who was meant to be a typical character belonging to the Sicilian countryside — such as the hero of his *Liolà* — could only express himself in Sicilian.

It was with Pirandello's *Liolà* that I brought the Catania Stabile Theatre to London from Sicily for the 1970 World Theatre Season. Written in Sicilian on one of the playwright's trips to his native island in 1916, this ironic and uproarious comedy of deception is one of his best works. As Professor Eric Bentley has said of it, 'It has a quality all can appreciate, the more so for its rarity in both life and art today, and that is joy. It lies tantalizingly in between the extremes of beatitude and bestiality, which are increasingly the postulates of our world.'

Turi Ferro, who directed the production and took the title role, is a man of great charm and intellect, and is dedicated to the Sicilian theatre. He has, with Mario Giusti, the dynamic administrator, crusaded for the theatre of Catania. My three visits to Sicily led me to understand how, of all theatres in Italy, this one is perhaps the happiest and most fortunate through the directorship of these two enlightened men. Their theatre became a *stabile* in 1958, and *Liolà* was their greatest success, running for ten years. Its triumph throughout Italy enabled them to tour many foreign countries, including Latin America, and the culmination of this success was their London appearance, audiences finding that time had dulled none of the spontaneity and vigour of the production. Turi Ferro triumphed as Liolà, the rustic Don Juan who leaves little souvenirs of his amorous exploits all over the place—a role that almost every great comedian, including Eduardo and Peppino de Filippo (under Pirandello's direction), as well as Vittorio de Sica, has played. The rest of the cast were also magnificent: Umberto Spadaro as Don Simone, the grasping old landowner, incapable of producing his own children; the marvellous Ave Ninchi as an artful old schemer; and the whole supporting cast. They came together to create a joyous evening of an unfamiliar Pirandello.

When the curtain came down on their last night at the Aldwych (their 242nd and final performance of this production of *Liolà*), and after Turi Ferro and Umberto Spadaro had taken repeated curtain calls, I shook hands with Spadaro, remarking that he had had as much success this time as on his previous visit. He looked up with his large bloodshot eyes and said slowly, deliberately and with a wry look of mischief, 'Thank you—I come here every sixty years.'

Umberto Spadaro, born in 1904, had last appeared in London with the Grasso Troupe at the age of six in 1910. A true son of the stage—his father, Rocco, was a well-known character actor with the company of Giovanni Grasso—Angelo Musco was his godfather. He had been destined to become a comedian, but his deeply expressive features, his gestures, his way of moving, the remarkable intonation of his voice—which reminded me of Raimu, the great French actor—made him one of the most generally sought-after actors in the Sicilian theatre, until the cinema took him away from the stage for many years.

The first thing Spadaro had done on arrival in London was to give me a copy of the *Daily Mirror* dated 1910, and costing in those days one halfpenny. The headline read CHILDREN OF THE SICILIAN ACTORS NOW PLAYING IN LONDON IMITATE THEIR PARENTS ON THE STAGE, and on the front page were photographs of Spadaro, aged six, with his seven-year-old sister Gina imitating the leading lady of the company, Signora Marinella Bragaglia, and Umberto, already in the footsteps of fame, imitating Grasso himself. Thus in May 1970—sixty years and two and a half months later—Spadaro had returned to London and the West End.

There is a tradition of the children of closely knit companies in Sicily growing up with the theatre and being initiated to the stage as early as the age of three. This continues to hold true for the Catania Stabile and in *Liolà* one of an engaging trio of illegitimate sons was played by Turi Ferro's own four-year-old son Guglielmo, a mischievous black-haired rascal who quite won the hearts of the London audience. These youngsters were already proficient new members of the company, and with the veteran Spadaro in London was his own three-year-old son. Who knows, perhaps in sixty years' time he will be playing his father's part for English audiences!

10

Greece, Ancient and Modern

When I went to Athens in 1963 to negotiate for the Greek Art Theatre's production of Aristophanes' *The Birds* for the 1964 World Theatre Season, my goal was a tiny basement underneath one of the innumerable cinemas in Stadium Street. After a seemingly endless search I arrived at the cinema—the home of the Greek Art Theatre.

The blonde usherette directed me down some dark stairs leading to a small hall decorated with photographs of former productions. I turned left along a narrow corridor to a dressing-room impregnated with tobacco smoke and inundated with coffee cups, in the middle of which a middle-aged man with a Socratic countenance, in old slippers and a deep blue shirt, sat at a desk. When I knocked at the door he looked up, and his face, with its high brow and short hair tinged with greyness, reminded me of an old lion who had carried for many centuries the agonies and ideas of other worlds. From the Socratic mask there suddenly burst a look of radiant pleasure. He got up and embraced me warmly.

In Greece Karolos Koun is a legend. He is the most consistently creative man of the Theatre. Everyone seems to know him, from taxi-drivers to politicians. His small theatre is a laboratory for actors, musicians and designers. Koun sees his company as a family. They in turn look upon him with devoted love as their guide, mentor and custodian, who has given them freedom through his disciplined protection. During all our meetings, alone or with other people, he showed himself utterly dedicated to the immediate project, never allowing a slackening of pace for himself or his company. I realized the truth of what Ionesco had said, that this company existed 'to make the play live. They take over the ideas, agonies and the very worlds of other people.'

Koun told me there was to be a rehearsal that evening of Aristophanes' *The Birds*, and, observing the heaped papers and

234

the hovering actors, I resisted further attentions and we agreed
to meet at seven o'clock. After ascending the stairs and finding
my way out of the empty cinema, where a war film was being
shown, I abandoned myself to the streets and the soul of the city.

The *Blue Guide* bluntly informs us that Athens is not a beautiful
city. Architecturally it is certainly a mess, and modern hotel
investment has further scarred the pattern of the place. For a city
dominated by the miracle of the Parthenon, it is strange to find
so much dreary functionalism of design. This is the first thing
that strikes you, yet the setting is magnificent, a natural site for
a great city at the sea's edge. I looked up at the Parthenon and
thought of the millions of people who had witnessed this calculated vision of perfection; this life-force which had reigned
through the centuries, dominating land and sea; this 'love of
beauty in simplicity' which Pericles had demanded of the architect
Phidias.

When I returned, the rehearsal of *The Birds* had already begun.
The tiny semi-circular theatre vibrated with the haunting sound
of Manos Hadjidakis's music, which took the traditional choral
passages and transformed them into lyrical melodies in which
Eastern cadences and sad sweetness alternated between Byzantine
and Russian folk-music. The feathered chorus, choreographed by
Zouzou Nicoloudi, was like an ecstatic carnival as it stamped,
danced and sang, the individual members clicking their fingers
like pop singers. I was stunned by their youthful vigour and virtuosity. The lyrical music of Hadjidakis's score and the inventive
delights of Zouzou Nicoloudi's choreography, with its partridges,
pigeons, owls, water-hens, jays and larks, revived 'the Bird cult',
which Aristophanes had re-created from primitive religion. But
in Koun's dynamic approach ritualism had been dismissed and
each member of his chorus assumed an individual characterization.

Throughout the excitement Koun sat silently hunched. Only
now and then a cigarette was raised to his lips, while his brown
eyes darted around unsparingly. The pace continued, his eyes
narrowed and suddenly he stood up, his weary body becoming
a bustle of energy as he chastized an actor over some little detail
of holding a goblet; over some inappropriate expression or distracting movement that for him threatened the sublimity of the
performance.

When at last even Koun felt satisfied with the evening's work, a taxi was called and various members of the company, including whatever designers, choreographers and composers happened still to be available, were crammed and hammered into this spring-less vehicle to bump towards the port of Piraeus, driven by a mad driver more interested in his St Christopher than in the fact of oncoming traffic.

We would often have our conferences at Piraeus, with its bright fishing-boats and small yachts, where we sat in the cool evening air at rough tables, drinking *retsina* and the Piraeus *ouzo* —which, I was told, was as individual as the port itself—the sleepy silence of the sea broken only by the laughter of boys in the corner *taverna*. The table was always set with plates of shrimps, squids, goat's cheese, hunky loaves of bread, and yoghurt mixed with oil and finely chopped cucumbers, which, Koun assured me, was a powerful aphrodisiac. Sometimes there would be Turkish ham served straight from the frying-pan, fried cheese, plates of spicy olives and grilled octopus.

Koun would explain how the modern Greeks were fortunate enough to live among and absorb, day by day, the very forms, rhythms and sounds that had been observed by Homer, Aeschylus, Sophocles, Euripides and Aristophanes. 'No matter how many centuries have gone by, or whether we believe or not that our race has undergone certain alterations, we cannot ignore the fact that we live under the same sky, that the same sun shines upon us, that we are nourished by the same soil. The geological and weather conditions that influence and shape our everyday life and mode of thinking, the seashores and the distant line of the horizon, the stones and sun-dried mountains, the long sunsets, the nights, the days, and high above all this, the sky, firm and clear—these are all the same. But if Aeschylus, Sophocles and Euripides were to direct their plays today, they would, I am sure, take into consideration contemporary theatre, contemporary stage conditions and the mentality of the contemporary theatre-goer. They would not have remained attached to dead forms that no longer serve their purpose.'

It was amazing to learn from Zouzou Nicoloudi, the beautiful dancer and choreographer of *The Birds*, that it was little more than a century since their liberation from the Turkish yoke, and the theatre, like all other arts, was just beginning to regain consciousness of its existence. In other countries there were centuries of tradition to go by, but Greece, having lost the tradition entirely, was faced with the problem of creating her arts anew. The earliest attempts were based on indiscriminate imitations of foreign art both good and bad, the influences of which Zouzou felt could still be traced. Dance fared no better than theatre. Efforts were made to transplant foreign ballet to Greece, which resulted in middling or bad imitation.

But then something happened. In 1927 a Greek poet, Angelos Sikelianos, with his American wife Eva, strove to revive the Delphic idea, and decided to arouse the interest of international culture in a unique gathering at Delphi, the aim of which was to assemble all eminent cultural personalities of that time for a world-wide exchange of ideas. For the first time in two thousand years the chorus of Greek tragedy sang the verses of Aeschylus to Byzantine music and danced to the rhythms of the traditional folklore. Peasants came down from the summits of Parnassus, bringing with them their traditional musical instruments, and for the first time an exhibition of folk-art was organized.

The Delphic Revival was a great breakthrough. As Zouzou explained, 'We rediscovered the unlimited treasury of our traditions, the roots of which go far back and have their beginnings in primeval religious worship—deep roots which have managed to survive four centuries of slavery. We still find them unbelievably alive in popular song and dance, in religious rituals, and especially in the very characteristic Greek rhythms. The traditional Greek metres are basically odd, and the same rhythms are to be found in the ancient metres. It is truly extraordinary that today they still exist in the songs of our country as well as in our dances, and it is perhaps the lack of symmetry which gives Greek music its lively and primitive character.'

Ancient Greek drama evolved from the dithyramb, a hymn connected with the worship of Dionysus. Originally fifty singers and one leader sang and danced in honour of the god. Gradually the leader came to speak a few lines and the song and dance acquired a plot. Drama was born, and to the one actor a second was added, and then another.

In seeing various productions in Greece I had been interested in the use made of the chorus. In the last production I had seen, the plot had come to a stop at their entrance; the chorus started their action, and then ceased while the plot continued. I mentioned this to Zouzou, who said she felt this was a mistake. 'The presence of the chorus should be so strongly interwoven with the action that entries should not create a break in the continuity of the action, but on the contrary should be a dynamic extension in space, and this movement of the group as mass should be the first choreographic consideration. The movement should not be a sequence of postures that appear copied from representations on museum vases, giving an impression of mummified figures. The artist who painted those vases caught a fleeting movement full of life, and one has the impression that the figures will dance right out before us! We, on the contrary, often try to reconstruct the movement from the figures, and the result is a lifeless group of moving limbs and spoken words lacking pulsation and providing no emotion. The elaboration which goes into minute details must always have absolute justification.'

One evening Manos Hadjidakis, the composer of the incidental music to *The Birds* and to Jules Dassin's film *Never on Sunday*, took me to hear *bouzouki* playing and singing and dancing. He showed me the small cafés and shops which he had frequented as a young man, entranced by the 'glass-like echo' of the *bouzouki* and by the insistent, penetrating sound of the *baglamas*, dazed by the grandeur and depth of the melodic phrases—a stranger to the performers, young and without strength, who had suddenly 'believed that the song I was listening to was my own, utterly my own story'.

When his funds ran out he applied to Koun for a job and stayed with the company for a year. He continued to write music, taking as his inspiration the traditional folk-songs he had discovered in his youth in the *bouzouki* cabarets, then unpretentious, unfashionable and without star names or exploitation by the tourist industry.

The main singer that night, who led the traditional long line of performers on the stand—singers and *bouzouki* players in the front row, behind them guitars, drums, piano and the electric violin—seemed truly inspired and earned the acclamation he received. His voice was guttural and virile, his songs of lamentation completely untheatrical, undramatized. Suffering is accepted as a part of destiny in the art of the *bouzouki*, yet without any element of self-pity or masochism. Powerful, but not rousing, its concern is to catch the precise feeling of the listeners' despair, but without rendering it defeatist or self-indulgent. It is the music of man who will persevere despite his fate, but who needs the cry of his song in order to continue.

Another great collaborator of Karolos Koun's is the designer and painter Yannis Tsarouchis. One of the most delicate of Greek painters, he is certainly the most distinguished and versatile stage designer in Greece. He has exposed the modern in the classical, and has created a personal mythology of contemporary types, as in his splendid decors for *The Birds* and *The Persians*.

I spent many hours in his studio watching him at work. When he conceived the first design for *The Persians* he showed it to me, and I said it was wonderful. 'You are wrong,' he said, and turned it over still wet on to a piece of blotting paper; the resulting image produced all the dark, mythological antiquity of Mycenae.

The Birds is set in Cloud-cuckoo-land, an airborne Utopia created by the birds midway between heaven and earth. To it flock a procession of fantastic earthly figures – bad poets, double agents, bureaucrats, parricides and parasites of every sort. From heaven the angry gods descend—Iris, Poseidon, Heracles—but are treated with scant respect while birdland continues in festive song and dance. *The Birds* is an amalgam of music-hall, satire, propaganda, lyricism, slapstick and bawdy humour. Above all, it is fun and celebration—an example of the exuberance and irreverence of the Greek temperament which can still delight us after more than two thousand years.

Of his designs Yannis said, 'I have tried to accompany the production with a setting wholly based on a sense of correspondence between present-day and ancient Greek life. I humanized the nest of Epopos, making it a strange country mansion, just as all the birds in Aristophanes are strangely humanized. I made the sky in this work black, because, besides being unwilling to reproduce ancient scenery (of which we are, in any case, totally ignorant), I felt that to imitate by any material means the sacred air of Greece would be sacrilegious, particularly where a classical Greek play is concerned. I preferred instead to introduce the colour of the sky in some of the plumage of the birds or in the costumes, and in a number of these I have followed the ancient models of Aristophanes' age very closely wherever it does not conflict with the spirit of the production.'

Koun has always relied on Yannis's deep knowledge of theatrical culture, and the little I know of Greek classical theatre is the result of many, many discussions I had with him. He is a wonderful companion, if one can find him, reminding me with his continual expression of wonder of a lost clown—an impression he accentuates by a small ill-fitting hat perched on the top of his head, making him look like a seagull.

Before he left Greece to settle in Paris he gave me some of the marvellous designs from his collection—mementoes I shall always treasure of an enchanting companion and a wonderful painter.

The London production of *The Birds* had been a great success, and it seemed important that the Greek Art Theatre should return to consolidate this; in fact they were the only company from the inaugural year to return for the second season. In 1965, as well as *The Birds* they brought with them *The Persians* of Aeschylus.

The *Sunday Telegraph*, who were sponsors for the 1964 and 1965 World Theatre Seasons and whose Philip Ashworth and Duff Hart-Davis were such enthusiastic fellow-workers in launching the whole World Theatre venture, decided to commission a special team to cover the whole operation for the second year. With Ian Dallas as reporter, and Peter Keen as photographer, our expedition to Greece set out in September 1964. Dallas's brief was to compile a World Theatre preview, describing in detail how each of the visiting companies worked at home. He watched from the wings as plans for the 1965 visit took shape: 'The forces of the Greek first wave were assembled and the array was formidable. Rehearsals contained that same thrill that must exist at the Royal Astronomical Society when Hoyle's mathematics etch out a new vision of the universe. With the elation went caution. Koun and Daubeny would sit huddled in conference.' Peter Keen went out to photograph the actors as they re-created a moment of history by standing on the Sound at Salamis—the place from which the Persian forces had watched the annihilation of their fleet in 480 B.C.

The Persians is a great popular war play by a great warrior, who directed it, choreographed it and composed the music himself. It marked the height of Aeschylus' popularity. He had played a prominent part on the battlefield at Marathon in 490 B.C., as he had ten years later at Salamis, the battle which, as Herodotus

62 (*left*). Kabuki Theatre, Japan: the author with Baiko (Tokyo, 1967)

63 (*centre*). Nō Theatre: Manzaburo Umewaka being helped on with his costume backstage (1967)

64 (*bottom*). Nō Theatre: eight-year-old Hisaharu Hashioka with Kenzo Matsumito in performance (1967)

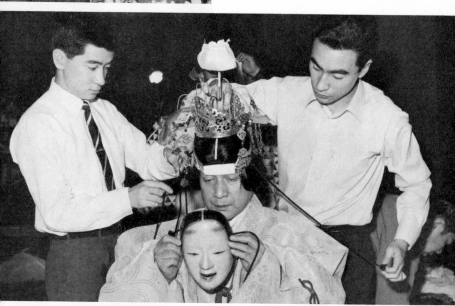

(*far left*). Bunraku: the author receiving
truction from Monjuro Kiritake and puppet
pan, 1967)

(*top left*). Bunraku: Monjuro Kiritake and
ppet in performance (1968)

(*centre left*). Warren Finnerty of *The Connection*
mpany outside Wyndham's Theatre (London,
51)

(*bottom left*). The author with Lee Strasberg
ew York, 1965)

(*above*). James Baldwin and Abraham Albert
nio at dinner with the author in London (1965)

(*right*). The author with members of the
gro Ensemble Company at the Aldwych
eatre (1969)

(*below*). The directors of the Negro Ensemble
rald S. Krone, Douglas Turner Ward and
bert Hooks (1969)

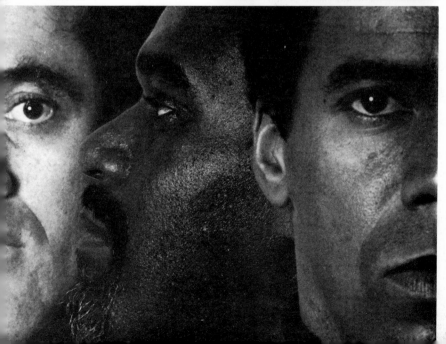

72 (*above*). A World Theatre Season first night at the Aldwych Theatre, London

73 (*right*). Molly Daubeny with Noël Coward and the author at Les Avants, Switzerland (1969)

74. The author outside the Aldwych Theatre during the World Theatre Season

puts it, 'saved Greek independence'. When *The Persians* was first performed in the Theatre of Dionysus there were two days of celebration in honour of the author, who was borne through the city in triumph as though he were Themistocles, the commander-in-chief, himself.

Aeschylus is known to have written some ninety plays, of which only seven survive. *The Persians* is probably the earliest extant, and no one was better qualified to write such a war tragedy. Step by step the action mounts towards its tragic climax: the agonizing wait for news from Greece; presentiments and fears of the Chorus of the Elders and of Queen Atossa (mother of King Xerxes, the leader of the expedition); the announcement of the Persian defeat and the tremendous description of the sea battle by the messenger; the lament and invocation of the dead king, Darius; and the appearance of the Chorus bewailing the humiliation and destruction of his army and his splendour. The catastrophe to the Persians is triumph for the Greeks; so the play is at the same time a tragedy and a paean to victory. This was exactly what Koun achieved in his memorable production.

During the rehearsal period for *The Persians* I watched Jani Christou, the composer, at work. In writing the music, he said, he was not interested in contributing mere background effects. What attracted him was the possibility of using the chorus as a means of generating the raw material of tragedy—the primitive, basic emotions.

'This I have tried to do by setting words and lines in such a way as to create patterns of sheer self-sustained vocal sound of varying complexity. Actual chanting was a secondary consideration and, wherever it is used, occurs as only one of several other "acoustical" happenings. For instance, there are frequent places in the score calling for several members of the chorus to deliver different bits of text, simultaneously and with different dynamics.

'None of this could have been possible without Karolos Koun, who had the formidable task of making it all appear spontaneous and natural. When I first told him how I intended to write for the chorus, I expected him to reply that that sort of thing is all right for a highly trained group in some contemporary opera company but not for the theatre. To my surprise he simply said, "Let's try it!" We did, and it seemed to work.'

Q

It was over lunch one day with Michael Cacoyannis, the Greek film director, that I received a particularly illuminating view of the contemporary theatre in Greece. He told me how the instinctive understanding of the Greeks for tragedy had been harnessed to a deliberately created stylistic approach, which originated with Photos Politis in the 1930s and continued to make its impact, without undue surprises or disappointments, in the hands of such expert producers as Dimitrious Rondiris and Alexis Minotis. To call the style of these productions 'classical' in the purely academic sense would be false. Centuries of slavery and silence lie between the birth of the great tragedies and their reappearance on the Greek scene. An apter description would be 'an evocation of a classical style, in keeping with modern Greek sensibilities'.

Greek revue, on the other hand, sprang directly from the subsoil of Greek humour and political satire, and reached its peak of glory in the years before the war, when an army of brilliant comedians and satirical writers provided the most vibrant form of living theatre. But between these two extremes lies the main body of seething, fighting, gallantly aspiring or meekly compromising (according to its commercial needs) Greek theatre. Or perhaps I should say Athenian theatre, for, with the exception of Salonika, which boasts a National Theatre of its own and two resident companies, Greek theatrical activity is restricted to the capital, with touring expeditions fanning out in all directions. This theatre, which operates on the usual commercial pattern, is very much alive in terms of a steadily increasing public interest. A company that does not find a hit will scrape through by putting on four or five plays in one season (staging costs in Greece are still low enough to be recoverable within a matter of days). But the overwhelming majority of these plays are foreign—predominantly French, English and American—and the almost total absence of original, exciting playwrights, who should supply the natural breath of a country's theatrical life, is a great drawback.

Greece continues to produce outstanding actors, of whom the greatest today is, in my view, Dimitrios Horn. The most eclectic of performers, he can jump from Shakespeare to Hadjidakis's musical, *Street of Dreams*—in which he danced and sang—with the consummate ease and assurance of a Fred Astaire. Before founding his own company in 1952, he had worked with Elli Lambetti, one of the most important actresses in Greece, and

George Papas, who died a few years ago. Obviously the strong personality of this actor had made a great impression on Horn. When Horn formed his own company he did, among other things, a production of *The Late Edwina Black*, with a formidable cast: Horn as the husband, Papas as the detective, Lambetti as the young girl and the late Christina Kalogerikou (then over seventy-five years old) as the maid. The play had been a West End success for me in 1949, and Horn had seen my London production with Catherine Lacey, Raymond Huntley and Stephen Murray. His company lasted three years, during which it toured Egypt, Cyprus and Turkey, and, with Lambetti as Ophelia and Papas as Claudius, Horn did a particularly distinguished *Hamlet* which excited the admiration of Lawrence Durrell, who after seeing it brought two exquisite ceramic plates round to Horn's dressing-room as a tribute. Lambetti and Papas made up the strongest team that existed at that time in the commercial theatre. After this they disbanded, and Horn did wide repertory work with leading Greek companies.

After he had left drama school Horn had begun his professional life in 1940 with the Greek National Theatre, which, headed by Alexis Minotis and Katina Paxinou, I brought to the 1966 World Theatre Season. Originally founded in 1900 by King George I of Greece, this great company was reopened in 1932, under state auspices. Alexis Minotis became the company's artistic director, and was shortly joined by his wife Katina Paxinou, a former opera singer and perhaps better kn wn to the British and American public for her film performances, particularly in *For Whom the Bell Tolls* and *Rocco and His Brothers*. Minotis formed the backbone of the company, and it is he who has been mainly responsible for maintaining their high standards. As he told me, he has always felt the revival of the ancient Greek tragedy to be 'a kind of national duty'. Since then they have presented plays from the world repertoire at their home theatre in Athens. Their main concern has always been the revival and reinterpretation of the ancient Greek classics, many of which they have performed in the open air in the Theatre of Herodes Atticus at the foot of the Acropolis as part of the Athens Festival, and in the vast 16,000-seat theatre at Epidaurus.

One of the company's greatest triumphs, their epoch-making production of *Electra* with Katina Paxinou, had been seen in

London in 1939, together with *Hamlet* with Alexis Minotis. These
two productions are still remembered, yet despite the company's
many international tours, which had built up the ensemble's fine
reputation, the 1966 World Theatre Season was the first time
London had seen them since that time. The three productions
they brought to this season, *Hecuba* by Euripides and *Oedipus Rex*
and *Oedipus at Colonus* by Sophocles, were all directed by Minotis,
who also played Oedipus in the two dramas.

In *Oedipus Rex*, as the ill-fated king of Thebes, who is driven
to put out his eyes by the terrible realization that he slew his own
father and took his own mother as wife, Minotis was partnered
by Paxinou as Jocasta. In Sophocles' last play, *Oedipus at Colonus*,
said to have been written when the dramatist was ninety years
of age, Minotis showed the blinded Oedipus in a wholly different
frame of mind, purged and healed and seeking the eventual peace
of death at the sanctuary of the Eumenides. To all three of the
National Theatre's productions Minotis's direction brought an
austere and telling simplicity, particularly effective in his fluent
control of the Chorus. The company's greatest triumph certainly
came with Katina Paxinou's outstanding performance in the
title role in Euripides' brutal tragic classic, *Hecuba*, probably
written in the same year as *Oedipus Rex* (about 425 B.C.). Her portrayal of the tragic Trojan queen, cruelly avenging herself on her
Greek captors, was superlative, breaking from moments of still
calm into the agonies of tragic grief. Paxinou more than lived
up to her reputation as the great tragedienne of Greek theatre.

After Koun's first two successful visits to the World Theatre
Season at the Aldwych, I had suggested to Peter Hall that he
might be asked to do a major production for the Royal Shakespeare Company at Stratford. My own choice would have been
Oedipus with Paul Scofield, but this was not possible, so Peter
offered him *Romeo and Juliet* for September 1967, by which time
the Greek Art Theatre would have made its third visit.

He had many worries about his production—all the more so
since this was his first one outside Greece. I had by this time
gained an insight into the way Koun creates a production.
Conversation with him at these moments takes on a living
rhythm with a counterpoint of themes, ideas and thoughts, of
questions overlapping and supplanting one another. At moments

he would become exalted with some new idea—a man with a mystic illumination—only to be slapped down by some creeping ghost of doubt. At these crises of helplessness he would turn to some trusted colleague for reaffirmation. This had happened even with *The Birds*, which was already an established success in Athens, and when he put on in London *The Persians* (1965), *The Frogs* (1967) and *Lysistrata* and *Oedipus Rex* (1969), all as world *premières*, I stood by like the family doctor in constant consultation, and was often able to help him without offending his professional pride.

Now, while preparing for *Romeo and Juliet* at Stratford, he once again confided his worries to me. 'I don't want to disappoint you or Peter Hall in any way, and above all I don't want to add some trivial *Romeo and Juliet*, but to *try and do something special* with the play. That is why I must believe in what I am doing, and not act on the impetus of sheer ambition or do something that would merely flatter my vanity. I know my inhibitions, and I know that I must feel passionately sure of what I do in order to get properly worked up and let myself go. You know me and understand what I mean.'

Yet, despite his trials and difficulties, he finally succeeded in producing a new illumination of Shakespeare's play. Koun interpreted *Romeo and Juliet* as a sombre, doom-laden tragedy of fate. He saw Verona as a decaying, gloomy city steeped in manifestations of evil and hate which are purged by the sacrifice of the 'star-crossed' lovers. Koun's vision of grim foreboding and his famous control of ensemble detail produced something quite stunning and original. As Alan Brien wrote in his review in the *Sunday Telegraph*:

> Gone is the sunny Mediterranean dazzle of Zeffirelli and Peter Brook. The days are hot but almost as overcast as the nights. As might be expected from the director of *The Frogs* and *The Persians* in the Aldwych World Theatre Seasons, the proles of Verona who gather silently to watch their betters fight and frolic provide a memorable human backdrop to the aristocratic tragedy. And Mantua, in the aftermath of the plague, is vividly established by a few apathetic, hobbling cripples haunting the dark alleys.

His mature, deeply perceptive reading, and the fine performances of Ian Holm and Estelle Kohler, made this a prime example of the cross-fertilization of creative ideas which the World Theatre Seasons have so often engendered. Alan Brien concluded his review with the following words: 'The magisterial fluidity of the action, the striking contrasts between the duellers and revellers and their world outside, the careful individualization of the tiniest roles—all this is unmistakably his own. Here is one of the great Shakespearian productions of our generation.'

In 1967, when *The Birds* and *The Persians* were about to descend on London once again, bringing with them *The Frogs*, the colonels' revolt broke out in Greece. The telephone rang, and there was Koun asking me to come to Athens immediately. He obviously could not go into details as the lines were tapped. Leaving the Bremen Theatre playing Wedekind's *Spring Awakening* and Bob Muller's *Die Unberatenen* at the Aldwych in the capable hands of their director, Peter Zadek, I immediately flew to Athens, and went straight to see him. He broke the news that the company still had not received permission to leave the country. What should he do about the scenery? If it did not leave immediately it would not arrive in London in time. We tackled the first problem by dispatching the lorry-driver with the scenery and costumes. He spoke only Greek, but he set off at once across Europe, his destination 'Aldwych Theatre, London'.

Then, weaving my way between tanks of every calibre, I made straight for the British Embassy, hoping for some help from the Ambassador. Standing in the cool drawing-room, with the distant throb of the tanks below in the square, I felt as if I had stepped into the enamel glaze of a society comedy by Somerset Maugham with settings by Cecil Beaton. Cool, poised and detached, they listened to my story. When I finished I was told that there were no diplomatic relations between the two countries, and help from the Embassy was impossible. There the conversation ended. I was politely shown out by the butler. It had been like talking to effigies in a waxworks.

Standing in the street, by now completely oblivious to all the turmoil around me, I decided to enlist the aid of Mr Close of the British Council. I went to his flat, where he helped me to draft a passionate appeal to the colonels. Then once again I wove my way between the tanks, to deliver it to the Foreign Office, and tottered up the hill to Dimitrious Horn's flat, expecting arrest at any moment. Two days later the permission came through!

Thus the Greek Art Theatre arrived in London for their third visit. In 1968 there was no Greek representation at the World Theatre Season, but in 1969 Koun was back for the fourth time, now with two entirely new productions. While preparing for this visit he wrote to me with his characteristic frankness and fervour, 'I am in a fever to get things organized for the World Theatre Season.' He was impatient to complete all his work and preparations, including his productions of *Measure for Measure* and *Waiting for Godot*, for that year's season in Athens, so as to be able to 'concentrate for the six following months on *Oedipus* and *Lysistrata*, to which I want to give my full self, both for the creative urge and for the idea of strong productions of Ancient Greek Drama at the World Theatre Season ... To be honest, at times I am getting panicky and then again regain my self-assurance. I expect that as soon as I get somewhat on the way things will go well.'

In fact the Greek Art Theatre once again astounded London with Koun's masterly interpretation of Sophocles' *Oedipus Rex*. Stately, even sombre, the play, hailed by Aristotle as the most perfect Greek tragedy, was spelt out relentlessly. Giorgios Lazanis was a reserved and calculating Oedipus, keeping his destiny to himself, while Angelika Kapelari was a powerful Jocasta.

As a contrast, Koun gave us Aristophanes' *Lysistrata*. The Athenian women, under the resolute management of Nelly Angelidou as Lysistrata, refuse sex to their men until they stop fighting, taunting them with modern Greek songs and dances and snapping their fingers to the beat. Pahidon Patrikalakis's inventive, vivid set, his masks and his colourful, mischievous costumes — making the characters look chubby and ridiculous in their multi-coloured robes, their grotesque battle-tunics or their matronly aprons — set just the right note for Koun's production. This anti-war comedy, written against a background of bloodshed, famine and misery, carried the same message for 1969 as it had in 411 B.C.: 'Make love not war!'

Koun is one of the great directors in the theatre today. His first visit to London brought his work international fame, and his influence expanded throughout Europe. His company is a unique memorial to a unique and much-loved man. In the classic theatre his work has given focus and immediacy to the ancient Greek drama, revitalizing it and rescuing it from a tradition in which it had seemed to have become fixed so immutably.

Koun's great friend, the poet Elytis, has said of him, 'One day, when we are gone, people in the corridors and back-stage will be talking of the "Age of Koun". Historians will justly associate him with that dawn which appeared on the Greek horizon about 1935 and which marked a profound renaissance.'

I I

Berlin and Eastern Europe

The war had been over for ten years and I had been to Germany several times before, but on the day in 1956 when I flew to Berlin to arrange the first visit to London of Bertolt Brecht's Berliner Ensemble I felt a distinct sense of uneasiness. Partly it may have been the effect of taxi-ing in on the vast grey apron of Tempelhof Airport, that frowning monument to the Third Reich's cult of arid grandeur, partly the uncanny neatness of the streets that led to the city's then still-ruined centre. Their garbage bins were ranged scrupulously with the tidiness not of life but of a stage-set arranged ready and waiting for a sinister drama to be enacted, and their window-boxes were as bright as children's toys. As we drove towards the Brandenburger Tor and finally past the Tiergarten, with its gaping, shell-pocked villas and the thin undergrowth thrusting out of the sandy Prussian plain, I reflected how infinitely remote it all seemed from the Germany of Max Reinhardt's heyday in the decade before the Nazis' rise to power.

In my opinion Max Reinhardt was the greatest figure in modern German theatre. His genius was as universal as his taste for life. There was no consistent Reinhardt style, but a continuous fusion of detailed ingredients of production into a rhythmic whole. Drawing from the influences around him, he was at one with Gordon Craig in proclaiming the theatre as an all-embracing art to which actors, authors, musicians, designers and craftsmen all had their various contributions to make. But he went further than Craig ever did, because of his unfailing ability to draw on any period, any school of acting or design, any spirit or mood of any age that would suit him best. The hallmark of a Reinhardt presentation was the rightness of whatever choice he made.

If Salzburg after the First World War became the artistic Mecca of the world, it was due entirely to Reinhardt's influence. From his magical palace, Schloss Leopoldskron, just outside the city he ruled in style, his art supreme throughout Europe. He had been fortunate in his moment. Stanislavsky was already pushing realism to the verge of symbolic pattern and simplifying the ensemble of acting to a degree hitherto unknown. The Russian Ballet was bringing forth new and vivid blooms. Reinhardt became the great eclectic director of the day, borrowing from Baroque pageant, the Elizabethan apron-stage, the medieval mystery, the theatre of the ancients and the Nō plays of Japan. As James Laver has written of him in his admirable book, *Drama: its Costume and Décor*, 'Reinhardt's importance lies in his capacity for using all the possible means of theatrical presentation, each at its appropriate moment, in order to get the maximum effect from each piece, and to fuse the manifold ingredients of theatrical production into a single jewel. No one has quite taken his place.'

London acclaimed him with *The Miracle*, which Cochran presented at Olympia in 1911, and *Oedipus Rex* at Covent Garden in 1912, a production which began a fresh revival of interest in Greek tragedy and which led ultimately to the exciting and dynamic productions of Karolos Koun. Yet the years of triumph were to end in 1933, and his letter of resignation from the Deutsches Theater addressed to Goebbels's Ministry is a masterpiece of underplayed irony:

I came to the 'Deutsches Theater' in 1895, as a subject of the old Austro-Hungarian monarchy. So, for nearly four decades I have worked for this institution, as actor, teacher, director and administrator. It is not for me to assess the value and influence of my work. But here are the undisputed facts. During this period the 'Deutsches Theater' has been the leading German theatre at home and abroad. All major isms and trends in current drama have begun at this theatre ...

My love of the German character is unshakable, though at present spurned. Truth, determination and straightforwardness are natural German characteristics. So I am confident that my bond with Germany which I have to advertise, grateful though I am, cannot be denied.

But New Germany cannot stand seeing a member of the Jewish race in an influential post. I am Jewish and even if personally unaffected I should be obliged to protest at the atmosphere of intolerance. A theatre withers without public good will and patronage.

To decide to sever my connection with German theatre was not easy. I lose a harvest of thirty-seven years' hard work. I lose my home. But as the state is determined to create a situation where I cannot fulfil my work, it is only logical that I hand my work over to the state, is it not?

It is part of Germany's wealth, and my satisfaction at having contributed the best years of my life to its betterment eases the bitterness of my departure ...

By a sad touch of irony Reinhardt ended his days running a school of drama in Hollywood, yet his influence was as universal as his genius. Through Erwin Piscator, the initiator of 'epic' theatre, he is directly linked to the work of Bertolt Brecht.

During many of my post-war visits to Berlin I called to see Erwin Piscator at his home and later in his office at the Free People's Theatre. Brecht had once referred to him as 'one of the most important theatre men of all time'. I found that he seemed to have lost little of the fire, enthusiasm and enormous good humour which had sustained him through the difficult times of the 1930s. 'How is it you look so young?' I once asked him. He laughed, and with a wave of his arm indicated the three or four pretty girl secretaries who were sitting in his office. Short, pink-faced, blue-eyed, with a massive shock of white hair, he seemed untroubled by age even two or three days before his death in 1966.

On this occasion we talked for hours about the German theatre between the wars, and the part Piscator himself had played with his multi-media concept, the 'epic' theatre. He told me how an experience during the First World War, when he had found himself unable to advance in the face of enemy attack, had convinced him that the theatre in which he had been trained was entirely unsuited to the realities of the world. Accordingly, after being discharged, he founded his Proletarian Theatre in 1919. Here he expounded *Zeittheater*, where art came nearer to journalism and immediate actuality. 'The word *Zeittheater*, or present-day theatre, has a somewhat ominous sound,' he told me. 'But I have always considered the "present-day theatre" as a very serious, authentic theatre, which represents a view of the problems of the times.' At the Volksbühne, which he ran from 1924 until 1927, he further enlarged his ideas of 'epic' theatre.

Berlin was astounded by the scope, originality and sheer technical brilliance of the productions which Piscator launched at the Theater am Nollendorfplatz. For his production of Toller's *Hoppla Wir Leben* he shot nearly ten thousand feet of film, using four projectors and massive settings. *Rasputin* was played inside a vast globe which split to reveal two stage levels. So much heavy machinery did he pile on the stage that it was necessary during his two-year tenure to use reinforced concrete to support the creaking boards.

His last work at the Volksbühne was *Thunder over Gotland*, for which he was finally dismissed. He described for me the setting he had used in this play about a revolt by fishermen in the year 1400, and how he had introduced film of Lenin and the Chinese Revolution. The amalgam of art and politics which 'epic' theatre provided did not amuse the authorities.

I discussed Brecht's work with Piscator on numerous occasions. 'We were brothers,' he said. 'He had a tremendous sense of humour but he also had a great sense of taking things away and using them for his own purpose.' In Piscator's view, Brecht had alienated himself from the German character. ' "Germans", Brecht would say, "are emotional and pathetic." Brecht could have been this too, but he made the opposite of it. He was a mixture of reasoning and sobriety. Where he could have described actual events, Brecht's plays were only rarely concrete. When he wrote his "political poetry … he always wanted to write for eternity, valid for all times".'

Piscator spent the years of Nazi dominance in exile, first in Moscow and later in New York. 'The bad thing was that the Nazis continued some kind of theatre art—in a way they simply returned to the old style. Nothing new was developed; there were neither new plays nor new methods. I was asked by Goebbels to return. I said, "Not until Goebbels has gone." '

The most important figure to emerge in the post-war German theatre, however, is Boleslaw Barlog, who was responsible for reviving and rebuilding the Schiller-Theater in West Berlin, which reopened its doors to the public in 1951. His company is today probably the best in Germany. Under his direction they presented two remarkable plays at the 1964 World Theatre

Season: Max Frisch's *Andorra*, with the brilliant actor Martin Held playing the main role, and Goethe's *Clavigo*.

In November of the same year they travelled to New York, where they appeared at the Lincoln Center in the newly opened New York State Theater. Their production of Schiller's *Don Carlos* and Zuckmayer's *The Captain of Köpenick* met with resounding success.

Carl Zuckmayer is among Germany's most interesting playwrights. Born in 1896, he worked with Brecht in the 1920s, and his favourite targets have always included nationalism and Prussian militarism. In 1970 London had a chance to see the Schiller-Theater's presentation of *The Captain of Köpenick*. This, with *The Devil's General*, is perhaps his most revealing work. More than any other contemporary plays, they show an artist's understanding of the character and mood of Germany's traumatic destiny.

The Captain of Köpenick deals with the Germany of Kaiser Wilhelm, and is based on an actual event reported in the newspapers. A shoemaker, Wilhelm Voigt, steals an officer's uniform and leads a squad of soldiers to the Town Hall, where the mayor is arrested and the building raided. As a satire on German bureaucracy and the cult of militarism it is successful and extremely amusing.

The Schiller also brought with them in 1970 for two packed matinées Beckett's *Krapp's Last Tape*, one of the most acclaimed World Theatre Season presentations, directed by the author himself with Martin Held giving a riveting and definitive interpretation of this formidable monologue.

Meanwhile the main problem of the post-war German theatre has been a shortage of good native material. But today at last the situation seems to be changing. It is perhaps significant that the most outstanding of the younger generation of authors and playwrights appear to be preoccupied with the themes of guilt and atonement. Of these the best-known are Peter Weiss, author of *The Investigation*, a moving, poetic reconstruction of the Auschwitz trials, and Rolf Hochhuth, whose *The Representative* condemned the lack of positive action on the part of the Papacy in opposing Hitler's 'Final Solution' for the Jews. Both these plays were first shown in West Berlin in productions by Piscator.

One other author, though far less well-known, who should perhaps be mentioned in any brief survey of post-war German literature, is Wolfgang Borchert, who during and after the war worked in a Hamburg theatre and cabaret. After being severely wounded at the Russian Front, he was sentenced to death for making 'defeatist' remarks about the regime. Yet the Nazis pardoned him and returned him to the east—in itself only one degree less than a death sentence—from where he was in the end discharged with his health broken. He died in Basel in 1947 at the tragically early age of twenty-six, but not before he had written some of the most heart-rending poetry and stories, as well as one play. His message, totally tragic, desperate and pessimistic, flows from his pages like tears of blood: it is a despairing plea for justice, understanding and sympathy addressed to a cruel, self-destructive and unconcerned world.

It was this aspect of Germany's legacy which was uppermost in my mind when I went to negotiate for the Berliner Ensemble to come to England. Past the frontier, every landmark in East Berlin carried the marks of sudden, mindless savagery. There, on what remained of the Unter den Linden, stood a stumpy annexe which was all that was left of the Adlon, the grand old hotel where Escoffier concocted sauces for Kaiser Wilhelm II. There, on what remained of the Friedrichstrasse, stood the Ministry from which Goebbels had broadcast hate and defiance over Europe's airwaves. The rest of what had once been the heart of Berlin's night-life was rubble—Lotte Lenya told me that after she saw it on her first post-war visit to Berlin she had gone to bed and cried for a week. In the desert of broken brick which had been Hitler's Chancellery garden was the burned-out bunker where he and Eva Braun had died and Goebbels had given poison to his sleepy children. The new buildings of the Karl Marx Allee, shoddily expressionless in their impersonal modernity, drew attention to the horrors they were intended to mask like cheap, whitewashed tombstones.

It was a relief to cross the slow-moving Spree to that corner of an older, dowdier Berlin, where Brecht had set up his homespun banner, which billowed out over the brick façade of the Theater am Schiffbauerdamm like the sails of one of the barges which still plied their way sluggishly through the heart of the city. It seemed appropriate that he should have ended his years of exile here by this crumbling brick quayside, where a cynical, urban working-life lived side by side with ships and sailors and the peasant tang of vegetables. This was the same theatre where he and Kurt Weill had had their great successes of the 1920s—the theatre which had housed *The Threepenny Opera, Happy End* and the embattled Berlin *première* of *Rise and Fall of the Town of Mahagonny.* Here Brecht had evolved his unique style of production in a theatre where, instead of drowsing in evening dress and plush-seated gentility, audiences could 'smoke and think'—Brecht regarding the two activities as inseparable—about the pungent, harshly lit scenes, as clear-cut and combative as boxing-matches, which his plays laid before them. No one would have leaned further backwards to avoid being called sentimental, but surely an element of nostalgia was involved in Brecht's decision in 1948 to cast in his lot with the Communist regime in East Germany and to return to the shabby playhouse by the canal where he had first become famous.

While it recognized him as its greatest cultural treasure, the East German regime mistrusted and patronized him. They suspected his cosmopolitanism, subtlety and ironic scepticism. The works he offered as propaganda were sternly criticized, not only in East Germany but also in Russia and Poland, where, after a visit in 1952, the Minister of Culture accused him with dismay of undoing the Government's entire *Kulturpolitik.* No matter how stubbly he let his chin grow, how proletarian the leather jackets and flat caps he wore, he stood out as uneasily in Eastern Europe as a wolf running with police dogs.

His one security, the trump-card in the tense game he was forced to play after Stalin's death, was his greatness and its growing recognition. In 1954 and 1955 he had taken his Ensemble to Paris, where I first saw them astonishing audiences with the stark power of his production of *Mother Courage* and the discipline and versatility of his actors. The East German Government might dislike the effect of his plays on their own citizens, but they saw the prestige-value of their success in other countries and the propaganda uses of the first spreading ripples of a Brecht cult.

It is one of the major ironies among many in my dealings with the Berliner Ensemble that, although the visit to London which I arranged with them was to make Brecht's reputation in the English-speaking world and establish his company on the international scene in a way that both made its position at home impregnable and revolutionized the English theatre, I was never in fact to meet him. At the time of my visit to Berlin he was on one of his trips abroad, and a week before his company set out for England in 1956 he died.

My link with his work and my ally in East Berlin was almost as great, baffling and contradictory, and certainly as steely nerved: the woman to whom he entrusted the management of his company, his wife Hélène Weigel.

She was rehearsing on stage when I arrived at the theatre. I waited in the foyer while one of Brecht's young lieutenants went to fetch her, watched silently and with a kind of sullen suspicion by two more. While they may have realized the use to their master of Western contacts like myself, it was clear that they did not for that reason like them.

Then Weigel arrived, and for the first time I felt welcome. She looked smaller than she had done on stage when I saw her as Mother Courage in Paris: a tiny, gaunt woman, her hair brushed back austerely from a long, bony face. Its lines followed contours of seriousness, trouble, even depression, but now it was thrown back in a brilliant smile of greeting which bared her teeth to the gums. There had been coarse humour in her performance as Courage, a certain harsh gaiety as well as pathos, but nothing to prepare me for such warmth. Her eyes fixed deeply on my face as we shook hands. Behind them I sensed a mind swiftly posing questions, and answering most of them simultaneously. But in the splendid power of that smile I felt able for the first time in Berlin to lower my guard.

She took me into the auditorium to see the stage and a little of their rehearsal. I cannot remember now what play it was—it was not by Brecht, and there were no costumes or scenery to help my memory to identify it. They were still at an early stage of their customarily lengthy rehearsal period: playing fragments of scenes and breaking off to discuss their effect, trying out tiny bits of business and rejecting them. Evidently their characterizations had not yet set in rigid moulds. They were offering tentative fragments of impersonation, not so much acting as telling alternative versions of a story to see how they worked. 'Now, if he were this kind of person, he would have done it *this* way. On the other hand, if he were *that* sort of character, here's what would have happened.' As they worked away in their rehearsal clothes— nondescript pullovers and suits—against the bare brick back wall of the stage, bewildering little flashes of narrative flared to life in their voices and gestures, only to be snuffed out again as they broke off for further discussion.

The Berliner Ensemble's visit to London was to unleash prolonged and profound debate about the Brechtian method of acting—its philosophy, its aim, its techniques and effectiveness. But I think my clearest glimpse of what it was about came while I watched that rehearsal in East Berlin. With his love of all natural crafts—weaving, leather and bronze—Brecht wanted to share with his audiences the craft of the actor: to remind them at every point that what they were seeing was not real life, but players creating an artistic effect.

I could see why, although their lives had diverged in many respects, he still revered his wife as an artist and entrusted his company to her. She was a master-craftsman; her authority in that company of craftsmen was absolute. In theory the process of rehearsal was democratic. Every point of interpretation was subject to discussion. The actors would break off to argue, each putting his own point of view. But when she had listened to them all and then had had her say, the argument was over. It was not only that she was Brecht's representative, the administrator of the company and their employer. Her authority was her own, implicit in her character and the impatient, incisive confidence with which she imposed her clear-cut interpretations on their tentative thoughts.

She dropped the mantle of authority as we left the theatre to talk more intimately at the little house which she and Brecht had divided between them—he occupied the two upper floors, she the lower ones. She was all charm and solicitude, exercising the art, for which Viennese women are famous, of making one feel uniquely interesting. She talked about her family in Vienna, her early days in the theatre. Like me she had been an admirer of the great actor Werner Krauss, and when he played in the film version of Lion Feuchtwanger's novel *Jew Süss*, which gave the original story an anti-semitic twist, she went in person to his flat to tell him in scorching terms what she thought of the disgrace he had brought on his profession.

At that time I had leased the Palace Theatre in London for a two-year season of foreign companies. The Berliner Ensemble would fit neatly in at the end, just before reopening their own

R

autumn season in Berlin. The plays had still to be settled: *Mother Courage*, of course; perhaps *The Caucasian Chalk Circle* and Brecht's version of Farquhar's *The Recruiting Officer*. I still had doubts about transferring some of the company's effects from their own intimate auditorium to the vast spaces of the Palace Theatre, but these would be details best settled with Brecht himself. We left it that either I should return to Berlin or he would come to London ahead of the company.

Brecht, of course, never did come to make these final arrangements for his company's visit. I opened my paper one morning to read that he had died of a heart-attack in Berlin the evening before. A state funeral had been ordered. It was not possible to speak to Weigel herself on the telephone, but by mid-morning she had transmitted assurances that the visit would take place as arranged, so I gave the news to the evening papers.

A day or so later, the Ensemble published Brecht's last message, a notice about their planned London trip pinned back-stage at the Schiffbauerdamm:

> For our London season we need to bear two things in mind. First we shall be offering most of the audience a pure pantomime, a kind of silent film on stage, for they know no German. Second: there is in England a longstanding fear that German art (literature, painting, music) must be terribly heavy, slow, laborious and pedestrian.
>
> Hence our playing needs to be quick, light, strong. There is not a question of hurry, but of speed; not simply of quick playing but of quick thinking. We must keep the tempo of a run-through, and infect it with quiet strength, with our own amusement. In the dialogue, the exchanges must not be offered reluctantly, as when offering somebody one's last pair of boots, but must be tossed like so many balls. The audience must see that here are a number of artists working together as a collective ensemble to convey stories, ideas, bits of art to the spectator, by a common effort.
>
> Best wishes for your work.

He had set great importance by this English visit. Lotte Lenya, who visited Berlin a week or two before his death, told me how all the while they talked the theatre was filled with deafening hammering back-stage, metal on metal, as scenery was prepared and crated for the journey. They were forced to shout at each other. 'Now you understand what it means to live behind an Iron Curtain!' Brecht yelled at her, grinning. His words happened to boom forth in a sudden lull in the uproar. Swiftly he looked round to make sure that no one had overheard.

In some ways Brecht's death gave the Ensemble just the impetus he would have wished for their English debut. In the fortnight between his burial, close to the grave of Engels, and their arrival in London, the British press overflowed with long obituaries and appreciations of the man and his work. Even if you had never heard of Brecht before, you were made aware that Europe had lost a major poet and dramatist. In one of the most glowing tributes, Sebastian Haffner wrote in the *Observer* that Brecht was probably the nearest equal to Shakespeare yet produced by world literature — 'indeed, if one believed in the transmigration of souls, one could be tempted to think he was Shakespeare reborn'.

But the first hints of a reaction to the adulation showed in the news stories which appeared on the morning of the opening and which tried to make out that the actors had been difficult at a photo-call the previous afternoon. In fact the company, having left East Berlin by special train at half past nine on Saturday morning, had been held up half the night by a delayed ferry at the Hook. They had embarked at two on Sunday morning, crossed the North Sea in weather which prostrated many with sickness, and arrived at the theatre on Sunday afternoon at the same hour as a mob of press photographers was milling in the foyer. Reasonably enough, the Berliners refused to be photographed until they had had time to lunch and repair their appearances. Yet that was a sufficient basis for the popular papers to spin it out into a small drama of Communist obstinacy and artistic haughtiness.

The delayed arrival barely left time for lighting and dress rehearsals, deficiencies having to be overlooked as a consequence of the wearying all-night journey. On the opening night the theatre was packed. All fashionable and theatrical London had come to see the source of the fanfare. But the curtain had not been up long before I could sense, from my place at the back of the stalls, a shifting and fidgeting in the auditorium. The performance was not coming across. Interpreting Brecht's instructions too literally, the actors were throwing away their lines. It was indeed very close to a pantomime—something remote, a silent film. As soon as the curtain fell for the interval I pushed through the pass-door and called them round me on the stage. Through an interpreter I told them that they would have to speak up; that they were underplaying almost to vanishing point, nine-tenths of their words were inaudible, and unless they made some effort to get through to the audience the season would be ruined. Some of the younger actors eyed me furiously. This, their eyes blazed, was the veracity which had won the admiration of Europe. Were they to compromise it for a bourgeois Englishman who preferred melodrama? I half expected a mutiny, but Weigel kept silent, her face expressionless. When the curtain rose again every word was audible, and ripples of appreciation began to run through the audience. An understanding and rapport began to feed back to the actors, who worked up a speedier, more confident style.

At the end, however, the applause was mainly for Weigel. Her performance as Courage had remained constant in its steely authority and purity of tone. One by one she registered the hammer-blows with which the years of war beat down the canteen woman's splendid vitality, robbing her of one child, then another, until, as she walks away from the body of her favourite son, the big careless laugh she turns on life freezes into a silent, terrible scream like that of a horse in Picasso's 'Guernica'. At the end, as she trundled her wagon alone into the gathering snow, the image she created was awful and pitiless. Face wizened, back bowed, she shrank into the likeness of an immensely aged tortoise, its blind, reptilian will to live forcing its frail shell of egotism once more into the path of war and its engines.

Next morning the notices were all praise for her and for Angelika Hurwicz, who played the part of the dumb daughter Kattrin, which Brecht had written for his wife twenty years earlier as a role which she could play anywhere in their exile without having to master new languages. 'Acting in the grand manner!' exclaimed the *Daily Herald*, and *The Times* critic confessed: 'However unwilling we may be to enter into the spirit of thesis drama conditioned by Marxism, the compulsion of the exquisite playing is not to be resisted.' Yet much of the time the acting was used as a stick with which to beat Brecht. But for the acting, several critics implied, the play would have been shown up as 'a tedious, dragging chronicle' (J. C. Trewin) or 'something between Dr Caligari and an illustrated lecture on road safety' (whatever Milton Shulman of the *Evening Standard* meant by that).

Kenneth Tynan, a great champion of the Ensemble, wrote a somewhat muted notice in the *Observer*, and seemed rather to see it as an opportunity to observe the impact of Brecht's concepts on a sophisticated West End theatre audience, commenting that 'the beauty of Brechtian settings is not the dazzling kind that begs for applause. It is the durable beauty of *use*.' He went on to quote Eric Bentley's remark that 'Brecht does not believe in an inner reality, a higher reality, or a deeper reality, but simply in reality'. This, he said, was 'something for which we have lost the taste: raised on a diet of gin and goulash, we call Brecht ingenuous when he gives us bread and wine. He wrote morality plays and directed them as such, and if we of the West End and Broadway find them as tiresome as religion, we are in a shrinking minority ... "I was bored to death," said a bright Chelsea girl after *Mother Courage*. "Bored to life" would have been apter.'

I myself stood rather with those who enjoyed the Ensemble's performances without fully grasping the theory behind them, although I did not suppose that this proved the theory worthless or empty. Entertaining members of the company at home, I often asked them if they could explain the mysterious 'A (alienation)-effect' to me. In the course of several after-theatre parties during their London season I never found one actor who was able to do so, and several, smiling openly, confessed that they had never understood it themselves. One veteran actor in particular won our hearts. He was a tall, stiff-backed old Prussian of marvellously Imperial courtesy who, as he bent over my wife's hand to kiss it, clicked his heels with the punctilious charm of a vanished age. One night I put my question to him. Without a word he brought his heels together, shrugged, bowed and smiled broadly and apologetically.

The comments which said most about the Ensemble's impact on London had nothing to do with interminable discussions on the 'A-effect'. One was a parenthetic remark in *The Times* that, whatever one thought of the plays, 'we may well sigh for theatrical conditions in which an English company could attain to the same pitch of team acting, at once flexible and precise'. The other was the answer John Osborne made to a reporter who stopped him in the theatre for an opinion on what he had seen. 'I can't talk about it yet,' replied Osborne briefly; 'there's too much to think about.' Whatever the critics wrote about Brecht and his company, theatrical people recognized their importance and the lessons they had for the English stage.

The London performances had been successful enough for Hélène Weigel to agree in principle that there should be a return visit before too long. During the following years of alternating political frost and thaw we kept in touch, and from time to time I would fly to Berlin to see the Ensemble's latest productions. In 1962, when I was planning my first World Theatre Season, I decided that the time was more than ripe, and once more made the pilgrimage through Checkpoint Charlie, now flanked by the hideous brick and barbed wire of the Berlin Wall. As always, Weigel was as charmingly welcoming as her young lieutenants were dour.

I wanted to persuade her to bring *The Threepenny Opera*, which they were preparing to revive. It seemed to me the purest work of the young Brecht's anarchic comic genius; the one most likely to break down a British audience's fear of him as a heavy, didactic Marxist moralist. It would provide a long-overdue re-examination of the glittering work which had first made Brecht's name. She was reluctant at first, as there were political difficulties. By the criteria of the regime, it was a nihilist work of dubious moral effect, contaminated by its association with the days of Germany's decadence and frivolity and the unchecked crime and sexuality of Berlin under the Weimar Republic. These could be overcome by pointing out the advantages of another successful visit to the West, where its possible corrupting influences would be unnoticeable, but it would also be a demanding vehicle for the company, heavy in its requirements of a full chorus, an orchestra, and dancing and singing from principals not primarily trained for them. She did not feel that they could undertake more than five performances a week, and I tried to demonstrate that, to make a profit in a rented theatre, seven would be essential.

After a visit to Buckow, where she and Brecht had shared joint cottages, and further, sometimes stormy, meetings in Berlin, I persuaded her that the Ensemble's revival would put London at her feet. There was then the difficulty of getting permission for

the company to visit Britain again—relations between East and
West had been icy since the building of the Wall—but she left all
that in my hands. Politics, she told me, could not come between
us. Whatever the world chose to do, we were allies, and whom
could allies trust if not one another? She held out both hands to
take mine in parting, smiling with a brilliant, urgent intensity.
I shall always remember her with that smile; as if she were thereby
trying to pour into me a current of will forcing me to believe, to
forget, to respond and obey. It was the last time we were to meet.

As it turned out, I was unable to get visas for the company to
visit London that year. The decision by the Foreign Office not to
allow their visit was deplored and protested against by George
Devine, Michael Redgrave and Sybil Thorndike among many
others, but there was little I could do. I began to look for something to take its place in my first World Theatre Season, and
once again it was a Brecht production which took me behind the
Iron Curtain.

In the autumn of 1963 I visited Warsaw to see the Polish Contemporary Theatre in their presentation of Brecht's *The Resistible
Rise of Arturo Ui*—which I had been told was one of the finest
things seen in Eastern Europe since the war—and to meet their
director, Erwin Axer. My first visit was a hasty one, and I had
little time to discover the miracle which the Poles had wrought
from the rubble of their destroyed capital. I saw *The Life Annuity*
by the nineteenth-century Polish playwright Alexander Fredro
and *Arturo Ui*, and signed a contract before returning to London.

Axer's production of *Arturo Ui* was certainly the finest I have
ever seen. Dominated by a superb performance from the great
Polish star, Tadeusz Lomnicki, it had been the highlight of the
previous season in Warsaw. Indeed, it was so successful that the
Russians had chosen Axer to direct the play in Leningrad, again
with Lomnicki, who was to play in Polish while the rest of the
company played in Russian. It was an unprecedented step. I felt
confident as I flew back that London would also acclaim it, so
many critics having assessed it as even better than that by
Brecht's own company.

Suddenly, a week later, a cable arrived from Warsaw:

'WEIGEL REFUSES PERMISSION FOR PRODUCTION ARTURO
UI IN LONDON STOP SHE FEARS VISIT WILL LIMIT AUDIENCE

FOR BERLINER ENSEMBLE'S OWN VISIT NATIONAL THEATRE
IN SEPTEMBER 1964 STOP PLEASE CONFIRM.'

I was dumbfounded. Whether or not Weigel was legally in the
right, she was wilfully preventing a company of fifty Poles from
visiting London in a great production. She knew how hard we
had tried since 1956 to arrange for a return visit from the Berliner Ensemble. Everything possible had been done to persuade
the Government to allow the company in, but, as the Home
Secretary, Sir Alec Douglas Home, had informed me, it was
impossible to obtain travel documents because of a NATO agreement to restrict East German travel.

I rang Suzanne Czech, Brecht's literary agent in London, who
was as shocked as I was, not only over Weigel's decision, but
over the news that negotiations were under way with the National
Theatre. However, in 1962 Weigel had herself given me written
permission to bring over Jean Vilar's French production of
Arturo Ui. Now—perhaps it was jealousy over Axer's success,
perhaps anger at the impossibility of obtaining visas—she had
effectively vetoed the Polish production and outflanked myself
and the Royal Shakespeare Company in negotiations.

All this left me more determined than ever to present Axer's
company. I flew again to Warsaw to start a long series of discussions in the little theatre which the company had occupied
since their arrival in Warsaw from Lodz in 1949, and Axer and I
talked late into the night. We finally arranged for the company
to present *The Life Annuity* and introduce London audiences to
the plays of Slawomir Mrożek through two one-acters, *Let's Have
Fun* and *What a Lovely Dream*. Born in 1930, Mrożek is Poland's
Ionesco, a brilliant and daring satirist. His plays find one of their
most persistent sources of humour in exploring the immense
gap between the world of reality and that recognized by Communist rhetoricians and bureaucrats. Though he has lived outside
Poland for several years, his plays have had continued popularity
in Eastern Europe. Yet before the Contemporary Theatre's visit
he was probably best known in England for his short stories.
The two short plays served as an introduction which was later to
result in Trevor Nunn's full-scale production of Mrożek's most
famous play, *Tango*, at the Aldwych in 1966. But the original
productions received mixed notices. *Let's Have Fun* and *What*

a Lovely Dream, which would, one suspects, have been received with roars of laughter by a Polish audience, left the English theatregoer slightly puzzled. In *The Life Annuity*, however, Tadeusz Lomnicki as Latka the money-lender gave an extremely lively and stylized performance, finding an effective foil in Tadeusz Fijewski, whose expressionless face and mechanical movements meant that Latka's state of over-excitement broke over him like waves on a rock.

I returned to Warsaw in November 1965 to see Adam Hanuszkiewicz at the Polish Popular Theatre. One of the plays I wanted his company to bring to London was Roman Bratny's *The Columbus Boys*, subtitled *Warsaw '44–46*, which documented the author's experiences in the holocaust of horror during the German destruction of Warsaw and in the struggles of the immediate post-war period. Hanuszkiewicz introduced me to Bratny, and together they guided me through the play's vivid and terrifying background.

Hanuszkiewicz collected me from my hotel early on the morning after my arrival. I had reached the hotel the night before in the dark and knew nothing of my immediate surroundings. Emerging with Adam into the daylight, I was confounded by the mellow beauty of an old city—a city which had been deliberately and systematically murdered by the Nazis, so that virtually nothing and no one remained. When Marshall Zhukov's Russian armies finally crossed into Warsaw on January 17th, 1945, of the 1,300,000 people who lived in the city before the war 800,000 had perished. Today Warsaw is a miracle: a phoenix city risen from the ashes, alive and thriving. There is something uncanny and unreal about this modern antique town—and something profoundly moving. Adam drove me to meet Roman Bratny at a small café, and over coffee he began to explain the background to his play.

Hitler's invasion, swift, decisive and brutal, had been met by a tragic, courageous defence. While in the opening days of the war Britain was dropping pamphlets on German civilians, the Luftwaffe was raining bombs upon a defenceless Warsaw. When the Russians joined the attack in support of the Nazi-Soviet Pact, Molotov declared: 'Poland, that bastard of Versailles, has ceased to exist.' Hitler's original plan to save two hundred thousand Poles as a labour force was soon abandoned. In the policy of

destruction which followed, over six million Poles perished
—about a fifth of the population. Bratny described how Hitler
had ordered 'the annihilation on the spot of the Jews, the intelli-
gentsia, the clergy and the nobility of Poland; it is useless to load
the Reich with this burden, absolutely useless to send these elements to the concentration camps in the Reich.'

With the memory of many horrendous statistics burning in
my mind, we drove to the former Gestapo Headquarters, now
the Ministry of Education. As we entered the courtyard of this
large austere building, which had remained untouched throughout the bombing, we were conducted through an iron door on
the left which led to the cells. At the bottom of the steps a flame
burnt, and, like that burning on the tomb of the unknown
soldier, it would never go out.

We then drove to Paviak itself. On one wall of its central
entrance-hall are engraved columns of the names of S.S. officers
—dead, captured or missing—recorded for posterity in a terrifying hymn of hatred. I asked Bratny about Poland's 'crucifixion
complex'. 'You have war memorials of honour and love,' he
replied; 'we keep memorials of hate.' Outside in the courtyard,
in the snow, stood one of the few trees to survive destruction.
It was covered with plaques of remembrance.

Bratny also insisted that I see the site of the Warsaw Ghetto,
in the area of which the ground stands several feet higher than its
surroundings because, below the concrete, lie the broken stones
of houses and the bodies for whom no individual burial was
was possible. It was here that Bratny had witnessed one of the
most pitiful and terrifying episodes of the war when, on April
19th, 1943, the Warsaw Jews had risen against their Nazi tormen-
tors. In the twenty-seven days of fighting which followed,
thousands were killed, and the ghetto razed to the ground.
General Stroop's message to Hitler at the end of the uprising had
been that 'The Jewish quarter of Warsaw no longer exists.'

I have dwelt in some detail on this day in Warsaw because it is,
I think, important in explaining the background to contemporary Polish theatre. That such a vivid and vital theatrical
tapestry should be created so rapidly after the ravages of war is
surely astonishing. Warsaw was hammered. Nearly 40 per cent
of the country's wealth was lost, and public buildings, documents,
archives almost totally destroyed. 'A lower race', declared the

invaders, 'needs less space, less nourishment and less culture than a higher one.' The last public theatrical performances were given in Warsaw on September 5th, 1939—four days after the Nazi invasion. Theatre became divided between the front-line theatres and clandestine performances given in private homes in the cities, where secret schools were established for actors. In the six years that followed, actors and directors—and audiences—continued to risk their lives to prove their faith in the theatre. All of Warsaw's eighteen theatres were destroyed; equipment, costumes and scenery smashed, burned and looted. Yet, in the face of this devastation, the illicit Council of the Theatre met regularly and fervently to plan a theatre which would reach all classes of society. Even as the Nazi occupiers were driven from Warsaw, the little theatre groups, which had taken refuge in the country, swept in with a touching, perhaps even crazy, persistence, performing on makeshift stages of planks fixed in corners of buildings whose walls were propped up by wooden buttresses and iron bars. At Craców and Lódź theatre groups began to work again.

From the first days after the liberation no one doubted that Warsaw would be rebuilt. It was an almost unbelievable concept, made feasible only by the discovery of the city plans, immaculately preserved from destruction. From all over Poland the population of Warsaw returned, and the great process of renaissance began. On January 1st, 1946, Warsaw's Polski Theatre reopened its doors for public performance. By 1948, only three years after the end of the war, Poland had forty-eight theatres and five opera houses. By 1965, Hanuszkiewicz proudly told me, there were sixty-nine theatres and nine opera houses.

The maintenance of a tradition of revolt, perseverance and continuing struggle has been a vital element in the re-establishment of Polish theatre. Through the three leading directors (with whom I was to become great friends), Axer, Hanuszkiewicz and Dejmek, I have discovered at first hand that this tradition has not been allowed to die. *Avant-garde* groups flourish throughout Poland, from the semi-professional satiric theatres in Warsaw, of which the Syrene is my own favourite, to the work of Jerzy Grotowski's Theatre of 13 Rows in Wroclaw. Like his contemporaries in Poland, Grotowski's theatre of movement, contortion and involvement has linked itself closely to the Polish background.

His production of Wyspiański's *Acropolis*, early in 1967, was set in Auschwitz, just as in the 1950s another director, Skuszanka, had placed *Measure for Measure* inside a barbed-wire barricade surmounted by watchtowers. These productions, set against the terror to which Hanuszkiewicz had introduced me, clung to the heart and haunted the memory.

It was the brilliant young actor Zbigniew Cybulski who introduced me to another aspect of the Polish renaissance: the enormous advances in the world of film which ran parallel to the growth of the theatre. Born of the newsreel, which had documented the tragedy of war and the optimism of its aftermath, the Polish cinema has developed rapidly from the intensely patriotic films of the early directors, among them Wanda Jaknbawska and Aleksander Ford, to the sophistication of Andrzej Wajda.

Cybulski was the star of Wajda's *Ashes and Diamonds*, a film of beauty and high pathos. He played the young gunman determined to uphold the orders of the exiled Polish Government, giving a performance of dazzling brilliance. The film's tragedy of life destroyed by circumstance was, for all his admirers, compounded by Cybulski's own tragic death, not many months after I met him, in an accident on a railway station in Warsaw.

Two of the productions that the Popular Theatre brought to the 1966 World Theatre Season emphasized the Polish background: these were the 1901 classic, *The Wedding*, by Wyspiański, and Bratny's *The Columbus Boys*, which remains for me the highlight of their visit with its evocation of the Polish struggle above and below the streets of Warsaw.

When the Polish National Theatre came to the 1967 season, they brought with them an even earlier link with history, Wilkowiecko's *The Glorious Resurrection of Our Lord*, one of the few texts to survive the destruction of the Polish archives. It seemed fitting that such a play should be brought by Poland's oldest theatre, founded in 1765 by the last king of Poland, Stanislaw August. The National Theatre had reopened in 1949 under Kazimierz Dejmek, a student of Leon Schiller, Poland's great theatrical influence and himself a director of the National. *The Glorious Resurrection of our Lord* reaffirmed Schiller's aim to create a progressive, popular and truly national theatre. Dejmek proved that the miracle play can exist as a living modern idiom. He has continued Schiller's search to renew the spectacular and romantic Polish heritage, opening out into world classics and modern plays. His productions have been praised for their combination of artistic experiment with the spirit of 'fighting theatre' — a phrase coined by Schiller during his war-time lectures. Dejmek no longer runs the National Theatre, and his place has been taken by Hanuszkiewicz.

In the previous year, when the Polish Popular Theatre were our guests, the season had been due to open with a visit from the Théâtre National Populaire. Only a few days before the details were to be announced, I received news that it was impossible for the company to come. The opening week therefore stood empty. Hurriedly I booked a flight to Prague, where I had heard the Czech National Theatre were doing a production of *The Insect Play* by the Čapek brothers. The following morning I flew to Prague with my friend Michael Halifax, general manager at the Aldwych at that time.

The baroque, secret dreaming of Prague was awakened for me by the hand of Kafka, becoming an image of the private consciousness which is his world. This is the city where he was born and where he spent his lonely childhood. Here, among the romanesque houses of the burghers, beneath the hundred spires, it is still possible to discover the buildings around which Kafka wove his tapestry of unnerving dreams. The labyrinth of narrow winding streets, squeezing alongside the mellow-hued houses with their steep-tiled roofs and iron-clamped walls, converges on his castle.

And in Hradčany Castle, where we then stood, high on the hill overlooking the city, the bad dreams came to life. Here the Nazi rulers had reigned. Here in the courtyard the body of the S.S. General Reinhard Heydrich had lain in state after his assassination by seven young Czechoslovak parachutists on May 27th, 1942. As a reprisal, the whole of the village of Lidice was razed to the ground, its inhabitants systematically massacred or deported to Hitler's death-camps. Probably more than any other atrocity, in a war full of atrocities, Lidice jolted the conscience of the world.

We visited the crypt of St Cyril's Church, near the Vltava River in Resslova Street, where four of the parachutists had been slowly and brutally exterminated by the S.S. Outside, bullet holes surround the ventilation slot which led to the crypt, and floral tributes commemorate the patriots' bravery all the year round. Even on that afternoon, twenty-four years later, the horror of that June day seemed grimly immediate.

It did not take me long to realize, even on my first visit, that a combination of old city and modern progressive theatre is, in fact, symbolic of the state of theatre in Czechoslovakia itself, where old and new struggle one against the other. The established theatrical tradition tends towards conservatism, exemplified by the Czech National Theatre. Yet, as in France, where the Comédie-Française stands in an identical position, this is not a harmful factor, for tradition has created the high standards for the revolutionary to reject or emulate. Otomar Krejča once described the Czech National Theatre to me as a 'huge factory', and, he went on, 'you cannot achieve concentration of purpose in a factory'. And so, like many others before him, he broke away to form his own small, closely integrated company.

The larger, more conservative companies can, however, provide a vital asset denied experimental groups: marvellous facilities for work. Thus Josef Svoboda, who with Ladislav Vychodil at the Slovak National Theatre ranks as one of the great designers not only in Eastern Europe but in the world, has the opportunity to reach a technical standard he could not achieve elsewhere. It was in the Czech National Theatre's workshop that I first met him. It was unlike anything I had seen before—a veritable conjuror's cave, where a designer could weave spells and create magic with equipment that would turn any English designer green with insatiable jealousy. It was here that he created the brilliant multi-mirrored set for *The Insect Play*. There on a table stood the model of the set which he later presented to me in memory of the production's great London success. The way his decor evolved is very interesting. As the play deals with insects, there were two possibilities. First, to set the stage to suggest nature with the cast performing in street clothes, or secondly, to suggest a human environment and dress the cast as insects. The problem with the latter concept is that though the costumes may be perfect, it would never be possible to disguise the fact that the cast are people. The producer, Miroslav Macháček, decided to try the first possibility. But here again there was a problem, since the days of real grass and trees on the stage are over. Then Josef Svoboda produced a yellowing little book on conjuring published in the last century. It described a technique for making people vanish by using tilted mirrors. By adopting this method, Macháček was able to make the actors seem to float on air, perch on flowers or disappear completely.

Like the Polish, the Czech theatre has a tradition of outspokenness and revolt. The intense patriotic fervour of its playwrights has made the theatre a form of prolonged cold war between progressive and reactionary forces. Many people have told me of the requirements imposed by the Party immediately after the war, when Stalinist policy demanded a culture to reflect Party aesthetics and Socialist realism, and so held back the progress of theatre in Czechoslovakia. It was only after the 'thaw' following Stalin's death that modernity came into the open on the stages of Prague.

By and large the Czech arts have always been linked with everyday life—particularly from the early nineteenth century, when they first came to be used as an ideological and political weapon in the struggle for national emancipation. Theatre has always formed an integral part of the general cultural scene. More than that: it used to be—and to some extent still is—almost a place of worship. It is significant that in popular parlance the Czech National Theatre is called 'our chapel'. When its superb house was burnt down in 1881 it was a national tragedy. People wept in the streets, and it was rebuilt within only two years from private donations in which the whole nation participated. The nation's gift to itself is its motto, engraved in large gold letters above the stage. It has been a place of pilgrimage for country people from near and far, a symbol of the Czech cultural heritage and of national unity.

The Theatre on the Balustrade followed in the wake of the release from the Stalinist period of 'desiccated, didactic and dehumanized art'. It was founded in 1958 by Vladimír Vodička, its administrator, and Ladislav Fialka, the brilliant mime, who had already been leading his own troupe since 1953. In 1959 the triumvirate was completed by Jan Grossman, who became artistic director of the drama group.

One evening, after seeing Fialka's troupe at the theatre in the beautiful old quarter of Prague, I dined with these three directors in one of the tiny cellar restaurants near the theatre. We talked first of Fialka and his mime group, whom I had just seen in

The Fools. Unlike most modern mimes, Fialka does not work alone, but as the leader of a closely knit, compact group. It was obvious from watching the dreamlike qualities of *The Fools* that it was the result of an evolution which the group had worked out for themselves among themselves.

'We felt sometimes as though we were doing something which had no logical sense,' he told me. 'But we knew that this was the key to the sense of everything. We felt like fools, and I gave this title to the performance.' Fialka's mimes are exquisite blends of pantomime, dance and drama. 'But for us', added Grossman, 'the most important thing is the audience. We aim at creating a kind of dialogue between actor and audience, so that both can be personally involved in what goes on on stage.'

In their little studio theatre it is undoubtedly easier to attain this relationship than in the large auditorium of the Aldwych, but his superb production of Jarry's *King Ubu*, which came as part of the 1968 season, illustrated perfectly the aspects of the Theatre on the Balustrade which have made it such an exciting and respected theatre throughout Europe. The impeccable timing was a tribute to the long hours of discussion and rehearsal which precede every production.

Grossman himself is a tall, loose-limbed, pink-faced man, with a careless, comic demeanour which is like the behaviour of a schoolboy who is determined to trick life without losing his own peculiar sweetness and grace. But underneath this air of abandonment he is an obsessionalist, whose imagination reaches fever pitch through human gaiety and upheaval. He is a director who has the capacity to reveal the already familiar as though for the first time, enlightening every production with his own extraordinary vision. A pioneer of the *avante-garde*, he is a master of invention and satirical comedy.

For their first appearance in London in 1967 Grossman's drama group had brought a dramatization of Kafka's novel *The Trial*, the story of Josef K, who 'without having done anything wrong was arrested one fine morning'. Grossman attempted to do more than merely present Kafka's story on the stage; he had tried to capture an aspect of Prague which had always fascinated me. This was the Prague which had existed as an entity in Kafka's mind during his years of spiritual exile in Berlin; the Prague of a man at the mercy of his own fears, and cut off from the world by a destructive process of self-examination and the agony of his sense of guilt.

The Czech breakaway movement which established progressive private theatres off the beaten track steadily grew in the post-Stalin years. Young theatres and technological theatres now came to life, including the Black Theatre, the Semafor Theatre and the Svoboda/Radok Laterna Magika Theatre. Variety, mime, ballet and dance groups formed together to create the State Theatre Group, a central body which could help to co-ordinate this new movement.

One member of this group was, until recently, Otomar Krejča's Theatre Behind the Gate, one of the youngest of the 'profile' theatres of Prague. Now its rapid success has assured it a direct state subsidy. I spent several days in the little theatre that the company share with the Laterna Magika at the end of an arcade off Wenceslas Square. I watched Otomar Krejča at work, and began discussions with him which we continued when the company visited London for the 1969 season.

Krejča is a tall, thick-set man with a strong, firm handshake. Immensely friendly and gregarious off stage, he rules the company's artistic policy with an iron hand. He is a man of acute sensitivity. Watching him rehearse their production of *The Three Sisters*, I saw the great respect with which he is treated by the entire company, from the youngest student to Czechoslovakia's oldest working actress, the ninety-year-old Leopolda Dostálová, who had been in the first production of *The Three Sisters* in Prague sixty years before, and had appeared in the title-role of Karel Čapek's *Mother*.

Between 1950 and 1960 Krejča had been director of the National Theatre. Its restrictions, however, burdened him greatly. Not only was his artistic scope limited by the traditional demands of an established national theatre, but he was increasingly subject to pressure from authorities, who 'found the incompatibility of his aesthetics most irritating'. He left the theatre, taking with him the team that had already been establishing a small studio theatre within the National—the dramaturge Karel Kraus, and two of the young stars, Marie Tomášová and Jan Tříska, both of whom would be spellbinders in any capital of the world.

'When we established the Theatre Behind the Gate', he told me, 'we defined its aim very simply. We wanted to do only what we ourselves considered to be essential. We wanted to do only what, right from the start, would give us satisfaction and happiness in our work.'

'But what sort of audience are you aiming at?' I asked.

'Not everybody.' He paused, then added, 'Only those who are capable and willing to understand what we are saying about ourselves and to recognize themselves in us.'

Like the Theatre on the Balustrade, one of the main principles of Krejča's company is to provide long and intense periods of preparation for each new production. 'We do about two productions a year,' he told me, 'usually rehearsing for four or five months with at least one month for dress rehearsals alone.' The result is a beautifully orchestrated and totally integrated whole.

The results of this dedication, concentration and hard work were seen to perfection in Krejča's wonderful production of *The Three Sisters*, which aimed, as Krejča himself told me, at capturing 'the futile endeavours to escape from reality to the illusion of a more beautiful world to come, the struggle for the preservation of self-deception'. Certainly it was one of the greatest productions I had ever seen. I shall always remember the final scene as the sisters, caged in their exile, sweep across the stage like birds. *The Times* summarized this great theatrical event: 'The pre-requisite of a masterpiece is that supreme arrogance and absolute humility should be inextricably intertwined in its creator. *The Three Sisters* is a masterpiece, and if the World Theatre Season were to bring nothing even remotely approaching the excellence of the production by the Theatre Behind the Gate from Prague ... it would be a memorable one.'

In a letter from Prague on the company's return home, Krejča and Karel Kraus wrote to me, 'Thanks to press reports and our own memories, the wonderful experience of our stay in London is still fresh in our minds. The applause of the audience and your own words convince us that we did not harm the good reputation of your World Theatre Season. All the expressions of appreciation we have received are an inspiration for our further work here in Czechoslovakia.'

The idea of a closely linked ensemble is nothing new to the Czech theatre; it has always worked along these lines. There has never been anything even remotely resembling the commercial theatre, either during the Austro-Hungarian Empire, the First Republic, or now. All Czech theatres have been run from the beginning as repertory theatres, subsidized by state or city. Thus a degree of experimentation on the big official stages has formed an integral part of the Czech theatre tradition. But the most meaning-ful experiments have been carried out by the smaller ensembles. The ensembles of the present time, originally sharing one stage, began to differentiate themselves and to multiply. Through their freshness and spontaneity, their refusal to accept ready-made formulae—philosophical, social or theatrical—they have pro-vided a new and welcome outlet for truly creative energy.

'The most important thing about these ensembles is that they have managed to attract the public, above all, by their consider-able demands on the intellect,' I was told by Jan Grossman, who started the present movement with his work at the Balustrade. 'These ensembles achieved the greatest response in so far as they diagnosed burning current problems, based on the authentic feelings of contemporary man. The most striking characteristic of this intellectual and analytical theatre is that these problems are posed and demonstrated not in a didactic way, but as an appeal for a dialogue. The dialogue between the stage and the audience is what this so-called "Appellative Theatre" is after. It considers man to be a social being, fully and decisively engaged in all the social processes; it approaches man, however, from the standpoint he himself takes towards these processes as an in-finitely complicated individual. The social relevance for this approach lies in its appeal for a common search for a solution. It does not attempt to instruct the public, or to provide any ready-made answers. The favourite artistic expression of both prose and drama is satire, the predominant characteristic of young intellectuals their inexhaustible sense of humour. It is of many shades and hues, from the earthy and rather rough humour of Bohumil Hrabal, the subtle humour of Ivan Vyskočil, the highly sophisticated humour of Václav Havel, to the gentle, almost fey humour of Miloš Macourek, and the challenging humour of Alena Vostrá's *Whose Turn Next?*

'The Czech theatre of today, drama and satire alike, is concen-trating its energy on an honest search for truthful answers to our common problems; on chipping away the hardened deposits of formalized thought which separate modern Man from reality.'

To give an impression of what their ideas have achieved in their productions, one could hardly do better than quote some of Ronald Bryden's review of Grossman's production of Kafka's *The Trial*, which catches completely the tone, character, timing, impact and acrobatic effects of this ensemble:

> Through the skeleton of scaffolding flit Kafka's figures of urban phantasmagoria: pallid clerks in bowlers, anonymous officials, child-whores in short frilly dresses or the sexless leotards of Picasso's blue acrobats. I mean flit: Jan Grossman's actors move with a speed and precision which turns them into glimpsed, illusory flickers. They dive from blind staircases, swing from doorways and rafters. Each uses his body like a circus-performer: as the enigmatic nurse temptress Leni, Marie Malkova whips round the stage in an asp-like glide which would torture an untrained pelvis. As Joseph K, Jan Preucil, a stocky actor with the jaw, deep-set smallish eyes and finicky negligence of a young Olivier, somersaults backwards over a bed in his garrotting by his unknown executioners, to collapse with head hanging and agape halfway into the pit.
>
> We have nothing in our theatre to match this total physical versatility. If the National and Royal Shakespeare show signs of approaching it, we have Mr Daubeny's previous international seasons to thank for the knowledge that is now part of the equipment of an actor in the first world class.

For the 1970 World Theatre Season Czechoslovakia was represented by one of the most interesting of the younger theatre companies of Europe. This was the Činoherní Klub (which translated means 'Drama Club') of Prague, a group formed in 1965 by two students at the Prague Academy of Dramatic Art, Jaroslav Vostrý, now their artistic director, and Ladislav Smoček, whose play *The Picnic* was their first production. They subsequently built up a repertoire that included work by O'Casey, Albee, Camus and Pinter.

Their aim from the beginning has been to work as a group, and for the actors to extend their own personalities into the parts that they happen to be playing; in this way a continuing creativity is formed out of an interaction and exploration of one another's individuality. The result is a marvellously relaxed, completely controlled timing that fuses with an infectious sense of spontaneity and enjoyment. As Vostrý defined his aims, 'I was looking for a whole group of theatrical personalities to produce performances which were expressions of their own selves.' Thus they found 'a curious fluency in which actors became playwrights, directors actors, through which a highly personal style could be evolved'.

The first play they put on in London was an interpretation of *Mandragola*, that ingenious comedy by Machiavelli. Jiří Menzel, the director of the much-admired Czech film *Closely Observed Trains*, produced it, combining moments of downbeat disillusion with manic bursts of dazzling acrobatics. It was followed by *Whose Turn Next?* by Alena Vostrá, Vostrý's wife. This wryly satirical comedy concerns a group of students who hang out in a Prague night-club, indulge their fantasies and seek ways of baiting the older generation, partly to strike a rebellious pose and partly to try to assure themselves of their own reality. One of the older generation, in the shape of an obtuse worker, gets Offside, the group's ringleader, at his mercy, proceeding to out-flank him by a casual use of muscle. 'Stupidity', he tells him, 'must be punished'. Jiří Hrzán, playing Offside, by turn mocking or put upon, or straight-jacketed in a wrought-iron plant-stand, gave a performance that bordered on comic genius.

Their season in London finished with *The Government Inspector*, Gogol's great comedy that demolishes the corruption of Tsarist bureaucracy with its magnificently effective shafts of black humour. The production was a triumphant vindication of the company's methods. Working on a broad canvas, they presented a wonderfully grotesque portrait of the petty tyrannical officials and their pathetic victims in a Russian provincial town, whose guilt makes them totally vulnerable to the brainless clerk from St Petersburg whom they fearfully imagine to be the visiting government inspector. The fawning and bullying grotesqueness of the main protagonists, however, was perfectly balanced by a display of style, and the result, in the words of Irving Wardle, writing in *The Times*, 'surpassed any interpretation to which a British company would or could aspire'.

The Činoherní Klub of Prague had shown themselves to be the inheritors of the best of their country's theatrical traditions. Their work had upheld a right to constructive dissent and social criticism within a collective society. 'It filled the audience with a sense of triumph', Ronald Bryden wrote in the *Observer*, 'simply to know that such freedom of personality survives in Czechoslovakia.'

12

Irish Theatre. Ingmar Bergman

In the spring of 1962 we had come to Dublin for eight weeks to rehearse Peter Ustinov's *Photo Finish*, in which Peter himself starred, together with Diana Wynyard and Paul Rogers, and which was to open at the Saville Theatre in London in April. We were there mainly because of Peter's tax problems, and at ten o'clock on March 5th we were gathered together for our first rehearsal.

Photo Finish, Peter's fifteenth play, was 'an adventure in biography'. As Sam Kinsale, a writer aged eighty, is putting the finishing touches to his autobiography, he is joined by his prosperous self at sixty, his sarcastic, esoteric self at forty and his innocent, aspiring self at twenty. Together the four characters re-examine their collective life.

Peter and I had already spent three months together in London dissecting sets, examining costumes and auditioning actors. Exploring facial landscapes, intonations, gestures and build, we had sought for germs of resemblance in faces for the three generations that *Photo Finish* required, and felt like plastic surgeons, examining eyes, measuring noses, peering at nostrils. It was the first play we had done together, and it was for me an historic event.

All Peter Ustinov's writing contains a powerful sense of recorded experience conveyed beneath overtones of humour and serio-comic thunderclaps. His sharp ironical wit saves his sense of pity from deteriorating into sentiment. He balances his humour between the earth and the moon, between St Peter and the Devil. In such plays as *House of Regrets*, *The Love of Four Colonels* and *Romanoff and Juliet* his characters move in a hinterland between illusion and reality, failing to dodge a satirical aim which can have the unsparing precision of a well-handled machine-gun. 'I have just finished a third of my new novel,' he once said to me; then he recounted every detail of what he had written while mapping out with topographic clarity the unwritten two-thirds. His way of working is like Racine's, who, when asked how his new play was going, replied, 'I have finished it, I have only to write the dialogue. There remains only the physical labour.' Yet, with all his quick-witted brilliance, his values affirm people. He has never lost his apprehension for the human race or the sound of his own heart-beat. Although Ustinov can make the mistake of pleasing people without pleasing himself, he remains contagiously and irresistibly sympathetic. Where life throws a cat and a mouse together, his heart invariably goes out to the mouse.

As raconteur and impersonator he has no equal. Record and TV audiences all over the world have been captivated by his imitations of German generals, English tourists, Bosnian diplomats, American music critics and French sports cars. Through what he calls 'a musical ear which enables me to get under the skin of a nation's aesthetic sense', he has exploded all the language barriers, and can establish a relationship on the basis of a language he cannot speak, even as he can give a musical recital without an instrument. Others found empires of literature, but Ustinov is on the way to founding an empire of human contact.

It was exciting to work in Dublin, even though it is at first glance a drab city, in spite of its rose-coloured squares which open and close between dark lacerated alleys described by O'Casey as 'slinky with shame'. Even then, in 1962, I was reminded of Kitchener's most melancholy recruiting slogan, 'The trenches are safer than the Dublin slums.' Those long, monotonous rows of crumbling elegance seem bored and exhausted by two hundred years of turbulent history.

Yet no one could long remain un-fond of this city of famous sons—Swift and Sheridan, Shaw and Wilde, Yeats, Joyce, O'Casey and the young Samuel Beckett. Brighton Square, Joyce's birthplace, is a proper place of pilgrimage, as is the Martello tower which features in the opening pages of *Ulysses* and is now a Joyce museum. In the streets of Dublin you are surrounded, as Stephen Dedalus and 'stately, plump Buck Mulligan' were, by the whole of Joyce's Irish world. To the east, the broken rocks and the 'snotgreen ... scrotumtightening sea'; behind, the Wicklow Hills; to the west, the tall stucco houses on the front at Dun Laoghaire, and the city spreading out behind them; and north, across the bay, Joyce's beloved Howth, where, in Pagan mythology, Grainne seduced the reluctant Diarmuid, and where Molly Bloom, among the rhododendrons, thought, ' ... well as well him as another and then I asked him with my eyes to ask again yes and then he asked me would I yes to say yes yes my mountain flower and first I put my arms around him yes and drew him down to me so he could feel my breasts all perfume yes and his heart was going like mad and yes I said yes I will Yes.'

One evening Peter Ustinov, Anew McMaster and Micheál Mac Liammóir gave a benefit performance for the family of a stage-hand who had met with a fatal accident during a performance in the theatre. It was a solemn evening. Peter walked through his concert recital, Anew recited a few Shakespearean sonnets with histrionic breeding and Micheál contributed a portion of Ireland's history with a short selection of its major poets.

When I dined with the three performers over candlelight in the Green Room, I asked Micheál to expand his performance into a full-length show which we could put on in London with his already famous Oscar Wilde sequence, *The Importance of Being Oscar*, for a short season of international theatre at the Aldwych. He agreed, and thus *I Must be Talking to my Friends* went on as a companion to the Oscar Wilde piece in 1963.

I had originally met Micheál by accident. He had telephoned Peter Ustinov, and I had picked up the receiver. 'Is that you, Peter darling?' Micheál's voice, immediately recognizable, had inquired. I was somewhat surprised by this affectionate greeting, but when he asked me to lunch the following day I accepted the invitation with alacrity. When I came into the restaurant he looked up at me with a startled expression. It was not until we had almost finished an enchanting meal that he told me he had invited the wrong 'Peter'!

This was the beginning of a long and firm friendship. Apart from his Irish loquaciousness, Mac Liammóir has the gift of the mythical Gaelic storyteller, who carried in his mind all the legends of the earth and sea and sky, of the visible and invisible, and who told them at the fireside. This was the bard of Celtic tradition, and Wilde himself had something of the quality. When Micheál speaks in his beautifully modulated, soft-edged voice, the world as we know it seems a drab place; he becomes like a great actor showing up a poor play. He has a quick, leaping, impulsive heart, that understands the spirit of folly and wisdom in human nature and illuminates characters, conflicts and countries. He senses a continuity between past and present. As Hazlitt said of Coleridge, 'He talked on for ever; and you wished him to talk on for ever.'

The Importance of Being Oscar had been inspired by an idea of Peter Ashmore, out of which, with the help of his partner Hilton Edwards, Mac Liammóir had devised a theatrical biography of Oscar Wilde. In this show Micheál displayed his flair as an actor, biographer and wit. It was formed from a series of excerpts set in a chronological pattern, linked by a commentary, as the episodes rolled forward with the inevitability of Greek Tragedy.

Micheál has traced the origins of this triumphant piece of theatre back to his childhood when, as a boy of eleven, he inquired of his father the identity of Oscar Wilde. 'My father, the most charming man, made one of the many major mistakes of his life.' The boy was told that Wilde murdered people's souls. 'But what did he do? Was he a murderer?' 'The man was guilty of a far greater sin, God forgive him, than the sin of going to bed with bad women. He turned young men into women.' It was a fatal answer. 'Questions are never indiscreet: answers sometimes are.' Never had Wilde's own aphorism been more true. Mystery is a spur to the imagination, and the effect on the boy was dynamic. He became a sleuth, and carried out his own private investigations, but at every inquiry he drew a blank. One evening, as he was changing trains at Charing Cross, he grasped his sister's arm. 'Look—there is one of his books,' he whispered, transfixed in front of a locked bookstall. What could be more tantalizing than this quivering Dickensian atmosphere of trains and hansom cabs, particularly as he was playing Oliver Twist at the time, earning good money—£2 10s. a week—as a boy actor, under the majestic auspices of Sir Herbert Beerbohm Tree at His Majesty's Theatre? There was, however, a middle-aged dresser at the theatre, to whom, at the first opportunity, he again fired his fatal question: 'Why did they put Oscar Wilde in prison?' The dresser knew the answer, and Micheál describes the incident in a brilliantly funny sprint of dialogue. But it was only after several years that he realized that the man was confusing the Ballad-singer of Reading Gaol with Jack the Ripper. It took him in all three years of investigation to solve this gigantic mystery, and his fascination with Oscar Wilde is consequently well ingrained. Since the first performance of *The Importance of Being Oscar*, Micheál has lived with Oscar's attendant spirit. It is indeed a ghostly companionship, and I sometimes fear that the puppet will be taken over by the strength of the puppeteer.

It was W. B. Yeats, with his passion for nationalism and the national traditions, who drew Micheál back to Ireland and inspired him to learn the Irish language. 'Probably the Irish theatre would not exist at all', he once told me, 'had it not been for Yeats's inspiration. He was essentially not a theatre man, but he was one of those who saw a pressing need to serve the country in his own medium of expression.'

Most Irishmen of great promise before him had followed the traditional route of emigration to England and America—from Swift, Farquhar, Congreve, Goldsmith and Sheridan to Wilde, Shaw and O'Casey. Oddly enough, as Micheál has pointed out, all masters and elegant practitioners in the art of comedy and wit are 'a strange contrast coming out of an historically dis-tressful and poverty-striken country'.

In Dublin in 1928 Mac Liammóir had founded the Gate Theatre in association with Hilton Edwards. It sprang partly from the work of the Dublin Drama League, a group founded in 1918 to bring international contemporary classics to the Irish stage and which presented plays by, among others, Pirandello, D'Annunzio and Eugene O'Neill. The Gate's policy remained to encourage young Irish dramatists by putting them in touch with what was going on in the wider outside world of experimental theatre.

'Micheál decided he wanted a theatre in Ireland,' Hilton Edwards told me. 'I wanted a theatre anywhere at all. I thought there was an open market. I thought here I had come to a town, in which there is no grocer's shop—there is a baker, a butcher, a fishmonger, but no grocer. We said, all right, we will set up a grocery store. Our definite intention was to bring to Ireland the plays it was not seeing.' One of their producers in the early days was a young man called Denis Johnston, who later blossomed into an experimental playwright of some importance, and whose best play, *The Moon in the Yellow River*, was produced at the

Gate in 1931. The theme of this play was, appropriately enough, the impact of industrial sophistication on an easy-going romantic community immersed in its traditions. The Gate Theatre has to this day remained one of the dominant influences on the Irish theatre.

Among the Gate's most notable achievements was the discovery of the young Orson Welles, who after the death of his father in America, had landed in Galway in 1931 with a few dollars, which he had invested in a horse and cart so that he could tour Ireland as an 'itinerant painter'. Sweeping into Dublin in due course, he demanded an audition, 'a very tall young man', as Micheál remembered him, 'with a chubby face, full powerful lips and disconcerting Chinese eyes'.

'I've acted with the Guild. I've written a couple of plays. I've toured the States as a sword-swallowing female impersonator. I've flared through Hollywood like a firecracker. I've lived in a little tomato-coloured house on the Great Wall of China on two dollars a week. I've wafted my way with a jackass through Connemara. I've eaten dates all over the burning desert and crooned Delaware squaws asleep with Serbian rhapsodies. But I haven't told you everything. No; there wouldn't be time.'

He was cast as the Duke in a production of *Jew Süss*, which was a huge success. The next year he returned to America and some years later he founded the Mercury Theater there.

Micheál and Hilton had met in 1927 in Anew McMaster's Shakespearean Company in Ireland. McMaster had had a successful career as an actor in London and Australia in the 1920s. Then a sudden row blew him back to Ireland to tour with a little company round the smallest towns—the tiny, almost illiterate villages all over the south and west.

There were many such small companies travelling through Ireland in those years between the wars; Dobell's, Carrickford's and Jack Walsh's were three. Cyril Cusack acted on tour with his stepfather's troupe, the Brefni O'Rourke Company, from about 1917, and he recollects those early days as 'perhaps the most fruitful and the most enjoyable of my career'. The company travelled from village to village, town to town. 'In each town we played a week, a different play each night. It was mostly melodrama in those days, beginning with the inevitable *East Lynne*.' Cusack also toured with the O'Brien and Ireland Company, specialists in Boucicault's melodramas. He remembers performances that were taken so seriously that 'not only would the villain be booed on stage, but some of the locals might even wait for him at the stage door to do what they might to him—one had to be rather careful in those days playing the villain.'

Anew McMaster broke away from the tradition of melodrama. He wanted to take Shakespeare to the Irish countryside, and after a few unhappy months his productions began to attract a surprising public. At one stop, where he announced he was to give a performance of Daphne du Maurier's *Rebecca*, an elder of the village rose in protest. 'We are very backwardy in this place. Why wouldn't you give us *Julius Caesar*?'

To McMaster all life was a fantasy. His wonderful wife Marjorie did all the booking; managed the wardrobe; painted the drapes; helped to adjust the scenery; dealt with the staff. He endowed this gypsy life with a noble grace, sailing through all problems with a majestic indifference. At times his humour almost destroyed him. It was of a grotesque, fantastic and unpredictable nature, and often ruinous. He reminded me of Tati's Monsieur Hulot, for I often saw him, then aged sixty-eight, march into the sea, tall, fit and remarkably youthful. He was, in Harold Pinter's words, 'a devout anti-puritan. He was a very great piss-taker! A jealous guardian of his love and understanding of acting, he resented the use of the new-fangled producer—"a lot of silly little boys from Oxford or somewhere, don't know their stage from their elbow." '

Enniscorthy in County Wexford, Cahirciveen in Kerry and Dunmanway in County Cork will never forget him. Pinter, who toured with him for two years, recalls in his little book, *Mac*, that McMaster was, 'at his best, the finest Othello I've even seen. His voice was unique, of unequal range.' At one place, where the hall was full, Marjorie rushed in as he was making up for Macbeth with the words, 'No more seats,' and promptly removed the last seat in the room, upon which 'Mac' was sitting, to place it in the audience.

Today the days of the touring companies are over, and the dominant influence on Irish theatre remains, as it has been since 1904, that of the Abbey Theatre. Up till the turn of the century Ireland, having anonymously contributed her distinguished exiles for two hundred years to English theatre and literature, herself remained an enigma.

Beyond the highly successful, skilfully constructed melodramas of Dion Boucicault—the dramatist and actor-manager who was born in Dublin in 1822 and died in New York in 1890—there had been little sign of an Irish theatrical tradition on its home ground. W. B. Yeats sought to change all this.

In 1898 Yeats had, with Edward Martyn, George Moore and Lady Gregory, founded the Irish Literary Theatre. Their purpose was to give expression to the Ireland that each one of them knew in reality, and not in romantic fiction. They were to revitalize the myth and passion of Irish history and character. English actors had had to be imported for their early productions, including Yeats's *The Countess Cathleen*, because no suitable group of actors existed in Ireland at the time. Then a company of amateur Irish actors, led by two brothers, Frank and William G. Fay, joined forces with Yeats and Lady Gregory to form the Irish National Dramatic Society.

The Abbey Theatre itself became a triumphant reality after the society had taken some of its plays to London and they had been seen by that great enthusiast, Miss Annie Horniman. In 1904 she put up the money to buy the old Mechanics' Institute in Dublin and to convert it into a theatre for the society's use. And in 1907 J. M. Synge's *The Playboy of the Western World* put Ireland on the stage at last.

In the decade that followed the Abbey's opening in 1904 it became not only the most exciting theatre in Europe but also the first true repertory theatre; later still, when Lady Gregory obtained £850 from the state, it became the first state-subsidized theatre in the English-speaking world. The Fay brothers, working with Yeats, evolved a unique style of presentation that had an almost classical emphasis, sets and actions being cut back to sparse indications and the weight of production falling on language and its declamation. When Cyril Cusack joined the Abbey in 1932, he was joining a company with a very strong tradition. 'We had personalities—names that are still well remembered—Barry Fitzgerald, who later went to America; F. J. MacCormick, who was one of the purest actors that I have ever worked with; and Maureen Delaney among them.'

It was late in 1921 that a rough manuscript arrived at the Abbey from a builder's labourer then living in a Dublin tenement. It was *The Shadow of a Gunman*, which opened two years later, and brought to light the playwright who was to dominate the Abbey of the 1920s: Sean O'Casey. Through O'Casey, though he changed the venue from mountains to slums, all the rich barbarities of Synge seemed to flow, but with something added. For following that descent from the windy heights to the darkest streets, from scarlet petticoat to black straw hat, a still warmer passion and laughter and wild pity lit the characters with fire; his characters were less beautiful, less abstract, less poetic and archetypal than those of Synge, but with that they were all the more terrible and familiar, funny and ferocious. O'Casey was perhaps the first writer after Gorky to celebrate the magnificence of poverty, the fierce and raw reality of suffering. In Brendan Behan's words, 'O'Casey's like champagne, one's wedding-night or the Aurora Borealis or whatever you call them—all the lights.'

Then, after both *Juno and the Paycock* and *The Plough and the Stars* had had their *premières* at the Abbey, in 1928 Yeats and Lady Gregory rejected *The Silver Tassie* on the grounds that it was 'too abstract'. Though the theatre continued with the earlier plays, and eventually put on *The Silver Tassie* itself, none of O'Casey's later plays were performed by the Abbey until after 1964. O'Casey himself moved to live permanently in England, the final break with the Abbey coming in 1958 when the Dublin Theatre Festival had to be abandoned because of religious pressure which demanded cuts in *The Drums of Father Ned*. Angered by this abandonment of the festival in the face of such opposition, O'Casey refused to allow any further professional Irish productions of his plays.

I had wanted to present a season of his work in London, and was already in touch with the playwright at his house in Torquay, when plans for the first World Theatre Season began to take shape. I decided to bring to my first World Theatre Season the Abbey Theatre playing O'Casey, and for this purpose I determined to repair the breach between Ireland's national theatre and one of its finest playwrights.

I was delighted and honoured to receive a letter from O'Casey's wife Eileen, in which she said:

I am thrilled that you have chosen to bring Sean's two plays, *Juno and the Paycock* and *The Plough and the Stars*, over from the Abbey Theatre to be presented at the Aldwych in the World Theatre Season this year. Sean, I know, is also happy that his plays are to be presented in London. I know he has written to you.

I am doubly pleased because, after the Bishop of Dublin had banned *The Drums of Father Ned*—which was written for the Tostal—Sean banned the performances of all his plays in Dublin. Joyce and Beckett were to have been performed, as you know, that year, but they withdrew their plays in protest.

Sean took a while to decide to lift the ban. I know it was his great respect and admiration for the work you have done in the theatre, and the fact *you* have chosen his plays to come to the Aldwych, that made him decide to do this. Having decided, he could hardly let down the Abbey players by not allowing them to perform and rehearse the plays in Dublin before coming to London.

Although I have always felt that Sean should do exactly as he wanted about his own work, I am delighted he has written to Ernest Blythe, saying he will lift the ban temporarily. I am most pleased that the younger generation in Ireland can now see his plays. There is no doubt that this gesture of his is entirely due to you.

In the months preceding their visit, O'Casey became my one great telephone friend. We never met, but we rang each other almost daily, and seemed to talk for hours. He was very happy that two of his plays should be chosen that year to honour Shakespeare.

'The best way to honour him, of course,' he wrote to me, 'is to know and love him; but it is good and proper to honour him in a tribute from one who loves true men and true poets. You have done richly in assembling this tribute in London. I am grateful to you for thinking of a place for Ireland and for me among those who come bearing the gold, frankincense and myrrh of Drama as an offering to the Poet!'

But when I actually went with John Francis Lane to see the plays in Dublin I experienced a degree of dismay. The Abbey Theatre Company were performing at the old melodrama theatre, the Queen's, while they awaited completion of their new building, which was to open in July 1966. After the old Abbey had been burnt down in 1951, the company, crossing the Liffey to the Queen's, had suffered a deterioration of spirit. It was hardly surprising. The place was like a drill-hall and, however full it might be, always felt empty. The productions seemed crammed with faults: some poor acting and very poor sets. The actors always looked cold.

I argued bitterly with the Abbey directors, insisting that changes must be made before the productions came to London. When I described my problems to O'Casey he wrote of one of the directors, 'He is a mass of obstinacy, so full of his own import-ance that he will listen to no one; insensitive, too, utterly im-pervious to anything said to him. He hasn't the faintest idea of what is Drama, and less about the art of actor; he has become a human limpet fastened to the Abbey Theatre.'

The plays, nevertheless, arrived, despite a strike threat by the Abbey Players themselves, and were received by a muted press. They were, however, enormously succeessful. We had full houses every night and long queues for return tickets.

'I accept the praise in your letter with humility,' O'Casey wrote to me, 'for, looking back at the plays and all else, like Gogol, I find little to brag about, but remain dissatisfied that all could not have been better shaped and the plays given a fairer habitation on the stage.'

The Abbey returned to London in 1968, with Dion Boucicault's melodrama *The Shaughraun*, a production which at last gave me the chance to present Cyril Cusack in London, in the role of Conn, the Shaughraun himself. It proved a triumph for the Abbey, and marked the revival of interest in Boucicault. It was strange that this author, so ignored by the early Abbey, should have been responsible for the Abbey's re-emergence. As Cyril Cusack said of *The Shaughraun*, it was 'an essentially theatrical experience, which would appeal to a truly sophisticated and a truly simple audience'.

In his production Hugh Hunt re-established melodrama in its nineteenth-century form, capable of stirring a contemporary public as deeply as it had their grandfathers. The format had re-mained constant: the villain was villainous, the heroine virginal, the hero noble and bold.

Nineteenth-century melodrama had reached its peak with Grand Guignol, that most sophisticated torture chamber, which caused Paris audiences to thrill to themes of violence, murder, rape and suicide. It was a pleasure which was carried forward into the 1920s, as Sybil Thorndike and Lewis Casson tortured and murdered their company at the Little Theatre with inventions borrowed from the Black Museum of Scotland Yard. And melodrama, with Tod Slaughter in *Maria Martin*, thrilled millions with that actor's feats of daring.

Tod Slaughter was the McMaster of melodrama in England. His company engaged in barn-storming tours with a repertoire of plays which revealed him as the octopus of melodramatic theatre. I had first seen him at Farnham when I was fourteen. He was playing Sweeney Todd on that evening, and in the story of the Fleet Street barber who murdered his customers and sold their bodies to the neighbouring pie-shop to be made into meat pies, Slaughter revealed all his cunning resourcefulness. I still remember the terrifying hint of malice which he concealed behind a mask of benignity. When in 1951 I was casting *The Gay Invalid*, it had been Tod Slaughter to whom I gave the part of Dr Slaughter, and discovered not only a friend but also a fine actor with a sharp sense of satirical comedy.

Meanwhile, in 1968, the success of *The Shaughraun* was immediate. Cyril Cusack wrote to me on his return to Dublin that it had been

a sudden revolution, a conspiracy of circumstances. As, indeed, the very beginning of the Abbey was a conspiracy of circumstances, of poetry, of politics, of acting quality. How it originates—where it comes from, I don't know, but the company had suddenly effloresced, and when it came to London with this very vital Boucicault play, we found a terrific reaction—a joyous reaction—and an arrival for us at any rate into the theatre of true theatre-goers.

Boucicault's full-blooded piece about the laughter-loving Irish peasantry, with its lugubrious and sophisticated irony, formed a strange contrast to the wintry world of Ibsen's black comedy *Hedda Gabler*, which followed it at the Aldwych and marked the second visit to London of a production by Ingmar Bergman. In 1959 I had brought to the Princes Theatre his production of Goethe's *Urfaust* with the Malmö City Company, with whom, as a director since 1954, he has staged such memorable productions as *Peer Gynt*, *The Merry Widow* and *Macbeth*. The

T

cast of *Urfaust* included Toivo Pawlo as Mephistopheles, Gunnel Lindblom as a touchingly beautiful and youthful Margaret, and Max von Sydow as a splendidly sensual Faust. It was a stunning stage production framed by three Gothic arches with projections at the back to convey the changes of scenery—which achieved a severity of style recalling the woodcuts of Dürer.

When I first met Bergman in Paris in 1959, he was on his knees hammering nails into a rostrum on the stage. He got up and looked at me, a lithe, youthful figure, with steady eyes like jets of flame. I had an impression of a simple carpenter possessed by an evangelical vision.

Bergman, known outside Sweden mainly for his work in the cinema, is a great theatre director who displays a great delicacy of composition. His patience and subtle power of improvisation help to give his actors a sense of relaxation. However much he denies that he is neither psychologist nor intellectual, he shows a rare instinct with his actors, with whom he becomes very emotionally involved. He will overlook technical faults if the performers are reproducing what he demands; he does not stop to analyse why characters behave as they do.

One might say that he inherits his sexual anxiety from Strindberg, his spiritual anxiety from Kierkegaard and his philosophic anxiety from Kafka. There is perhaps no living artist so profoundly appalled by life's brevity, a philosophy summed up in his manifesto on his work in the cinema, *Each Film is my Last*.

His *Hedda Gabler*, with the Royal Dramatic Theatre of Stockholm at the 1968 World Theatre Season, proved that there is no greater interpreter of Ibsen. In much of Bergman's work he deliberately over-simplifies in order to elucidate; in his production of *Hedda Gabler* he stressed the psychological motivations of the heroine, which Ibsen had intentionally left in doubt. Played against a stark set of Venetian blood-red, with a token panel in the centre of the stage to indicate two rooms, and sparse matching furniture edged in black, Bergman dispersed the cobwebs of suffocating Victoriana which always tend to surround the play. He made both actors and playwright project with steely strength and superb control. Gertrude Fridh as Hedda revealed the suppressed desires of a man-eating tigress, with the needs, greeds and passions of a predatory animal that crushes its victims before devouring them. It was a marvellous performance which created in Hedda a complete woman. Trevor Nunn, the brilliant young artistic director of the Royal Shakespeare Company, said in a speech at the British Council, 'Ingmar Bergman's production of *Hedda Gabler* has made a deep impression on us because it demands that we reassess all our old preconceptions of Ibsen and because it points the way to the future.'

My first understanding of Ingmar came when, after arriving from Malmö in 1959, he accompanied me to the Swedish Embassy for a press conference. The entrance was jammed with journalists, and he at first refused to go in, reluctantly entering only through a back door, from where we were escorted to the Ambassador's private study. He hated publicity, he said, and seldom gave interviews. 'When I have finished something I have done with it. It bores me stiff. That is why I hate discussing it with a lot of strangers. It is awful to be questioned about one's meanings and interpretations.'

While the clamour below grew in intensity, he told me about his father, Dean Bergman, who was for many years Sweden's most famous preacher, as well as about his maternal grandmother, who showed him his first movie. 'I was sitting on the carpet, when suddenly I noticed shadows moving over a painting of Venice opposite me. The shadows contracted and dissolved in curious shapes, and there I was, seeing my first film. I felt I had entered a new dimension, and it was very wonderful.' We talked about Camus, P. G. Wodehouse, Pirandello and Kafka, bowler hats, Strindberg, puppet theatres and umbrellas; and, for some reason, the sad, infantile delight that transforms second childhood into a private fantasy of expressionism. He had started his career as a director for children. He loved children, with their sense of wonder and discovery; and 'those first surprises that invade childhood'. 'I must see Madame Tussauds,' he said. 'That must be our first visit.' Then with his charming laugh he gestured me to the door to face the wolves below. I had detected no hint of the visionary laughing noiselessly at his own secret thoughts. When he left London he sent me a note, an expression of affection:

Dear Peter,
To come to London, to work for you, to come to your house, to feel friends with you, I thank you so much,
INGMAR

During his ten days in London he told me that he admired David Lean's films, and so I brought them together over dinner. David's most recently completed film at that time was *The Bridge on the River Kwai*, and as he had never seen a Bergman film he had hurried off to see *Wild Strawberries* that afternoon. Bergman listened with humility while David Lean, the master craftsman and editor, talked at length about *The Bridge on the River Kwai*; then he asked David, 'Have you ever seen one of my films?' David admitted that he had just come from *Wild Strawberries*, which was the only one. 'Did you like it?' asked Bergman nervously, and Lean replied, 'You can do certain things better than anyone in the world, but if you had cut'—he mentioned a particular sequence—'you would have achieved a much more exciting effect.' Bergman said that as soon as he got back to Stockholm he would run the film again. It was a fascinating meeting, in which this tense, swift-tongued Swede, who turned out film masterpieces on a shoe-string in his own country, chose to play the pupil.

All his leading themes are orchestrated in *Wild Strawberries*. Here the guilty eroticism of *Smiles of a Summer Night* is heightened into mystery, and the confrontation with death, so coldly symbolized in *The Seventh Seal*, is pitched as human tragedy. The film forms a series of confrontations—of youth with age, of lust with frigidity, of life with death—and its images are unforgettable.

Bergman also has a strong romantic vision. Many years later he told me in Stockholm of an indelible memory from the days at the Princes Theatre with *Urfaust*—'I loved it, it was so dirty.' While rehearsing there in 1959 he had wandered up to the dress circle to inspect one of the spotlights. 'Through a tapestry of heavy coloured dust I found a boy and girl embracing. I was enchanted.'

In the English script edition of *Wild Strawberries* (1960) Bergman wrote:

A lot has been said about the value of originality, and I find this foolish. Either you are original or you are not. It is completely natural for artists to take from and give to each other, to borrow from and experience one another. In my own life, my great literary experience was Strindberg. There are works of his which can still make my hair stand on end—*The People of Hemsö*, for example. And it is my dream to produce *Dream Play* some day. Olof Molander's production of it in 1934 was for me a fundamental dramatic experience.

This ambition has since been realized, and Strindberg's *Dream Play* is at the time of writing to be a star item in the 1971 World Theatre Season.

There are many modern artists who have cast a cold eye on death. And Bergman's genius is that he makes us look as well, however reluctantly. There are things better not talked about, but he has talked about them. We can only be grateful. He is the Strindberg of contemporary theatre.

13
The Orient—China and Japan

In 1955 London saw for the first time the unsurpassable vision of beauty and sorcery which the Peking Opera reveals in its unique form of production. It is a form which has no contemporary parallels; carries no message for those standing outside. Time and place cease to exist in a world that is ruled by gods, monkeys, frogs, dragons and fishermen.

The Chinese drama, like the Greek and Japanese, derives from primitive religious ceremonies, and abounds in acrobats, jugglers and dancers. It began in remote antiquity, but during the third century B.C. it is thought to have relied entirely on improvised comedy and acrobatics similar to the *commedia dell'arte*. Then, during the Han dynasty (140–87 B.C.), when a clairvoyant brought a dead empress back to life by casting her shadow on a screen, it gave birth to a new kind of play—the shadow-play—that can still be seen in China and Greece today. This theatre, together with the puppet-shows manipulated by gloved puppeteers, continued as an entertainment throughout the various dynasties. Then, for the first time, actors came to wear masks painted on their faces, and it is amusing to record that the mask was originally a device adopted by a great general as part of his armour to convey a facial aggression that his delicate features lacked. These performances go back to the Yüan dynasty of the late thirteenth and early fourteenth centuries, for it was then, about a hundred years before Zeami created the Nō plays in Japan, that China, under its Mongol rulers, produced its greatest drama. The Yüan plays were to become the source of all traditional Chinese theatre and, in particular, the direct ancestors of the Peking opera.

When the curtain rose on the performance in London, it revealed a brilliant turquoise carpet which burst into a garden of flaming colours. The greatest pageantry that the East had to offer had begun. In memory this entertainment appears as a series of tracking shots of piercing beauty, whose visions of unguessed wonder still haunt the mind. Its subject-matter was drawn from a deep well of history and legend, mirroring the beauty, cruelty, taste, serenity and violence of a succession of periods. The fabulous tapestry unfolded itself in mime, opera, recitations and miraculous acrobatics, drawn from the myths and symbols of many dynasties. Coloured scarves dipped and swayed to the clashing of gongs and cymbals, the jumping of monkeys, the flashing of swords and the swirling of acrobats, the gorgeous costumes of sulphur-yellow, crimson and gold.

Back-stage another world was revealed. I made great friends with the monkey king, Wang Ming-chung, who spent nearly two hours on making up, ringing his eyes with bright crimson and silver circles and applying gold to his nostrils. Under the shell of this terrifying make-up, however, Wang Ming-chung showed a shy manner, stealthy authority and a compulsive kindness.

I also watched for hours the training of the acrobats, who taught me to stand on my head while they held on to one leg. I watched the generals, one of whom looked as fierce as Picasso's 'Portrait of Vollard' before he had applied his beard. He talked to me a great deal in French and English, his smooth, faintly smiling face sensitive, moody and intellectual. All beards denoted age, he said. The long ones conveyed prestige, the coloured ones nobility and refinement. 'But when you see me with my beard up', he said, 'it means catastrophe.' A moustache symbolized cunning. The mimetic gestures quite clearly indicated their meaning without having to be explained. But the colours of the masks required an intricate vocabulary to portray character and emotion, just as the colour of costumes indicated rank, social order or nobility, and the cymbal and gong denoted the character of the drama.

I did not find it possible, however, to concern myself simply with aesthetic or dramatic considerations during the visits of Chinese groups. When two years later, in 1957, I presented the Formosan company in London at Drury Lane, I found myself unwittingly embroiled in a political row. The Chinese Government saw in the visit of a group from Nationalist China an insult to the Chinese nation. The *chargé d'affaires* in London issued a statement declaring that the aim of the visit was 'to slander the

Chinese Government and to undermine the friendly relations between the peoples of China and Britain under the cloak of cultural activities'. The Britain–China Friendship Association also weighed in with their support. However, when the *chargé d'affaires* added that the company was really part of Chiang Kai-shek's air force, only the *Daily Worker* carried the revelation with any degree of confidence in its truth.

As it emerged, several members of the company had once been part of the Peking Opera before 1949, when they crossed over to Nationalist China. No doubt this fact still rankled with the mainland Chinese, though it in no way affected the success of the company. 'I'm glad I've lived to see it,' A. E. Matthews told me delightedly after the first night. 'Better than television; it's better than me!' But, in contrast with the Peking Opera itself, the Formosan acrobats seemed under-trained, and marvellous scenes, which danced and spilled over with light—full of harsh, conflicting shadows of menace—were replaced by a gorgeous, but less resonant display of ceremonial pageantry.

The mime, character and acting of the members of the Peking Opera had shown a technical resourcefulness that seemed to be second nature. Their gestures and rhythm gave each character a life and soul of its own, each scene a split-second timing that contained a counterpoise of tension and humour. When I remember this extraordinary entertainment I call to mind a living montage. There is the scene at an inn where two people hunt each other with murderous intent in pitch darkness on a brilliantly lit stage; they miss each other by a hair's breadth and make one's spine tingle and hair stand on end; when the candle arrives, the audience swoons with relief. The monkey king, Wang Ming-chung, eats the heavenly peaches of immortality which he has been sent to guard, only to be routed by the generals in a breathtaking battle. The maiden beguiling the old boatman to row her downstream to her lover shows her wit and hypnotic beauty, while the slow motion of the non-existent boat rocks dangerously, making everyone feel seasick. The dance of victory throws up yellow scarves that unfurl above the blue like endless Catherine wheels. The pheasant's feathers of the bearded generals shake as they take up their position in the great revolt, the acrobat fighters leaping between, around and over each other like monkeys in a zoo, with a timing, energy, elevation and rhythm that defies all the rules of physical limitation. In the finale the acrobats disappear in one fantastic backward leap over a high wall.

Since Mao Tse-tung promoted his 'Cultural Revolution' in 1966, the iconoclastic teenage Red Guards, promoted as a public image, have seemed to shatter the cultural fabric of the oldest existing civilization. While silence continues to reign behind the Great Wall of China, it can only be from Japan, through the Nō, Kabuki and Bunraku, that our younger generation will learn the mystic art of another world.

Before I went to Japan in 1967, I had not gone out of my way to find out anything about the country. Like an opium-smoker, I was reconciled to what would happen. I was about to enter a golden labyrinth of myth and imagination.

After eighteen hours in the air, my senses sharpened as we approached the twinkling lights of the fairy-tale city of glowing lanterns and paper houses called Tokyo. I had been invited by the Japanese Ministry of Education to spend a few days in their country following the unparalleled success of the Nō Theatre on their first memorable visit to London earlier in the year, and with a view to bringing the Bunraku puppet theatre to the next London season. But now, as we landed, I thought the pilot had made a mistake, and the people at the airport reinforced this impression. My eyes sought in vain for a traditional Madame Butterfly; most of the women looked like fashion models from *Vogue*, and the rest could have stepped out of *Coronation Street*. The men all wore neat black suits and sombre ties, like mortuary attendants in New York; everyone was impeccably gentle and polite.

I went through Customs and found awaiting me a reception committee from the Hashioka and Umewaka Nō families dressed in brown kimonos. In my exhausted state they looked so odd that I thought it must be me at London Airport who was receiving them. They all stood together in an old-fashioned way, as if posing for the family Brownie. Waiting with them was Robin Duke, the elegant and charming cultural attaché, who brought me back into focus, and I was then introduced to Mikkio, my interpreter, a young man with a huge grin and horn-rimmed spectacles. We piled into three cars and set off at full speed along the four-lane highway. Even on that fleeting journey, I suddenly realized that Tokyo was neither all lanterns and paper houses nor merely iron and cement, but that, more than any other capital city, it still managed to be all things to all men. Japan has never discarded the old when she has taken on the new. In the shadows of office blocks and hotels I glimpsed little wooden shops, and when we passed a rickshaw being pulled under a railway bridge that served one of the 150 m.p.h. bullet trains, the conjunction of old and new seemed strangely exciting.

Arriving at an extremely modern hotel, I was shown into a bedroom which had all necessary comforts without losing the sparse, economical essence of Japanese taste. The floor was softly carpeted all over. On the walls were three prints of famous Samurai warriors or Kabuki actors. A red lacquer table stood on a small square of rush matting, and the bed, like something from a Feydeau farce, was large and brassy. The lighting shone, a delicate amber, on the table, upon which were two red roses, poised like benign virgins in a green vase, representing the first of many encounters with the delicate art of Japanese flower-arrangement.

The next morning at ten o'clock Mikkio arrived at the hotel. He was to prove a delightful companion, with his eye for the small gesture and the little scenes of delicate reality which conformed to his sense of theatrical fantasy. He read out with mounting enthusiasm a schedule of events in a voice that reminded me of a Noël Coward parody of Dickens's Mr Jingle. In his excitement he showed a tendency to forget his verbs, but he had an encyclopedic knowledge of his country, better than any guide-book.

'Ambassador call—nice man—lunch tomorrow' (huge smile). 'Now we walk—see shops—Ginza—give you first scent of city yes? Then Hashioka—special show written for you—Ambassador there—Kabuki troupe—lunch with Umewaka—go Kyoto very fine—Nara very beautiful—judo—karate—Sumō—modern theatre—tea ceremony—relative Imperial family—show flower-arrangement—go now? Explore Ginza—tonight welcome dinner in your honour—Geisha girls—very lovely—we now explore?'

My first exploration was disappointing. Japan's breakneck industrial progress after the devastation of the war had produced a conglomeration of buildings. As we walked along I saw women in beautiful kimonos wandering through the Balenciaga and Dior salons. Mikkio told me that their husbands spend anything up to twelve hours a day in their offices giving Japan's run-away economy an extra push. He informed me that later they would relax in bars, cabarets or geisha parties, according to their taste and the size of their expense-accounts. And the worker, Mikkio told me, is looked after from the cradle to the grave by industrial firms, whose owners act as godfathers, supplanting even the deep elemental family roots. I was to find out that the Japanese have a passion for becoming Westernized and an obsession with remaining traditional. The younger generation have also acquired a stronger and taller physique through Westernization, and throughout my visit I was conscious of a bitter clash between the two cultures. Nowhere were its paradoxes more evident than at dinner that evening with the members of the Department of Culture, the first official engagement of my visit.

We sat upon cushions round a low table in a large private room of a Japanese restaurant. A geisha girl sat on each side of me, one to feed me while the other wiped my face with a small towel. This cult of cleanliness has its origins in the Shinto abhorrence of defilement from dirt, blood and death. Shinto is the native religion of Japan, characterized by ritual ceremonies at planting and harvest times. The food on the table was beautifully set out, intended to appeal to the visual sense as much as to the palate. A great many little dishes were carefully arranged to give the best effect of shape and colour, even slices of carrots being shaped into cherry blossoms. It was a gastronomic exhibition, and I was still feasting my eyes when the two geishas motioned that I should start. I was slightly apprehensive when offered a small rice-cake topped with raw fish, but this proved delicious. It was then followed by *sukiyaki*—thin strips of beef cooked in a rich sauce with vegetables—and then by *tempura*, which was so appetizing that it would be little more than an insult to describe it as, basically, fried fish. Many other delicacies with strange-sounding names were placed before me, each one proving that *haute cuisine* in Tokyo could compete with the best in London or Paris. The two geishas offered me saki, and became distraught when I refused to drink. The gentleman next to me noticed this and informed me that 'the Japanese love drink', but, he admitted, masking his face with his hand, 'we are the world's worst drinkers.' This was illustrated quite clearly when a single glass of lager-type beer brought a fiery flush to his saffron complexion. I asked him to tell me more about saki, the traditional Japanese drink made from rice. It was obviously a matter for consideration, for he fell into a deep silence. Taking another sip of beer and composing himself for the announcement, he then proceeded to give me a short lecture on this traditional drink, which looked to me very like a European white wine—except that it was warmed in small china bottles and then drunk from tiny dishes like saucers from a doll's tea-set.

Twittering like birds, the two geishas chattered to me while their eyes watched every movement I made. I knew from my friend on the right that the geisha is a poetic symbol of unchanging Japan. But for me, I am afraid, with their thickly whitened faces and necks, they created the uneasy impression of being like pieces of Turkish delight at the end of a toothpick. They are not prostitutes as Westerners suppose, but the residue of the great courtesans and *demi-mondaines* of Japanese legend. As students (*maiko*) they are trained at Kyoto, where I saw their little wooden houses, where dancing, deportment, singing, flower-arrangement and the social graces are taught. Any geisha worthy of the name will be the mistress of a patron as rich and important as her looks and personality will attract. They are costly toys, and most Japanese men are unable to afford the dubious delights of their company. Apart from their oriental glamour, they leave an impression as asexual as the dreadful Bunny girl.

Returning to my hotel at the end of the evening, I saw how the workaday, functional Tokyo of the daylight hours had metamorphosed into a dazzling, flashing sea of coloured lights, the little rubbish-filled alleys signalling their many attractions with their night-time neon signs.

On my second day in Japan I was introduced to the Kabuki theatre. The Kabuki is to the Nō what Boucicault is to Shakespeare. It is a fabulous spectacle, easily comprehensible and bursting with vitality and colour. Kabuki draws mainly on the legends, epics and suicide-tragedies of old Japan. Its acting style sometimes extends to the presentation of plays by Molière, Scribe, Edmond Rostand and Marivaux.

It began as a woman's art. The first of its dance-dramas, presented near Kyoto, was performed by a dancer from the famous Izumo shrine. In subsequent decades Kabuki became a vehicle for courtesans seeking to display themselves before their customers. So severely did the Government view this state of affairs that in 1631 the Tokugawa shogunate was forced to ban women from the stage, but then the young men who took over their roles began to cause as much corruption as the women before them and were outlawed in turn twenty years later. As a result of these two events, Kabuki developed as a theatre using only men as actors and began, through force of circumstance, to evolve its unique style. By the end of the seventeenth century Kabuki had taken the form we see today.

As with the Nō, the Kabuki's influence has extended into our own Western theatre. Paul Claudel, for six years French Ambassador to Japan, wrote that 'The long hours I spent at the Kabuki Theatre were for me a veritable professional school of dramaturgy.' Claudel's contact with the theatre in Tokyo influenced him deeply, and he wrote a play for the Kabuki, *The Woman and her Shadow* which was performed in 1923. There is strong evidence also that his massive drama *Le Soulier de satin* drew heavily upon his theatrical experience in Japan.

The first thing that struck me about a Kabuki theatre was the enormity of its scale and the strange proportions of the theatre itself: shaped like a letter-box with a copper-, green- and black-striped curtain covering the stage. Stretched on either side of the auditorium down to the stage is an aisle at the same level, which is known as the *hanamichi* ('flower path') and along which the characters in the play can make entrances and exits. Before the curtain, warning clappers sound the alarm. When it was pulled back I was surprised by the indifference of the audience; the exquisitely costumed actors had to battle against a continuous background accompaniment of chattering, eating and rustling of programmes in the undimmed auditorium. This continued until the moment that they had been waiting for—the appearance of the star performer, the legendary and stupendous Baiko VI. To a silence born of amazement, he slowly ascended from the bowels of the earth with all the regal grace of Britain's late Queen Mary, into a blaze of brilliantly coloured confusion.

Baiko is Japan's greatest living *onnagata*, or female impersonator. It is an art which is learnt from early childhood and represents a meticulous skill, the secrets of which are handed down from father to son; the *onnagata* actors are also part of a long tradition going back into history, and Yoshizawa Ayame I, who lived from

1673 to 1729, was the artist usually regarded as having brought the art to a peak of perfection. He made every effort to become like a woman, even in his day-to-day life. Segawa Kikunojo (1693–1749), also highly regarded as a dancer, was an actor who never played a male role. As an *onnagata* became older, he warned, he must be careful, since as he lost his beauty he would find it more difficult to become truly like a woman; yet it is said that he remained very beautiful, even after the age of sixty. Iwai Hanshiro V (1766–1847) was known as the 'great star with the thousand *Ryo* (million-dollar) eyes', and contrasted gentle feminine roles with those of vampires and murderesses, becoming famous for his creation of such melodramatic roles.

After Baiko's performances I was escorted across the stage, with its colossal revolve, by a *kurombo*—a dedicated student-servant attached to one of the masters. At Baiko's dressing-room he requested me to remove my shoes and, opening the door, bowed low. Baiko knelt with grave dignity in front of his brilliantly illuminated mirror. He had just been playing a naughty nanny on whom the gods had taken their revenge by removing her arm. He bade me welcome by gesturing to a cushion beside him. I sat down and we confronted each other in the mirror. He slowly turned to me with a brilliant smile and remarked, 'Two arms, two men.' It was to be the seal of our friendship. He asked me about London, Laurence Olivier and Westminster Abbey. As he removed his make-up he told me that to be a Kabuki actor required all the skills of mime, dance, singing and deportment. 'The most vital aspect of the Kabuki', he explained, 'is stylization, and this is the quality which is instilled, particularly in the *onnagata*, from the beginning of their long training.' Baiko's performance that afternoon reminded me of Eisenstein's observation that true stylization grows from within.

As I left the theatre after this wonder-inspiring theatrical experience, I thought how true was the meaning of the word *kabuki*—'extraordinary drama'. Extraordinary indeed!

If Kabuki is a spectacle, Nō is an art, and of all the arts in Japan that of Nō is perhaps the most elusive, esoteric and exciting. Even in modern Japan, Nō continues to occupy a world of its own: its actors are born and brought up within it and live according to its traditions, as if the entity of Nō is the all-absorbing reality, and everything outside mere make-believe. It has been through Professor Pat O'Neill of London University, whose charm, friendship and enthusiasm have led me through the dark laby-rinths towards a glimmer of understanding, that I have come to have some familiarity with this, the oldest of the traditional forces of the Japanese theatre.

The history of Nō stretches back to the fourteenth century. Founded by Kan-ami, and developed in its theory and aims by his son Zeami, Nō began in a style much rougher than the refined shape we see today. Originally presented out of doors, the plays often had the air of a pageant, with actors dressed in armour and riding horses. Nō originally drew its form and materials from the ritual dances of the temples and the folk-dances of the countryside, from Buddhist scriptures and the abundant sources of Chinese and Japanese poetry, myth and legend. From such beginnings emerged the traditional Nō stage, bounded on its four corners by four pillars supporting a shrine-shaped roof. A pine tree which formerly stood behind the stage remains to this day upon the backcloth. The Nō plays are usually divided into five pieces: the god-piece, the battle-piece, the woman- or wig-piece, the mad-piece and the devil-piece.

The writings of Zeami, which have become the dominant influence in the development of Nō, were more visionary than realistic. 'Forget the theatre', he wrote, 'and look at Nō. Forget Nō and look at the actor. Forget the actor and you will grasp Nō.' In time, Zeami's ideals became those of Nō itself, and were slowly attained to little by little by each succeeding generation of actors. Thus, while Nō has remained basically unchanged since the time of Zeami, it is today closer to his dreams than anything he himself can ever have known. And those critics and members of the London audience in 1967 who found themselves confused by the mysteries of Nō could take comfort in the know-ledge that they seem equally strange to most Japanese. The ordinary Japanese citizen can understand Nō singing no more easily than the Englishman in the street can understand *The Canterbury Tales* in their original pronunciation.

Trained from childhood within family groups, the Nō players ignore restrictive realism. They are taught to convey the essence of the character they are playing, not to give a close imitation of any particular person. It is this suggestive rather than realistic aspect of Nō that has attracted so many Western directors. Copeau was deeply influenced by it. 'The Nō', he wrote, 'appeared to be the application of the music, dramatic and plastic studies upon which, for three years, we have nourished our students, so much so that their various improvisations, the goal of these studies, was related in style to the Nō much more than to any contemporary work.' Benjamin Britten's *Curlew River*, with its libretto by William Plomer, was based upon *Sumidagawa*, and W. B. Yeats also wrote his own Nō-type *Plays for Dancers*, one of which, *At the Hawk's Well*, was translated and performed in Japan as a Nō play with considerable success.

Yeats took his study of the Nō theatre very seriously, and for the English production of *At the Hawk's Well*, which was presented before Queen Alexandra at a charity performance in Mayfair in 1916, he was aided by Michio Ito, a Japanese dancer, who undertook to take the part of the hawk. At Regent's Park Zoo Ito created a stir among the visitors as he tried to learn the behaviour of the hawk. After the unfortunate bird had been prodded with an umbrella, Ito leaped about before the cage in such a way that many imagined him to be either insane or else a member of some strange Oriental bird-cult.

In view of its esoteric basis, it had been with some trepidation that I had arranged to bring a Nō group to London in 1967, the practical arrangements for their visit being helped enormously by the energy and understanding of M. René de Berval, a distinguished and charming Frenchman with a long experience of Japan and the East, who acted as manager for the group. In the event I need not have worried, for the performances created an enormous impact. Audiences in London seemed ready to accept that a stage art from an alien culture that had taken over six hundred years to develop to its present style could not be completely absorbed during a mere two or three hours in the Aldwych Theatre. Some who saw them were utterly bored by the Nō plays, and only came to life during the comic *kyōgen* interludes; but the majority, like myself, were captivated by the indefinable magic in the total dramatic effect. Part of the fascination lay in the utterly strange means by which this effect was achieved. Many people made several visits so as to arrive at a fuller understanding of something they had previously been able to know only through translations. Nō is now universally recognized as one of the great theatres of the world.

The leading Nō player in the group was Cumas Hashioka, who has had his skill recognized by receiving the Government designation of 'Intangible Cultural Asset'. On my later visit to Japan I was invited to a special performance in my honour at his house in the company of the charming British Ambassador, Sir John Pilcher.

Hashioka is a pale-complexioned man with a toothbrush moustache—unusual for a Japanese. He speaks excellent French, which he learned in his early years with the idea of teaching it if he failed to succeed as a Nō player. Born as the eighth generation of a Nō family belonging to the Kanze School, he invariably wears Japanese costume, and, like his profession and mode of dress, his house was also traditionally Japanese. The main room where we talked together was my first experience of a purely Japanese-style room, and my first impression was of its bareness. It was empty except for a low lacquered table, a few cushions on the floor on which we sat, and an alcove with a hanging scroll behind a flower-arrangement. But, as we sat there, I came to feel more and more that everything in the room was just right. The floor of springy padded rush mats was comfortable to sit on, and nothing else could have been introduced into the room without spoiling the total effect. My initial impression of bareness changed to one of spaciousness, and I wondered if perhaps the hundred million Japanese crowded into their small islands, and in particular the ten or eleven million of them who live and work in Tokyo, did not compensate for the conditions in their world outside by creating a little haven of space for themselves within their own homes.

The Nō performance was given in Mr Hashioka's own theatre, which was attached to the house—part of his heritage as the head of one of the main families in the most important of the five schools of Nō. The roofed stage was polished to a dark glow, in rich contrast to the traditional green pine tree on a gilt ground painted on the back wall; and a surround of grey pebbles separated the auditorium from the stage. There the master rehearsed and trained his pupils. Today, he told me, he had a set of Nō dances and a comic *kyōgen* play, which had been arranged as a celebration of my visit. Mr Hashioka's son, who was about eight years old, also performed that day, as he had with the company in London. He is the ninth generation of Nō players in his family line, and its traditions seem secure with him.

The very word Nō means 'refined accomplishment', and the performance which the Hashiokas gave for me was exactly that, the graceful slow movements beginning to hypnotize me again as they had done in London. For many moments the actors remained quite immobile. It is a theatre of vivid contrasts, of abstruse dream-like movements and taut drama.

Everything is concentrated on the main actor, the *shite*; it is ensemble work with a star system. The leading player is always the centre of attraction, and nothing must be allowed to distract from this concentration. Jean-Louis Barrault described the powerfully intensive results in his *Journal de bord*. 'The *shite*, strikingly immobile, has opened wide his fan. His inner life is there offered to all: his soul unfolded. While the chorus chants the torments of his character in unison, he makes the fan undulate and tremble. We have the impression that these emanations from the soul literally come from the object itself. The soul quivers. Our eyes are riveted on the fan.'

'Drama', wrote Paul Claudel, 'is something that happens.' Nō is someone who happens. The performance in that little theatre was a beautiful and moving experience.

To understand the art of Japanese theatre it is necessary to appreciate something of the vast influence that Buddhism has had on Japan over the centuries. The Japanese do not appear to be, by Western standards, a deeply religious people, in that they are extremely tolerant of different beliefs and seem to take their own easily and with enjoyment rather than with the solemn formality associated with the Church in Europe. Yet it was clear that, ever since Buddhism became important in Japan in the seventh century, the ideas and attitudes initiated by the original Buddha in India had gradually permeated the life and mentality of the Japanese as deeply as the teachings of Christ have in the West. The concept of Nirvana, the Buddhist paradise, has produced the same reliance on an after-life as in Christianity, but the fundamental Buddhist belief in reincarnation must have played a very large part in the readiness of the Japanese to resort to suicide, whether as *kamikaze* pilots or soldiers in war, or as ordinary individuals in society who use it as a form of protest or escape. Even for me, the atmosphere of timeless peace and comfort which seemed to envelop the Buddhist temples and shrines was as real as that to be found in the quiet of an Italian church, and I could imagine the strength of spirit of those who managed to achieve enlightenment through contemplation after the fashion of the Buddha, one of the three greatest religious teachers the world has known. When I linked this with the military traditions of sacrifice and stoicism of the *samurai* class, I felt that I was approaching an understanding of at least one side of the Japanese character. The heroic stories of the warriors who fought and died in the bitter civil wars from the eleventh century onwards became an influential element within the military families in the generations that followed, and although their standards and traditions were ruthlessly misused by the twentieth-century militarists, it was not difficult to see how the formidable combination of *samurai* bravery and Buddhist spiritual discipline had developed, and to be impressed by both the inner peace and the outward manifestations of that great religion.

I had brought a very different company to London as part of the 1968 World Theatre Season and, although less well known than the Nō, the Bunraku puppet theatre achieved almost as great a success.

Bunraku is closely akin to the Kabuki, for they share the same history and most of their writers and plays. Puppets are known to have existed in Japan since the first half of the tenth century, but it is not clear what form the earliest ones took. A mention in the fifteenth century may refer to hand-puppets; but when puppets became increasingly popular in the sixteenth century, it was in the form of simple puppets manipulated by handling the dolls from outside in much the same way as the present Bunraku dolls are worked. Bunraku dolls derived from the island of Awaji, where the heads are still made and where there are local amateur groups which continue an old tradition of puppet-plays. Bunraku arose together with Kabuki in the early years of the seventeenth century, after Nō had become so much the monopoly of the ruling nobility and warriors that the ordinary people had to devise new forms of theatre for themselves. The first half of the eighteenth century was the golden age of Japanese puppetry, with important theatres, mainly in Osaka, competing with each other and with Kabuki to put on plays by gifted playwrights, including the great Chikamatsu. In the late eighteenth century a new theatre was set up in Osaka by a puppeteer from the island of Awaji called Bunrakuken Uemura, and it is from his name that the term Bunraku has been taken to indicate the professional puppet theatre in general. Gradually, however, Bunraku lost ground to Kabuki, until finally in 1963 the Bunraku Association, with Government help, took over the management to ensure the preservation of this unique theatrical art.

We in the West are accustomed to think of puppetry as not much more than an occasional minor entertainment, but Bunraku is from every point of view a complete and major drama-form. It presents a full Kabuki-style repertoire—with comparable spectacle and drama and a good deal more literary content—by means of three-foot-high dolls manipulated by puppeteers in full view of the audience against a virtuoso accompaniment from a chanter and a musician playing the three-stringed *samisen*.

These two, who occupy a shelf beside the stage on the right of the auditorium, form an entertainment in themselves. The flaccid but expressive twanging of the *samisen* creates the appropriate mood for the vocal pyrotechnics of the chanter, who, with his controlled power and range of expression, must be the ultimate in story-tellers. He begins quietly, as he sets the scene and narrates the early part of the play, but then, as the action on the stage develops, he also speaks for the characters themselves, sometimes switching phrase by phrase from the grating growl of a villain to the wheedling tremolo of the heroine. Then, as the climax of the act or play approaches, he either builds up to an explosive outpouring of words or, in a love tragedy, achieves his effect by a well-judged and restrained lament on the lovers' dilemma which can only be resolved by suicide.

The contributions of the chanter and musician, however, have developed over the centuries with the sole aim of heightening the effect of the action on the stage. Anyone seeing Bunraku for the first time must, to start with, find himself distracted from the play itself by the sight of the manipulators of the dolls, the main ones in formal Japanese dress and impassive of face and the others in black robes and hoods which completely cover their faces. But very soon the attention is drawn to the dolls alone, for as they move about the stage, fighting, loving, dancing, weeping and dying, they clearly take on a life of their own, like Petrushka in Stravinsky's ballet and with a similar supernatural effect. They make their way spontaneously about their world, intent on their own purposes, and the puppeteers behind them recede into a shadowy presence, seeming to be hovering deities trying to restrain the wayward actions of the creatures in their charge.

My dear friend Mr Monjuro, one of today's masters of Bunraku, showed me some of the secrets of his art and even allowed me an hour's precious manipulation. He was now sixty-eight, and three years before had been declared a 'National Treasure' by the Japanese Government—the highest award in Japanese art. Mr Monjuro has a gentle aristocratic demeanour, combined with a lively sense of humour. He told me of a Japanese proverb which says that it is necessary to spend ten years operating the foot of a Bunraku puppet and another ten operating the left arm before one can become a principal puppeteer. I asked him how long it had taken him. 'Ten years,' he replied.

Each leading puppet is operated by three men, two of them masked, all of whom appear on the stage; no strings are employed. Technically, the method of presentation is extraordinarily accomplished. The three puppeteers—one controlling the head and right arm, another the left arm and the third the feet—combine together so expertly and smoothly and with such delicacy of movement that in a surprisingly short while it is hard to see the doll as anything but an independent living entity. Artistically also the Japanese puppet theatre is important and intriguing. Though very much like the Kabuki in style and content, it is a kind of distillation of its best elements: the bombast and extravagance are reduced in physical scale, and the inevitable stylization invites a suspension of disbelief which often makes it more theatrically effective than the live Kabuki.

When the hectic whirl of my stay in Japan had come to an end and I was sitting in the plane leaving Tokyo, for the first time since my arrival it became possible to collect my thoughts, and to sit back and enjoy the cobweb of my impressions: the mountainous *sumō* wrestlers, whose contests formed part of religious divination ceremonies in the mists of time before Japan's recorded history began; the small, vicious exponents of *karate*, whose every blow or kick is designed to maim or kill; the art of Japanese swordsmanship, which, like fencing in the West, seems to be practised almost as much by women as by men; the gleaming sword-blades and intricate metalwork of their hand-guards displayed in the National Museum like works of art, as indeed they are; gentle, contemplative arts like flower-arrangements and the tea ceremony—basically simple things which in Japan have been raised through Zen Buddhist influence to the level of aesthetic cults; and the hot, noisy and crowded discotheques and jazz clubs of the entertainment district of Shinjuku—full of hippies, drop-outs and ordinary young people—which could have been in any big town in Europe or North America.

My strongest impressions were, of course, of the theatre. I had already become familiar with the main forms of Japanese theatre from the performances in London, and my visit to the country had enabled me to see them in their actual setting and to find out more about their background. I came to appreciate more, for example, the role of Zen in the presentation of Nō plays. This Buddhist sect of Chinese origin has had a tremendous influence on the development of poetry and many other arts in Japan. Its ideas and ideals are not easy to pin down; by turning the rational on its head or inside out it seeks to find truth on the path beyond the intellect, particularly through paradox. 'What would you advise if a man came to you with nothing?' one of the great Zen masters was asked. 'Throw it away!' was his reply. Zen is therefore more of an anti-philosophy, and its influence is best to be seen in what *we* might call its negative aspects: in emptiness, for example, which is such a feature of a Nō stage, in a black-ink painting, or a temple garden of raked sand and just a few rocks; in the silence, solitude and loneliness typified by a bare tree in winter; in the importance and significance of what is *not* said or done; and in restraint in all its forms. Nō is thus, in one sense, the theatrical expression of Zen.

I felt too that the apparently negative aspects of the Zen tradition might be the key to the mystery of the Japanese actor's art of timing. Many of the most dramatic and meaningful points in Japanese plays seem to be moments of silence and immobility. Such a moment interrupts the underlying rhythm of a performance, but when it occurs one feels that it was the only possible theatrical expression which fitted the situation at that moment. The pause or silence is held for just so long—usually longer than we in the European tradition would ever consider—and then, again at the only possible moment, action is resumed and life moves on a little further. Perhaps the secret of this perfected sense of timing is found in the use Japanese theatre makes of music, which imposes its own conditions: at certain points, and in certain theatrical situations, the music requires silence. In the Japanese forms of drama, tradition has led music, words and action to share such moments of silence and inactivity, and thereby to reinforce the effect of each individual element.

14

The U.S.A. — off-Broadway
and off-off-Broadway

When a play called *The Connection*, written by Jack Gelber and produced by the Living Theatre company, had opened in a down-town off-Broadway theatre in 1959, it had gathered a bad crop of reviews. Brooks Atkinson, then the doyen of American critics, dismissed it with the same pompous authority with which a now forgotten English critic once dismissed Ibsen's *Ghosts* in London. But such was the effect of electric shock that the play caused that within a month it was enjoying capacity audiences and being re-reviewed enthusiastically in the press. My ardent and ambitious assistant Michael White had read it, and Jerome Robbins had told me that it was the most brilliant piece of theatre he had ever seen.

I decided to fly to New York to see it for myself. The city had changed immeasurably since my first visit there directly after the war. Then it had symbolized the brash superficialities of a civilization that we in Europe had come close to losing. Now New York, for all its summer heat, seemed cold and soulless. The theatre also appeared to be struck by a kind of paralysis. Edward Albee's complaint that, while Broadway was presenting trifles which would better have been the concern of the smaller New York theatres, it was off-Broadway that was putting on the works which Broadway should have been taking up, carried considerable justification. Nearly every exciting new playwright who emerged during this dark period was indeed a discovery belonging to off-Broadway—the new arrivals including Albee himself, Jack Gelber, Murray Schisgal and Arthur Kopit.

Although off-Broadway was an institution going back to the beginning of the century, not since the 1920s had it seen such a frenzy of activity. In cinemas, churches, halls, basements — wherever it was physically possible to produce a play—tiny theatres sprang up. It represented a new flowering of experimental drama in the United States. Some production companies, of course, were fated like beautiful butterflies to have one glorious moment of existence before a quick and unmourned extinction; others, like the Circle in the Square, were more lasting.

Now in the late 1950s, in the era of a broad-minded mayor, a new theatre began to emerge — the underground theatre, previously harassed by the police and fire departments. As it gained acceptance, newspapers started to review its productions. A total freedom of expression incorporated vulgarity, ridicule and spectacle as the three main essentials of its formula; young people were not, it was said, interested in the theatre as an older generation understood it, and they felt the need to participate. The Living Theatre was part of this new concept. It had been formed originally in 1947 by Julian Beck and his wife, the actress Judith Malina. Their policy from the start was to present new, controversial and experimental plays; *Dr Faustus Lights the Lights* by Gertrude Stein was one of their most important early productions. Among other authors they presented were T. S. Eliot, Cocteau, Pirandello and Strindberg, all in productions which brought them a great deal of prestige. Their theatre on 14th Street, possessing only 162 seats, seemed to answer youth's demand for involvement. The actors spent as much time in the auditorium as on the stage, seeing the spectator as an enemy until he had proved himself a friend, the playgoer being subjected to insults almost to the point of physical involvement until he responded. On the evening when I went to see *The Connection* I found that the tiny claustrophobic room where it was being performed had an astringent atmosphere: huddled together, the audience seemed almost completely integrated with the actors.

Gelber's play represented a revolutionary break in the theatrical treatment of drug addiction. Other dramatists had dealt with drugs before, but always the authors had set the drama of the addict against a background of moral society. In such plays as Michael V. Gazzo's *A Hatful of Rain* the result was simply a conventional family conflict of father versus son which was merely heightened by the fact of the son's addiction. The addiction was thus seen as a weakness, as a flight from the world of responsibility, love and affection. These things may be a part of addiction, but they are far from the whole story. Gelber's drama took place in the inverted and closed world of the addict's society. Here the man not 'turned on' was the weakling, the coward. Here love was the 'pure' 'transcendent' freedom of marijuana, the saviour not the welfare worker but 'the connection', the mysterious link with peace, the bringer of heroin. The play carried a dedication 'to Thelma Godsen, dead of an overdose of heroin at the Salvation Army, 1957, and to all other junkies, dead and alive, in The Women's House of Detention'.

The dramatic idea behind the play is simple. Starting with a Pirandellian kind of alienation, Gelber tells us that he is presenting a play, that the author is here, and that the actors are all in fact real junkies. To get the money to pay them, he has promised them their fix with the money made by documentary film cameramen who will shoot the action. Thus the unbearable oppression of the addicts' tormented waiting for the 'connection' is formalized into a cool objective study of straightforward human pain. As a junky twists in the physical torment of withdrawal, a cameraman coolly kneels beside him, an arc-light shining as the camera whirls. The author looks at the audience and calmly says, 'That's what it is like. That's just what it is like.' We are left in no doubt, and the effect is shattering.

During the play the junkies, who are also jazz musicians, play cool post-Parker jazz that is hauntingly lonely and both breaks the overpowering tension of the physical action and contributes a unique dramatic element that the Western theatre, in contrast to the Japanese Nō theatre, has completely lost. While listening to the music the audience can regard the characters in repose, robbed of speech and slumped in their chairs or staring anxiously out of the windows: lonely figures who take on a kind of archetypal tragic dignity in their desolation against the angular structure of modern jazz.

The play contains only one serious inroad from the world of 'squares', and this character is introduced with an awe-inspiring stroke of theatrical genius. Just before the play's climax, Cowboy, the angelic and evil 'connection', arrives with the dope, bringing with him a shrivelled and ageing Salvation Army sister, Sister Salvation, who, suddenly confronted with human suffering, spiritual bankruptcy and desolation, tries to talk to the junkies in chastening, comforting terms. Her words of comfort fall in vain, like barren seed on barren ground, and in vain she sings of Jesus's mercy. But she has served her purpose. She has allowed Cowboy to enter the house without arousing the suspicions of the police. One by one the men leave the room to receive their fixes. Sister Salvation stands among them, bewildered, aware of the tension of those not satisfied, baffled by the sudden calm that descends on those who return. Knowing she has failed, she turns to go. But at the door she makes one last attempt to usher in their spiritual renaissance. Raising her hands in benediction, she announces triumphantly, 'You are not alone! You are not alone!' —then leaves.

It was only by going back to Brand's annihilation under the avalanche at the end of Ibsen's play that I could think of a worthy equivalent to Gelber's unforgettable image of human disaster. These men are lost. Not even their drugs can bring them peace or real paradise; only the negative paradise of a slow process of self-annihilation. As Virgil led Dante into hell, but could only guide him a certain part of the way, finally leaving him to proceed alone, so Gelber's character of the 'author' can only go so far in communicating the torment of those condemned men. Finally he himself has to succumb to the drug's cycle of addiction —otherwise he simply cannot comprehend the experience. Genet once said that if St Vincent de Paul had really loved the galley-slaves he would not only have taken their place at the oars, but would have committed the same crime as they had done. How else could he know them? For if we cannot love them, in the end it is they who must forgive us.

After seeing the play, I hastened the same evening to meet its author, Jack Gelber. For someone who had been described as 'the playwright of the beat generation' he was hardly what I expected: a man in his late twenties, elegant, small and quietly spoken. During the turmoil of *The Connection*'s subsequent history we were to become close friends. On this occasion we talked far into the night and I saw something of his personality—the views, outlook and beliefs of a character of smiling charm and a gentle humility.

Did he, I asked him, see his work as having any specific social message? 'If there has to be some social message,' he replied, 'I suppose it's about addiction. Look at what Sam says in the play—how he used to think that people who worry too much about the next dollar, the aspirin addicts, the vitamin-takers, were all hooked worse than him. And Solly tells him, "They are—you happen to have a vice that's illegal." '

The oldest of three sons of a Jewish tin-smith, Gelber grew up on the south and west sides of Chicago, graduating with a degree in journalism from the University of Illinois. He kicked around for two years in San Francisco and held a fantastic array of jobs in New York, including that of a mimeograph operator at the United Nations, before writing *The Connection*, which he finished in one week. 'It was my first attainment I was pleased with,' he said. 'I felt I had been worthy of myself.'

When, after nightmarish difficulties, I brought *The Connection* to the Duke of York's in London in February 1961, complete with the original cast of eight actors and musicians, it landed like a bomb. It encountered the most hostile reaction that any play can have met in a London theatre for many years.

While the acting was certainly a feat of minutely observed naturalism, I felt the first-night audience withdrawing drastically from that sense of involvement that had made the New York evening so haunting and memorable. A conventional theatre obviously upset the balance of rapport between cast and audience.

The effect on the actors was only too evident. Although in the interval Warren Finnerty, who played Leach, said he felt that, if nothing else, he was getting across to the audience, many of the other actors were quite obviously disturbed by what was happening. Gelber commented, 'I always felt that the British were a civilized people. At least I was always informed that you were.' There was little I could do except feel angry and disgusted. The gallery were operating as a law unto themselves. They were refusing to give a serious play a fair hearing—or, indeed, any sort of hearing at all.

The curtain came down at the end to a conglomeration of applause and boos. The audience had certainly contained many who were deeply moved by what they had seen, by the isolation and despair depicted. Yet, as the audience drifted away, an angry throng of about eighty hecklers remained gathered on the pavement outside. As my wife and I joined them, the arguing was turned directly on to us. The crowd began to demand their money back, claiming the play was a disgrace which had only been put on to make money for the management. 'My opinion of the gallery tonight is very, very low,' I told them. Predictably they chorused back, 'So is ours of you!'

A rather confused policeman pushed his way into the crowd to ask us all to move on. 'This is a peaceful discussion,' someone shouted at him. 'Move on yourself.' Even more confused, he walked off up St Martin's Lane. My wife became engaged in bitter conversation with a woman called Sophie, who was calling the play 'sheer filth' and demanding the return of Noël Coward and her money. Lady Listowel, who was in our party, promptly handed her three shillings—the price of a gallery seat. One by one we were joined by the actors. The arguments began again and repeated themselves continuously, until slowly the debaters drifted away. We went on to Ronnie Scott's Club with the cast to celebrate in whatever way we could during what remained of a shattered evening.

The *Evening News* reported the incident next day: 'Has a manager ever before come out into the street after a first night and boldly challenged an angry audience? Peter Daubeny did just that. After hearing *The Connection* booed and heckled by the gallery, Mr Daubeny made a dramatic appearance in St Martin's Lane. Chaos followed!'

The play's eight-week run became filled with every kind of incident, but as ordeal followed ordeal the cast virtually became part of the family. We suffered with Carl Lee and James Anderson the indignity of racial discrimination. Gelber was particularly concerned for the sake of the Negro actors. 'Everyone insists there's no colour bar, but there's certainly one here. It is all very hypocritical because it's so cool. In America you know who your enemies are.'

But the cast's exuberant involvement left us with few dull moments. If it was not one of them believing himself to have become a real drug addict, it was another blowing his bugle at full blast throughout the night in Eccleston Square. It was Warren Finnerty, the Oscar-winning star, who got so involved with his role that he imagined he had turned into a genuine junkie. I sent him to my doctor, who pronounced him to be suffering from nervous exhaustion. He was immediately shipped back to New York. Then the theatre tried to stop the play by imposing an injunction, because box-office takings had failed to reach the specified break figure, and so we ended up with a hearing in the High Court and won. One happy result of this troubled production was that it launched Michael White, who had been my assistant for five years and who wanted to become a producer. I had therefore decided to let him co-present the play to give him his first chance as a West End manager, as I believed in his talent and intuitive flair—a belief which was subsequently endorsed.

When Shirley Clarke later filmed *The Connection* it was shown in the fringe of the Cannes Film Festival, and caused a great sensation in its own right. London, which had not been ready for such a piece of raw poetry on the stage, finally came to its senses and flocked to see it at the Academy Cinema in a belated tribute to Gelber's talent.

In 1963 I was again in New York, this time to negotiate to bring to the World Theatre Season an acknowledged legend: the Actors' Studio Theater and its inspiring spirit, Lee Strasberg.

To talk about Lee Strasberg is to talk about one of the greatest influences in modern theatre. His influence on many of the younger generation of American producers and directors on off-Broadway or off-off-Broadway has been far more profound than many of them no doubt would care to admit today. Like many prophets of modern culture, he seems to have been outstripped by the headlong advance of a turbulent *avant-garde* which affects not to take him seriously—as children must reject a powerful parent before they can assess their own individuality or before they can return to admitting the validity of what he has taught them.

My own impression of Strasberg on our first meeting was of a certain melancholy. He made me think of an outdated 'angry young man' with cerebral acne dying of a creeping common sense. As we became friends I realized that my initial reaction had been entirely wrong. Like a skilled psychiatrist he penetrated the dark subconscious of the American mind, releasing cherished inhibitions with clinical detachment. I was to learn that he could inspire a fresh, sharply focused vision in the world of American acting which the English actor would reject.

'The Method', as Strasberg's teaching style has come to be known, has its basis in the work of Stanislavsky. As a young immigrant from Austria, making a living in New York in, to use his own words, the 'human-hair business', Strasberg had seen the Moscow Art Theatre on their first visit to America and had been deeply impressed. His own career began as a young actor with the Theater Guild in 1926, and Harold Clurman in his great book *The Fervent Years* (*The Story of the Group Theater and the Thirties*) recalls him in the lead in a production of Pirandello's *Right You Are If You Think So* as

> a young pale-faced man of intellectual demeanour. He was very short, intense-looking with skin drawn tightly over a wide brow. He spoke with a faint foreign accent, had a large head with rather curly hair, a face that expressed keen intelligence, suffering, ascetic control, with something old, withdrawn and lofty about it. We not only studied these productions but debated them with passion. We sought out exotic examples of theatrecraft.

In 1931 Strasberg was one of the co-founders, with Cheryl Crawford and Harold Clurman, of the Group Theater, and a year later they were joined by Elia Kazan, other members of the Group including such diverse talents as Irwin Shaw, William Saroyan and Luther Adler. Strasberg and Clurman's decision to break with the Theater Guild had been precipitated by a feeling that it offered no opportunities to young actors to train. Their growing need to develop was ignored. While the Group continued to take shape in their absence they went with a group of actors down to the country and set to work. 'The adoration of the actors for Lee Strasberg seemed to me to have the effect of inflating his ego with what struck me as a sense of total mastery,' Clurman remembers. As Strasberg's style of direction began to make itself felt, it seemed, in Clurman's words, like 'a miracle'. The system represented the 'open sesame' of the actors' art, a key to that elusive ingredient of the stage: true emotion. And Strasberg was a fanatic on the subject of emotion. Everything else was secondary to it. He sought it with the patience of an inquisitor and was outraged by trick substitutes, and when he had succeeded in stimulating it he husbanded it, fed it and protected it. It was something new to most of the actors, something basic, something almost holy, and Strasberg became its prophet.

In 1934 he visited Russia, and in Moscow was deeply moved by Meyerhold's productions. On his return he directed *Gold Eagle*

Guy and produced, with Clurman directing, *Awake to Joy* and Clifford Odets's *Waiting for Lefty*. The Group was active during 1934 and 1935, and Odets became a theatrical vogue. Both plays were enormous successes. Dramatists of a wide range of personalities and attitudes had their plays produced, including, besides Odets, Paul Green, Maxwell Anderson, J. H. Lawson, Dawn Powell and Sydney Kingsley. But the Group remained a training-centre as well as a theatre, riding the giddy wheel of theatrical vicissitudes, on the one hand being publicly praised for its vision and integrity, and on the other often finding itself emotionally and economically worn out.

In 1937, following Strasberg's production of Paul Green's *Johnny Johnston*, which folded in spite of rave reviews, the Group Committee sat in judgment on their directors. Not even Strasberg escaped censure, and it was advised that he be relieved of all but artistic tasks. Clurman and Cheryl Crawford were also censured, and all three directors resigned. Clurman, however, then rescinded and announced the Group's continuation, and in the same year Strasberg took over all Group affairs. Its last production was *Clash by Night* in 1941 with Tallulah Bankhead, Sylvia Sydney and Luther Adler, directed by Strasberg. The shock of Pearl Harbor finished everything.

The Actors' Studio itself came into being in 1947, when Tennessee Williams's *A Streetcar Named Desire* was in rehearsal in New York, bringing Strasberg, Cheryl Crawford and Kazan together with Robert Lewis. To the spark of enthusiasm carried over from the Group Theater days, this small group, with their intense love of theatre, added the sense of vocation that a community of religious zealots might have for a particular faith. There has still never been anything like it in the entire history of theatre. At the start the Studio formed in effect a school for professional, mainly young, actors. Later, towards the end of the 1950s, it established other classes for theatre workers, including play-wrights and directors, besides putting on private productions of plays. The legend the Studio created round itself was enhanced in the early days by the growing list of young actors trained in 'the Method'—Marlon Brando, James Dean, Paul Newman, Eli Wallach, Geraldine Page and Shelley Winters—who entered films and injected into cinema a new and remarkable style which caught the public imagination.

By the time I made my quest to the Actors' Studio in 1963, Cheryl Crawford, a woman of vitalizing energy and immense charm, was only working on the periphery, and Kazan had severed his connection. Lee Strasberg, however, remained very much in control. He lived in a spacious flat in Central Park West which commanded a view of the whole of Central Park. But my immediate attention was caught not by the view, but by books, which were everywhere, filling shelves, piled high in top-heavy columns, strewn across tables and chests. Mixed with them lay spools of tape and the recording machines on which he recorded his 'seminars' at the Studio, while music played unceasingly.

Strasberg talked at length and with a certain absent-mindedness due not so much to forgetfulness as to his agility of mind. He has an ability to turn conversations into what one actor described to me as 'a monologue with interruptions'. He can catch words and improvise upon them like a jazz musician with a tune.

As we talked he began to describe to me the true purpose of the Actors' Studio. 'At the start we didn't aim at providing a sense of the theatre. We simply wanted a place where actors could solve the problems they had discovered on stage, or on the screen. It was a place to experiment with oneself, simply to help an actor use his talent.' He paused momentarily. 'You see,' he continued, 'a career must develop in public but one's talents only grow in silence.'

The one qualification for entry into the Studio is talent. But the result is not a mere powerhouse; it is a place where you go to try. As Geraldine Page explained later, 'If an actor says he wants to do Hamlet standing on his head, nobody looks surprised. They simply say, "Let's see it."' 'It is a place', in Strasberg's own words, 'where an actor can fall flat on his face.'

At his invitation I spent a week watching the Studio at work in the little church hall on West 44th Street. As I arrived just before eleven the main hall was already filling up with actors preparing to watch the first scene. The hall is a simple, unpretentious room, painted white, encircled by a gallery. From the gallery seven or eight spotlights shine down on the acting area.

In the centre of the front row Strasberg sat in a director's chair, his name embossed in gold on the back. Behind him was the ever-present tape recorder to record his comments after each brief scene had been acted out. Each work was followed in attentive silence, and at the end there was no applause. The performers simply explained what they were trying to do, and the whole audience then began to discuss what they had seen. The basis for discussion was not the quality of the acting but the extent of the actor's achievement and progress. An actor gets from the Studio only what he takes to it—the will to improve must come from within.

Finally Strasberg himself rose to speak. The tape recorder clicked on and he began to sum up what we had seen as well as the following discussion. His voice is dry, monotonous and entirely lacking in rhythmical tone; yet he exerted a spell-binding authority. In a matter of minutes Strasberg had discovered faults none of us had noticed in one of the performances which had seemed particularly brilliant. He analysed, laid bare and healed in one operation. Geraldine Page, sitting next to me, turned to me and said, 'Where else in the world could you see a performance like that and then have criticism as valuable as that? By God, that's why we keep coming back.'

It was obvious that Strasberg has an almost hypnotic effect upon his pupils, who hold him in god-like reverence. After the next scene, in which a young Negro was trying to extend his range, Strasberg launched a most brutal attack upon the actor's style. He demolished him, and, having done so, destroyed him again. A few minutes later the Negro went up to Strasberg. 'Thank you, Mr Strasberg,' he said, 'that was really wonderful.' Next morning I asked Lee why he had been so harsh. 'Was I harsh?' he replied. 'I didn't think I was.'

A respect for his opinion is almost universal among the actors who work with him. Shelley Winters told me how Marilyn Monroe would fly for the day from California to discuss a problem with him, flying back the same evening. 'For me', Eli Wallach once told me, 'Lee has been the actor's conscience, guide, voice in the wilderness.' ' He made it possible for the world to open up for me,' said Kim Stanley. 'Through his teaching, he gives you tools that make it possible for you to accomplish what *you* want to do.'

Talking specifically about the Method and its significance for American theatre at the present time, John Fernald, a great teacher, has said that he believes that the Method—the actual title—has tended to become a little old-fashioned today. Yet the basic idea behind the Method—that the actor must think truthfully and feel truthful — remains absolutely fundamental to any American actor's way of thinking, as indeed to any English actor's way of thinking. Where the two attitudes diverge seems to be that often in America people imagine that feeling right and feeling truthful is the same thing as conveying these attributes to the audience, and forget that it is impossible to convey them without the proper technique with which to do it. The Method can still work, in Fernald's view, provided you go on from there.

For the 1965 World Theatre Season it was arranged that the Actors' Studio Theater should bring to London two plays: James Baldwin's *Blues for Mister Charlie* and their new production of Chekhov's *The Three Sisters*. The Actors' Studio Theater was a relatively new departure for Strasberg, and his production of O'Neill's *Strange Interlude* in March 1963 was the first time the Studio's work had, so to speak, 'gone public'. It was a natural development. During their 1957–8 season the Studio had given birth to a Playwright's Unit, then in 1960 to a Director's Unit; now there was to be a Production Unit. 'Our actors', Eli Wallach remarked, 'rarely tie themselves down with a company or group. They want to be free to accept work in the open market.' The Actors' Studio Theater permits this freedom, but also demands an agreement for a minimum four-month engagement. It is a tribute to Strasberg that artists eagerly accept these terms, together with salaries far lower than they could otherwise command.

In order that arrangements could be finalized for their visit to the Aldwych, it was necessary to sign a contract with the company almost a year before their arrival. Several stars declared themselves ready to risk the loss of film and theatre offers for the chance of coming to London. But though the company which eventually arrived included some great actors and actresses, it was not the company I had seen do *The Three Sisters* in New York. Diana Sands had been replaced, and neither Geraldine Page nor Shelley Winters had been able to come. It was not until the cast-lists arrived a few weeks before the production opened that I realized what had happened. I had no reason to expect, however, that the company would be subjected to the hysterical abuse which was in the event showered upon them by critics and gallery alike.

Their two-week stay began with James Baldwin's savagely bitter play, *Blues for Mister Charlie*, at a time when I was myself seriously ill in hospital. This play gave voice for the first time to a new dimension in hatred of the injustice of white society in the United States. It was passionate, violent and profoundly sincere. 'You're going to make yourself sick with hatred,' his grandmother says to Richard Henry, the young Negro in revolt. 'I'm going to make myself well with hatred,' he replies. 'I'm going to learn how to drink it—a little every day in the morning, and then a booster shot late at night.' 'The play for me', James Baldwin wrote in his introduction, 'takes place in Plaguetown, U.S.A., now. The plague is race, the plague is our concept of Christianity: and this raging plague has the power to destroy every human relationship.'

As a friend Jimmy Baldwin never missed the moment of spontaneity. As a writer he sustained that power, bitterness and passion which gave him that great force as a crusader to assault the mighty forces of white supremacy. He visited me in my illness, and I would receive his splendid poetic splinters of humour and passion that never failed to ameliorate my clinical frailty. He would peer round my door with the latest gossip, and however much violence was raging around him (more often than not the result of bumping into Lee Strasberg at the Savoy, where both were staying) his huge eyes would roll with laughter and his mouth extend into a beautiful row of white piano notes from which he spoke the music of Bach and 'swing'. He is probably the most articulate man I have ever met. All this may sound trivial, but he never failed to penetrate the psychic structure of people, nor wavered from his crusade for the cause which he ruled as a champion and wrote for as a poet.

The bigoted clichés of rabid segregationists depicted in the work were nicely supplemented on the first night by two members of the British National Party, who began shouting at the cast during the second act. Their cries of 'Filth, why don't you go back to Africa' echoed through the theatre. 'I was scared for a moment,' Jimmy Baldwin told me afterwards. 'I thought my cast might get lynched.' But the players continued. As the director, Burgess Meredith, commented, 'The shouting just spurred them on.' In character, the cast turned their attention on the hecklers, one line of the play being directed to the circle: 'Ain't you people had no education?' As someone said to me later, the 'plague' of Baldwin's play seemed to be loose in the auditorium that night. 'We are walking in terrible darkness here,' Baldwin had written in April 1964 in the preface to the New York edition of his play, 'and this is one man's attempt to bear witness to the reality and the power of light.'

The full vent of fury, however, broke over *The Three Sisters*. Perhaps too much was expected of the Actors' Studio, which, rightly or wrongly, had been seen by many as a permanent repertory company providing the creative inspiration for all American theatre. Thus, when the curtain rose on *The Three Sisters*, many critics and most of the audience were expecting something corresponding to jewel-like perfection. When it came down a few hours later, what they had seen seemed to them under-rehearsed and poorly assembled. The gallery, with the display of bad manners for which it is too often renowned, showed its own disapproval with shouts and boos. The critics displayed theirs over the next few days. Almost in unison, they declared the Strasberg method to be merely a fraud, and the production nothing but an unmitigated disaster. The *Sunday Times* described the performances of Kim Stanley and Sandy Dennis, both great stars individually, as 'ludicrous and painful'. 'I could barely restrain myself from screaming aloud', wrote Bernard Levin in the *Daily Mail*, 'with the pain of my throbbing nerves.' Finally, in the *Observer*, came the most outraged notice of all from Penelope Gilliatt, who launched a bitter and savage attack on the whole company. 'The admirable World Theatre Season's last dismal task', she wrote, 'has been to mount the suicide of the Actors' Studio.'

It would be foolish to maintain that Strasberg's production was without fault. Equally it cannot be left unsaid that, as Ronald Bryden noted at the time in the *New Statesman*, and as several commentators have written since, there were elements in Strasberg's production which were admirable and even brilliant. George C. Scott's fine timing gave a new meaning to a number of the play's more difficult lines, and Bryden recognized in Kim Stanley's Masha one of the finest performances he had ever seen on the English stage. Indeed, Strasberg's production, while far from perfect, revealed a depth of understanding of Chekhov which is rarely witnessed. It captured, as one commentator wrote, 'the dichotomy between coarseness and refinement'. For these reasons alone, Strasberg's *The Three Sisters* deserved more consideration than most critics were prepared to give.

'*The Three Sisters*', as Francis Wyndham wrote, 'is a masterpiece so full of meanings that no one production could give them all equal value.' In their determination to fall over themselves with negative expression, the critics denied whatever positive values the production contained, and audiences attending the play after reading the first-night notices were perhaps surprised to discover some virtues.

Any consideration of the Method raises the whole complex question of acting styles, how much they are formed by the intellect, how much by instinct or intuition. For Laurence Olivier, for instance, acting is the art of persuasion—the actor persuades himself first, and through himself the audience. At one end of the scale the actor is important as the illuminator of the human heart, and at the other a scavenger of the tiniest little bit of human circumstance—often stored in the mind for as long as eighteen years before being used in a role. 'Out of a little thing you've seen somebody do, something causes you to store it up, and it can be the illuminating key to the whole bit of characterization.'

As Olivier himself has told me, his methods are the antithesis of the Method and would be heresy to the Strasberg school. He considers himself to be among the class of actors, which also includes Alec Guinness, for whom acting requires a peripheral approach—approaching roles from the outside rather than from within, as the Method actor does. 'The actor who starts from the inside is more likely to find himself in the parts he plays than to find the parts in himself.' For him it is naturalism or truthfulness that comes first—the same naturalism mastered by Alfred Lunt and shown to brilliant effect in those famous overlapped conversations with his wife Lynn Fontanne. What they called overlapping was a technique for speaking to each other as people do in real life. During their apprenticeship Chinese actors are taught to throw their voices about an octave higher than normal. The treble twang of their delivery on the stage leaves no doubt that they are acting; a rigid frontier is drawn between the stylization of the theatre and the realities of ordinary life. With the Lunts, however, this process is entirely reversed. Abjuring the 'naturalism' of a Gerald du Maurier golf-house locker-room technique, which smelt perhaps more of the theatre even than did

Bernhardt's 'golden voice', they act with an ease so cunning, so admirably adapted to the dimensions of the place in which they are playing, that reality and dream merge insensibly.

Olivier, remembering their achievements, has paid tribute to the enormous amount that Alfred Lunt taught him by example in the field of naturalistic acting and with the 'marvellous overlapped conversations'. 'They must have rehearsed it for millions of years, it was delicious to watch, and they carried on their own tradition in that way for many, many years.' Lynn Fontanne told me that 'It is necessary for an actor to have an outside eye and an outside ear. Thus you can look at yourself.'

We saw earlier how Strasberg's techniques for internalization are based on the work of Stanislavsky. One of his earliest positions was as an actor at the American Laboratory Theater, which was run by two members of Stanislavsky's company who had remained behind in New York after the Moscow Art Theatre's visit in 1923. Yet, as I discovered from talking to him, he is careful not to link his work too often with that of Stanislavsky. Although derived from the Russian's teaching, the Strasberg system remains a highly personal phenomenon and, as he told me, he has found a great deal of Stanislavsky's work formal and academic. As he has said so often in his sessions at the Studio, 'I want to give Stanislavsky credit, but I don't want him to be discredited by anything I do.'

When in 1968 I spent a week in New York with the Negro Ensemble I caught a glimpse of the tumultuous range of American theatre from off-Broadway to off-off-Broadway. My guide through that maze of cults and frenzied activity was Gerald Krone—himself a producer of forty-three off-Broadway shows—whose knowledge of the New York theatrical scene knows no bounds. During the years since I had last been in New York a revolution had taken place: the tiny arena theatres, the churches and cellars of the off-Broadway theatre had gained an unexpected respectability. As the rock of Broadway seemed to crumble, off-Broadway had increased its standards, its costs and its audience; it had, in short, often become a commercial proposition. Today playwrights are less concerned with a Broadway production, and ticket agencies are taking the unprecedented step of booking off-Broadway shows.

The American theatre is still in search of a standard, and in seeking that standard it has seized an opportunity to do or try anything. The latest craze then was nudity. *Hair* had been the first to present the naked body on the theatrical stage and to say, 'Look at us; we're different. We can do anything we want and no one can stop us.' By comparison with what followed, however, *Hair* seems almost a family show. Nudity is firmly in fashion. Kenneth Tynan's opportunist review *Oh! Calcutta!* took the theme up where *Hair* left off, and justified its commercial intentions by playing nightly to full houses.

I had earlier discovered the work of the Living Theatre with *The Connection*, and, despite the company's exile in Europe, they remain a potent force in New York, that terrifying play about life in a U.S. Marine glasshouse, *The Brig*, being another of their landmarks. One of the fiercest theatrical arguments still raging concerns the extent of involvement to be demanded of an audience, an argument that was sparked off by the Living Theatre's performance of *Paradise Now* at the Brooklyn Academy of Music. And the theatre of involvement flourishes; though its audience is caught up not in the harmless tasks of cheering the hero and hissing the villain, but in activities of a far less inhibited nature.

With Gerald Krone as mentor, I travelled through these American laboratories of theatrical experiment. From John Vaccaro's Theater of the Ridiculous, which regards murder on stage as the ultimate aim in a search for theatricality, to the Theater of Bestiality, from the Artaud-motivated and Grotowski-influenced Open Theater of Joseph Chaikin and Jean-Claude van Itallie to the calm simplicity of the Bread and Puppet Theater. Grotowski is currently the strongest influence on the easily affected off-Broadway theatre. Stories about him are told everywhere, his theories expounded and re-interpreted. The training to which he submits his actors in Poland and the acrobatic nature of his performances have taken New York by storm.

The prevailing mood, as I discovered it, was one of anarchy. The backwoods of American theatre are today rejecting the premises of a previous generation of actors and directors. Only a total dissolution of order will bring a new sense of order. What matters now is not how the director chooses to interpret *Hedda Gabler*, but whether the actor feels like taking off his clothes and throwing his shoe at a lady in the third row.

Certainly one of the most interesting, if not the most disciplined of productions, was *Dionysus 69*, a version of the classical legend put on by the Performance Group. The Group was founded by Richard Schechner, who acknowledges Grotowski and Peter Brook as his main influences. To see the play you entered what turned out to be a garage, a dark, dreary location which made very little attempt to say it was anything but a garage. Scaffolding had been erected and covered with planks, chairs, bits and pieces of cloth and carpeting to provide seating for the audience.

Dionysus 69 was a production which changed almost weekly, and it made its attempt to involve the audience by the actors rushing through their midst and trying to drag them into a circle of squirming humanity in the middle and to engage them, and one another, in sexual acts, as far as they were able to go. In Schechner's view the playwright must be a part of the company, 'someone who writes something which the company then takes over and does with it what it needs to do'. Not unnaturally this has led to some resentment among the new playwrights, who see little relation between what is on the stage and what they think they have written. The view that what the playwright writes is not important seems, however, to be a misinterpretation of Grotowski's intentions. While Grotowski certainly alters the works of playwrights considerably, his stated purpose remains to bring out, in terms of the actor as an instrument, psychologically, emotionally and physically, the playwright's true intention.

To see *Geese* by Gus Weill we had to go to McDougall Street, in the heart of Greenwich Village — a crowded street of old tenement houses in what had once been a pleasant residential area. There, above a café, was the Players Theater, seating over two hundred. Sitting in its long narrow auditorium was like looking through the wrong end of a telescope or down a tunnel. The play was made up of two separate acts, and the author's avowed intention was to write about love. The first act was about a typical 'American family', in which a mother and father reveal themselves as an unhappily married couple who married only for the sake of their young teenage son. The son and an older school friend enter down the aisle together, chattering. The older boy seduces the younger one, and thereafter the boys stay nude for the rest of the play. The parents argue all night while the boys continue making love upstairs, and the act ends with the younger preparing to come downstairs in the morning to tell his mother what a wonderful love he has found. In the second act the daughter of a wealthy family returns with a school chum, with whom she is have a lesbian relationship. This one also involved nudity, but, oddly enough, only from the waist up.

Geese had received bad reviews, but was playing to full houses. A duet of plays at the Gramercy Arts Theater, however, called *Eros* and *Witness*, which also featured nudity from the waist up, with an attractive actress named Sally Kirkland, closed after about six weeks in spite of respectable reviews. It seemed that nudity was not enough!

Playing at the United Church of Christ was a play called *Riot*, which featured its own attempt at audience involvement. At one point the actors charged the audience with real bayonets, stopping just short of transfixing the front row! While it did not run long, it threw up for the critics many questions of interest on the whole subject of audience involvement. Where *Dionysus 69* had tried to draw the public in on the action, *Riot* represented a murderous attack on its audience.

No visit to the New York theatre scene, then or now, would be complete without taking account of The Circle in the Square. Their early successes were with revivals of Eugene O'Neill's plays, and they have close links with Lee Strasberg's Method. Their director is Theodore Mann, and the acting talent they have produced includes Geraldine Page, Jason Robards and Dustin Hoffman. Probably their work was as responsible as that of any other institution for interesting the critics in what was going on in the small theatres during the 1960s.

The Café La Mama, a small basement coffee-house on Second Avenue, is often seen as the home and birthplace of the off-off-Broadway movement. Under the inspiration of Ellen Stewart, who has become something of a legend, it provided a platform for essentially short evenings of work where the actors were not paid but passed a hat round afterwards. It grew out of a tradition of coffee-shop poetry readings and presented that kind of informality. At the time I was there they were in the process of moving into a grander establishment on 4th Street.

Ellen Stewart first made her appearance in New York from Louisiana in 1955, when she came to study fashion design, and

gave birth to 'La Mama'. She then proceeded to rear her discoveries, who included such primary playwrights as Rochelle
Owens, Leonard Melfi and Jean-Claude van Itallie, and such
directors as Tom O'Horgan, director of *Hair*. Like the Greek
Art Theatre and the Negro Ensemble, she now has the support of
the Ford and Rockefeller Foundations; support that has enabled
her to buy and convert the present building, which opened in
1969 with *Caution: A Love Story*, a musical romance based on the
Windsors. She presents around forty plays a year, each costing
less than a hundred pounds, and hates long runs, money-making
and the slickness of professionalism equally. Ellen Stewart has
created a new beat-shock theatre that can often be toneless,
shapeless and horrific. But she recognizes the importance of
actors and directors, and her primary concern is to foster, nurture
and develop her dramatic babies. If anyone, she is the mother-
figure of off-off-Broadway and undoubtedly the founder of a
theatrical cult that probes the meaning and self-indulgence of the
adolescent obsession. One of her playwrights aptly described her
as constituting the 'love-energy of La Mama'.

Running right through American theatre is this sense of the
underground at work, with its associations linking it back to the
hippie and drug sub-cultures. There is what Jerry Krone described to me as the 'communal theatre' leading to the 'communal
action theatre' and the 'theatre of revolution'. The people involved in these movements feel that theatre should be the means
of provoking revolution within society, working under cover
like a kind of cultural yeast, in such a way that it will in the end
actually change that society in a very real sense. As Julian Beck
has been quoted as saying, 'We will be successful when our
audience walks out of the theatre and makes the revolution.'

The upsurge of the Negro theatre is an understandable example
of the theatre as a revolutionary expression. One movement
within the Negro theatre is actively concerned with the further-
ance of Black Power. This, however, was never the objective of
the Negro Ensemble Company. Tucked away in the St Martin's
Playhouse in Greenwich East Village, the problem they were
attempting to remedy was that of an environment in which Negro
artists would no longer find themselves all the time addressing
almost exclusively white audiences. Its aim, in short, was to
establish a permanent Negro repertory company—a theatre

which could concern itself with black problems, black life, and provide a home for the Negro artist.

The Negro Ensemble was very closely related to the off-Broadway and off-off-Broadway movements in that it represented a coming together of a group of actors in what was essentially a social rather than an artistic coalescence. They were there to express the point of view of a particular social grouping within the framework of the theatre at large; to express a new-found pride in the quality of 'blackness' which had hitherto represented a stigma.

In the week that I spent in New York early in 1969 to discuss arrangements and to choose plays for the Negro Ensemble's visit to the World Theatre Season later that year, I spent several days with the company. Watching them at work, I discovered the extent of their training programme, which embraced not only acting and design but dance, karate and musical technique. The enthusiasm of the Ensemble for their London visit was running high. I made a variety of suggestions as to how I felt the company's work might be improved for London, and presented the director, Michael Schultz, with a critique of what I had seen.

Perhaps the most impressive aspect of their work that I discovered was when I went to a performance of Ray McIver's musical morality *God is a (Guess What?)*, which the company were to bring to London. Douglas Turner Ward, the Ensemble's artistic director, had told me that he had hoped, when the Negro Ensemble had first been formed, to achieve a 35 per cent black audience. That night, and, as I later learned, almost every night, the audience was nearly three-quarters black. And indeed it was for this incredible achievement that the company were awarded a Tony Award just before their European visit, 'for developing new talent and new audiences'.

McIver's play was a stylized morality play which lashed out at bigotry and oppression with a tone that was mischievous, blasphemous and witty. The Ensemble's other production was Peter Weiss's *The Song of the Lusitanian Bogey*, which launched a bitter attack on the white man's oppression of the Negro, taking as its example the Portuguese colonization of Mozambique and Angola. Both were directed by Michael Schultz. To many critics the Ensemble's brand of black militancy was too strident and too much a diatribe against white society. Questions were even asked in the House of Commons as to whether the organizers of the World Theatre Season might be prosecuted for inciting racial hatred against the whites of this country.

Clive Barnes, in New York, had written quite simply, 'We could send no better troupe. This is a marvellous company.' But the attitude of the critics in England revealed at least a certain amount of ambivalence. While many of them appeared to enjoy the performances and encouraged people to go and see them, there was a distressingly prevalent attitude of condescension about the notices which the productions received. Perhaps the critics were not able to adapt themselves to seeing the productions against the social background which gave rise to them; perhaps they were even profoundly offended, whether they knew it or not, at the material contained in the plays, feeling that it might somehow foster racial conflict in Great Britain. People in England are on the whole reluctant to recognize the existence of any black problem in their midst, as the Negro actors in *The Connection* had discovered eight years earlier. Yet the members of the Negro Ensemble on their visit to London found a remarkable similarity of experience with those black people whom they met in England.

'It may be all very well and good for white people to say that the problem doesn't exist,' Jerry Krone commented. 'But talk to the black people here and they will tell you that the problem exists.'

One of the actresses with the Negro Ensemble, Rosalind Cash, kept a diary during her stay in England, which was later printed in the *New York Times*. It is a direct, eloquent and dignified testimony to what she felt and discovered about England.

I have a faint tired memory of pounds and shillings and pence and not knowing what I was spending. Then a ride through the English countryside. Green, green, and grey skies ...

While not performing I visited all the exotic restaurants I could find, and went to the local discotheques to dance my head off with some of the most beautiful black people from the West Indies and African countries ... They have great self-assurance and flair in their speech and dress and in the way they dance and talk. Unlike a lot of the English whites we met, who can be so god-damned RIGHT — like Goldwater. You can't argue with them ...

The first-night reception had been warm, but then, during
a performance of *Lusitanian Bogey*, shortly before the run ended,

> At the beginning of one show we were hooted down by a
> group in the audience. Just a lot of voices from all over the
> theatre. And leaflets thrown from the balcony ... anti-black
> leaflets ... pro-Rhodesia ... pro-Portuguese. Shouts. 'If you
> were white you'd be thrown off that stage, you bastards.'
> 'Portugal is our Atlantic ally.' 'Go home, niggers.' ...
> I felt so frustrated. I couldn't see who was doing it ...
> But we kept going. Then it would get very silent. And that
> was most frightening because I didn't know what was about
> to happen. A bomb? Then more shouting. I wanted to be
> made of steel. I was crying from despair. It's not going to
> change—this hatred. These people really think they are
> right.
> During intermission, I remember that one of the actresses
> in our company was crying very hard. She said, 'You know,
> we get so comfortable ... we're in a famous company ... we
> have jobs ... we travel round the world ... and then all the
> old wounds open up. It's all the same. We forget.' The
> reality of what we were doing and really saying in that play
> came back to us again. We knew what we were about
> again.

These few words from an unknown actress are not only the
cry of a black artist. They express the insecurity of every artist in
the world of theatre. Leaflets, shouts and bombs will continue to
be thrown until we learn to love each other instead of each
other's country. But with what compulsion do we return to the
theatre again and again, with all its unforeseen elements of
anguish and joy.

I have been twenty-nine years in the theatre, and I have just
presented my two hundredth production in London, Montherlant's *La Ville dont le prince est un enfant*. I have been stage-
struck since a boy, and throughout the drift and debris of a
million events flashing by like a single heart-beat, I have touched
hands with death, held hands with love, and beheld the touchstone
of magic—the theatre.

AFTERWORD

By the time this appears Peter Daubeny and I may not be on speaking terms, so I'd better write it now, if you follow me. Another World Theatre Season will be on us, and the seasons are difficult times for theatre critics as well as for Peter. Nothing in the London reviewer's normal round prepares him for these polyglot annual marathons. London's theatre year sets a pattern of expectations and responses which we've learned to deal with without excessive strain on ourselves or our vocabulary of superlatives. Plays and performances are 'competent', 'interesting', 'polished', 'entertaining' or 'gripping', in ascending order. At the top is 'outstanding', for anything which stood out from those categories in some way which we'll have to work out later. We don't expect to face more than two or three times in a twelvemonth the sort of theatrical experience which demands full, disarmed attention, a virgin alertness, and eventual measurement against our ultimate critical weapons: 'memorable', 'historic' and 'masterpiece'.

Into this neat, settled round burst the seasons, bringing not merely two or three extra opening nights a week, but a crashing bombardment of the most exacting theatrical quality. Night after night, week after week, we're exposed to the international stage's heaviest artillery: to the classics of half a dozen dramatic literatures, in performances we'd need to see half a dozen times to take in fully. It's as if, after ten months' diet of snacks, canapés and puff-pastry, we were suddenly crammed with giant collops of bloody beef. A surfeit of protein makes us liverish, tetchy and querulous. We defend ourselves from this onslaught on habit and cosiness by complaining about our seats, the programmes, prolonged scene-changes. Now and then, exhausted, we simply cut off our attention, like a deaf man switching off his hearing aid. Immediately we do that, the preposterousness of the whole thing overwhelms us. What on earth are we doing, huddling in the dark among an audience full of superior expatriates, struggling to follow a performance in a foreign language, our ears glued uncomfortably to a baton-shaped transistor squeaking a jerky English translation, in order to describe it the following Sunday, when the company's already left for home, to readers most of whom couldn't care less? What is it all in aid of? What does Peter Daubeny think he's achieving, spreading these feasts of alien caviare before a tiny metropolitan minority of caviare-fanciers year after year?

We know he asks himself the same questions. Sometimes toward the end of a particularly arduous season, goaded beyond endurance by some notice in which we have worked off our battle-fatigue by carping at one of his imports, he puts them rhetorically to us over the telephone, asking why he should go on combing the world for pearls to cast before insensible swine like ourselves? What is the point of his exhausting himself flying about the globe, moving heaven, earth and suspicious governments in order to bring some small, uneven but uniquely representative company thousands of miles to London, simply for them to be told that their scenery arrived looking tired and crumpled? Do we realize that it had been rescued from a Gravesend warehouse only an hour before the curtain rose? That the leading lady had laryngitis, picked up crossing the Carpathians in a draughty sleeper? That the rest of the company were still recovering from the worst Channel crossing in fifty years, the lighting-chart had been lost in transit, and the Ruritanian ambassador has just spent an hour on the telephone explaining why Ruritania is breaking off cultural relations with Britain? Can we suggest one good reason why he should not throw up the whole business?

Can we? It is hard to suggest a single one: the balance of international good will and ill will promoted by exposing foreign companies to the erratic mercies of London critics must be slender. The number of people who can see any particular production is minuscule—I once wrote that no one interested in Chekhov should miss the Moscow Art Theatre's clumsy but fascinating attempt to re-think *The Seagull*, and received a furious letter from an Oxford lady, who had tried vainly for three months to procure a ticket, cancelling her subscription to my newspaper. No: there *are* reasons justifying Peter Daubeny's labours, but they are scattered and diffuse, noticeable over the long run of subsequent British theatrical activity.

Take his importation of Brecht's Berliner Ensemble in 1956. At the time it seemed a modish teacup furore of Hampstead intellectuals, insignificant beside the native revolution launched by Osborne's *Look Back in Anger*. To appreciate its impact you have to cast your eye over the whole following decade: at the epic-theatre form of Osborne's *Entertainer* and *Luther*; the structure of John Arden's *Serjeant Musgrave's Dance* and *Workhouse Donkey*; at the whole style and output of the Royal Shakespeare Theatre in the 1960s, including Peter Brook's famous *Lear*, Peter Hall's and John Barton's cycle of Shakespeare's history plays in 1964. The work of a whole generation of British playwrights, directors and actors was radically affected by that three-week season at the Palace Theatre, and the ripples of its influence are still spreading.

Or take the two visits of the Comédie-Française, in 1959 and 1964, with productions of Feydeau's great farces *Le Dindon* directed by Jean Meyer and *Un Fil à la Patte* directed by Jacques Charon. Their most direct consequence was the National Theatre's brilliant mounting of *A Flea in her Ear*, under Charon's direction, in 1966. But beyond that, one can trace a revived interest among British playwrights and directors in the possibility of farce as a form, a new willingness to regard it as respectable. In addition to commercial productions of Feydeau and Labiche, there have been some notable revivals of classic British farces: Pinero's *The Magistrate*, Ben Travers's *Cuckoo in the Nest* and *Thark*. It does not seem too much to connect with them the sudden rise of Joe Orton, putting farce to new, satirical use in *Loot* and *What the Butler Saw*, and Peter Shaffer's small, brilliant excursion into the form in *Black Comedy*.

The list is endless. The Moscow Art Theatre's superb adaptation of Gogol's *Dead Souls* prompted Peter Hall to revive *The Government Inspector*, with Paul Scofield as Hlestakov, in an unashamedly derivative production for the Royal Shakespeare Company. The National Theatre has mounted three productions directly inspired by World Theatre successes—an adaptation of Dostoyevsky's *The Idiot*, modelled on the Leningrad Gorky Theatre's version starring Smoktunovsky as Prince Mishkin; Carl Zuckmayer's *Captain of Kopenick*, brought to London by the Schiller-Theater of Berlin in 1970; and Ingmar Bergman's production of *Hedda Gabler*, which he simply re-created for the

National in the summer of 1970. The visit of the Nō Theatre in 1967 obviously influenced enormously Peter Brook's production of Seneca's *Oedipus* at the Old Vic a year later, as well as, indirectly (he did not see it, but was struck by a description of its performances), Edward Bond's satirical Japanese fantasia *Narrow Road to the Deep North*. Josef Svoboda's revolutionary mirror-set for the Czech National Theatre's *Insect Play* sparked off at least four British imitations I could mention, and led to invitations to design, superbly, a Covent Garden *Frau Ohne Schatten* and National Theatre *Three Sisters*. The Abbey Theatre's astonishing, mockery-free revival of Dion Boucicault's melodrama *The Shaughraun* resulted in a new wave of interest in the old nineteenth-century form, and a splendidly comic mounting of his *London Assurance* by the Royal Shakespeare Company. And so on.

But the greatest influence Peter Daubeny's long career as an importer of great foreign companies has had on the British stage, I'd say, has been its demonstration of the value of such permanent ensembles, of the quality of performance an ensemble alone can achieve. More than anything else, it was his presentation in London of the Comédie-Française, the Barrault–Renaud troupe and Brecht's Berliners which created the climate in which Peter Hall was able to set up the permanent Royal Shakespeare Company, in which the old dream of a British National Theatre was finally realized under Laurence Olivier. If his World Theatre Seasons have subtly fed vivifying foreign influences into the British theatre's bloodstream, it is largely because it now *has* a bloodstream—a central, continuing core of subsidized classical repertory—which can absorb them and feed them into the theatre at large.

Is this enough for him? Sufficient justification for those long, lonely journeys from capital to theatrical capital, wading through scores of dim foreign-language productions to find the occasional masterpiece which will travel, struggling with interpreters, stony officials and volatile theatrical temperaments simply in order to set up another eight to ten weeks of imported drama each spring at the Aldwych? He would have to be a supernaturally strong, far-sighted and resilient man for such scattered, piecemeal and long-term results to compensate for all the crises and disappointments; and although he glosses over it in this book, most of us know that his war-wound and subsequent operation for a brain

tumour have left him frail, often ill, easily depressed and exhausted, unable to concentrate for long periods of time without
frequent rests and an armoury of medicines which must travel
with him everywhere. It must seem to him often that, like
Sisyphus, he is rolling a colossal boulder single-handed up a
mountain, compelled to start again at the bottom every time he
seems to have reached the top, that the whole enormous effort
takes place in a void, with no visible result and no audience even
to applaud his struggle with futility; that no one else really cares.

Perhaps that is what keeps him going. I suspect it is precisely
the fear that no one else cares that sends him off each year with his
suitcase of pills and notebooks, bumping around the world from
airport to airport to look at Indian dance-troupes, obscure Balkan
repertories, rebellious little *avant-garde* companies performing in
basements in Prague or Harlem. Somebody has to care. If he did
not, who else would see them and bring them to light? Who else
would pursue the dream of a world theatre?

London, 1971   RONALD BRYDEN

Index